AF505827

Against Theory of Mind

Also by Ivan Leudar

VOICES OF REASON, VOICES OF INSANITY
CONVERSATION ANALYSIS AND PSYCHOTHERAPY

Also by Alan Costall

DOING THINGS WITH THINGS: THE DESIGN AND USE OF
EVERYDAY OBJECTS

Against Theory of Mind

Edited By

Ivan Leudar
University of Manchester, UK

Alan Costall
University of Portsmouth, UK

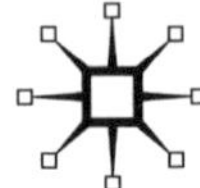

First published 2009 by
PALGRAVE MACMILLAN

Palgrave Macmillan in the UK is an imprint of Macmillan Publishers Limited,
registered in England, company number 785998, of Houndmills, Basingstoke,
Hampshire RG21 6XS.

Palgrave Macmillan in the US is a division of St Martin's Press LLC,
175 Fifth Avenue, New York, NY 10010.

Palgrave Macmillan is the global academic imprint of the above companies
and has companies and representatives throughout the world.

Palgrave® and Macmillan® are registered trademarks in the United States,
the United Kingdom, Europe and other countries.

ISBN-13: 978–0–230–55273–9 hardback
ISBN-10: 0–230–55273–0 hardback

This book is printed on paper suitable for recycling and made from fully
managed and sustained forest sources. Logging, pulping and manufacturing
processes are expected to conform to the environmental regulations of the
country of origin.

A catalogue record for this book is available from the British Library.

Library of Congress Cataloging-in-Publication Data

Against theory of mind / edited by Ivan Leudar, Alan Costall.
        p. cm.
    Includes bibliographical references and index.
    ISBN-13: 978–0–230–55273–9 (hardback)
    ISBN-10: 0–230–55273–0 (hardback)
    1. Philosophy of mind.   I. Leudar, Ivan, 1949– II. Costall, Alan.

BD418.3.A33 2009
128′2—dc22   2008042700

10 9 8 7 6 5 4 3 2 1
18 17 16 15 14 13 12 11 10 09

Printed and bound in Great Britain by
CPI Antony Rowe, Chippenham and Eastbourne

Contents

List of Contributors   vii

1   Introduction: Against 'Theory of Mind'   1
    Ivan Leudar and Alan Costall

Part 1 Theory and History

2   On the Historical Antecedents of the Theory of
    Mind Paradigm   19
    Ivan Leudar and Alan Costall

3   'Theory of Mind': The Madness in the Method   39
    Alan Costall and Ivan Leudar

4   'Theory of Mind': A Critical Commentary Continued   56
    Wes Sharrock and Jeff Coulter

Part 2 Applications

5   Participants Don't Need Theories: Knowing Minds in
    Engagement   91
    Vasudevi Reddy and Paul Morris

6   Specifying Interactional Markers of Schizophrenia in
    Clinical Consultations   108
    Rosemarie McCabe

7   The Roots of Mindblindness   126
    Stuart Shanker and Jim Stieben

8   Who *Really* Needs a 'Theory' of Mind?   144
    Emma Williams

9   Do Animals Need a 'Theory of Mind'?   167
    Michael Bavidge and Ian Ground

Part 3 Alternatives

10 Closet Cartesianism in Discursive Psychology   191
    Wes Sharrock

11   A Dialogical Approach in Psychology: An Alternative to
the Dualism of ToM   209
Ivana Marková

12   ToM Rules, but It Is Not OK!   221
Daniel D. Hutto

References   239

Author Index   263

Subject Index   269

List of Contributors

Michael Bavidge: Centre for Continuing Education, University of Newcastle upon Tyne, UK.

Alan Costall: Department of Psychology, The University of Portsmouth, UK.

Jeff Coulter: Department of Sociology, Boston University, USA.

Ian Ground: School of Education and Lifelong Learning, University of Sunderland, UK.

Daniel D. Hutto: Department of Philosophy, University of Hertfortshire, UK.

Ivan Leudar: School of Psychological Sciences, The University of Manchester, UK.

Ivana Marková: Department of Psychology, The University of Stirling, UK.

Rosemarie McCabe: Queen Mary, London, UK.

Paul Morris: Department of Psychology, The University of Portsmouth, UK.

Vasudevi Reddy: Department of Psychology, The University of Portsmouth, UK.

Stuart Shanker: Milton and Ethel Harris Research Initiative, York University, Canada.

Wes Sharrock: School of Social Sciences, The University of Manchester, UK.

Jim Stieben: Milton and Ethel Harris Research Initiative, York University, Canada.

Emma Williams: Department of Psychology, The University of Surrey, UK.

1
Introduction:
Against 'Theory of Mind'

Ivan Leudar and Alan Costall

The 'Theory of Mind' (ToM) framework has been associated with one of the fastest growing bodies of empirical research in psychology over the last 30 years, and has also given rise to a range of different theoretical positions and elaborations within those positions. However, the approach has remained unusually self-enclosed, avoiding any sustained engagement with alternative explanations of social action such as discursive psychology or socio-cultural psychology. By comparison with the wealth of articles and books published by proponents of ToM, the critical literature on ToM is rather limited, consisting of a few articles and monographs taking issue with its assumptions (e.g., Hobson, 1991; Carpendale and Lewis, 2004), methods (Dunn, 1988; Reddy, 1991, 2007) and empirical findings (McCabe, Leudar and Antaki, 2004; McCabe, Leudar and Healey, 2005; Ochs and Solomon 2007). There is, however, also important recent work within the philosophy of mind directed against ToM (e.g., Zahavi, 2006; Hutto, 2008). To our knowledge there exists not a single published response in which proponents of 'Theory of Mind' address systematically and carefully the objections to their programme. Indeed, critical studies are either ignored or subjected to considerably more methodological scrutiny than confirmatory findings. 'Theory of Mind' has become so much a part of the furniture in developmental and cognitive psychology that it is now largely confused with the very phenomena it was introduced to explain.

The term 'Theory of Mind' was coined in the 1970s, in relation to research on intentionality in non-human primates, to refer to the ability to impute mental states to others and to oneself (e.g., Premack, 1976, Premack and Woodruff, 1978). This capacity came to be known as 'mind-reading' or 'mentalising' (e.g., Whiten and Perner, 1991), and is now widely regarded as essential to both self-reflection and coordinated social action. The reason the term 'theory' was invoked is that interpersonal understanding was claimed to be a *theoretical* accomplishment, involving a person constructing and using a 'theory' about the nature of minds. Applying such a theory to observable behaviour was claimed to enable the individual to interpret that behaviour in intentional terms as the outcome of specific, underlying mental states.

The original 'Theory of Mind' framework was a development of philosophical cognitivism and especially of the conception of 'folk psychology' (see, e.g., Dennett, 1971 and 1987; Bennet, 1976; Stich, 1983; Fodor, 1987; Goldman, 2006). 'Theory of Mind' promised to provide empirical confirmation of the philosophical claim that our ordinary, commonsense understandings of mental life amount to a contingent empirical theory of mind (e.g., Wellman, 1990). Yet the treatment of children and adults as *theoreticians* – or *as if* theoreticians – is not actually an empirical discovery at all, but a background assumption inherited from Chomsky's theory of language (see Leudar and Costall, 2004b and the next chapter in this book). Furthermore, the assumption that social action entails such 'mindreading' – and hence theorizing – individualized the problem of social understanding, thus making the study of intentional social activities seem no longer the preserve of social psychology, but of cognitive psychology instead. This essentially cognitive approach has been widely adopted by developmental psychologists to explain the development of social cognition (Bretherton, McNew and Beeghly-Smith, 1981; Perner and Wimmer, 1985), and has provided the basis of influential accounts of psychiatric disorders such as autism (e.g., Baron-Cohen, Leslie and Frith, 1985) and schizophrenia (e.g., Frith and Corcoran, 1996).

The original version of 'Theory of Mind' theory has, over time, been joined by a number of alternative theories of social understanding that have also been included under that original heading, so that the kind of theory proposed by Premack has now to be referred to by the awkward expression, *'Theory* Theory of Mind', or TToM. One of the earliest alternatives to TToM postulated a biological module, a 'Theory of Mind Mechanism', or ToMM:

> evolution has equipped the human brain with a special module, a theory of mind mechanism (ToMM), that helps normally developing children to attend to the invisible mental states of others [...] This social instinct owes little to general reasoning powers [...].
>
> (Leslie, 2000, p. 61)

According to this particular alternative, it is theorizing once again that in effect allows us to make sense of one another, but, in this case, thanks to a biological implant, rather than our own intellectual powers. 'Theory of Mind', in this version, is intelligence by proxy, deriving not from God (as in pre-Darwinian instinct doctrine) but from cognitivism's current *deus ex machina*, natural selection:

> We are 'mindreaders' by nature, building interpretations of the mental events of others and feeling our constructions as sharply as the physical objects we touch. Humans evolved this ability because, as members of an

intensively social, cooperative, and competitive species, our ancestors' lives depended on how well they could infer what was on one another's minds. Precisely because such an interpretative system does model the world in terms of unobservable entities (thoughts, intentions, beliefs, and desires), it needs to be coupled to confederate modules that can construct a bridge from the observable to the unobservable. *Unobservable entities are invisible to association-learning mechanisms, but they are 'visible,' over the long run, to natural selection.* As chance created alternative cognitive designs, this process 'selected' those that implemented the best 'betting' system.

> (Tooby and Cosmides, 1995, p. xvii; emphasis added)[1]

There are also a variety of 'simulation theories' which deny the involvement of theorizing of any kind, either personal or subpersonal (i.e., neural), and yet these too are, nevertheless, routinely characterized as part of the Theory of Mind approach (e.g., Gordon, 1992; Harris, 1992; Goldman, 2006; cf. Gallagher, 2007). Finally, to make life even more difficult, the expression 'Theory of Mind' is no longer presented in the textbooks and the research literature as referring to any kind of *theory* at all, nor even a specific *set of theories*. 'Theory of Mind' is now widely presented as a relatively neutral, uncontroversial 'construct', or well-established fact:

> Theory of mind (TOM) is a multi-faceted construct that captures the capacity to make inferences about others' mental states, such as intentions, emotions, desires, and beliefs. Over time children come to realize that such mental activity is not obvious to another person.
>
> (Barr, 2008, p. 188)

> children's ability to understand the person-specific nature of emotions is critically connected to their developing understanding of people as *psychological* beings with internal mental states, what is known as a 'theory of mind' [...].
>
> (Thompson and Lagattuta, 2008, pp. 320–1)

> ['Theory of mind' is] the 'everyday' ability to understand other people's beliefs, thoughts and desires in order to explain and predict their behaviour. With the ability to infer mental states, like the true and false beliefs of oneself and others, children become more capable of participating in a wide range of conversational and social interactions.
>
> (Pring, 2005, p. 2)

There are now, therefore, grounds for a great deal of confusion surrounding the term, 'theory of mind'. What exactly, then, is our present book, *Against Theory of Mind*, supposed to be *against*? The criticisms and objections to be presented in this book are explicitly directed at TToM and ToMM. The real target is, however, a wider schema, which we will refer to as *ToMism*.[2] We are against a set of assumptions and more implicit, insidious, commitments that pervade the, by now, extensive schema of ToMism. We are against the dogmatism of ToMism and the way it keeps presenting its starting assumptions not as *assumptions* at all, but as well-established, inescapable facts of the matter. Two such assumptions are crucial:

1. *Indirectness.* In making sense of one another, we need to bridge a gulf between what we can 'directly' experience about other people, and what is going on 'in' their minds: 'our sensory experience of other people tells us about their movements in space but does not tell directly about their mental states' (Meltzoff, Gopnik and Repacholi, 1999, p. 17).[3]
2. *Detour.* The presumed gulf between people can only be crossed by inference, theorizing, simulation or some other kind of 'detour' (Asch, 1952, p. 144).

Within ToMism, these theoretical assumptions are simply not a matter for debate. They are truths to be universally acknowledged. They remain unnoticed even in the following recent attempt at a 'rigorously agnostic' definition of 'Theory of Mind':

> We will henceforth use the acronym ToM, to refer to *any* cognitive system, whether theory-like or not, that predicts or explains the behaviour of another agent by postulating that unobservable inner states particular to the cognitive perspective of that agent causally modulate that agent's behaviour. We believe this construal of ToM *senso lato* is about as broad and minimalist as possible without losing the distinctive character of the capacity in question.
>
> (Penn and Povinelli, 2008, p. 394)

This definition unites ToMism around the unexamined distinction between mind and behaviour while allowing for a plurality of ways in which the gap between the two can be bridged.

The *indirectness* and *detour* assumptions were not, of course, invented by the ToMists. For example, these assumptions have long been basic to the 'social cognition' approach within social psychology. The social cognitivists certainly had their own *a priori* reasons for supposing that making sense of other people (as opposed to objects and physical properties) might be 'difficult':

> It is generally no more difficult to judge the height of a person than it is to judge the height of a bookcase. The same is true of weight, skin color, or style of clothing. It is also fairly easy to make judgments about

somebody's social role. [...] But person perception becomes more difficult when we try to infer internal states – traits, feelings, emotions, and personalities. [...] Judgments of such internal states as emotions, personality traits, and attitudes are often *extremely difficult*. The person's internal state cannot be observed directly – it must be inferred from whatever cues are available.

(Taylor, Peplau and Sears, 1994, p. 51; emphasis added)

However, the social cognitivists largely presented themselves as addressing an essentially *empirical* matter. They claimed that it was on the basis of their actual research that we had to conclude that people's judgements of one another are deeply unreliable, not simply because internal states cannot be directly observed, but also because, as a matter of empirical fact, people are subject to a host of selective biases when dealing with one another (Smith and MacKie, 2000, p. 85).[4] Yet, the social cognitivists were surprisingly undogmatic. Their mainstream literature acknowledged the existence of an alternative tradition of research, largely stemming from Gestalt psychology, that argued that meaningful qualities of people's actions are manifest in their actions, and, more generally, in the ways they relate to the world and other people:

The quality of their actions imbues persons with living reality. When we say that a person is in pain, we see his body as feeling. We do not need to 'impute' consciousness to others if we directly perceive the qualities of consciousness in the qualities of action. Once we see an act that is skillful, clumsy, alert, or reckless, it is superfluous to go 'behind' it to its conscious substrate, for consciousness has revealed itself in the act.

(Asch, 1952, p. 158)

Remarkably, such claims were never (well, hardly ever) dismissed as heresy, but presented as a serious theoretical option, and even as a possible complement to the mainstream inference-based approach. Furthermore, the social cognitivists did not simply dismiss objections to their own research methods. Critics pointed out that the experimental studies were, as a rule, far from natural, involving highly contrived situations in which participants merely *observed* someone else (or, more usually, a film, video or even a picture of that person) with whom they had no real involvement at all. Furthermore, the very 'tasks' involved in these studies rendered the business of making sense of one another as abstract and overly intellectualized. As Ulric Neisser complained:

The theories and experiments [...] all refer to an essentially passive onlooker, who sees someone do something (or sees two people do something) and then makes a judgment about it. He (this is the generic passive *he*) doesn't *do* anything – doesn't mix it up with the folks he's watching, never tests his judgments in action or interaction. He just watches and makes judgments. [...] When people are genuinely engaged with one another, nobody stops to give grades.

(Neisser, 1980, pp. 603–4)[5]

The social cognitivists, to their credit, have been sensitive to such criticisms, even if, as committed experimentalists, they have found it very difficult to do much about them. One could even regard the way the social cognitivists routinely ignore their own empirical conclusions as a kind of open-mindedness. For, of course, in order to assess the reliability of other people in making sense of *other* other people, the researchers had to allow that they themselves, at least, must be in a strong position to know what those *other* people *really* think and feel.

It is striking how differently the assumptions of *indirectness* and *detour* have played out in the context of ToMism in contrast to the 'social cognition' approach. First of all, despite their persistently disparaging references to non-psychologists as, for instance, 'the folk', 'ordinary people', or even 'naïve people' (Goldman, 2006, pp. 4, 230, and 258), the ToMists have been remarkably egalitarian in their insistence that they should not exclude themselves from any claims to be made about how people in general are supposed to make sense of other people. The majority of ToMists insist that psychologists in their research and 'ordinary people' in everyday life share exactly the same *problem* when making psychological sense of others. Thus, in their attempts to make *psychological* sense of other people, 'ordinary people' and the psychologists are supposed to be in precisely the same epistemic position, and must, therefore, solve the problem of other minds in fundamentally the same way: by somehow going *beyond* the limited data immediately available to them.

Unfortunately, it is precisely the inclusive claim by the 'Theory Theorists' that has rendered ToMism a self-enclosed scheme, robustly immune to counter evidence. Given we are all supposed to be only *really* able to relate to one another on the basis of theory (or some logically equivalent substitute mechanism), then obviously any investigation into whether anyone is *really* able to understand another person should test them under experimental conditions *where theorizing or quasi-theoretical capacities would be essential*. Most notably, this was the very point of the 'false-belief' task, a test of a person's ability to 'meta-represent' (i.e., simultaneously to represent someone's thoughts and also whether those thoughts actually correspond to reality).

As Jerome Bruner pointed out long ago, this new research procedure was not simply an investigatory tool but also a *criterion* of understanding other minds. Along with many of the other experimental procedures within ToMism, the experiments themselves were *stipulative*, defining the very phenomenon they claim to investigate:

> I was struck at the European Conference on Developmental Psychology
> held in Scotland in 1990 that theory of mind researchers seemed to have
> got stuck on the criterion of false belief [...] To equate grasping other minds
> with getting a False Belief Diploma at Graduation Day is to oversimplify its
> form and function. To equate 'having' a theory of mind with grasping the
> epistemological distinction between true and false belief obscures the con-
> tribution of the three or four years of development that preceded it.
>
> (Bruner and Feldman, 1993, p. 269)

The false-belief task no longer enjoys its once central, definitive status within ToMism, not least because of its problematic relation to autism. One of the important initial claims of the ToMists had been that the theory approach explains the nature of autism (Baron-Cohen, Leslie and Frith, 1985). An inability to meta-represent was supposed to account for the difficulty people with autism have in relating to other people. However, it was soon discovered that many people diagnosed as autistic were found to be able to pass the false-belief test (Boucher, 1996). Furthermore, there was, in any case, an obvious problem that should have been noticed from the very beginning. Those who do lack the capacity to meta-represent – very young children, severely learning impaired adults, and, one might add, even dogs and cats – nevertheless have no great difficult getting on with other people: they do not appear to be autistic (Boucher, 1996; see Bloom and German, 2000, for a recent criticism of the false-belief task).

Within ToMism, however, the basic conviction has remained that it is only on the basis of experimental evidence that we can determine whether a particular individual is *really* able to understand other people. And from within the schema of ToMism, the reasoning seems obvious and compelling. Given the indirectness assumption, then it is only under the contrived and controlled conditions of an experiment that the capacity to make sense of other people could properly be tested. For, of course, according to ToMism, *genuine* understanding of other people inevitably requires some kind of psychological detour (such as inference), and so the greatest care must be taken to prevent the person being tested from resorting, instead, to 'some surface-level strategy' (Sodian and Frith, 1993, p. 174). So, in order to study how people *really* make sense of one another, it is obvious that they *must* be studied in contrived experimental situations, in order that they *should* make the required detours.

In short, the ToMist experiments are a *fix*. This, in itself, is not the problem, for the whole point of experimental control is, indeed, to fix things: to stop *certain* things happening and getting in the way in order better to study the *essence* of the phenomenon under investigation. The trouble arises when investigators assume from the outset that they already know the essence of the phenomenon under study (and, indeed, that the phenomenon has a unitary essence). From that point on, what counts as 'contaminating' or 'incidental' factors can no longer arise as a serious and substantive scientific issue. And, yet, there is always the danger that what is eliminated as an 'extraneous variable' (to use one of Skinner's favourite terms) may actually be rather important, as in the following parody of operant psychology:

> The completely controlled experiments [...] begin with the invention of the Brittlesparse box. It has no lever. It has no food. It has no subject. To operate it the box is hit. It breaks. By thus eliminating the organism completely a parsimonious science of Stimulus (hitting box) and Response (breaking box) is achieved. [...Thus] complete control and prediction is possible. If you hit the box it breaks. If you do not, it does not.
>
> (Rudin, 1959, p. 114)

This brings us to one of the main critical issues raised in the following chapters, the ToMists' exclusion, in their research and theory, of *other ways* that people – adults as well as children – might actually deal with one another *without the help of 'Theory of Mind'*. It is not as though the ToMists did not soon discover that subjects lacking 'Theory of Mind' are sometimes able to 'cheat' by resorting to 'surface strategies' even in the supposedly crucial tests of the attainment of 'Theory of Mind'. Furthermore, there has been growing recognition within ToMism of the *derivative* status of 'Theory of Mind' in relation to both normal development and autism:

> mind-reading theories have increasingly moved back from seeing lack of a theory of mind, or of metarepresentational processes, as the primary cause of autism, identifying, rather, the precursors of a theory of mind [...and] have increasingly converged with socio-affective theories (Hobson, 1993).
>
> (Boucher, 1996, p. 228)

Nevertheless, ToMism continues to treat 'Theory of Mind' as the *one* true form of social understanding, and all other kinds of relating to other people as the *mere* appearance of the real thing. This is why the ToMists distrust or else simply disregard research based upon real-life social interaction: from their perspective *real-life* studies can (somewhat paradoxically) only provide evidence about the *appearance* of sociality, they could never confirm its *reality*.

The resolute faith in the priority of experimental evidence stems from the very schema of ToMism itself. For the experiment has a dual role within that schema, not just as the favoured objective method but also in providing the highly persuasive model of what psychology – along with the rest of science – should be *about*. According to the model, the purpose of scientific research is to take us beyond the *surface* of things, beyond their *mere appearance*, to a hidden reality beyond: for example, atoms' structure, genes, or cognitive mechanisms. In this very process, however, the tradition of scientific empiricism, while proclaiming the crucial value of empirical evidence, has long been in the business of undermining the primacy of experience:

> The universe is not as it appears in common experience; its nature and structure do not lay themselves open to perception; on the contrary, they have to be uncovered by means of mathematical notions. In reality, then, the universe is not as it seems to be, but as it is conceived and constructed by the mathematical physicist.
> (Gurwitsch, 1978, p. 72; see also Blackmore, 1979)

Gurwitsch traces the revival of a Platonist dualism of appearance and reality to the physics of Galileo, where the realm of appearance 'is assumed to be subordinated to the other and to lead a merely borrowed existence [...] to be explained in terms of the domain of higher order' (Gurwitsch, 1978, p. 84). However, according to Gurwitsch, it was Descartes who made this dualism fundamental to the philosophy of the new mechanical science. Critics of cognitivism and dualism may have, therefore, identified the wrong target and the Cartesian *mind-body* dualism may not, after all, be the most fundamental problem. Even Descartes himself, at least in his scientific writings, proved remarkably open-minded about this dualism (Cottingham, 1992). The Cartesian *appearance-reality* dualism may indeed be more fundamental in generating the many dilemmas of modern psychology.

It is on the basis of this opposition of appearance and reality, that ToMism assimilates the problem of how *psychologists* make sense of 'ordinary people' to how, for example, physical scientists come to theorize about atoms.[6] Yet the move is not as straightforward or innocent as it can appear. First of all, there is a profound problem concerning what the psychologists take to be the *data* for their theoretical inferences: for the available evidence, according to ToMism, is entirely disconnected from the hidden mental structures it is supposed to reveal (see Costall and Leudar, Chapter 3, this volume). In addition, there is an obvious, if seldom noticed, *lack of* analogy between the way physicists study the properties of matter, and psychologists conduct experiments on people. As Danziger (1989) has argued, psychological experiments cannot be thought of as experiments in, say, chemistry, because they inevitably involve social interactions. Before the psychological experiment can even begin, researchers must already have related to 'subjects' in an effective way in order to obtain their participation, and then their agreement to follow the experimental instructions (cf. Wieder, 1980). And this point applies equally to those subjects who the experimenter presumes to 'have' a Theory of Mind as to those who do not, such as young children and people with autism or schizophrenia. Thus, the experiments on 'Theory of Mind' presuppose the existence of effective modes of mutual understanding that are not of the detached and inferential kind that is the focus of actual research.

Before the advent of ToMism, cognitive psychology treated the problems of how psychologists study people, and how lay people make sense of other people as being quite separate. The textbooks had separate chapters for each issue, namely an initial chapter on the nature of psychology as a science, and another chapter coming much later in the text – once all of the 'harder' aspects of the discipline had been dealt with – on social psychology. ToMism is almost unprecedented in assimilating the problem of how 'other people' make sense of other 'other people' into its own methodology, a methodology that, as we have just concluded, has to allow for non-theoretical modes of mutual understanding, but does not. The upshot is that ToMism became caught within a theoretical and methodological circle where, despite all of the research conducted within this schema, the starting assumptions of *indirectness* and *detour* could never themselves arise as a fundamental issue for investigation. Furthermore, given the restrictive methodological limitations imposed by that very schema, these assumptions simply could not become empirical issues at all, for the experiments have, all along, been grounded upon those assumptions. Two central issues to be raised in the following chapters, therefore, concern how ToMism has managed to lock itself in such an anti-empirical loop, and how psychology can break out of its enchanted circle.

However, the most fundamental issue addressed in this book concerns the way ToMism has, through its methodological commitments, reformulated the traditional dualistic problem – or, to be more exact, *mystery* – of other minds (see, in this volume, Leudar and Costall, Chapter 2; Costall and Leudar, Chapter 3, and Shanker and Stieben, Chapter 7). Now, modern psychologists are very insistent that they are not *ontological* dualists, they do not suppose that there is one kind of 'stuff', matter, on the one hand, and another, quite different kind of 'stuff', mind, on the other. Nevertheless, in their insistence that making sense of another person *must* involve a two-stage process, the observation of '*mere* behaviour' and the inference from such observable data to hidden mental states is the cause of a different kind of dualism. For they keep talking themselves into *epistemic* and *methodological* dualisms, based on the opposition of *appearance* and *reality, surface* and *depth*, and *behaviour* and *mind* (see Leudar and Costall, 2004b). For, despite all the talk of cognitive revolution, the 'official' concept of behaviour they unwittingly invoke is that bequeathed by neo-behaviourism, a concept of behaviour as meaningless movement, physically measurable, and the antithesis of mind. Such data, so construed, could not constitute any kind of evidence for mind. In fact, the way the ToMists present 'the problem of other minds' is inconsistent. In relation to 'ordinary people' they gleefully talk the problem up as highly intractable, and in this way 'Theory of Mind' has come to seem a truly intriguing field of research. Once they invoke the reassuring analogy of the theoretical scientist, however, all of the mystery is suddenly and mysteriously supposed to be dispelled.

In conclusion, the paradigm of ToMism is one of the most recent, and certainly most influential, outbreaks of 'scientism' in psychology. It is motivated by the wish to appear scientific rather than by the urge to do justice to the complexities of the phenomena it studies. This is indicated not just by the methods of investigation, but also by how ToMism pre-conceives the very phenomena it investigates. It conceives of psychology as a natural science and investigates intentional agents using methods of natural science, pre-empting the investigations by thinking of the children and adults as themselves proto-scientists, who treat other people with detachment, objectively, and in an intellectual mode. These presuppositions are built into the methods of investigation, such as, for instance, the false-belief task. The more ecologically sound observational and analytic methods, such as conversation and discourse analyses, are widely dismissed as providing no more than anecdotal and subjective evidence. Yet, most of the Theory of Mind experiments substitute abstract puzzle-solving for situated, collaborative and embodied management of intentionality, with the result that they never really investigate the phenomena they are ultimately meant to explain (see Rose McCabe's comments in Chapter 6). The relationship between the experiments and the theories is anyway not as straightforward as imagined in falsificationism. Experiments do not simply 'test' theories but also in their design reproduce the unnoticed assumptions of the theories, and so the theories, one might say, *co-produce* the results. This is very much so in the 'false-belief task'. The logic of ToM is to intellectualize intentionality and to put detached abstract reasoning about detached mental states on centre stage; in the false-belief task, the cooperative participants cannot but *observe, infer and predict* rather than engage the characters in the experimental scenarios, and ask them questions, or formulate the happenings (these being some of what might happen in less constrained social interactions). In other words, the central presuppositions of ToM framework are embodied in its experimental techniques rather than actually tested, and so ToMism is not an empirical but a metaphysical system, and as the philosopher Geoffrey Warnock has warned:

[...] metaphysical systems do not yield, as a rule, to frontal attack. Their odd property of being demonstrable only, so to speak, from within confers on them also a high resistance to attack from outside. The onslaughts of critics to whom, as likely as not, their strange tenets are very nearly unintelligible are apt to seem, to those entrenched inside, misdirected or irrelevant. Such systems are more vulnerable to *ennui* than to disproof. They are citadels, much shot at perhaps but never taken by storm, which are quietly discovered one day to be no longer inhabited.

(Warnock, 1969, pp. 7–8)

Do our criticisms of ToM research mean that we – the editors of this volume – are *anti*-scientific, methodologically and in the sense that the Enlightenment thought of science as helping people to understand their world and themselves, and changing both for the better? No, but this does depend on what science is deemed to be. To our mind, defining scientific psychology by its method – 'scientific psychology is experimental, and scientific psychologists should test subjects!' – is dogmatic, not scientific. Science started in opposition to authoritarian dogmatism and aimed to combat it through developing systematic methods of enquiry that would be adequate to its phenomena. The complication is that the phenomena studied in different scientific disciplines are not all of a kind and so one has to think about sciences in the plural, rather than about unitary science (cf. Feyerabend, 1999) – and it is futile to try to define what all such methods have in common (it is certainly not testing subjects).

Our contention is that, because of its subject, psychology cannot entirely emulate natural sciences without losing its phenomena. This is of course not a new idea – the contention was implicit in the methodological pluralism of Wundt (see, e.g., Rieber, 1980) and sharply formulated by the philosopher and historian R. G. Collingwood now over 70 years ago in his attacks on 'modern psychology' (see Collingwood, 1940, 1946, 1994). For reasons that are still pertinent, Collingwood argued that sciences need to devise and use their *own* distinctive methods adequate to their *own* phenomena.[7] This in turn requires that a science does not prejudge the phenomena it studies, and does not reconstruct them in accordance with its methodological strictures, as behaviourism did in its way, and the research within ToMism does in a different but closely related way. How is this relevant here? One argument of this book is that ToM research does not understand the phenomenon it investigates – human intentionality exercised in social settings. ToMism warps intentionality into abstract problem-solving that takes place in a vacuum. So exactly what aspects of intentionality are lost in ToM research, and what research methods are more appropriate than the false-belief task and the other experimental paradigms within ToMism?

The chapters in this book, read together, indicate answers to these questions. Most review, analyse and critique specific domains of research on ToM: Ivan Leudar and Alan Costall on communication; Rose McCabe on schizophrenia; Vassu Reddy and Paul Morris on child development; Stuart Shanker and Jim Stieben and Emma Williams on autism; Michael Bavidge and Ian Ground on animal communication. These chapters are, however, not just critical assessments of available research – they are also calls for alternative ways of doing research on how people engage each other as people. These alternative research programmes indicate the aspects of social experience that are lost in the Theory of Mind research.

Sharrock and Coulter in Chapter 4 argue that rather than learning to theorize about other people's minds, children learn how to use what ToM sees as 'psychological' language in interactions with other people. In Chapter 12, Hutto similarly argues that rather than thinking about ToM as a theoretical variant of folk psychology, intentionality has to be thought of in narrative terms – children, for instance, do not learn to (folk-)theorize about others in psychological terms, but instead acquire narrative resources to understand them appropriately. Consistent with this, Leudar and Costall in Chapter 2 argue that the theory of ToM is a restricted, impoverished and intellectualized model of communication. Reddy and Morris (Chapter 5) note that ToM investigations are typically in the third-person perspective and call for a move towards second-person perspective and 'engagement' – this necessarily stresses children's involvement in situations where they learn and develop. Shanker and Stieben (Chapter 7) propose research which is essentially in Vygotskian and socio-cultural tradition, but with an emphasis not on cognition but on emotions – the researcher needs to track children's participation in early, emotion-filled social interactions since it is disengagement in these and the resulting lack of social enskillment that are the first steps towards autism. Williams (Chapter 8) shows that what people with autism find difficult is acting as skilled experts in engagements with others, and instead they act as strangers detached from them and taking recourse to formal rules. Bavidge and Ground (Chapter 9) invite the readers to think about animal behaviours not as carrying information that would allow inferences about invisible psychological states, but rather as expressive in the Wittgensteinian sense, that is, as constitutive aspects of the phenomena.

All of these critiques of the ToM programme, and the proposed changes in direction of research, stress that investigations cannot start with the situation where the person is an individual *detached* from others and requiring some universally valid *intellectual* means to transcend the gulf that always separates him or her from others. There are, of course, some alternatives to ToMism in contemporary psychology that take as their subject not solipsist mental states, but situated and meaningful activities. Chapters 10 and 11 focus on two of these alternatives. Wes Sharrock (Chapter 10) discusses discursive psychology (and the conceptual problems with which it struggles). Ivan Marková (Chapter 11) explains dialogism in psychology and shows that other people are never simply objects of knowledge, but are co-participants in acts of knowing. These two alternative approaches investigate the ways people engage each other *in situ*, the resources they have for doing this and how they use them.

One important theme of this book, then, is to set out basic characteristics required of theoretical and methodological alternatives to ToMism. We need to be clear, first, that no-one in this book is denying that sometimes, in our interactions with others, we resort to inference, simulation and perhaps, occasionally, even something resembling theorizing. But people relate to other people in a *diversity* of ways, and only some of these are of a specifically linguistic or propositional kind. Second, we are not claiming that people are infallible in their dealings with other people. They are. But the source of fallibility is not the supposed 'privacy' of other minds. It is a question, not of hidden depth, but of breadth – in our view ToMism is looking for intentionality in the wrong place. Thoughts, feelings, desires, hopes and so on, cannot be 'observed' in people's heads – not even with the help of a PET scanner or a resort to theory. Descriptions of activities vary in the kind of detail provided, and 'intentional talk' specifies *biographic* and *circumstantial* particulars pertinent to the activity, not details of *hidden mind/brain* events (Sharrock argues this cogently in Chapter 10). Wittgenstein expressed the idea as follows:

> Why do I want to tell him about an intention too, as well as telling him what I did. [...] because I want to tell him something about *myself*, which goes beyond what happened at the time.
>
> I reveal to him something of myself when I tell him what I was going to do. – Not, however, on grounds of self-observation, but by the way of a response (it might be also called an intuition).
>
> (Wittgenstein, 1997, §659; emphasis in the original)

And Stephen Toulmin developed the idea as follows:

> What makes it so difficult to 'say the last word' about anyone's state of mind is no longer simply the *formal* possibility that he is deliberately concealing his feelings and intentions. Rather, it is the *substantive* possibility that we are failing to recognize the broader contexts within which the fuller significance of his conduct needs to be judged, and so are failing to see the whole picture. [...] The philosophical doubts and difficulties that arise in this way are, as a result, not the purely formal and general doubts of the skeptic; they are the substantial and specific hesitations and reservations that properly hedge around the interpretations that one human being places on another's feelings and actions in practice.
>
> (Toulmin, 1976, pp. 191–2)

This means that the alternatives to ToMism must essentially be ecological. Epistemically, they have to go beyond both behaviourism and cognitivism, and especially beyond the Cartesian conceptions of mind and behaviour. The two have to be considered parts of a unified phenomenon – situated activity. Methodologically, the alternatives to ToMism have to move beyond investigating isolated individuals in artificial settings, towards investigating them in circumstances that combine proximal settings, personal life biographies and culture at large (see Leudar et al., 2008a, b). So in our reaction to the ToMist claim that making sense of other people is indirect, requiring inferences about unobservable mental states, we are not claiming, instead, that intentions, emotions and feelings are directly *observed*. In challenging the priority of the experiment as the source of evidence about how people make sense of other people, the emphasis should not simply be upon studying social interaction 'in the wild', but on taking on board the *different ways* people relate to one another in real interactions. The term 'observation' implies not just a single perceptual modality, but the very detachment that has become definitive of sociality within ToMism. 'Observation' implies a spectator theory of how we know one another. The point being made throughout this book is that knowing people in real life – and also investigating how people know people in real life – requires going beyond mere observation, to getting involved instead. Socio-cultural, Dialogical, Discursive, Historical and Ecological psychologies are small steps in the right direction.

Notes

1 What Tooby and Cosmides signally fail to explain is how these 'unobservable entities' are somehow miraculously 'visible' to natural selection. Compare and contrast their claim about the all-seeing powers of natural selection, and the Duke of Argyll's nineteenth-century account of the nature of instinct in birds, and other animals. In this case, the 'Agency' in question is the all-knowing Divine Creator:

> All the knowledge and all the resources of Mind which is involved in these instincts *is a reflection of some Agency which is outside the creatures which exhibit them*. In this respect it may be said with truth that they are machines. But then they are machines with this peculiarity, that they not only reflect, but also in various measures and degrees partake of the attributes of Mind. (Argyll, 1884, p. 106; emphasis added.)

2 We have taken the term ToMism from Sharrock and Coulter (2004) but, unlike them, we are using it in a much more inclusive way referring not only to TToM.

3 Such a disconnection between people is now simply taken for granted, as in the following title from a recent book on social understanding, *Other Minds: How Humans Bridge the Divide Between Self and Others* (Malle and Hodges, 2007).

4 Funder (1995) characterized this approach as an 'error paradigm', and rightly so, for while it has been very effective in explaining why we happen to *mis*understand one another, it has remained rather at a loss to account for how we might ever manage to relate effectively to one another.

5 Neisser's observation is especially telling, because it was part of a commentary upon some studies claiming to adopt an alternative, 'ecological' approach to social knowing.

6 This move, of course, was made long before the rise of ToMism. It is the standard way the introductory textbooks explain the logic of psychological research:

> Saying that our knowledge of other minds is theoretical rather than observational means that we study mind in the same way as a chemist studies the atom. Atoms are not observed directly, but their properties can be inferred from observable events. (Hebb, 1958, p. 3.)

7 Collingwood argued that not all sciences can be *natural* sciences. He presented history – his subject – not as a Humanity but as a science with its own methods

that were developed for rational study of activities of people in the past. He concluded that history, so defined, required an 'internal' perspective on such activities. If, instead, it used methods of natural science, it would lose essential aspects of its subject. Collingwood argued forcefully that psychology conceived of exclusively as a natural science was not in a position to study higher mental processes, such as thinking, because these were self-critical and criterial, with the criteria being historically contingent. According to him, for this reason the scientific study of thinking had to use historical methods. His view was that Psychology was founded in the seventeenth century as a natural science of emotion and perception to supplement criterial disciplines, such as history, ethics and logic, and there already were disciplines which had adequate methods to study higher psychological processes. Collingwood therefore saw no need to develop psychological methods that would be adequate to a study of thinking, for example. We agree with Collingwood that the methods of the natural sciences cannot be used to investigate higher psychological processes but not with his belief that such methods already exist in ethics, logic and history.

Part 1
Theory and History

2
On the Historical Antecedents of the Theory of Mind Paradigm

Ivan Leudar and Alan Costall

In this chapter we discuss the historical origins and conceptual debts of the theory of mind paradigm (ToMism).[1] We argue that this paradigm should be thought of as a model of communication. We find that ToMism has roots in Noam Chomsky's psychology, and Paul Grice's work on meaning. It is based on their ideas, inherits some of their problems but adds little new. What is new in ToMism in fact makes matters worse by profoundly intellectualizing social interactions. We find that it inherits and tries to solve the Cartesian 'problem of other minds'. Not surprisingly, it fails to solve this unsolvable problem.

The problem of other minds

'How do we know that another person is angry? [...] Do we ever know?' (Austin, 1979, p. 76). A sceptic would answer that we can never know *directly*, but that we may infer the anger and believe that the person is angry with varying degrees of uncertainty. John Austin found the sceptical answer not just wrong, but worse, an answer to an ill-conceived problem. The general questions: 'How do we know that other people have minds at all?' and 'How does a child learn that other people have minds?' are even worse. They bring back into psychology the 'problem of other minds' and in posing that problem, in Austin's words, we step even further away 'from the garden of the world we live in' (ibid., p. 90). This is to say that the problem of other minds is not a natural one, but 'iatrogenic'; not a natural fact about human beings, but a consequence of a philosophically inspired rethinking of what it means to be a person and what it means to engage with other people. Our starting point here is that the 'problem of other minds' is not something that arises universally in every interaction between people, but is created through thinking about people as minds and bodies, a dualism reproduced in psychology as the contrast between 'cognitions' and 'behaviours'.

It is customary to blame Descartes for starting the problem off in philosophy, through dualism and the use of systematic doubt. Here is Gilbert

Ryle's distillation of what he called the 'Cartesian Myth':

> Every human being [...] has both a body and a mind. [...]
>
> Human bodies are in space and are subject to the mechanical laws which govern all other bodies in space. Bodily processes and states can be inspected by external observers. So a man's bodily life is as much a public affair as are the lives of animals and reptiles and even as the careers of trees, crystals and planets.
>
> But minds are not in space, nor are their operations subject to mechanical laws. The workings of one mind are not witnessable by other observers; its career is private. Only I can take direct cognisance of the states and processes of my own mind. A person therefore lives through two collateral histories, one consisting of what happens in and to his body, the other consisting of what happens in and to his mind. The first is public, the second private.
>
> (Ryle, 1949, p. 13)

The problem of other minds arguably arises when we divide the world into mental and material domains which are incommensurable and where any person's mind is hidden from everyone else, and yet reading such hidden minds is essential for understanding one another. Contemporary psychology claims to set aside the 'Cartesian Myth'. Yet, even though it explains mind as a mechanism and claims to be materialist rather than dualist, it inherits the problem of other minds in distinguishing mind from behaviour and in assuming that mental states are essentially private, whereas behaviours are not. In fact, both the categorical behaviour/mind distinction and the privacy of mind presupposition are formulated in ToMism very much in the way Ryle found them in Descartes. Behaviourists in their determination to be scientific failed to notice that they adopted a definition of behaviour that is basically Cartesian, and were themselves responsible for the modern dualistic meaning of 'behaviour'. The cognitive revolution, which aimed to bring back mind into psychology (Bruner, 1990, p. 1), actually maintained the problem of other minds. No wonder that Bruner has called for a renewed cognitive revolution focused on 'meaning-making' (ibid.). Cognitivism reinstated the legitimacy of scientific inference to the unobservable, but retained the conception of behaviour as logically separate from mind, and so regarded behaviour very much as evidence of an essentially unobservable mind. Behaviourism and cognitivism, despite their avowed materialism, both operated in what is a Cartesian framework for thinking about people – epistemically they remained Cartesian.[2] In psychology, the problem of other minds is not usually stated explicitly or in formal philosophical terms but is instead implicit in theories, methods of investigation and in the language of psychology itself (see Costall and Leudar, Chapter 3 in this volume). The problem is inscribed in the language of psychology which sets apart behaviour and mind and then tries to put them together again along Cartesian lines – with the behaviour providing the data for psychological inference.

Our claim is that the problem of other minds is not a fact which people must somehow get around in interacting with each other. Now, one might ask what our *evidence* for this claim is. This, however, is not a sensible question. What empirical evidence could there be for the existence of the 'problem of other minds'? The fact is that the problem is not an empirical scientific discovery by psychologists or anybody else. It is rather what R. G. Collingwood might have called an 'absolute presupposition' of modern scientific psychology (see Collingwood, 1994). The question, therefore, is how we can decide whether this presupposition is warranted and useful? Although experiments cannot help, conceptual therapy may (Wittgenstein, 1997, p. 232ᵉ). The way out is to subject this dualistic presupposition to historical and conceptual analysis to see when and where it is coherent or whether in fact it always leads to troubles.

Wittgenstein and Austin both argued cogently that behaviour is not an arbitrary, 'colourless' sign of 'mental states', but is instead constitutive of emotions, beliefs and wants (Wittgenstein, 1997; Austin, 1979, ch. 4). For this reason, one can 'notice and grasp' directly that others are in pain, or act with particular intentions. Inferences are, moreover, not required because, as Goffman (1979) pertinently noted, intentionality is 'given off' by participants, who make their behaviour 'monitorable'. More recent ethomethodological and conversation analytic work indicates that conversations are organized so as to make experiential aspects of activities noticeable, obviating the need for inference (Suchman, 1987; Edwards, 2006). People can of course lie and occasionally hide their feelings, beliefs and intentions. However, it is *hiding* one's experience – keeping it private – that is the real accomplishment, not *revealing* it. This indicates that our knowledge of others is not in the first place a matter of detached and theory-driven inference, but of engagement in organized joint activities.

This way of thinking is not possible if one starts with the unexamined presupposition that behaviour is just bodily movement without intrinsic intentionality, the way of thinking that relocates all that is alive and intelligent to the hidden mind. As has been made clear in ethnomethodological studies, this psychologized way of talking about pain, beliefs and desires – as referring to private and hidden 'mental states' – is inconsistent with how experiential words are used in everyday life (see Coulter, 1989, 1992; Bilmes, 1992; and Sharrock, Chapter 10 in this volume, for a discussion of this point).[3] Kurt Danziger in his book, *Naming the Mind*, demonstrated how modern psychology has taken over terms from everyday psychological discourse, such as personality, memory and intelligence, subjected them to radical transformation, and has thus given them a unity and abstraction they never previously possessed (Danziger, 1997). The language of experience has been subjected to the same transformation in psychology and the problem of other minds is partly of psychologists' own doing rather than inherent to human nature.[4]

So what is to be done about the problem of other minds? One can analyse it and its historical roots, and, as Austin did, then wisely set it aside (Austin, 1979, ch. 4). Or else one can try to solve it once and for all. The 'Theory of Mind' paradigm is the most recent and influential attempt in psychology to do just this. If behaviour is merely a 'clue' to an unobservable mind, then something is needed to bridge the gap, and, according to ToMism, that something resembles the theoretical leap that scientists make when drawing inferences from observable data to hidden structures. On this view, in order to understand other people as beings who experience the world and themselves in it, all of us in everyday social life must engage in theorizing or something functionally equivalent to it. Since such understanding is central to our social lives and distinguishes human social interactions from those observed in other species, by implication it must be such theorizing about mental states that holds human social life together. A long tradition, arguably going back to Plato, but ascendant since the sixteenth century, prioritizes theoretical knowledge of universals over practical knowledge of culturally and situation contingent matters. In rethinking philosophy Descartes in fact set up geometry and systematic doubt as paragons of knowledge (see Toulmin, 2001).

The theory of mind paradigm is a part of this tradition. It intellectualizes mundane social life – assuming that such life depends upon theories to be enlightened, effective and in many respects possible (cf. Nehamas, 1998; Ryle, 1999). Ter Hark has noted that this theoretical solution of scepticism assimilated ordinary knowledge claims about other minds to procedures of scientific inference:

> By transforming ordinary use into a form of hypothetico-deductive entailment, Fodor and Churchland have made propositions about other minds and propositions about mathematics and physics into similar instruments – the way out of the sceptical problem is to recognize that we measure with different instruments.
>
> (Ter Hark, 2001, p. 215)

This is a step in a right direction but in our view not far enough. In everyday life people rarely 'measure' each other, whatever the instruments. Personal experiences in everyday activities are noticeable without any resort to mediating theory-based inferences (cf. Merleau-Ponty, 1973, p. 9); and we mostly manage our dealings with other people without measurements and inferences. Our everyday use of language is a practical matter. As in natural science, we can use everyday language to describe, explain and predict the actions of others. These three are, however, just some amongst many speech acts, none of which are actions of solitary observers oriented to but disengaged from the world of others, but rather conversational activities done *with* other people. In fact, thinking about 'Theory of Mind' as an objective way of representing people and their deeds, rather than engaging them communicatively, is the point where ToMism profoundly intellectualizes everyday social life by inappropriately applying the attitude of natural science to the mundane. The remedy is only possible if we think of ToMism as a theory of communication with a very restricted scope. The rich variety of ways people engage with others in conversation – hinting, requesting, explaining, protesting, cajoling, endearing oneself, interpreting, advising, to name a few – is, in ToMism, contracted to explaining and predicting the behaviour of third persons!

In fact, Descartes himself insisted that we will never comprehend the mind-body relation just by 'meditating' and 'studying things that exercise the imagination'. He may have set up geometry as a paragon of human knowledge and regarded mind and body as distinct substances, but he also took it for granted that mind and body are thoroughly 'intermingled' – the mind is not in the body like a pilot in a ship. Rather, the union of mind and body must be lived to be understood: 'it is just by means of *ordinary life and conversation* [...] *that one learns to conceive the union of soul and body*' (Descartes, 1954, p. 280, emphasis added; see Tibbetts, 1973).

We take it therefore that the 'problem of other minds', as reformulated within ToMism, is not a universal human burden but instead a problem which makes sense and becomes acute in specific historical and cultural conditions. There is a way of turning the problem of other minds into a research topic of historical psychology and we would have liked to be able to summarize here the findings of the research on circumstances in which that problem is acutely experienced by participants in social interactions. Unfortunately the cultural and historical contingencies of the 'problem of other minds' have not been recognized in psychology (see more on this in the next chapter).

Why is the epistemic Cartesianism, implicit in present-day psychology, not noticed more often, and why is Neuro-Cartesianism so attractive to psychologists who deem their work scientific and materialist? In what follows we shall examine some of the historical sources of ToMism to understand how this frankly dualistic approach has come to seem in psychology so plausible as the solution not just to the traditional 'problem of other minds', but also the problem of how in fact we all, as 'just plain folks', typically make sense of one another.

Since it is not an empirical discovery, ToMism needs to be understood in the historical context of studies of communication and language in psychology. These, we shall see, are Cartesian in the sense just outlined. ToMism follows in their tradition, without resolving the issue, nor ever noticing its quandary. We find that ToMism is historically contingent on both the cognitive psychology of Noam Chomsky and also the pragmatics of Paul Grice.[5] We argue that both prepared the ground for ToMism conceptually even though their influence is not widely acknowledged in the subsequent literature.[6]

'Theory of Mind' and communication

Before turning to Grice and Chomsky, we first turn to the origins of the dualistic conception of communication that pervades psychology, and for which Grice and Chomsky have been taken to provide the 'solution'. Psychology tends to borrow from other disciplines – from logicians, logics to study reasoning; from linguists, grammars to study language; and from computer scientists, theories of computation for human cognition. The study of communication in psychology obtained a significant impetus after the Second World War from the developments in communication technology and in information theory (Wiener, 1948). These provided psychology with concepts for research on communication such as, for instance, 'information', 'code', signal', 'channel', 'capacity' (e.g., Broadbent, 1957; see Vroon, 1987).

One can apply information theory radically, and acknowledge only those meanings that are expressible in its language. Claude Shannon put it as follows.

> The fundamental problem of communication is that of reproducing at one point either exactly or approximately a message selected at another point. Frequently the messages have meaning; that is they refer to or are correlated according to some system with certain physical or conceptual entities. These semantic aspects of communication are irrelevant to the engineering problem. The significant aspect is that the actual message is one *selected from a set* of possible messages.
>
> (Shannon, 1949, p. 33)

Echoing Shannon, Colin Cherry (1957) noted that information theory was concerned with signals and their transmission, but not with their meaning for the users. In contrast, information theory as it was applied in psychology to communication, retained both 'information content' and 'meaning' – with the latter being psychological states, such as 'notions', 'ideas' and 'desires' and the meanings had to be inferred from the information content. In the resulting model of communication neither the information content nor the psychological meanings were 'visible' but had to be decoded and inferred, and the understanding of 'messages' consisted in going beyond what is observable and depended on complex cognitive activities. This model of communication sets participants in communication the same task as ToMism would – bridging the gap between signal (linguistic or non-verbal behaviour in face-to-face interactions) and meanings (mental states of others). Historically, the information theory based model of communication prepared the ground for *telementational* models of communication.

A lucid proponent of these at the time was Michael Reddy (1979). He argued that the commonsense meta-language of English consists of a set of 'conduit metaphors', such as 'putting (thoughts) into words', 'getting (one's feelings) across' and he criticized this metalanguage from a standpoint of 'radical subjectivism'. According to him, 'no one receives anyone else's thoughts directly', nor can anyone literally 'give you an idea' – these are 'locked within the skull and life process of each of us' (ibid., pp. 286–7). Anticipating the simulation thesis, Reddy argued that language helps 'one person to construct out of his own stock of mental stuff something like a replica, or copy, of someone else's thoughts, a replica which can be more or less accurate, depending on many factors' (ibid., p. 287). On this account of communication, meaning is once again *hidden*. It is not in the open, and so has to be inferred. But then, we wonder, how does anyone – children or adults – ever know that there is *anything* to be inferred either in general or on a specific occasion? The substance of the *telementational* account of communication and social interaction is as follows: individual social behaviours are caused by their doers' mental states, and properly understood in terms of those states. Organisms do not react directly to the behaviour of others, however, but instead to the occluded 'mental states' which these indicate. On this view communicative behaviours mediate interactions that are effectively mental! This way of thinking about communication is notable in ToMism. Thus, according to Astington, for instance, 'Social interaction is really an interaction of minds, of mental states' (Astington, 1994, p. 43).

The telementational account is, then, not a discovery made within ToMism – all that it contributes is the hypothesis that one needs a *theory* to cross the gap between observable behavioural evidence and hidden meaning.[7] The question is how the telementational model of social interaction became so firmly established in contemporary psychology. Our argument is that this was partly through the work of Chomsky and Grice.

Chomsky and theory of mind

Chomsky and the status of theory in ToMism.   Chomsky is fabled for having delivered modern psychology from behaviourism. His influence on psychology was indeed considerable, even though, from our point of view, somewhat Mephistophelean. In marginalizing behaviour, Chomsky reinforced the Cartesianism implicit in scientific psychology, and even though he did not actually write about it, he nevertheless provided a niche for the theory of mind and has been credited with doing so (e.g., Smith, 1999, pp. 25–6). Moreover, as we see it, his programmatic formulation of the pragmatics of language prefigures the theory of mind.

Chomsky and the status of behaviour in ToMism.   The behaviour of individuals in the theory of mind framework has the status of observable 'evidence' to be used in inferring their occluded mental states. A crucial part of Chomsky's psychology is what is now referred to as 'the poverty of the stimulus' argument. Usually, and especially in developmental psychology, this is taken to mean that the 'language input' (i.e., the talk of other people) does not contain sufficient information to specify a grammar of the language for a child (cf. Pullum and Scholz, 1992). The poverty of the stimulus is, however, conceived in somewhat broader terms by Chomsky, presumably following from his rejection of behaviourism (Chomsky, 1959). Chomsky did not just argue that children cannot induce a grammar from 'language input' without an innate endowment. He also disdained the use of a language corpus as an adequate source on which to base linguistics (e.g., Chomsky, 1964; cf. Sampson, 2002). He argued that the object of traditional linguistics, the language, is an abstraction and hence not a proper object of study (e.g., Chomsky, 1976, ch. 2; 1984, ch. 2). He was doing cognitive psychology instead (see, e.g., Chomsky, 1976, p. 36; 1980a, p. 4).[8]

With respect to ToMism, it is crucial to note that Chomsky viewed behaviour as evidence of knowledge, but not as a *criterion* of knowledge. The following text, written by Chomsky in the 1980s, presumably relates to his debate with Quine but could have been a response to Wittgenstein's comments on the same issue (Chomsky, 1969; Quine, 1969; Wittgenstein, 1997):

> [...] one might attempt to characterize the knowledge of language – perhaps knowledge more generally – as a capacity or ability to do something, as a system of dispositions of some kind, in which case it is perhaps not unreasonable to think of behavior as providing a criterion for the possession of knowledge. In contrast, if such knowledge is characterized in terms of mental state and structure, then behavior simply provides evidence for possession of knowledge, as might facts of an entirely different order – electrical activity of the brain, for example.
>
> (Chomsky, 1980b, p. 5)

Chomsky thus acknowledged that behaviour *may be* thought of as either evidence or a criterion of knowledge, depending on one's ontology (see also Chomsky, 1980a, p. 48). Somewhat dogmatically, however, the 'fact of the matter', as far as he was concerned, is that behaviour *merely counts as* evidence:

> But I see no reason to deny that there is a fact of the matter, however difficult it may be to establish, on that *behavior is only one kind of evidence – sometimes not the best, and surely no criterion of knowledge.*
>
> (Chomsky, 1980b, p. 6; our emphasis)

The poverty of stimulus argument then chimes with a neo-Cartesian epistemology. It sets up behaviour as *evidence*, and *poor* evidence at that, for mental states. Theory of mind inherits this conception of behaviour and the problems of other minds it carries.

Nobody needs to be reminded of Chomsky's distrust of the notion of learning (when he writes the word, it is more often than not in inverted commas). Indeed, his striking entry into psychology involved demonstrating that the behaviourists' notion of learning would not account for language acquisition (Chomsky, 1959). Human language could not be acquired sentence-by-sentence through an equivalent of a 'finite state automaton'. What was acquired, he argued, were rules of language, organized in a grammar capable of producing a bounded infinity of sentences. In 1958, in the preface to his *Words and Things*, Roger Brown wrote that acquiring a language is learning a system, and to know a language is to know its rules (Brown, 1958, viii). Brown located the beginnings of Psycholinguistics to the early 1950s, singling out an interdisciplinary meeting of psychologists and linguists at Cornell University in 1951. Notably, the participating linguists were 'descriptive linguists' not 'generativists' – that school of linguistics did not yet exist (Brown, 1958, the preface). Brown's comments on the origins of psycholinguistics are cogent but he was less persuasive when he took credit for turning Chomsky towards psychology:

> Following Chomsky's talk there was an exchange that went something like this:
>
> Brown: 'It sounds to me as if a transformational grammar might be what children learn when they learn their first language.'
>
> Chomsky: 'Oh, do you think so?'
>
> (Brown, 1970, p. 17)

In fact, Chomsky seems to have regarded himself as engaging in psychology from the outset (see Chomsky, 1986). His critique of Skinner's *Verbal Behavior* (Chomsky, 1959) was addressed to a psychological audience already prepared for the ideas it conveyed – but it amplified and focused them.

Chomsky contributed significantly to the acceptance within psychology of the notion that language is a system of grammatical rules (e.g., Greene, 1972), and to the extension of this way of thinking to other psychological 'faculties', for instance the ability to think and reason (see Johnson-Laird and Wason, 1977). Premack and Chomsky engaged in an ardent debate on whether the acquisition of such language was restricted to humans, or shared with other primates. An interesting passage in the seminal article on theory of mind by Premack and Woodruff (1978), however, reveals an affinity: they accepted that the theory of mind consisted of rules (albeit not as tightly structured as a grammar of English) which are not learnable through associative mechanisms (Premack and Woodruff, 1978). In other words, like generative linguistics, ToMism is explicitly opposed to behaviourism, and specified as a system of rules internal to the individual. The influence of Chomsky is clear, if unacknowledged. But the affinity goes further. Premack and Woodruff define theory of mind thus:

> In saying that an individual has a theory of mind, we mean that the individual imputes mental states to himself and others. [...] A system of inferences of this kind is properly viewed as a theory, first because such states are not directly observable, and second because the system can be used to make predictions, specifically about the behavior of other organisms.
>
> (Premack and Woodruff, 1978, p. 515)

The terms Premack and Woodruff use here to describe how individuals accomplish understanding severely intellectualize the matter. Even so, does a 'system of inferences' used to predict behaviour or a 'rough kind of system with which we all work' necessarily count as a theory? In fact, the term 'theory' is used rather flexibly by Chomsky. In his writing, linguistic competence conceived as a grammar is a tacit theory. But a grammar can be an aspect of a theory of language in two senses. It is formulated by linguists to describe and explain language behaviour (and this sense we take to be relatively uncontroversial). For Chomsky, however, grammar is also a psychological object:

> To know a language, I am assuming, is to be in a certain mental state, which persists as a relatively steady component of transitory mental states. What kind of mental state? I assume further that to be in such a mental state is to have a certain mental structure consisting of a system of rules and principles that generate and relate mental representations of various types.
>
> (Chomsky, 1980a, p. 48)

In this sense, the grammar of a language is 'known' by lay individuals. But is it to be thought of as a theory? Chomsky seemed to think so when characterizing language acquisition as hypothesis testing. Some developmental psycholinguists at the time wrote of children learning to speak as 'little linguists' (cf. Thomas, 2002). Indeed, Jerome Bruner (1978), although deeply critical of Chomsky's claim that knowledge about language learning could be regarded as independent of any wider knowledge of other people or the world,[9] nevertheless had no objection at all to an intellectualized way of thinking of language learning:

> I would take the view that the child's knowledge of pre-linguistic communication, related as it is to world of action and interaction, provides him with tell-tale cues for constructing and testing hypotheses about the

meaning and structure of the discourse into which he quickly enters. He does, as LAD would have us believe, have a stunning capacity to infer and to generate rules, indeed to over-generalize them.

(Bruner, 1978, p. 83)[10]

Even in Bruner's formulation, children learning to talk behave as proto-scientists.

It is clear that, in practice, children and linguists are doing very different things, and the relationship between linguistic competence and linguistic theory is not really clarified in Chomsky's work (cf. Searle, 1972). We suspect that explaining language in very general and formal terms (as, e.g., 'a grammar', or a 'projection problem') obscures important differences between what children do when learning language and what linguists do as scientists when studying language.[11] Even at the time, the way Chomsky spoke of grammar as known by lay speakers of language was controversial (see, e.g., Stich, 1980), and Chomsky of course did not argue that ordinary folks know language in quite the same way as generative linguists do. As Chomsky put it, the lay 'theoreticians' merely *'cognize'* the grammar of a language – their knowledge is not reflexive, but provided as a biological structure (a language module, perhaps). This knowledge, if it should be regarded as knowledge at all, is then inevitably tacit and inaccessible to consciousnesses. It is of course debatable whether the unconscious rules of grammatical competence postulated by Chomsky count as rules in the everyday sense of the word (see Chomsky, 1969, and 1976, pp. 179–95; Hacker, 1988; Quine, 1969; Searle, 1980).[12]

Chomsky thought in this way of other 'faculties', not just language. He wrote, for instance, that the term 'theory' 'covers general common sense and belief' (Chomsky, 1969, p. 53), and this seems to be a relatively fixed element of his psychology. In an apocryphal story in his *Reflections on Language*, he considered that even face recognition might reflect an implicit theory:

> S might study, for example, the ability of his subjects to recognize and identify complex physical objects and predict their behaviour under various circumstances. He might find that there are qualitative differences in their ability to recognize human faces and other objects of comparable complexity. This investigation might lead S to attribute to his subjects, as an element of common sense, an abstract theory of possible faces and a system of projection which (abstracting away from memory restrictions and the like) enables the subject to predict how a face will appear under a range of empirical conditions.

(Chomsky, 1976, pp. 139–40)

In summary, Chomsky proposes a partial symmetry between expert and lay 'knowledge', just as it appears in ToMism subsequently (see Costall and Leudar, 2004). The affinity between Chomsky's ideas and ToMism is clear and it is actually occasionally acknowledged explicitly in ToMist writings: 'Infants have an implicit theory of mind [...] in the same way that two-year-olds have an implicit theory of grammar' (Astington, 1994, p. 47).[13] Chomsky's work seems to have prepared the ground for the 'theory' in 'Theory of Mind'.

Chomsky's pragmatics, Grice and ToMism.   Chomsky explicitly declared his linguistics to be in Cartesian mode (Chomsky, 1966). He did not, of course, sign up to all aspects of Descartes' philosophy. He endorsed Descartes' reflections on human linguistic creativity (Chomsky, 1966, pp. 3–6). Where the creative use of language indicated immaterial soul to Descartes, to Chomsky it implied a recursive grammar which, like the soul, was unique to humans. Since grammar is a psychological faculty realized in the human brain (an aspect of 'mind/brain' in his later writings), Chomsky is a materialist, whereas Descartes was an ontological dualist. Chomsky did, however, import into psychology other aspects of Cartesianism, namely the categorial distinction between behaviour and mind. Even though he wrote that he did not believe 'that bodies are Cartesian automata' and accepted that the concept of 'the body' is historically evolving (Chomsky, 1980a, p. 6), he also argued, as we have seen, that behaviour is not constitutive of the mind but just evidence for mental states, *and poor evidence at that.*

Do individuals have a privileged access to their own mind in Chomsky's psychology? Shanker (2002) has pointed out that with respect to the organization of the language faculty, Chomsky could hardly argue this since such knowledge is, according to him, tacit in individuals, 'cognized' in his terms, and only accessed through scientific investigation conducted by generative grammarians. Chomsky, nevertheless, endorsed an essentially telementational notion of communication, and hence also the notion that one human mind is occluded from another and only revealed, indirectly and ambiguously, in language and other behaviour. As a consequence, Chomsky accepted that in everyday social interactions, our minds are occluded from one another and so became committed to the traditional problem of other minds. One important link between Chomsky's work and 'Theory of Mind' is then through his conception of language use, i.e. *pragmatics.* Chomsky conceived of the human cognitive system as consisting of autonomous and biologically fixed modules, or in another context 'competences' (Chomsky, 1980a, 1980b, see Smith, 1999). The core modules in his psychology were 'linguistic competence', 'conceptual competence' and 'pragmatic competence'.[14] 'Pragmatic competence' provides arguably a direct historical connection to 'the theory of mind'.

Grice and theory of mind

Chomsky had little to say about 'performance' and did not carry out sustained work on pragmatic competence, but sketched this out as follows: pragmatic competence 'underlies the ability to use such [grammatical] knowledge along with the conceptual system to achieve certain ends or purposes' (Chomsky, 1980a, p. 59). Chomsky in fact endorsed, if somewhat tentatively, Grice's version of pragmatics: 'Pragmatic competence may include what Paul Grice has called a "logic of conversation"' (ibid., pp. 224–5).[15] But what kind of pragmatics was Chomsky endorsing here?

Grice's own work turned on two ideas – 'non-natural meaning' and 'implicature' (Grice, 1957, 1968, 1969, 1975). The former is the idea that effects in linguistic communication are accomplished by means of intention recognition, and a communication is successful to the extent that communicative intentions are recognized.[16] The latter idea was that listeners infer implicatures so as to preserve the validity of maxims of conversation.[17] Initially it was just about possible to understand Grice's work not as cognitive psychology, but rather as an exercise in philosophical logic and about mundane reasoning taking place in talk. After all, Grice was a philosopher, concerned with defining linguistic meaning, and was doing this partly by comparing different types of meaning. As a philosopher, he would, quite properly, have nothing much to say on how intentions defining non-natural meaning are 'put into' utterances or inferred from them. According to this interpretation, Grice should be regarded as writing about the logic of language games and was certainly not concerned with psychological questions, such as how children move from communicating in pre-linguistic ('perlocutionary' in the terminology of developmental pragmatics) mode to linguistic ('illocutionary') mode.[18] Grice's latter work, however, makes this non-psychological reading impossible to maintain (Grice, 1982, 1989). Grice (1989) writes of communication as the production of psychological states by one person in another. For instance:

> [...] a certain psychological state Ψ^1 in certain circumstances is followed by a certain utterance U, made in certain circumstances, which in turn, if the circumstances are right, is followed by a particular instance of a further psychological state Ψ^2, a state not now in the communicating creature but in the creature who is communicated to.
>
> (Grice, 1989, p. 287)

The operation of such creatures as I have been talking about is at least in certain circumstances going to be helped and furthered if there is what one might think of as shared experience. In particular, if psychological states which initially attach to one creature can be transmitted or transferred or reproduced in another creature [...], that would be advantageous.

> (pp. 286–7)

In fact, Grice himself even considered if this psychological exchange might be underwritten by what could count as 'a theory':

> The laws I have mentioned are vulgar laws. The kind of theory in which I think of them appearing would not be a specialist or formalized psychological theory, if indeed there are such things; I am perhaps not very comfortable with the word 'theory' being applied to it. It would be the rough kind of system with which we all work, and the laws in it are to be thought of as corrigible, modifiable and *ceteris paribus* in character.
>
> (p. 285)

Grice's 'non-natural meaning' became a part of John Searle's definition of speech acts – their essential condition – and thereby influential, especially in cognitive science and in developmental psychology (Searle, 1969; McShane, 1980). The reworking of Grice in speech act theory is itself an important precursor to 'Theory of Mind'. Approaching pragmatics from the direction of speech acts, one is inferring not what a speaker's communicative intention happens to be, but what speech act was issued. But speech acts are organized in a system and theorized (Searle and Kiefer, 1980). This sort of pragmatics thus implicitly postulates a *theory* of interpretation – something explicitly declared in theory of mind theory. Thus, although Searle took issue with Chomsky's conception of rules and innateness (see Searle, 1972, 1980) and did not see himself as describing psychological competence, his conception of speech acts did nevertheless afford a link to ToMism. In fact, much of the work in developmental pragmatics in the 1970s and 1980s used speech act theory (see, for instance, the work brought together in Ochs and Schieflin, 1979).

Even in the absence of explicit references to theory of mind in Grice's writings, we are tempted to speculate whether Grice's work did not just prepare the conceptual ground for ToMism but was also subsequently revised by it. Some followers of Grice – Sperber and Wilson (2002), for instance, now refer to the inference of communicative intentions as 'mind reading', and postulate a ToM 'brain module' that would be dedicated to doing relevance-theoretic pragmatics. Gricean pragmatics is here assimilated into the theory of mind framework, even to the extent of offering speculations about its evolutionary origins (cf. Sperber, 2000; Wilson, 2000). Grice's reluctance to think of maxims of communication as being a theory (as noted above) indicates that he would have been unlikely to accept that there is a *formal* theory, with which one can bridge the Cartesian divide between persons. His approach, nevertheless, assumes such a divide and, endorsed by Chomsky, provided psychology with a system which mentalizes communication.

Unlike the link to Chomsky, the historical link of ToMism to Grice is frequently acknowledged. Astington, who has adopted a pragmatics based on

Gricean principles, has written:

> Social interaction is really an interaction of minds, of mental states, but we have to communicate those states to others. We have to let the other person know we want something, or that we want them to believe something, and so on. Human beings are not mind readers, not in any telepathic sense anyway, and in order to know what is in another person's mind we have to give that information to one another. ... You have your thoughts, your beliefs, desires and so on, and I have mine. We share them in language, in the talk that passes between us.
>
> (Astington, 1994, pp. 45–7)

Baron-Cohen wrote:

> Speech Act Theorists such as Grice (1967/1975), Austin (1962) [*sic*], and Searle (1965) had argued that a theory of mind is also essential for normal communication, both verbal and non-verbal. Put simply, the argument is that all communication requires both participants to take into account the background knowledge and presuppositions of the other person in the dialogue, as well as their intentions in communicating. Such mental state attribution is necessary, it is argued, if a dialogue is to respect the conversational rules of pragmatics – if it is to be appropriate and relevant to the social context (Sperber and Wilson, 1986).
>
> (Baron-Cohen, 1992, p. 10)

We have seen that Grice was ambivalent about the need for a *theory* of mind to underpin intentionally mediated communication and neither Searle nor Austin have ever argued for a theory of mind.

Baron-Cohen (1988) unfortunately does not provide a clear and cogent outline of the relationship between pragmatics and theory of mind. He implies that he does not equate pragmatics with the theory of mind, and instead regards having a theory of mind as a *precondition of* pragmatics (see Baron-Cohen, 1988). What, then, according to him, is a theory of mind (in addition to knowing what beliefs and intentions and so on are, that is)?

Theory of mind seems to entail instrumental means-end reasoning about actions in general (cf. Bilmes, 1986) and so it is about more than just communication. It is presumably required not just in conversation but also on occasions where we just observe other people, without communicating or engaging them, and we observe them not just as physical objects but as intentional beings.[19] And yet this is an orientation to others imposed in typical theory of mind experiments and in general appropriate in natural science – it detaches the observer from the observed and assures objectivity. Developmentally, however, such objectivity could hardly be said to be normal or desirable, and it cannot be where the child could start to make sense of other people – children learn about others in engaged interactions in their families, and only eventually may learn to apply what they learned there in becoming invisible and observing others. The observer–observed detachment is also rare in everyday interactions between people – observing intentional beings tends to turn into engagement, in which the observer and the observed mutually constitute each other. These are some reasons (in addition to the historical points we made above) why we say that theory of mind is better thought of as a theory of communication (but a wrong-headed one at that).

Looked at in another way, Baron-Cohen restricts the scope of pragmatics disproportionately. Pragmatics is not restricted to *linguistic* pragmatics – its aim is to account for the *varieties* of ways people reason *in situ* about what they themselves and other people *do*, what they intend and believe, and the circumstances in which they do so. Pragmatics usually does this by analysing everyday reasoning practices, such as those Grice described for deriving implicatures. Language mediated communications can be thought of a special case of coordinated social interactions, where the intentional interpersonal engagement is foregrounded through talking and mediates the interactions.[20]

On the whole, the relationship between ToM and relevance-based pragmatics seems fluid in ToMism but 'Theory of Mind' is about more than communication. Historically, it is clear that the relationship between Gricean pragmatics and ToMism is far from unilateral. Grice provided the conceptual grounding for the ToM, but his pragmatics were transformed (or at least some varieties of it were) in the process, and subsumed in a speculative modular and evolutionary psychology.

Conclusion

Our historical analysis demonstrates that there are affinities between Chomsky's psychology, Grice's pragmatics and the theory of mind paradigm. Chomsky and Grice mediated the Cartesian problem of other minds to ToMism in their theories of language and meaning. Chomsky further bequeathed to it the ideas that behaviour is an impoverished source of evidence about mind, and furthermore, that the Cartesian divide is to be spanned, not just in science but also in everyday life, by a theory. This formulation presents mundane understanding as a 'poor cousin' scientific endeavour, a form of scientific investigation, yet one which obviously lacks rigour (cf. Taylor, 1992, ch. 1). The common theme is the acceptance of the Cartesian divide represented in the distinction between 'mental states' and 'behaviour', with the former being treated as unobservable hypothetical states inferred on the basis of behavioural evidence. The Cartesian divide is conceived of as a universal fact about human beings rather than something which is historically contingent. These affinities are only occasionally acknowledged by ToMist researchers.

We have tried to avoid critique and focus on the internal logic of ToMism and its precursors and the links between them. It must be obvious though that we consider the intellectualization of everyday communication inappropriate. Everyday interpersonal understanding simply does not consist in using a theory to infer 'unobservables'. The issue is how people make sense of what other people do, and this is not just hard but impossible to resolve if one starts by assuming that people's minds are concealed and only knowable indirectly through *'behavioural* cues'. Such cues are said to be limited and unreliable since there is allegedly no systematic relation between what we observe about other people, and their 'hidden' thoughts and feelings. A host of experimental studies supposedly 'confirm' that people are inconsistent in 'encoding' their mental states and inaccurate in making psychological attributions (e.g., Fiske and Taylor, 1991). Conversation analytic studies, however, show that conversations are intricately organized so that individuals' contributions to social interactions incarnate intentionality and also, more often than not, in an unambiguous way (e.g., Pomerantz, 1990; Mandelbaum and Pomerantz, 1991; Drew, 1995). Moreover, if there really were no systematic relations between how people act and what they feel and think, it is not easy to see how anyone, even a psychologist, could determine the accuracy or inaccuracy of psychological attributions. An explicit connection should be made between how real people make sense of other people in everyday interactions, and the problem of how *psychologists* go about doing their kind of science.

The interactions between investigators and participants in psychological experiments are rarely analysed as dialogical engagements but there are exceptions, which show incongruity between the precepts and practices of experimental research. What participants do in experiments is demonstrably interactively contingent on what experimenters do (cf. Leudar and Antaki, 1996). We note a curious inconsistency: cognitive psychologists' accounts of mundane communication are modelled on the practices of experimental investigations, yet these same psychologists seldom notice that the experiments are themselves dialogical encounters.[21] The dialogicity of experiments is of course constrained, and interestingly in the same way that ToMism constrains the rich variety of engagements in conversation to prediction and explanation. The false-belief task, for instance, foregrounds mental states, induces explicit reasoning and requires participants to make predictions. One can say that in neo-Cartesian accounts of social interaction such as ToMism, and their empirical investigations, 'one does not encounter others' (Merleau-Ponty, 1973, p. 3).

The theory of mind paradigm is, however, caught in another, even more, serious conceptual problem. ToMism draws a sharp distinction between the mind and the behaviour, so that the former does not reduce to the latter. But it also holds that behaviour is the evidence from which mental states are inferred. The problem, then, is how can behaviour signify 'mental states' if it is an altogether distinct order of phenomena. How can the observed behaviour possibly *suggest* the presence of an inner mental state and how can it *justify* the attribution of a 'mental state'? The problem is of course a general one and not unique to ToMism – how can anything be evidence for something else? C. S. Peirce was clearly aware of this problem in arguing that the unity of a sign was provided by an 'interpretant'. Plainly, the connection between the evidence and the conclusion it supports needs to be understandable and 'warrantable'. But then we can also ask, how do I know that the warrant justifies the connection between the evidence and the conclusion and the justification is cogent? Stephen Toulmin argued some time ago that valid arguments are *grounded* (Toulmin, 1958). The problem for behaviour–mental state inferences in ToMism is that, with the two terms placed in separate and autonomous domains, such 'grounding' of the warrant connecting them is unattainable. Why should this be? What 'grounding' is may vary, but one kind is practical non-reflexive action. Looking at a computer monitor, for instance, I know that it has a far side which cannot be seen just now. The grounding connecting my experience now and the knowledge of the occluded part of the monitor is practical action – I could always turn the monitor round or walk round the desk, as I did when the connection failed. But what could be the grounding for the behaviour-to-mind inferences? – I certainly can't stroll from someone's behaviour to someone's mind and, as Sharrock and Coulter (2004) have argued, the theory necessary to connect epistemically 'behaviours' to mind is not learnable *in principle.*

Speaking about the relationship between 'language' and 'reality', and dealing with a like problem, Hilary Putnam wrote, 'The real worry is that sentences cannot be true or false of an external reality if there are no justificatory connections between things we say in language and any aspect of that reality whatsoever' (Putnam, 1995, p. 65).

Putnam's solution is to argue that language and reality are not autonomous, but 'interpenetrate' each other. What would this solution require from the theory of mind framework? Basically it would mean abandoning epistemic dualism and accept that intentionality and behaviour are not different in kind but aspects of the same phenomenon – activity. But then there would be no need for a theory of mind. What psychology requires is a good account of communication. What it gets, instead, is an over intellectualized account caught up in the spurious problem of other minds.

Notes

1 Under this term we subsume the original theory of 'Theory of Mind' (associated with the work of Premack, Baron-Cohen, Frith, Leslie) and the variants that it spawned, such as, e.g., the idea of an innate 'theory of mind module' (e.g., Leslie) as well as alternatives such as simulation theory (e.g., Gordon). (See, e.g., Premack and

Woodruff, 1978; Baron-Cohen, Leslie and Frith, 1985; Leslie, 1994; Gordon, 1992). ToMism is thus a historically coherent, but conceptually loose family of approaches which have in common the assumption that individuals are separated by a Cartesian divide that needs to be bridged in any communication. Several chapters in this book occasionally refer to this paradigm as 'ToMism' (the pun intended).

2 This is another respect, in which the behaviourist and the cognitive revolutions were hardly revolutions (Still and Costall, 1991; Leahey, 1992; Costall, 2006).

3 One of us has argued elsewhere that privileging a solipsist conception of 'mental language' leads to construing incorrectly whole cultures as being literally mindless (Leudar and Thomas, 2000, ch. 2).

4 It is important to mind one's language here. One line of argument here is that Cartesian dualism is not (just) a philosophical thesis, but is built into the language of psychology and into its practices of investigation. Were we ourselves to accept the terms 'mental states' and 'behaviour' in their usual psychological senses, and declare that the former *is* visible in the latter, we would maintain and propagate the dualism. So we avoid these terms and say that thoughts, intentions, fears, pains, jealousies, etc. (i.e., the family of specific intentional experiences) are 'noticeable and graspable', and this from how an action is done *in situ*. (The terms 'noticeable' and 'graspable' are borrowed from Merleau-Ponty, who used them to avoid tying understanding of others to the five senses.) Our empirical research is partly concerned with how interactions are organized to make experiences 'noticeable and graspable' (or occluded!).

5 We are of course not arguing that Cartesianism entered psychology just through the work of Chomsky and Grice. Freud, for instance, in his paper *The Unconscious* took the problem of other minds for granted in the social domain and argued that the same problem arose when one thinks about one's own (and other peoples') unconscious – the unconsciousness is an agency that one infers on the basis of evidence that is made meaningful and relevant in a theory provided by psychoanalysts (Freud, 1915).

6 Costall and Leudar (2004) investigated the comparable effect of the assimilation of Jean Piaget's work to mainstream developmental psychology.

7 One could think of ToMism as a rather late attempt to bring the Enlightenment to everyday mundane practices. There is, however, a way in which the two differ – the Enlightenment was reformist and assumed that mundane practices can be improved through scientific theories; ToMism on the other hand holds a more radical view – everyday social interactions are in fact *constituted* by theories, however inadequate these *folk* theories may be.

8 Not many psychologists though accepted that Chomsky was a psychologist – after all, psychology was defined by its method, experimentation. Psycholinguists did accept Chomsky's grammar as a linguistic description of language but insisted that its 'psychological reality' be tested *experimentally*. The criterion of the model being 'psychological' included the method of investigation. Doing experiments was the right method, using grammatical intuitions was not (cf. Broadbent, 1973, pp. 208–9). Roger Brown, however, also thought psycholinguistics should be an interdisciplinary science requiring psychologists to become sophisticated linguists (Brown, 1958).

9 The nativist corollary, that grammar 'grows' rather than is learned, however, was not as broadly accepted at the time. Roger Brown, for instance argued consistently that grammar of language is induced from a corpus (e.g., Brown, 1958, p. viii, see also Cromer, 1980; cf. Shanker, 2002).

10 'LAD' refers to Chomsky's proposed Language Acquisition Device.
11 Not all differences, however, always disappear. For example, Stanley Peters (1972) at the time emphasized that he considered it important that the linguistic corpus is unordered, but children experience language in an ordered manner.
12 Why should we take 'cognizing' to be a kind of *knowing*? This is a notable difference between Chomsky's and Descartes' conceptions of knowledge. Chomsky allows 'cognizing' (i.e., unconscious knowledge) whilst, according to him, it is crucial to Descartes that knowledge is accessible (Chomsky, 1976, p. 23).
13 Astington was characterizing the response of the 'theory theorists' to evidence of early understanding of other minds.
14 Chomsky could presumably endorse the modular version of the theory of mind, but not the 'theory-theory' version.
15 Grice, however, did not endorse transformational grammar (see Grice, 1982).
16 Grice's definition of 'non-natural meaning' was, roughly: Speaker $\underline{S}$ means something $\underline{x}$ by an utterance $\underline{U}$ if he utters it with an intention $\underline{I}$, wants this intention to be recognized and the recognition to be instrumental in achieving the intended communicative effect. Grice (1957) did not have much to say about natural meaning, except by exclusion.
17 The maxim of quality is in fact a precondition for the operation of the intentional mediation model of communication (Grice, 1989; cf. Leudar and Browning, 1988).
18 In developmental pragmatics the word 'perlocutionary' tends to mean 'instrumental' rather than what Austin meant by the word – an actual consequence of a speech act. The idea is that a child somehow moves from instrumental to conventional use of language and in this respect using language precedes ToM – conventional use of language involves attributions of intentionality.
19 Without this distinction we would presumably be either autistic or animists.
20 Sperber and Wilson (2002) are more clear than Baron-Cohen about the relationship between pragmatics and theory of mind. Pragmatics and theory of mind are subserved by independent brain modules, with their functional organizations described by relevance theory and by means–ends logic respectively. Sperber and Wilson's position is a notably Chomskyan one, even though in their writing they credit the notion of modularity to Fodor. Their relevance theory, however, ignores the varieties of mundane relevance, and instead individualizes, mentalizes and technicalizes the notion.
21 Conversation analytic studies of the engagements between experimenters and participants could throw many of these experiments in doubt, showing that built into them is what they suppose to test.

3
'Theory of Mind': The Madness in the Method

Alan Costall and Ivan Leudar

Research on 'Theory of Mind' has proliferated since the 1980s, and there are now many different *theories* of 'Theory of Mind'. Indeed, the name for this field of research derives from a specific theory which has now to be awkwardly referred to as the '*Theory* Theory of Mind'. According to '*Theory* Theory', *all of us* (psychologists and non-psychologists alike) are engaged in something akin to *theorizing* when making sense of one another: making inferences from mere behaviour to hidden psychological states that lie behind that behaviour. The main theoretical alternatives that have emerged to 'Theory Theory' deny that non-psychologists are *really* engaging in theorizing when dealing with one another: these include nativist theories based on postulated neurological 'modules', different versions of 'simulation theory', and several more radical and apparently 'anti-dualist' alternatives. So the term 'theory of mind' persists, yet now in a highly inclusive and confusing way. It is no longer presented as a body of contestable *scientific theory*, but as an established fact or else as 'field of study' with no particular theoretical commitments at all:

> ['Theory of mind' is] the 'everyday' ability to understand other people's beliefs, thoughts and desires in order to explain and predict their behaviour. With the ability to infer mental states, like the true and false beliefs of oneself and others, children become more capable of participating in a wide range of conversational and social interactions.
>
> (Pring, 2005, p. 2)

> Theory of mind as a field of study encompasses research that examines how people make sense of their worlds, of themselves, of others, of interpersonal relations – social and cognitive processes that are apparent in everyday life.
>
> (Garton, 2004, p. 80)

It is impossible to overemphasize the centrality of ToM in human civilization because ToM is necessary for the appreciation and transmission of culture in the form of novels, theatre, and song, and more generally for the maintenance of family and social life.

(Siegal, 2008, p. 22)

Despite the apparent diversity of the theories in the field of 'Theory of Mind' (or ToMism), these different theories nevertheless share, to varying degrees, the following specific assumptions:

1. Somehow or other we all *have* to engage in an inferential leap beyond what we can actually 'observe' about other people – their 'behaviour' – in order to relate to them truly as psychological beings with, for example, intentions, emotions and thoughts. It is only through such an intellectual or quasi-intellectual process that we can truly know other people as beings with minds.
2. Any development towards a proper understanding of other people, and engagement with them, consists of a single, all-or-nothing transition (or, as in the more Ptolemaic versions of 'Theory of Mind', constellations of such transitions).
3. Very young children and most other animals are incapable of properly relating to others as psychological beings or *really* communicating with them.
4. Very young children and most other animals may *appear* to relate psychologically to others, but this is indeed mere *appearance*. Despite their lack of the relevant 'Theory of Mind' capacity, they can, in effect, *fake* making sense of, and engaging with, others by resorting to, for example, the surrounding 'context' or the effects of mere conditioning.
5. Autism and schizophrenia can be understood as an impairment, or, indeed, in some cases the complete absence of the very 'mechanism' or 'capacity' for inference that allows the rest of us to make sense of other people. It is this assumption that has helped give the rather scholastic experiments conducted within the field of ToMism (e.g., on false belief) a sense of wider, practical significance.
6. Finally, and most fundamentally, there is supposed to be a *very* big problem inevitably facing people when they are making sense of one another, since there is a profound logical chasm between understanding 'mere' behaviour and truly understanding minds. And this problem, in effect, is *the traditional 'problem of other minds'*, 'a radical scepticism [...] regarding what we can know of these other minds (and, in its most extreme form, regarding the very existence of other minds)' (Kirschner, 2003, p. 278).

This chapter will not compare the relative merits of the various proposed *solutions* to the problem of other minds now available within the field of 'Theory of Mind'. 'The problem of other minds', based as it is on a *disjunction* of behaviour and mind is an impossible problem, and hence can have no coherent solutions (see also Leudar and Costall, 2004a, and Chapter 2, this volume). As Hammond and Keat (1991) have explained, if body and mind really are mutually exclusive categories, then 'no deductively valid inference can be made from statements about one such "part" of a person to statements about the other. In particular, one cannot validly infer, on the basis of knowledge of a body, any conclusion about a mind' (p. 205).

No wonder proponents of ToM talk coyly about 'mind-reading' (see Costall, Leudar and Reddy, 2006). On the assumptions of ToMism, it is truly a *miracle* that we can ever tell what other people are thinking or feeling, or, indeed, know that they have any kind of mental life at all. As Alan Leslie, one of the main proponents of ToMism, has tellingly put it: 'It is hard to see how perceptual evidence could force an adult, let alone a young child, to invent the idea of unobservable mental states' (1987, p. 422). This 'hard' task of reading other people's minds is claimed to be soluble, nevertheless, in a perfectly non-mysterious, naturalistic way. We are supposed to be able to leap the gap between the observable and the unobservable, thanks to the existence of special representational capacities, innate modules, or simulation. Yet, as with similar applications of the representationalist approach in perceptual theory, the postulated gap is *so* great there is absolutely no way the prior knowledge embodied in the representations could derive from either individual past experience or even that favourite *deus ex machina* of recent psychological theory, 'evolution' (e.g., Tooby and Cosmides, 1995, p. xvii). Not even natural selection can differentiate between differences that (as the ToMists insist) are supposed to make *no* difference (for an extensive criticism of theory of mind, see Leudar and Costall, 2004a).

Over the last three decades, psychologists have been cheerfully foisting the problem of other minds onto 'other people' (i.e., non-psychologists). And this is surely odd, because ToMism marks an unusual departure from the epistemological chauvinism that has traditionally pervaded most of psychology, since, according to the ToMists *we are all in the same boat*. Not only 'other people' but also the psychologists themselves in the course of their scientific investigations are supposed to confront precisely the same problem of other minds. Furthermore, we are all supposed to 'solve' it in ultimately similar ways: by somehow bridging the gulf between the only available 'evidence' – 'meaningless behaviour' – and the psychologically meaningful events hidden beyond and behind it. The only serious point that seems to be currently at issue within the field of 'Theory of Mind' concerns the relative merits of the different solutions. Yet it is the *problem* that is *the* problem. So, how did modern psychology resurrect the traditional philosophical problem of other minds without really trying, or even caring?

Methods, problems and theory

Methodology within psychology takes on a life of its own. Methods are typically discussed and evaluated in the abstract and in general, as in the continuing debates about the relative merits of qualitative and quantitative methods. Methods are also routinely used without much reflection about their compatibility with the theoretical or metatheoretical commitments of the researcher. Hardly any reference is made to the particular issue at hand. Thus, cognitive psychologists, for example, employ statistical techniques that presuppose the randomness of the variability of response within any experimental condition, even though, according to their metatheory, people are supposed to impose their own cognitive structure on any situation, and hence should respond to the 'same' situation in *systematically* different ways. Similarly, ecological psychologists still mainly use the standard experimental method of *imposing* conditions upon their subjects, despite their explicit rejection of 'stimulus-response psychology' in favour of an emphasis upon 'embodied agency'. And, the ritual of statistical significance testing persists many years after it was exposed as a thoroughly bad idea.

Unfortunately, within modern scientific psychology, methods, problems *and also theory* keep passing one another by. The perpetuation of methodological norms is seldom highly conscious and reflective. The process is insidious and local, and the effects are visceral. In contrast to the evaluation of theories, it does not usually happen out 'in the open'. It is mainly played out in the refereeing of submitted research articles and research grants, and in appointment panels in search of a 'sound' candidate. Even well-intentioned PhD supervisors, anxious about the career prospects of their students, will deter them from straying too far from the straight and narrow. Innovation is, for the most part, quietly put down.

The new cognitivism claimed to restore 'the mind' onto the scientific agenda. In fact, it failed to mount an effective challenge to the methodological imperatives of the behaviourism it also claimed to replace, or question the dualistic assumptions upon which that behaviourism was founded. The new cognitivism retained the stimulus–response formula, the hypothetico-deductive method and methodological behaviourism (see Neisser, 1997; Costall, 2006). Most importantly, the new cognitivism remained committed to an ideal of scientific objectivity based on a methodology of estrangement, and a concept of behaviour – 'mere behaviour' – as the antithesis of mind.

Estrangement as method

In the nineteenth-century, psychology (along with sociology) was at the spearhead of a new kind of scientific revolution and taken very seriously indeed. Scientists were finally getting their political act together as a new source of authority and social reform. The very term 'scientist' was coined in the nineteenth century to capture this new sense of professional identity. This aspiring elite, in order to consolidate its position, needed to be able to offer authoritative opinions not only about physics, chemistry, geology, and biology, but also about *human* affairs. Yet psychology faces a rather special difficulty as a science, since we all know – or *think* we know – a good deal about ourselves and other people without the benefit of psychologists. The New Psychology had, therefore, to establish its own epistemological distance from our 'common-sense' knowledge of ourselves, by developing its own distinctive methods, most conspicuously the psychological experiment, and also opening up uncharted territory, ranging from mental chronometry to the more exotic fields of hypnosis and mental dissociation.

Not least, the New Psychology had to transform the '*non*-psychologists' into '*non*-experts'. One important way that this was achieved was to transform the *intimate* knowledge people have of one another (and other animals) into a disqualification. Engagement, closeness, and *care* were no longer to be regarded as a secure basis for true psychological knowledge.

Here, for example, is James Sully putting mothers (if not fathers) in their scientific place:

> Her way of looking at babies unfits her from entering very cordially into the scientific vein. She rather dislikes their being made the objects of cold intellectual scrutiny and unfeeling psychological analysis. And she is apt to make a determined stand when the rash enthusiast for science proposes to introduce the experimental method as superior to that of passive observation. To suggest a series of experiments on the gustatory sensibility of a small creature aged from twelve to twenty-four hours is likely to prove a shock even to the more strong-minded class of mothers. [...] If, on the other hand, as is not unlikely, the mother herself gets in time infected with the scientific ardour of the father, she may prove rather more of an auxiliary than he desires. Her mental instincts impel her to regard her particular infant as phenomenal in an extra-scientific sense.
>
> (Sully, 1881, p. 546)[1]

Another group of 'amateurs', the pet owners and animal lovers, also had to be taken on, as in the following review by Conwy Lloyd Morgan of a book on the speech of monkeys. R. L. Garner, the author of that book, is put soundly in *his* place, this time through guilt by association with old ladies:

> popular and chatty anecdotes, with reflections thereon suitable for the delectation of elderly spinsters. [...] there is no evidence in his book that

he has, by a careful training in psychology, earned for himself the right of expressing a scientific opinion on this difficult question.

(Morgan, 1892, p. 509)

Although the 'third-person' method of experimentation has come to be largely identified with a commitment to objective detachment, this was not always the case even in relation to animal psychology. The new generation of experimenters were making a point of dismissing the earlier students of animal behaviour as old buffers relying exclusively on 'anecdotes' (an impression perpetuated in many of the current textbooks). Yet they knew perfectly well that their predecessors, such as Romanes, Lubbock and even Darwin, had themselves conducted meticulous experiments. Yet, when Darwin, Lubbock, and Romanes conducted experiments this did *not* entail detachment from their subjects, but quite the reverse. Lubbock, for example, made no secret of his *care* for his ants, bees and wasps:

It was Lubbock's supreme contribution, the basis of his psychological achievement, that he got to know individual insects intimately. It was a triumph of technique. When an ant died which he had kept for many years, the French paper which had a paragraph 'profoundly sympathizing with the great scientist on the loss of his aged and valued relative', showed unconsciously, perhaps, as much insight as humour. This attitude, this treatment of experimental animals as personalities, was justified in its results, and we venture to prophesy, will be increasingly justified in the progress of animal psychology.[2]

(Myers, 1929, p. xii)

And here is Leslie Stephen's telling comparison of Charles Darwin and Jonathan Swift:

Swift studied the manners and customs of his servants as Darwin studied worms. The difference was that Darwin had kindly feelings for his worms [...].

(Stephen, 1882, p. 200)

Francis Darwin, in his autobiography of his father, cited the above passage from Leslie Stephen with approval, and added his own recollections of Charles Darwin's relation to his subjects:

He could not help personifying natural things. This feeling came out in abuse as well as in praise – *e.g.* of some seedlings – 'The little beggars are doing just what I don't want them to.' He would speak in a half-provoked, half-admiring way of the ingenuity of a Mimosa leaf in screwing itself out of a basin of water in which he had tried to fix it. One might see the same spirit in his way of speaking of Sundew, earth-worms, &c.

(Francis Darwin, 1887, p. 117)

The shift within experimentation towards objectification initially oc-curred within the field of animal psychology. Now, given the wider pol-itical significance of the New Psychology derived from its role in the new 'scientific priesthood' (to use Francis Galton's term), it might seem odd that so much energy was devoted to experimentation with *animals*. Yet, such research did serve to impress and hence enhance the credentials of the new science. Even though the apparatus constructed by the animal researchers was conspicuously 'home-made' (compared to the 'brass-instruments' of the human experimenters), the greater degree of experimental control possible with non-human animals meant that (on paper at least) such studies looked like impressive, hard science.

There was, however, another crucial function of the animal experimen-tation: as a *distancing device*. By working with animals, experimenters could start to develop a sense of disengagement with their subjects not so easily achieved when dealing with a fellow human being. The psychologists were beginning to learn to treat their subjects – either human or non-human – as inanimate, insentient *objects*.

J. B. Watson was obviously a significant figure in furthering this process of objectification. His behaviourism has been widely characterized as the intro-duction into *human* psychology of the objective experimental methodology developed by the animal experimenters. As Watson put it, 'Behaviorism is a direct outgrowth of studies in animal behavior during the first decade of the 20th century' (Watson, 1929, p. 327). Yet experimentation *as such* had already been widely established within *human* psychology prior to Watson's behaviourist manifestos (Watson, 1913a and b), and 'introspectionism' had by no means been the dominant force that Watson claimed it to be (see Costall, 2006). As Woodworth protested:

so far from experimental psychology having begun as a purely intro-spective enterprise and needing young upstarts to force it into objective channels, it made its beginning with non-introspective studies of reac-tion time, psychophysics, and memory.

(Woodworth, 1924, p. 258)

Watson was keen that the new behaviourism should come across as hard, reductionist science, and yet he also wanted to convince the wider com-munity that it had wide practical implications for business, education and mental health. To this end, he astutely sold the methodology of estrange-ment from an *applied* angle. Being strangers to one another, he insisted, was now an important social issue, because of the rise of the new industrial cities, and the coming together of people with highly diverse backgrounds. Psychologists could no longer take anything for granted (e.g., Watson, 1924, p. xi). Henceforth, researchers would have to take the perspective of a 'stranger scientist' from 'some distant planet', and restrict their focus upon what people actually *do* (see Bakan, 1966).

There were other important issues concerning estrangement going on around Watson that he himself did not explicitly pursue. First of all, as the sociologist Georg Simmel argued, the new big cities and their organizations and facilities were not merely gathering places for strangers but also a kind of technology creating a new stranger mentality. The new cities had become overwhelming. As Sennet has explained:

> This excess of psychic stimulation, as Simmel called it, led men to try to defend themselves by not reacting emotionally to the people around them in a city; for Simmel this meant they would try not to react as whole human beings with distinct identities. [...] The market economy and the office and factory bureaucracies were the apotheosis of this fragmentation process, for in these socioeconomic forms the urbanite was most shielded from acting with other men as a full, emotional human being, most directed toward human contact in purely functional and rational forms. [...] What Simmel envisioned, concretely, was that a man could learn in a city not to feel tied to his job, or his family, or his friends, but finally to turn in on himself [...].
>
> (Sennett, 1969, pp. 8–10)

This move towards estrangement, however, was even promoted within the Protestant religion:

> The Protestant ethic was associated with an intense psychological separation of individual from individual. It had a theology which suggested that the thoughts, feelings, and wishes of each individual were a matter between himself and God alone, and not a matter for another man to concern himself with. It tended to substitute formal and contractual forms of relationship for intimate interpsychic contact. A too great interest in the inner life of another person not only exceeded the bounds of formal relationship, but was also a reminder of the odious Confessional of the Catholic Church. At the same time the Protestant ethic was associated with a vaulting thrust to master the world through industry and through science.
>
> (Bakan, 1969, p. 39)

Finally, there was also a serious problem about estrangement arising within science itself. The scientists were becoming strangers to one another.

With the expansion of science, the traditional personal networks based upon trust were increasingly undermined. One's scientific peers were no longer acquaintances, or (as in the case of Newton and Hooke) even enemies. The problem of communicating with scientific strangers led, in turn, to the emergence of a distinctly new scientific ideal of objectivity as 'aperspectival', the view from nowhere.

As Lorraine Daston has brilliantly argued, this sense of objectivity is relatively new within science. It did not emerge until the nineteenth century, when science was becoming highly international and conducted on an almost industrial scale, so that the relationships among scientists themselves were becoming more distant and impersonal:

> Aperspectival objectivity was the ethos of the interchangeable and therefore featureless observer – unmarked by nationality, by sensory dullness or acuity, by training or tradition, by quirky apparatus, by colourful writing style, or by any other idiosyncrasy that might interfere with the communication, comparison and accumulation of results.
>
> (Daston, 1992, p. 609)[3]

Although Daston makes no specific reference to psychology in her discussion of the development of this new sense of objectivity, Watson's insistence that psychology should be a science of *behaviour instead of mind and consciousness* is clearly part of this much wider shift towards uniformity and standardization. Even though introspectionism was hardly the dominant force claimed by Watson, there were fundamental debates about the reliability of introspection around the time of Watson's manifestos. And these debates largely concerned *the communicability and comparability of the methods between different laboratories* (most notably Princeton and Würzburg). Yet merely to redefine psychology, as Watson did, as a science of 'behaviour', was not enough. That, in itself, would not guarantee a methodology that could 'travel'. The concept of behaviour had itself to be radically decontextualized and divested of meaning in the cause of uniformity and communicability, for otherwise the same issues of situatedness and interpretation attached to the existing methods would remain. Behaviour had to be 'de-psychologized'. In order to be measurable, it had to be regarded as meaningless, mechanical movement and hence as the *antithesis* of mind.

Watson's role in 'the objectification of the subject' was hardly decisive. He did not entirely eliminate mind from science, conceding that consciousness is, after all, ' "the instrument or tool with which all scientists work" ' (Watson, 1914, p. 176). And he was a shameless opportunist (see Samelson, 1994). When Watson wanted to assert the strict scientific credentials of the new behaviourism, he would invoke his highly restrictive, 'official' conception of behaviour. But when he wanted to convince the wider world of the practical implications of the new behaviourism, his conception of behaviour could hardly be more inclusive, and redolent with meaning:

> anything the organism does – turning toward or away from the light, jumping at a sound, and more highly organized activities such as building a skyscraper, drawing plans, having babies, writing books, and the like.
>
> (Watson, 1930, p. 6)[4]

Behaviourism did not become a system until after Watson had left academia, most notably through the work of Clark Hull. It is now difficult to understand how Hull could have been taken so seriously – even by himself – were it not for the new obsession within science with detachment and uniformity.

Hull's claims for his new 'system of behaviour' were, to say the least, ambitious, given it was founded on a few simple behavioural principles gleaned from just a handful of rats:

> all behavior, individual and social, moral and immoral, normal and psychopathic, is generated from the same primary laws; that the differences in the objective manifestations are due to the differing conditions under which habits are set up and function. Consequently the present work may be regarded as a general introduction to the theory of all the behavioral (social) sciences.
>
> (Hull, 1943, p. v)

In contrast to Watson, Hull was resolute in his insistence upon the psychologist's complete disengagement from the subjects under study. As he explained, one important reason why psychologists had studied 'subhuman organisms' was the 'attainment of behavioral objectivity'. Yet, he complained, such objectivity 'often breaks down', even when dealing with rats. Here is Hull's preferred 'prophylaxis' against engagement:

> A device much employed by this author has proved itself to be a far more effective prophylaxis [against subjectivism]. This is to regard, from time to time, the behaving organism as a completely self-maintaining robot, constructed of materials as unlike ourselves as may be. [...] *It is a wholesome and revealing exercise* [...] to consider the various general problems in behavior dynamics which must be solved in the design of a truly self-maintaining robot.
>
> (Hull, 1943, p. 27; emphasis added)

Hull's identification with the new scientific ideal of objectivity is also reflected in his attitude towards the very *style* of scientific communication:

> The so-called social sciences will no longer be a division of belles lettres; anthropomorphic intuition and a brilliant style, desirable as they are,

will no longer suffice as in the days of William James and John Horton Cooley. Progress in this new era will consist in the laborious writing, one by one, of hundreds of equations [...].

(Hull, 1943, p. 400)

Clark Hull was the personification of this new 'madness of objectivity' (Bolton, 1987, p. 245). Now, this would all be ancient history, but for one very important thing. The neo-behaviourist ideal of objectivity has remained the *official* methodological standard in the new cognitivism. Indeed, the new cognitivism came armed with its own powerful distancing device, the metaphor of the computer (see Weizenbaum, 1995).[5]

The cognitive 'revolution'

The rise of cognitivist psychology in the 1950s and 1960s is typically portrayed as a revolution. According to Newell, the crucial year was 1956 when 'the break with behaviorism happens across the board' (1995, p. 150). Certainly, many of the pioneering texts still convey a vivid sense of intellectual passion and a promise of change. Yet, there is also a clear sense of *continuity* – an acceptance of the methodological status quo.

Here, for example, is Miller, Galanter and Pribram's somewhat 'arch' account of the problematic position they found themselves in:

Our emphasis was upon processes lying immediately behind action, but not with action itself. On the other hand, we did not consider ourselves introspective psychologists, [...] yet we were willing to pay attention to what people told us about their ideas and their Plans. How does one characterize a position that seems to be such a mixture of elements usually considered incompatible? Deep in the middle of this dilemma it suddenly occurred to us that *we were subjective behaviorists*. When we stopped laughing we began to wonder seriously if that was not exactly the position we had argued ourselves into. At least the name suggested the shocking inconsistency of our position.

(Miller, Galanter and Pribram, 1960, p. 211; emphasis added)

One might dismiss such deference to behaviourism as merely a cynical ploy to placate the behaviourist old-guard (see Simon, 1995, p. 233). And yet, the new cognitivism not only continues to pay lip-service to the neo-behaviourist ideal of objectivism, but has incorporated this ideal into its own self-narrative.

It is true that the new cognitive movement did start out with radical intentions, and has made some difference in terms of the content of research (Tracy, Robins and Gosling, 2004). However, as many of the pioneering figures have more recently complained, in terms of *method*, the new cognitivism lost its way (e.g., Broadbent, 1980; Bruner, 1988, 1990; Neisser, 1997).

The cognitive psychologists soon found themselves caught up in psychology's long-standing anxieties about *method*. As James Jenkins has poignantly put it, they 'stopped looking at the world too early and tried to be scientists…they got precision at the cost of validity' (1986, p. 254). So, despite great hopes, the new movement failed to create an effective challenge to the methodological imperatives already established by the behaviourists. These, to repeat, include the stimulus–response formula, the hypothetico-deductive method, and an official commitment not just to methodological behaviourism but also to *a thoroughly objectified and, hence, dualistic conception of behaviour*:

> cognitive psychology lost out to the received view, with its operational and reductionistic methods […] the old won out over the new.
>
> (Garner, 1999, p. 21)

Despite all the talk about 'revolution', the retention of methodological behaviourism is openly acknowledged in the textbooks, and even celebrated as part of an essential synthesis, the combination of the research agenda of introspectionist psychology with the methodological rigour of behaviourism. Here is an early example, from Donald Hebb's influential textbook:

> If Watson's work is seen as [a] house-cleaning operation […], its importance becomes clearer. In the first place, he was right about rejecting introspection as a means of obtaining factual evidence; it is certainly true that one often knows much of what goes on in one's own mind, but there is an element of inference in this knowledge that we do not yet understand clearly (i.e., it is not factual evidence) and little agreement can be obtained from introspective reports. In 1913 the whole case for mental processes seemed to depend on introspection; if it did, the case was a bad one, and 'mind' had to be discarded from scientific consideration until better evidence could be found […] Paradoxically, it was the denial of mental processes that put our knowledge of them on a firm foundation, and from this approach we have learned much more about the mind than was known when it was taken for granted more or less uncritically.
>
> (Hebb, 1966, pp. 5–6)

Here is a much more up-to-date example, from the thirteenth edition of *Hilgard's Introduction to Psychology*:

> Because psychologists were growing impatient with introspection, the new behaviorism caught on rapidly […] The modern cognitive perspective is in part a return to the cognitive roots of psychology and in part a reaction to the narrowness of behaviorism and the S–R view […] Like the 19th century version, the modern study of cognition is concerned with

mental processes such as perceiving, remembering, reasoning, deciding, and problem solving. Unlike the 19th-century version, however, modern cognitivism is not based on introspection. Instead, it assumes (1) only by studying mental processes can we fully understand what organisms do, and (2) we can study mental processes in an objective fashion by focusing on specific behaviours (just as behaviorists do) but interpreting them in terms of underlying mental processes.

(Atkinson, Atkinson, Smith, Bem and
Nolen-Hoeksema, 2000, pp. 12–13)

George Miller has continued to make the same basic point, years after the 'old-guard' had surely retired from their watch:

The cognitive revolution in psychology was a counter-revolution. The first revolution occurred much earlier when a group of experimental psychologists, influenced by Pavlov and other physiologists, proposed to redefine psychology as the science of behavior. They argued that *mental events are not publicly observable.* The only objective evidence available is and must be, behavioral. By changing the subject to the study of *behavior,* psychology could become an objective science based on scientific laws of behavior.

(Miller, 2003, pp. 141–2; emphasis added)

To the extent that modern cognitivism is *really* committed to methodological behaviourism and also (as in the above quotes) to Hull's conception of behaviour as 'colourless movement', it is also committed, *whether it likes it or not*, to a stark dualism of body and behaviour – a dualism more extreme than Descartes could have ever envisaged (Costall, 2007). This is precisely the dualism celebrated by the ToMists, in their claims about how '*other* people' make sense of '*other* other people'. These claims are based on their own 'official' methodology, either explicitly as in 'Theory Theory' or else implicitly (and hence more insidiously) in their appeal to their own objectified conception of behaviour. If making sense of one another *really* requires the divination of 'invisible, intangible, abstract states' (Leslie, Friedman and German, 2004, p. 531) solely on the basis of 'mere' behaviour (as the ToMists insist), then the prospects for theorizing are indeed bleak. To repeat our earlier quote from Leslie: 'It is hard to see how perceptual evidence could force an adult, let alone a young child, to invent the idea of unobservable mental states' (1987, p. 422). Unfortunately, there is *no* way to bridge the gap between what we can experience of others and an understanding of their intentions, emotions and so on, given that the only grounds for such understanding is supposed to be behaviour *divested of all psychological meaning.* Removing 'the problem of other minds' to the distant evolutionary past, to the accompaniment of hand-waving about natural selection, hardly counts as a real explanation. In short, the ToMists who claim to have solved 'the problem of other minds' just don't understand the problem.

Three remaining questions

This chapter has argued that modern cognitive psychology remains committed to an official methodology fashioned during the period of neo-behaviourism, and that it is this methodological allegiance that makes 'the problem of other minds' seem so inescapable. But three obvious puzzles then arise.

The first concerns why the early cognitive psychologists were so slow to notice that they had saddled themselves with the traditional, dualistic, 'problem of other minds'. Why did this *not* become an issue as early, say, as the 1960s? There are several possible reasons. The first is that all the hype about 'cognitive revolution', and the overthrow of behaviourism, induced a remarkable bout of intellectual complacency that continues to the present day. The second is that despite some real innovations in research methods, the new cognitive psychologists were soon making concessions to the existing 'establishment' by way of methodology, and, as we have argued, such concessions tend to occur in a local and relatively covert way. Furthermore, cognitive psychologists have, in fact, been as shameless as Watson in wavering between their official objectified concept of behaviour, and a concept of *action* richly imbued with meaning.

The second puzzle concerns the *nature* of the emergence of ToM within psychology. Now, the very fact that ToMism eventually came to have such an influential place within modern psychology is, according to our analysis, hardly a surprise at all. It was a nasty mistake just waiting to happen. But why did it take off so relatively late in the day (i.e., in the late 1980s), and, initially, primarily within developmental psychology? Although the origins of ToMism as a theoretical option must be understood in relation to the work of Noam Chomsky (see Leudar and Costall, 2004b, and Chapter 2 this volume), we need to understand the strange role of another important figure, Jean Piaget, to understand *when* and *where* ToM actually took off within psychology (see Costall and Leudar, 2004, for a fuller treatment).

Initially, the cognitive psychologists in America and Britain had enthusiastically turned to the work of Jean Piaget for *theoretical* inspiration, but they quickly became obsessed yet again with *methodology*. Piaget's largely uncontrolled, naturalistic studies did not meet the exacting standards of American experimental psychology. So the agenda soon became that of 'Piaget bashing' (an expression widely used at the time): to determine whether young children, when tested under tighter experimental conditions, might be *more* competent and similar in their thinking to adults than Piaget had been claiming. In fact, the developmental researchers came to attribute such a range of remarkable competencies to neonates that the so-called 'developmentalists' seemed to be talking themselves out of a job. What was there left to *develop*? One answer the developmentalists could widely agree upon was that it is the child's capacity to *theorize* that develops, and that it does so across a range of *separate* domains, including the child's own competencies (meta-cognition), and so-called *physical* things (as opposed to so-called *social* things; cf. Costall, 1995; Costall and Dreier, 2006). Thus '*theory* theory of mind', as it was taken up within developmental psychology, was just part of this wider approach to 'the child-as-theorist':

> According to theory theory, children have the innate ability to abstract information from events and this helps them construct their theories. Within this broad predisposition, experience (evidence and counterevidence) contributes to the specific theory they construct. Consequently, the type of theory a child has would differ from one domain to another and would evolve at different rates in different domains. Not only would 6-year-old's theory of biology be very different from her theory of mind, but also one theory could be more advanced than another.
>
> (Miller, 2002, p. 424)

However, the adoption of the 'theory' approach in relation to children's understanding of *other people* involved a fundamental shift in the established conception of 'the competent neonate'. In relation to all the other domains, the child could still be regarded as relating *meaningfully* to the objects of its theorizing *prior* to engaging in such theorizing. The child thereby had some foundation of 'evidence and counterevidence' upon which to base the theory. But ToMism challenged the claim central to the initial construction of the young child as a 'competent neonate', namely in relation to his or her *interpersonal* understanding. Once the ToMists had explicitly reinstated 'the problem of other minds', the young child could no longer be regarded as *socially* competent. Any appearance of sociality in early development had to be dismissed as mere *appearance* (see Reddy and Morris, Chapter 5 this volume). Thus, the child's theorizing about minds, in contrast to other domains, *could* not be based upon existing 'know how'. Theorizing *had* to come first, but only to create the largely unacknowledged paradox about its own origins in development or evolution. To repeat, colourless movements, by their very nature, cannot constitute 'evidence' for mind. Behaviour, so conceived, is meant to be *meaningless*.

The final puzzle relates to a fundamental inconsistency with cognitivism since the rise of ToMism. As we have seen, the ToMists enthusiastically foist 'the traditional problem of other minds' onto children and 'just plain folk', while also insisting that this is the self-same problem they are addressing in the conduct of their own scientific research, in their own attempts to make sense of other people. Yet, despite the claimed epistemological parity between 'ordinary people' and the experts, this supposed symmetry proves distinctly one-sided. In connection with the conduct of psychological research itself, there is little evidence of any awesome chasm between theory and data of the kind that the ToMists attribute to 'other people'. The textbooks, for example, assure us that the leap from behaviour to mind is no more precarious than that, say, from X-ray diffraction patterns to hidden molecular structures:

> we know mind, and study it, as the chemist knows and studies the properties of the atom. Atoms are not observed directly; still less the electrons, protons, neutrons and so forth that – theoretically – compose the atom.
> (Hebb, 1966, pp. 10–11)

In fact, when we come to consider how psychologists actually interpret their results, there is seldom a hint of any difficulties, let alone mystery. Even the interpretation of the famous experiments on 'false-belief' task proves to be remarkably straightforward, despite the ToMists insistence upon the 'invisibility' of beliefs. In any case, most experiments are not even about intentions, beliefs or emotions at all, but the testing of micro-models of 'cognitive processing':

> Ironically, the 'hypothetico-deductive method' that was so strongly advocated by Hullian behaviorists half a century ago has become the stock-in-trade of their cognitivist successors. [...] The activity that dominates cognitive psychology today is not empirical exploration but something quite different: namely, the making and testing of hypothetical models. [...] research should always begin with a theory; not just any theory, but a specific model of the internal processes that underlie the behavior of interest. That mental model is then tested as thoroughly as possible in carefully designed experimental paradigms. [...] The aim of the research is not to discover any secret of nature; it is to devise models that fit a certain range of laboratory data better than their competitors do.
> (Neisser, 1997, p. 248)

In *practice*, the 'leap' from evidence to theory, within psychological research, is anything but heroic. It is mundane, often self-enclosed, and, at times, little more than platitude (Martin, Sugarman and Thompson, 2003; Neisser, 1997). But if the ToMists themselves are not dealing with 'the problem of other minds' in relation to their actual research methodology, then perhaps neither are 'just plain folk' relentlessly facing the profound problems when making sense of '*other* other people', as foisted upon them by the ToMists. *In practice*, none of us, when making sense of one another, may really be in the business of treating people as mere *objects* of theoretical speculation. If only the ToMists would stop being pompous and scientistic about their own methodology, and projecting their confused methodology onto the rest of us, we could learn how to give up trying to solve 'the problem of other minds', and begin to get over it instead.

Notes

1 Later, Sully changed his tack somewhat: 'Women – and particularly mothers – are [...] exceptionally well situated for carrying out a careful and continuous record of an infant's mental progress. On the other hand, the observation of the mental manifestations of an infant is especially difficult and is hardly possible save to one who has both undergone some methodical training in simpler kinds of observation and served a further apprenticeship as a student of psychology' (Sully, 1897, p. 408).
2 At this point, Myers refers to the ongoing research of von Frisch on bees and Köhler on apes. For a fine account of the reaction against the methodolatry of objectification within American psychology, see Pandora (1997).
3 This loss of trust has now overtaken many of the professions, where a perpetual spiral of standardization, assessment and externally imposed targets have come to replace professional judgement and wisdom. Charlton (2000) has documented a chilling example of this in relation to the managerial takeover of clinical practice in the British National Health Service.
4 See Kitchener (1977) for an extensive account of the different and often ambiguous meanings of 'behaviour' in behaviourist theories.
5 The power of this distancing device depends, of course, on the failing to notice that computers are not really 'alien' at all, but already part of our own lives and our representational practices (Costall, 1991).

4
'Theory of Mind': A Critical Commentary Continued

Wes Sharrock and Jeff Coulter

Introduction

The idea of 'Theory of Mind' is deeply dependent upon an array of uncritically adopted but contestable assumptions from contemporary philosophy of mind. We argue that some of these key assumptions carry tacit but implausible conceptions of the nature and role of language in the acquisition of 'Theory of Mind'. We seek to show that without these misconceptions the idea of a 'Theory of Mind' itself becomes superfluous.

Throughout this, and an associated chapter (see Sharrock, Chapter 10 this volume), we make use of the expressions 'conceptual' and 'grammatical' to indicate the nature of our approach to the problems involved here.[1] This approach is philosophical in nature, indebted most centrally to so-called 'ordinary language philosophers' but especially to Ludwig Wittgenstein and Gilbert Ryle. The approach is, however, not to be thought of as enabling a philosophical commentary on what are *scientific* and especially psychological matters. It is called 'grammatical' to hallmark the fact that it focuses on features of language and the way words are used to say things. Those we criticize are not much interested in the language and its use. They are inclined to think that the main business of language is to *refer* to things that are independent of it, and statements which feature expressions such as 'think', 'believe', 'imagine', 'perceive' and so forth must also be referring to something, namely occurrences in somebody's mind. Such occurrences would pose a substantial task for a psychology designed to discover what it is that we are talking about when we refer to a thought or an intention; what sort of occurrence takes place in the mind or the brain when we think, and how the different occurrences such as thinking, perceiving and the like, are organized and interrelated within the totality that is the mind.

The assumption, however, that all of us, on an everyday basis, use words such as 'intention', 'purpose', 'know', 'understand' and 'reason' to refer to occurrences 'within the mind' should be the problem addressed first. So are our putative references to these occurrences well founded? Is there anything that occurs within our mind or brain, with which the mind has come to be identified, that actually corresponds to the referring intentions of expressions like 'belief' and 'thought'? The 'grammatical' analysis casts doubt on this whole project for it questions whether psychological terms function referentially in the way that 'referring' is understood in the theory of mind paradigm. The grammatical approach asks about what it is that we are *saying* when we use such terms, and thus about how we *use* those expressions – where is it appropriate to say such things, and what sorts of responses are appropriate to them in everyday practices.

Thus, for example, if someone were to say to you, 'I thought the American presidential candidate, Hillary Clinton, would win the Iowa caucus', you could certainly understand them to be telling you that they have undergone a change of mind, and you could ask them when and where that happened. But you would not be asking at what millisecond the event of a rearrangement within their belief box had occurred or which precisely located synaptic configurations realized this rearrangement. You would understand that what you were asking could be answered by either (1) telling you that they had changed their mind before the caucus, having lost their original confidence in Hillary's persuasive power; or (2) after she lost the caucus – then they *knew* she did not win. Equally, if they were to give a location to where their change of mind took place, an answer like 'in the kitchen, whilst listening to the World Service and making my breakfast' would be appropriate.

When someone tells you such things, what sort of things are they thereby saying? Something like this, perhaps: that if you had asked them three weeks ago – before Hillary's polling leads started to weaken – they would have told you that Hillary would definitely take Iowa, but if you had asked them again in the days immediately before the caucusing they would have told you something rather different, perhaps that they were no longer confident that she would win, or, even that they were confident that her opponent, Obama, would. In a case like this 'I thought' tells you they had a change of opinion because what they would have told you initially would have been wrong. The difference between 'I thought…' and 'I knew…' prefixing 'Hillary would win the Iowa nomination', does not hinge upon the referential criteria for two different orders of occurrence in the mind (or mind/brain), but relates to the correctness of what they would have told you: if Hillary had won they would have *known* that she was going to win, but *because she lost* they are now only entitled to say that 'I thought she was going to win'.

This example shows that rather than referring to occult occurrences, the expression 'I thought…' is often used to indicate *a revision of views*, and 'I know' affirms the capacity to give correct information. The two concepts 'think' and 'know' have different grammars, but both have to do with one's capacity to give the right answers. Neither, however, nominates different 'states of mind', as is often imagined.

Having sketched out what is 'grammatical' about our approach, the main consequence for the issues discussed in this book can be stated: the disagreement between us and those we oppose *involves no disagreement in psychological doctrines*. The temptation is to construe the disagreement as one over the right kind of psychological theory. Many in the opposition incline towards 'mentalism', though they might prefer to identify their attachment as being to one of subsidiaries of mentalism, namely cognitivism. Their understanding of the history of psychology is that the only real alternative is behaviourism, and since we ourselves are so plainly out of sympathy with mentalism we must be behaviourists. Our defence against this is not: our psychological views are *not* behaviourist; rather, our position implies no psychological theory whatsoever. Hence, our disagreement with the mentalists is about 'grammatical' issues, ones in which the mentalists' supposed psychology entirely depends upon a misconstrual of the grammar of quite ordinary everyday words which are vital to the formulation of their doctrines. The disagreement is over how parts of the language work. The mentalists perhaps cannot acknowledge this and maintain the viability of their project.

Both the theory of mind theory (TT) and Simulation Theory (ST) stand within the broad 'mentalist' tradition of theorizing that we fundamentally reject. Our commentary here has a dual purpose: to mount some fundamental objections to these approaches and in turn to offer clarification of the scope and force of the 'grammatical' approach to the issues involved. Even though TT and ST regard themselves as rivals, the two share the general mentalist conviction that the minds of other individuals are not *directly* available to us.[2] One might well ask, as we shall, why there is a need for 'directly' here.

The mentalist tradition taken most broadly insists that another individual's mind – thoughts, intentions, beliefs et cetera – cannot be observed. We cannot imagine what those 'mental states' might 'look like'. Yet we talk with considerable confidence about what other individuals do think, believe et cetera. So what entitles us to talk in this way, to use expressions which are supposed to refer to events we cannot see? This is where the word 'directly' comes in. For mentalists, to directly access someone else's mind would entail having their specific thoughts, intentions et cetera in our perceptual field along with the bodily movements. When we say 'X thinks Y', we cannot be making a straightforward report, since the condition assumed by mentalists for making an observational report – that reported phenomena are present in our perceptual field – cannot be met. So, X thinks Y must be some other kind of statement, something like the sort of statement that scientists make all the time, namely a theoretical or hypothetical one. 'Theoretical' in the sense that one speaks of something as though it exists though one has as yet no definitive evidence that it does.

Thus, 'X thinks Y' is essentially a postulation that an event has occurred, that the thought Y has occurred somewhere in X's skull, though the hard evidence of having personally witnessed Y's occurrence is not available. However confident one may seem in saying 'X thinks Y' there must be a necessary tentativeness to it, for there is no conclusive evidence that 'thinking Y' is what went on in X's mind (or mind/brain). However, on the arguments just given, the whole business of attributing 'mental states' to other persons is provisional because, by their very nature, attributions are 'postulations' rather than reports. One has no conclusive evidence that there are any such things as thoughts, and so the question can arise, as it does amongst mentalists, as to whether anyone ever thinks anything, and whether 'thought' could possibly be a scientific term in good standing. Hence, for mentalists, one's relationship to 'other minds' is effectively that of a theoretician to an unobserved/unknown phenomenon, and the use of words that make up our everyday 'mentalist vocabulary' *must be* by default a piece of (speculative) theorizing on the user's part. TT and ST both belong to this framework, but TT takes the issue a bit further. It postulates that the mentalist vocabulary has an organization and is coherently structured in the way that scientific terminology is, that is, combined in a propositional scheme. The supposed ToM users are not merely theoreticians hypothesizing unobservable phenomena; when they make statements such as X is thinking Y, they are *applying* a systematic theory. Thus, TT unlike ST, takes it for granted that adult human beings understand other human beings on the basis of their possession of a theory regulating their ascription of thoughts, beliefs and intentions. That, for them, must be so, and two questions are thereby licensed: (a) Human children developing to normal adulthood must develop a theory of mind, but *when* do they do this, and *how?* (b) Is it possible that creatures other than human beings could have a theory of mind? What about the higher primates, for example?

All the above is manifest in a concise programmatic statement Janet Astington makes to describe the basic premise of the theory as follows:

> According to this [the theory theory] view, children's concepts of mental states are abstract and unobservable postulates used to explain and predict observable human behavior. The concepts are coherent and interdependent, and the theory can interpret a wide range of evidence using a few concepts and laws. The theory is not static, but is open to defeat by new evidence, that is, subject to replacement by a new theory [...] On this view, mental state concepts are theoretical entities that children postulate in order to explain and predict people's interactions.
>
> (Astington, 1996, p. 185)

Premack and Woodruff elaborate:

> An individual has a theory of mind if he imputes mental states to himself and others. A system of inferences of this kind is properly viewed as

a theory because such states are not directly observable and can be used to make predictions about the behavior of others.

(Premack and Woodruff, 1978, p. 516)

Before we take up these issues in detail, we begin our discussion with some general remarks about the position from which we shall be arguing, and the framework within which we develop our criticisms.

Experimental methods and conceptual confusions

The idea that many of the problems of the 'social and human sciences' are fundamentally conceptual is one that scarcely registers within the numerous enterprises included under that general rubric, and when it does, it is one that usually receives no further attention, let alone comprehension, being simply brushed aside. At the same time, to anyone who appreciates the priority of conceptual over empirical questions the correctness of the claim about the *centrality* (not exhaustiveness) of conceptual problems in these areas is amply confirmed by the confusion and ineffectiveness which commonly accompanies allegedly 'empirical' ventures. The pertinence of Wittgenstein's (1953/1958, para. 232[e]) comments on the psychology of his day, that the 'problem and method pass one another by', and that in psychology 'there are experimental methods and *conceptual confusion*', has not been diminished by the passage of many years, as Jan Smedslund (1997) has documented. Wittgenstein's remarks apply with a vengeance to the theory of a theory of mind and simulation theory – both are little more than compounds of philosophical misconceptions and inappropriate 'experiments'.

The quotations from Astington and Premack and Woodruff are opaque about the *status* of claims for a 'theory of mind'. Are these remarks clarifications of what it means to talk about 'mental concepts' or are they empirical postulations about the occurrence of processes in the minds of young children? Are they, that is, claims about the status of 'mental concepts', that these have the character of 'postulations' as opposed to, say, that of 'observables', meaning that the claim that 'mental state concepts are theoretical entities that children postulate' is validated by the more basic claim that expressions which identify 'mental states' have the character of theoretical terms? This, then, would naturally be a claim about how these words work *in the language*, which, if substantiated, would mean that children could be described as 'postulating' inner states just because they use these terms – there would be no need for them to engage in any further 'mental acts' or 'psychological processes' of making postulations.

If, however, the claim is about psychological processes currently taking place (such as events in the brain that are the thought that 'today is Thursday'), then the question is: what kind of evidential basis could there be for such occurrences other than children having learned the use of these terms?

If purportedly empirical claims about psychological processes in children are involved, then further questions arise. Is it not being assumed that the children who are supposedly postulating the theoretical conceptions they use to attribute mentality to others somehow happen to converge on the very same vocabulary that everyone else uses to express *their* theoretical constructions? To make this convergence anything other than an amazingly fortuitous occurrence, an account needs to be given of how *the language* features in the formation of individual theories of mind.

Why should the individual theoretical conceptions converge? One can resort to the last refuge of mentalism: the conceptions must be innate. Short of that, there is ambiguity: are we to envisage individual children as engaged in an effort to *originate* the language of 'mental states' or are they merely picking up a pre-existing vocabulary and its rules of application?[3]

The latter is obviously presupposed in the 'Theory of Mind' research. The implication is that children are engaged in individual theorizing but are doing so in terms of the ready-made language, but this seems confused. Why should any individual child suppose that *these* are the words to adopt to provide the medium of their mental attributions? The children are purportedly discovering and finding useful not only that other people 'have minds', but that all other people feature certain common 'mental states'. The problem is: how do small children *discover* that others have these specific kinds of mental states, rather than postulating *either*: (a) different others possess very different kinds of mental states, or (b) that quite differently conceived mental states than those named in the language are more explanatorily effective?

Let us suggest that 'Theory of Mind' theory only appears to work at all because it resorts to that old, well tried technique of the humanities and social sciences, namely that of depending upon what it knows about how things turn out to facilitate explaining why they turn out that way. Why should those attempting to learn not avail themselves of *any* words taken from the language as names for the mental states individuated by their theory? Even if children uniformly employ words from the so-called mentalistic sector of the language to make their postulations of 'inner states', why should we suppose that the word 'belief' adopted by one child as the vehicle for his postulations identifies an 'inner state' that bears any relation to the one that another child – or any of the rest of us, for that matter – supposes is identified by that same word? Why should one presume that the content of the child's theory of mind is the same as one's own even if the same vocabulary is used? After all, one's attributions to the child will be only applications of one's own theory of mind. Without such theoretically gratuitous suppositions, how could anyone conduct the standardized experiments which are designed to study how *children* deploy the 'Theory of Mind' in respect of, for example, 'belief' or 'knowledge'? – Only by means of the common language. But, then, what is to stop a child from adopting a *behaviourist* interpretation of supposedly mentalistic language, which the mentalists assume can be done? Why should a child suppose in the first place that there *are* any 'inner states'?

But, then, what precisely triggers in *all* children the determination that a theory provides the best, let alone an indispensable, means of, for example, predicting the behaviour of others? How could one actually demonstrate that adopting an 'intentional stance', to use Dennett's terminology, *is* notably successfully predictive *in comparison to other possibilities?* What are the specific explanatory tasks that the child *must* attempt that can *only* be resolved by postulating mental states? Having the picture of mental states as explanatory always before their eyes enables 'Theory of Mind' theorists to find these tough questions unproblematic, renders them incapable of conceiving things otherwise.[4]

If, however, something in the mentalistic vocabulary indicates that such words refer to inner states, then this means that the child can learn the mentalistic vocabulary without need for individualized speculation about inner states. Grant this, and then the question is, does acquisition of a 'theory of mind' consist in anything but *the acquisition of the relevant portion of the language?* Do studies of 'Theory of Mind' formation in children consist in anything beyond tests of the stages reached in acquisition of the language and its associated practices?

Compulsion to theorize

Writing – in a critical way – on psychology, we need to point out that our formal disciplinary affiliation as sociologists has nothing to do with our critique. Ours is not a move against psychology on behalf of sociology in the disciplinary turf wars. We are as sceptical of many of the pretensions and 'achievements' of sociology as of those of psychology.[5]

Our scepticism is deep and wide-ranging, essentially about the presupposed compulsion to theorize in the social and human sciences, including psychology. This must not be mistaken for any generalized hostility to theory, but only as a suspicion of an unreflective and unrestrained enthusiasm for theory, and thus of an inappropriately ready determination to construct theories where there is no basis for supposing that problems of understanding will be resolved by the construction of theories. We are also sceptical of the urge to theorize because it produces too many unconvincing products. Thus, there *is* significant evidence that the construction of theories *does not* resolve the problems of understanding in the continuing proliferation of unsatisfactory theories itself, although the persistent failure of theorizing to deliver is characteristically treated as showing the need for yet more theorizing. It is this disproportionate fixation on supposed explanatory problems that is the target of our argument. The availability of a multitude of 'social science' theories is just as much evidence for the view that theorizing itself does not, and, more importantly, will not, answer our 'real needs'.

Of course, and reciprocally, it often appears to those enamoured of theory that our own approach is *a priori* and unsatisfactory because lacking an empirical foundation.[6] However, any such response begs the question because it aborts the attempt to state our position. The *first* question is where the demarcation line between the empirical and the conceptual falls, or, put another way, what our understanding of the 'conceptual nature' of the issues actually is.[7] Those who are driven by the will to theorize, enamoured of the view that there is something potently 'empirical' about what they are doing, simply fail to appreciate the extent to which they misrepresent their problem situation to themselves. It is, therefore, hardly cogent for them to stand pat on *their* conception of the nature and relevance of the 'empirical'. Without denying that there are empirical aspects to psychology and sociology, nonetheless, in many significant cases, the crucial moves are made long before one arrives at the making of observations and inquiries.

The 'observable' and the 'unobservable'

We find in TT ('Theory of Mind' theory) and in ST (simulation theory) an adherence to the Cartesian conception of the 'mental' as belonging to a domain that is 'unobservable directly'[8] and we note too a tendency to construe the demarcation line between that which can and that which cannot be 'observed' about human conduct along empiricist-behaviourist lines. We may indeed refer to both as ToMism. Our approach originates in the subversion of the Cartesian framework by Gilbert Ryle and Ludwig Wittgenstein, to which the stock response has been that, like them, *we* must therefore embrace behaviourism, tantamount to endorsing a regressive, even reactionary, alternative to the resurgent mentalism of the last half-century. Thus, a key to the whole mentalist problematic is the attempt to impose on the use of the expressions 'behaviour' and 'observable' a narrow and restricted employment, insinuating that what are in a less arbitrarily gerrymandered sense *manifest phenomena* are accessible only through inferential postulations. Neither Ryle nor Wittgenstein, however, had any proprietary psychological theory in mind, so it follows that they could not affiliate themselves to behaviourism. Their shared concern was the extent to which language sources philosophical illusions and, especially in Ryle's case, with the ways in which the ensemble of illusions constituent of the Cartesian 'mythology' originate in superficially misleading features of the language we all speak. Cartesians were not, nor are they, concerned with specifics about how we speak, despite being led from the strongholds of Chomsky-dominated linguistics (see Chapter 2, this volume). Ryle was contesting the mentalists' claim that the mind/body problem is suggested by features of that language we speak, especially aspects of the ways in which we normally use words like 'mind'. *If* English speakers did speak of 'body' and 'mind' as inhabiting distinct orders of being, the former observable and the latter not, this could encourage us to wonder about the nature of the mind, supposing that an inquiry into its nature is needed.

If neither Ryle nor Wittgenstein could (in terms of their own approach) legitimately prescribe any psychological theory, behaviourist or otherwise, then any element of behaviourism present in their expressions should be attributable, rather, to the language. The title of Ryle's book, *The Concept of Mind*, does not feature that title to present a psychological system, but encompasses the description of the heterogeneous 'grammars' of a range of concepts – attention, understanding, intelligence, and so on. Therefore, *if* Ryle's description of the 'informal logic'[9] of these concepts is roughly correct (and not something extensively contested by detailed alternative descriptions), then it is the language being described that manifests what are, in the mentalist's understanding, behaviourist tendencies. But the idea that the language itself is behaviourist stands in direct contradiction to the supposition that the language is patently mentalist. One can, then, forget substantive psychology: the division is over the grammatical features of the language, which fact is merely disguised by the attempt to talk in terms of scientific psychology.

The heart of our argument is: central claims of TT are essentially about the language, about those terms purportedly constitutive of a 'folk psychology'. The key claim is that these are theoretical terms. This claim is, however, not backed up by sustained analysis of the language to establish that these terms do operate in the way that theoretical terms do, and there is no effective speci-fication of the theory within which these terms are purportedly housed. The time-worn distinction between 'theoretical' and 'observation' terms, drawn from the philosophy of science, is pressed into service because it is assumed that interpersonal environments exhibit a complete discontinuity between what can and what cannot be observed, and, since the 'mind' is 'unobserv-able', then it cannot be depicted by *any* 'observation' terms and so the words that depict it must be 'theoretical', where 'theoretical' mean 'speculative' or 'provisional' not 'constituent in a defined theory'. It is the inclination to think that the terms are theoretical in the former sense that encourages the thought that they must be theoretical in the latter sense. The supposed 'folk psychology' is the product of the projection of this assumption onto the language. The problem is, as we will seek to show, that this assumption does not project effectively onto relevant key features of the language. Hence the forceful nature of Ryle's discussion of the 'informal logic' or 'grammar' of some of the relevant expressions, a discussion evidencing the fact that, in the language as spoken, these terms do not operate in the ways in which the Cartesian and neo-Cartesian traditions assume they must do.

Ryle's most elementary point was: we do *not* ordinarily speak of mind and body as if they comprised a co-ordinate pairing in the way Cartesians imagined (see Cook, 1969). If we do not speak of mind and body as two distinct orders of being, then there is no need, as contemporary materialist neo-Cartesians assume, to correct Descartes' initial postulation of two distinct orders of being, insisting that there is only *one*. The behaviourist or materialist assertion that 'there is only one' was as objectionable to Ryle as the assertion 'there are two'. His challenge was not restricted to the dualism which Cartesianism distinctively expresses, but to the inclination to *count* which equally characterizes dualism's materialist opponents. A plague on both their houses! *All* depends on how we ordinarily do speak, the ways in which those features of language that Descartes found so suggestive are to be understood. The demonstration that our ways of speaking, our uses of language, embody neither dualist nor behaviourist suppositions – indeed, the demonstration that our 'ordinary language' functions in independence of *all* philosophical assumptions – does not require us to construct any theories, psychological or otherwise, but rather requires the piecemeal examination of the 'informal logic' of our concepts. Ryle's detailed investigations of the workings of numerous, assorted and distributed constituents of our everyday concepts and expressions pertinent to the Cartesian problematic did not require him to furnish a theory or theories, whether materialist, behaviourist or any other.

As Leudar and Costall (2004b) argued, the notion of 'behaviour' itself is one usually taken wholesale from behaviourism, but insofar as we do talk about 'behaviour', it is *not* the same thing as the behaviourists and their materialist/mentalist successors imagine that they are talking about. 'Behaviour' in the (inherited) behaviourist sense means that the things that people do are depicted by what Gilbert Ryle called 'thin' descriptions – only the physical motions involved are described, but 'thick' descriptions can also be given, so that, to use Ryle's own example, an up-and-down movement of the eyelid can also be described as a 'wink' and that is a description of what the eyelid does, but it is a description that involves a great deal more than reference only to the physical movement (Ryle, 1971, pp. 481–2).

Perhaps the critics of Ryle and Wittgenstein have no idea how to confront them on their own terrain? Even those who have some insight into Ryle's general strategy, such as Jack Bilmes (1986, 1992) and Alec McHoul and Mark Rapley (2003), seem to think that it is something that can be dealt with simply as a matter of counter-assertion: Ryle might have argued that 'ordinary language' is not 'mentalistic' in the requisite Cartesian sense, but they are confident that he was wrong, and that our language *is* (at least sometimes, in some people's mouths) mentalistic. The challenge which Ryle poses for them is, of course, to try to find a way of demonstrating that the relevant expressions do function 'mentalistically' since the status 'mentalist' cannot be simply and superficially read off the fact that certain words are being used (see Chapter 11 for this argument in more detail). ToMists embrace the idea that many concepts and predicates are patently mentalistic, even though Ryle and Wittgenstein gave alternative analyses to dispel this impression. Thus, there are usually no detailed arguments adduced to support this mentalist position, let alone any demonstration of the wrong-headedness of Ryle's and Wittgenstein methodological strategies or of the application of those strategies by many successors to the piecemeal portrayal of relevant parts of the language.

Take, for example, the notion of 'mental states' itself. These are claimed by ToMists to be 'unobservable' and 'hypothetical' in nature. But which concepts or predicates are we to subsume under this taxonomic rubric, and on what grounds? Consider our vernacular notion of a 'mental state'. Perhaps it can subsume such varied phenomena as grief, depression, worry, agitation, intense focus, distraction and others. Are these 'unobservable'? Are they available *only* via 'inference'? – surely not. One can *directly* discern someone's 'state of mind' on many occasions; as when one can see that someone is grief-stricken, depressed, distracted, 'high' on some drug, and so on, and only when some relevant contextual details are lacking and where observational details are unclear might one need to infer such 'states'. This clearly contradicts the dogma inherited from Cartesianism – any and all such 'mental states' are, essentially, 'unobservable', and thus might require some theory, or at least some hypothesis, within which to articulate their avowals and ascriptions in vernacular parlance. Further, ToMists seek to incorporate many more concepts and expressions than these under the rubric of 'mental states': they would include 'having a thought', 'intending', 'believing', 'knowing' and a host of others, heedless of the many arguments advanced by both Ryle and Wittgenstein showing how widely divergent their grammars are. Norman Malcolm (1977, ch. 10) drew attention to the misguided efforts made by theorists to force concepts that identify neither states nor processes into one side of the already inappropriate dichotomy of '(mental) states and processes' (see also Ryle, 1949, pp. 222–3; 1960, pp. 102–3).

Let us return to consider the variegated uses of the concept of 'mind' itself in our ordinary, practical discourse. 'It slipped my mind', 'he couldn't get her out of his mind', 'she has a sharp mind', 'he lost his mind', 'mind your Ps and Qs', et cetera all 'come to mind'. Cursory inspection of the ways in which such expressions function in our ordinary language belies the claim that any *single* conception or 'theory' might encompass them, let alone one as restrictive as their characterization as 'descriptions of mental states'. 'It slipped my mind' can be paraphrased without residue into 'I forgot (about) it'. 'He couldn't get her out of his mind' can mean: 'He was obsessed with her'. 'She has a sharp mind' can mean (among other things): she can reason with perspicacity, do many things intelligently. 'He has lost his mind' can mean (*inter alia*): he began to scream and shout for no good reason. Notice that the use of the term 'mental' is beginning to appear *otiose* rather than essential to our understanding of the ways we use such words and expressions.

The use of expressions such as 'intention', 'thought', 'belief' and so on are treated by the ToMists as hypothetical, as speculative, because they are located with respect to a demarcation between 'the observable' and 'the unobservable', which is simply and unquestioningly shared with behaviourism. But why should anyone accept the behaviourists' implausible legislation that we can witness only the movements of bodies and can hear only the sound waves that emanate from them? This very stipulative assumption encourages a distorted reading of the grammar of putatively 'mentalistic' expressions such that the deployment of those expressions is treated as *uniformly* hypothetical solely on the grounds that they feature those terms, regardless of the substantive nature of whatever they are used to assert. Thus, fundamentally, they are hypothetical because what they hazard is that thoughts, intentions and the rest actually might not exist, not just that this individual is currently thinking this or intending that, since no one has observational – direct – evidence that, for example, there are intentions (though some hope that brain imaging techniques will provide pictures of thoughts as they occur, or suppose this has already been done).

While ostensibly honouring the same demarcation between the observable and the unobservable as the behaviourist, however, the 'mentalist' tradition in practice honours it vastly more in the breach than in the observance. There is little thought about how far (if one takes it seriously) the idea that we observe nothing but bodily motions would reach, and how overwhelmingly impractical it would prove, not to mention the extent to which it would yield complete obstruction to the root idea that hypotheses about unobservable 'inner states' are required to explain and predict the behaviour of others. Moreover, it is not just a matter of the adoption of a large number of explicit assumptions which is involved here, but also of what is allowed to slip into the argument unannounced.

Suppose that we were to accept this demarcation, and insist that what we and the child observe are only physical movements: then we should be incapable of observing such things as instances of 'crossing the street', 'answering questions', 'looking in X's direction', 'addressing a letter', 'authorizing a check' and innumerable other doings, since such descriptions already involve 'intentional' characteristics. If we cannot observe 'mental states' and can only observe bodily movements then we cannot observe someone 'crossing the street', we can only observe a body positioned somewhere between one side of the street and the other, with its legs moving. We cannot even assume that the legs are moving so as to transport the rest of the body in any direction: 'crossing the street' anticipates further movements of the body, and characteristically indicates the directedness of the mover's steps. No more can we, if the ToMists are to be believed, ever observe another person observing events, for all we can see is a body with its eyeballs positioned in certain ways within their sockets. It is rather presumptuous even to speak of a body as 'facing in a certain direction' if there is even the slightest suggestion of a bodily orientation or direction of vision in that depiction. Of course, ToMists persistently write as if such phenomena as oriented bodies, ones which make responses and reactions to situations and persons, and that are engaged in the performance of actions with an oriented character, *are* matter-of-course observable phenomena. They treat these, though, as if they were the *explananda* of the theory of a theory of mind when, *by their own premises*, the observable *explananda* would have to be movements of the body identified in strictly physical terms.

TT in a double bind

We want to argue that TTs are apt to conflate the idea of a 'theory' with things that are not really theories at all, and, in addition, that the target phenomena for the postulated theories which children are supposed to develop, the 'inner mental states' of others, are chimeric. Consider the case of children who are asked to assess what other children will do when things those others have seen in a room are moved out when they are absent from the room. The kids in question understand that, after the objects were (secretly) removed, those who were temporarily absent from the room can now be ascribed as only 'believing' and no longer 'knowing' where the objects are located. Indeed so. But what is the role of 'theorizing' in this? And, more especially, what is the role of a 'theory about others' inner states' in such a scenario? Is the ascription of 'belief' meant to be construed as a deduction from a general theory of beliefs? Do the kids in question have the *capacity to articulate* any such general theory? No evidence for *that* is ever adduced.

We might try to formulate a sort of a 'theory'. It might run: 'when objects are removed from their locations unbeknown to prior observers of their location, such observers can now only legitimately be ascribed "belief(s)" about their location, not "knowledge"'. But this is a fact, not any sort of a (testable, defeasible) theory, nor, further, does the ascription of belief or knowledge involve determination of some configuration of brain states, but depends on whether a person is able to give a correct answer to the question: where is (say) the ball? Whether another child is in a position to give that answer depends on assessing what information is available to them, grasping that their information about the ball's location has not been updated in line with changes. And what sort of 'fact' is this? A *grammatical* one, a matter of understanding what 'know' means as opposed to 'believe', is a matter of understanding the rules for the ascription of 'knowledge' rather than 'belief' or vice versa.

The question remains: what is the source of the idea that children develop a 'theory of mind' at all? What could a 'theory of mind' be about? 'Mind', as we have argued, is either a vernacular notion (with ramifying uses, none of which require the preservation of this particular word in paraphrases thereof) or else a residue of Cartesian dualism, a theoretical reification.

If it is being used in the latter fashion, then it is no sort of genuine *explanandum* (either for children, lay adults or behavioural scientists) but, rather, a fallacy. 'Reification' is another way of saying this: a fallacy of what Whitehead succinctly called misplaced *concreteness*. *Res facere* is the Latin origin of 'reification', and it translates roughly into 'to make into a thing' or 'to treat as if a thing'. If a mind is not a thing of any sort then, again, we are dealing with a fallacy and not with an *explanandum*. And if there is no *explanandum*, then there is no need for an *explanans*.

TT argues that we all must be either lay or professional psychologists who need to appeal to 'mind' as a *theoretical construct* of something both unobservable and hypothetical if we are to understand how it is that we can 'predict and explain' human conduct in everyday affairs as in scientific practice. They claim that what Dennett and others have termed a 'folk psychology' is the phylogenetic and ontogenetic precursor of scientific psychology, and it consists in the array of interdependent 'mental' concepts/predicates in our language. We may call our 'folk psychology' a 'theory' because it facilitates predictions, and this is a hallmark of any genuine theory. Here, to justify this usage, TT is clearly appealing to the fact that many scientific theories have the property of predictive power. Nonetheless, note that predicting that sunlight in this forest interacting with the chlorophyll in the living green leaves of the plants over there will generate photosynthesis (a deduction from the *theory* of photosynthesis) is barely comparable to the assertion about children switching from 'knowing' to 'believing' in the above scenario.

In the senses in which we *can* predict what others will do in our everyday lives, neither a deterministic nor a strictly quantifiable probabilistic account can be legitimately formulated and defended as such. The history of positivism in the human sciences is a stark enough witness to this. 'In such-and-such circumstances, he is likely to do this rather than that' is certainly a predictive remark and, when justifiable, of considerable usefulness, but scarcely any sort of deduction from a prior nomological or stochastic theory.[10]

The idea of a theory of mind

Some proponents of TT (such as Premack and Woodruff) take the evolutionary aspect of the argument literally, and believe it appropriate to raise the question: 'does the chimpanzee have a theory of mind?' ostensibly as a genuinely *empirical* matter, requiring extensive ethological investigations. Any such studies can only *effectively* address the question of what specific capacities may legitimately be ascribed to non-human primates. For example, inquiries might reveal to what extent they are sensitive to the nature of human responses: even the casual zoo visitor can ascertain that some of these primates discriminate human intentions to some degree. One can make this a matter for a more technical inquiry by seeking to establish just what capacity for discrimination amongst what range of human reactions the chosen primates do possess. That they possess some such capacity is plain enough, and, however far it might extend, it will inevitably prove considerably more limited than what human beings are capable of. Clearly, however, how a particular species of primate responds to its human keepers is an *empirical* question and it will only be answered by seeing what, for example, apes and chimpanzees can do.

Whilst we do not deny that such studies are appropriately conducted; nonetheless, we want to call into question the *standard* of significance that is attached to these investigations within the 'mentalist' tradition from which they emanate. For these standards are themselves *a priori*, and involve appeal to a whole range of contestable preconceptions about what the point and possible achievements of such studies might be. Do we want to lump the range of capacities the primates are proven to have under the heading 'Theory of Mind'? Do we *need* to do this? Does it add anything to enumerating those capacities? Or is there an ulterior motive? It is, after all, widely claimed that such studies constitute investigations into 'the nature of the mind', and it is at this juncture that the notion of a 'theory of mind' ceases to be an innocuous (though never especially happy) turn of phrase, becoming instead the carrier of an overload of suppositions. The idea is that these studies will help to establish that some primates also possess what human beings possess, and that which children must either acquire or possess innately, namely *a theory*. It is *assumed* that possession of the capacity to make discriminations, for which the primates are being tested, must depend on the possession of a *theory*, although note that the inspection of primate responses does not itself provide any evidence for possession of a theory, save by showing that they have the capacity to make certain relevant discriminations. The conclusion that their behaviour evidences possession of a 'theory' follows only from the circular application of the prior assumption that a theory is the basis for *people's* capacity to understand each other.

Of course, the claim that a theory is the basis for *that* capacity is not something that itself is treated as a hypothesis and subjected to test, for how could it be? *People's behaviour shows only that they possess assorted capacities, dispositions, inclinations et cetera, and is not independent evidence that the capacity implements some theory.* It is only by treating the supposition that observable activities are not merely subsumable under, but are actually generated by a theoretical system as a given, that one can construe their activities as evidencing the application of the proposed theory. The claim that such theories exist is much more specific and speculative than the manifestly observable fact that people do have the relevant capacities, which fact can be secured quite independently of any understanding of what the bases for those capacities might be. People's behaviour is, rather, to be construed in TT on *the assumption* that it is expressive of a theory which assumption itself comes at the end of a long avenue of other (*a priori*) assumptions, being supported by the interlocking logic of these, rather than in any way necessitated by the nature of the behaviour itself.

One of the central neo-Cartesian assumptions which unites proponents of TT (and, we might add, most proponents of the notion that people possess a 'folk-psychological' theory) is the postulation of 'inner mental states' as facilitators of many of our ordinary capacities. We have argued that any such conception is essentially a philosophical *projection* onto the uses of aspects of our everyday vocabulary that philosophers have picked out as a supposedly unified collection of expressions, misconstruing those as an array of names for referring to hidden 'phenomena'. Even if we were to concede the existence of such phenomena, what difference would they make? Our uses of the vocabulary in question – our saying things to each other in accord with the grammar of the relevant expressions – would proceed apace without any of us having the slightest idea as to what such 'inner states and processes' might consist in. There is *literally* no work for such a notion to perform, for no-one even attempts to correct attributions of a 'mental' kind ('he thought that...', 'she intended to...', 'he remembered that...' and the rest) by scrutinizing anyone's insides – there is no evidence that users of them give any theoretical content to those terms. Doing this would be as obviously absurd as attempting to open up someone's intestines in order to see if he has 'guts' (in the sense of bravery or courage).

Our position is that the postulation of 'inner states' is a mere detour, which takes for granted and depends upon the children's capacity to deploy 'mentalistic' vocabulary and does nothing whatsoever to clarify what is involved in their mastery of those, nor how it is that the children are able to apply these terms in conventional and quite standard ways.

As so often in the social and behavioural sciences, the theoretically provided version of things is the very obverse of the theorist's own practice – it is not the identification of any inner states that enables the identification of what people are doing, whether or not they are thinking of X or intending to Y, whether or not they are depressed or elated, but rather, their conduct is treated as entitling us to ascribe 'mental states' to them. The ascriptions that we routinely make to others – and which proponents of TT also and indispensably make – are made on the basis of what people are doing in various circumstances, for, of course, we as speakers of the language have absolutely no idea what kind of inner state the 'mental state' terms might correspond to and accompany their doings; for instance, what inner state are we postulating when we attribute a 'thought' to someone? To say that we are attributing an occurrence 'in the head' says nothing whatsoever, for, according to this conception, all so-called 'mental states' occur in the head: so what *distinctive* inner state does the attribution of a thought identify? The mentalist psychologists must themselves understand how to apply those same vernacular terms to persons, independently of any idea of what 'inner states' would correspond to them, as a precondition of their speculations on what those states could be. *In the mouths of speakers of the language, the nature of the inner state plays no role at all – unless one reduces the supposedly empirical claim that such expressions make reference to inner entities to a tautology – the use of the relevant terms just is taken as evidence that they are being used in this way.*

Even so, the point cuts both ways, because without some comprehension of the nature of the inner state which individuates not merely the occurrence of 'a thought' but the occurrence of 'this thought', how are we to individuate the bits of people's doings that are purportedly underpinned by these – for mentalists, as yet – undifferentiable inner states? This either cannot be done (which would bring one, e.g., close to Stephen Stich's position that a scientific psychology would be a study of God-knows-what, but certainly could not be a study of beliefs), or it *is* done, but entirely independently of the attribution of an 'intermediary' inner state – we just are entitled, *because we can speak the language,* to say in appropriate circumstances of someone's saying 'We should take a holiday in the Seychelles' that he or she has 'offered a thought' and, equally, to add that our return to them, 'Not the Seychelles again!', shows that their thought is not our thought.

At the most, the postulation of inner states putatively corresponding to 'mental' expressions can only *accompany* the application of that vocabulary, since there are no means of determining the presence or character of inner states *independently of, or in addition to*, the grounds for intelligibly and appropriately asserting in a particular case that X believes Y, Z hates J, et cetera. Thus, the 'inner states' postulated are linguistically empty, but the words making up the 'mentalistic vocabulary' do have rules for their correct use (i.e., a grammar), and cannot, therefore, be ones which are *indispensably* associated with determinate conceptions of inner states. The postulation is idle, though this point is not a behaviourist counter to mentalism, but an argument about how the relevant parts of the language actually work.

Since one has no access to such inner states, one also lacks any idea what they could be like. One's use of this vocabulary thus absolutely cannot *depend* upon such a postulation. Moreover, in what sense could an attribution of inner states actually *accompany* our usage in ordinary language? The language would not demonstrably differ in how we actually talk to and about one another, whether or not there was any such accompaniment. The idea of our language embodying a 'folk psychology' is a wholly unnecessary shuffle superimposed on the problematic notion that we can demarcate a portion of our vocabulary as 'mentalistic'. Such a shuffle (involving the postulation of essentially 'intermediary' *inner* states and occurrences) is due to the fixation upon the 'mentalistic' portion as though it operated entirely in hypothetical mode, when, as we have seen, it does not do so. Much of this language operates in a way which is 'criterial' rather than hypothetical: someone's saying and doing thus-and-so in such-and-such circumstances just *does* entitle us to say that he knows this or believes that, and the distinction between the two does not hinge upon the identification of any inner state, but upon the matter of attribution. Par Segerdahl (1996) offers a useful illustration of this point:

> How does a child come to *believe* that his mother is in the kitchen? He does so in ways that are very similar to the ways in which he comes to *know* that she is in the kitchen. The difference is that the evidence is no longer conclusive. The evidence may be the fact that it is lunch time soon, or that the mother is not in the bedroom or that sounds are heard coming from the kitchen area, although the sounds are not the ones typically heard from the kitchen, and so on. This kind of evidence, and the correct distinction between what is conclusive evidence and what is merely inconclusive evidence, is something that children learn only late in their development.
>
> (Segerdahl, 1996, p. 156)

Muddles about modularity

One facet of the 'Theory of Mind' theory, the idea of partitioning a section of our language into a 'mentalistic' domain, underpins a further development: the postulation of cognitive 'modules' as advocated especially by Alison Gopnik (1996) in a move inspired by current tenets in 'cognitivism' derived from Chomsky and Fodor.[11] Chomsky's proposition that the human capacity for syntax in language could be distinguished analytically and ontologically from our capacity for semantics, led various theorists (notably Fodor) to elaborate a theory of the 'modularity' of human capacities (among them, grammatical speech, visual perception, pattern recognition, auditory perception and somatosensory perception). 'Modularity' theory in 'cognitivism' asserts that a human capacity for speech is encapsulated and distinguishable from a capacity for perception, and from other forms of conduct (e.g., non-verbal kinds) as well. TT is based upon an even more radical version of the modularity thesis, namely that our capacity for using a *portion* of our language (the so-called 'mentalistic' part) can be distinguished and studied independently from the rest of our linguistic capacities. However, if, as we argue, linguistic capacity more generally cannot comprise a discrete 'module', then *a fortiori*, neither can linguistic conduct employing the 'mental' vocabulary comprise a subsidiary, specialized one.

We need to clarify one issue here. Our discussion in this chapter is focused solely upon the notion of 'psychological' modules. Such modules as specified by discrete, lay 'theories' articulated internally by rules and representations, should not be conflated with neurophysiologic use of the concept of a neural 'module'. Whilst equivalently hypothetical in many of its specifications, the latter, biological, notion – related to the classical localization-of-functions hypothesis in neurophysiology – does *not* commit its proponents to any-thing like the apparatus of the 'inner information storage' models favoured by 'cognitivism', even if some of them try to attach their work to mentalism. For serious neuroscientists, the discreteness of a capacity is an empirically decidable matter to be established prior to a principled search for any sort of underlying neural mechanism which might facilitate its exercise (e.g., the capacity to walk, to masticate as a component of eating, to co-ordinate various motor functions, and the like). It is a matter of significant dispute whether or not neurophysiological theories of localizable neural structures subserving capacities can be extended to encompass the full range of human conduct, especially rational, intelligent, purposeful activities.[12]

There is, however, no requirement ordained by the neurosciences that we *must* construe such a range of human capacities and conduct in modu-lar terms. Indeed, there are logical obstacles to efforts to classify human capacities in this way. Consider the argument that speech and perception constitute informationally encapsulated modules because speaking and seeing, say, are distinctively different capacities. This position cannot be sustained, not least because so much of what we ordinarily, and properly, call (the exercise of) visual capabilities among human beings requires a mastery of linguistic resources.[13] In mastering and using natural language, there can be no neat separation of what are, in fact, varied and assorted capacities from our 'form of life', as Wittgenstein argued. To be able to, for instance 'tell the time', or to be able to 'order a meal at a restaurant' requires linguistic competence but they are not separable from the social practices, interactions and circumstances which variously comprise our everyday lives. We do not learn to speak, and somehow, independently, learn the vast and motley array of things that we do. That array includes the capacity to ascribe beliefs, to avow thoughts, to assign motives, to infer personality traits, to ascribe purpose to someone's conduct or a lack thereof, to recount dreams, to discern 'mental illness' and so forth. It is odd, we think, that it is this latter bunch of capacities which Gopnik and those who concur with her position seek somehow to 'modularize' into a 'Theory of Mind'.[14] By contrast, we argue that such practices *also* belong to the assortment of language-games we 'play' as intrinsic (not extrinsic, discrete, separable, independently analyzable) dimensions of our social existence. We would also insist that many linguistic articulations (e.g., 'want a cigarette?') can be handled by functionally equivalent *non-verbal* articulations such as: holding out a pack of cigarettes toward someone whilst shaking the pack so as to project one from the pack and waiting for his or her response. We now ponder the modularity thesis in this respect: how could such an argu-ment encompass the communicatively equivalent practice, given its vastly different mode of articulation, if, say, speech and non-verbal conduct are to be construed as represented internally (*sic.*) by different (e.g., modular) 'theories' of conduct?

Quasi-experiments

According to Wellman and Bartsch:

> Sensible prediction of [a] character's actions can result from utilizing the information about his belief coupled with information about his desire. We call stories such as this *Standard Belief* tasks. [Whereas 'Prediction Tasks' attempt to assess whether] children younger than 4 or 4 and a half years old are consistently inaccurate at belief-desire reasoning in that they predict that an actor with a false belief will search for an object where it really is, not where the actor believes it to be.
>
> (Wellman and Bartsch, 1988, p. 262)

Thus, in Astington's (1996) 'experimental' scenario, a child is shown two boxes: for instance, an *empty* Band-Aid box and a plain box *with band-aids inside*. 'A puppet appears with a cut on his hand, the child is told he [the puppet] wants a band-aid and then is asked where the puppet will look for band-aids. The typical response from three-year-olds is to predict that the puppet will look in the plain box where the band-aids are' (Astington, 1996, p. 191). In this scenario, the child mistakenly predicts the puppet character's action because the child confuses its *knowledge* with the puppet's understanding, for on the basis of normal belief attributions to the puppet, it would believe that the plasters would be in the Band-Aid box, even though there are, in fact, none there.

Such a quasi-experiment itself presupposes what is supposed to be at issue in it, namely the capacity of children to exercise a 'theory of mind'. For example, it is not entirely clear from the summary of the experiment whether the child does understand what it is supposed to – does the child actually understand what a 'Band-Aid box' is? After all, to understand what a Band-Aid box is involves understanding what its use or purpose is – the Band-Aid box in the experiment is not a Band-Aid box in the sense of containing band-aids, for it does not contain any; it is only a Band-Aid box in virtue of being a kind of box where band-aids are *supposed* to be kept. Thus, does the child understand the part that the Band-Aid box is meant to play in the experiment? Does the child understand that this is meant to play the default part of the place where people would normally go to look for band-aids in the first instance, and absent knowledge of the storage of band-aids in some other place? It is assumed that the child will make the connection between the cut on the puppet's finger and his 'wanting a band-aid' which, itself, involves understanding what the standard use or purpose of a band-aid is, and also to see that the puppet is purportedly an embodiment of the standard practice of finding a band-aid to place over the injury. But does the child understand that he is supposed to envisage the puppet as someone who does not already know where the band-aids are actually kept, and is therefore to be imagined as operating on the assumption that the band-aids will be in their appropriate place (in the Band-Aids box)? Is the child to assume that, unlike himself, the puppet does not know where the band-aids actually are?

Our point is not to highlight the questionable status of the 'experiment' as here described, but rather to bring out the extent to which the undertaking of the experiment just *assumes* and *utterly depends* upon the attribution of a capacity to make numerous and fine discriminations in other people's so-called 'mental states' in even quite young children: the child's capacity to do so is *a condition of* his proper participation in the 'experiment', of the child's understanding of what he or she is supposed to do. Secondly, we wish to point out that the child's capacity to understand what the experimenters intend he or she should do does not depend upon any sort of speculative theorization of the inner states of the experimenters, but rather upon his or her mastery of a variety of things that are acquired through participation in practices. The child has already learned something about the role that boxes play in our lives, about the significance of markings upon them (with brand names, for example) and about the connection between such identifications with the normative regulation of the use that is (to be) appropriately made of such boxes, not to mention the practice associated with the use of band-aids, such that the thing to do following a cut is to look for a band-aid. The child has also learned what questions and instructions are. If one accepted Chomsky-type innatist arguments, all that a child could possibly 'know' innately would be that certain utterances have an interrogative or imperative form, but even this would merely be a capacity to identify grammatically structural features of those utterance forms, and would provide no indication that anything was to be done in response to them, or what that might be. Third, and by far most importantly, the *officially* 'mentalistic' words – such as 'thought', 'belief', 'desire', 'intention', 'understanding' and the like – are thoroughly interwoven with the rest of the language, such that we are able to speak of a 'Band-Aid box' or of someone 'being asked [to do] something', 'understanding the situation', and in the innumerable other ways presupposed in the writing of even the cited brief description of the experiment.

In other words, there is no independent mentalistic vocabulary as such to be segregated from the language. Nor could the capacity to attribute beliefs, intentions, understandings and the like conceivably operate purely on the basis of theories about putative inner states and without any embedding in a culturally accumulated mountain of understandings of the ways in which practices are organized, of the kinds of circumstances in which, for example, a child should do what an adult – though not just any adult – asks him to do, and so on. Understanding that something is a 'question to be answered' is not a matter of understanding something 'inner' in addition to what is said or done in these circumstances, but is a matter of understanding *just that.* Of course, *in practice*, theorists of 'Theory of Mind' do not suppose anything remotely different from this. If they were to respond defensively to the suggestion that their experiment might not have been testing what they supposed it was testing – that the children might not have understood what they were supposed to in order to play their proper part in the experiment – they would *not* suggest that we should try looking deeply into the eyes of the children or drilling into their skulls or even having tomographic images made – they would naturally detail for us the things that they and the children said and did in setting up the 'experiments' to demonstrate that the children perfectly well understood what they were being asked to do. Indeed, the experimenters themselves did try to explain how they attempted to ensure that their tests tested for what they were designed to test (Wellman and Bartsch, 1988, p. 264).

Are we behaviourists?

One possible reply to our argument is to reiterate the old claim: but you are only ever talking about behaviour, so you remain, after all, behaviourists. In return: but this is a wholly tendentious description of our position, formulated in terms of the very position that we have rejected. Where does the 'only' come from, except from the supposition that the problem of mind resides in the question of whether there is 'behaviour' or something more?

The complaint that we 'only talk about behaviour' does not grasp the two-pronged nature of the strategy guiding our argument.

(a) If we stop thinking of behaviour as something that must be described only in 'thin' terms, and recognize that it can also be described in 'thick' terms, then the illusion that the line between 'the observable' and 'the unobservable' is to be drawn along the line of thin descriptions will evaporate, and one will stop thinking that 'the mental' is unobservable, obscured from view by bodily movements and accessible only as a matter of *inference*. A supplementary point is, we note, that mentalists are entirely disloyal to this principle in practice, not least because consistent application of it would render their position wholly impractical. It is not only mentalists who have insuperable difficulty in sticking to their own methodological recommendations about how we should speak in scientifically correct ways. Behaviourists face exactly the same situation (as Merleau-Ponty [1965, p. 226] observed about John B. Watson). This reinforces the point that we are as distant from behaviourists as we are from mentalists, and criticise *both* on the grounds that they do not securely articulate their supposedly 'technical' discourse with everyday ways of speaking that they, along with the rest of us, persistently – and unreflectively – deploy.

(b) Our argument is developed to do away with the twin, paired distinctions between 'inner'/'outer' and 'private'/'public' *in the form* that they
are cherished by the behaviourist/mentalist axis, and a view which
involves the idea that talking about (thickly described) behaviour can
be considered a matter of talking about 'the outer', adoption of obsolete
jargon to formulate a position that has moved beyond this vocabulary.
Wittgenstein explicitly reminded us all that any inner process stands in
need of outward criteria, whence we derived our point that the way in
which language works in (thick) description of people and what they do
is more akin to operating in a criterial way (i.e., their grammar involves
ways of telling one thing from another, whether a person is in pain or
only pretending, whether a person does or does not believe a certain
thing) and not to the hypothetical mode in which the behaviourist *and*
mentalist proponents construe our talk of others and, by the same token,
of ourselves (cf. Chapter 11 this volume). The argument that folk psychology is unnecessary is not premised in an argument that there is nothing 'inner' to be referred to. Rather, any 'inner' apparatus such as has
been postulated by mentalists, cognitivists and ToMists is simply surplus
to what is routinely accomplished by the use of the criterial organization of those expressions which attract the philosophical psychologist's
attention. Nothing in Ryle or in Wittgenstein prohibits the possibility
of reference to 'inner' states, or denies the actuality of such reference in
the language. This is, however, no concession whatsoever to the mentalists *or* materialists – the point is that these 'inner' states do not conform
to the neo-Cartesian conception of what is involved in speaking of the
'inner' according to the 'grammar' of everyday discourse.

The idea of a 'theory of theory of mind', then, becomes a mere surplus
artefact. Instead of needing to construct a theory of mind, children learn
to speak the language and to apply the criteria that are part of it, though
learning the language is not some single, unified or independent task, but
something that is done in and through learning to participate in a range
of diverse practices that make up the lives of whatever collectivities we
belong to. *De facto*, the theory of 'theory of mind' is an arcane, theoretically top-heavy way of redescribing phenomena which we can perfectly
well describe and understand independently of that or any other theory
from the human sciences. Strip away the apparatus of theory and it all
becomes clear what it is that a child learns when it purportedly 'acquires
a theory of mind': the language. That is, first, the child learns to use the
supposedly mentalistic vocabulary, and needs to learn nothing in addition
to that, in the sense of an additional theory. Second, the child's learning
of the supposedly 'mentalistic' vocabulary requires the learning of much
more of the language and of the activities that the language is used in – for
a simple example, the child has to learn that the word 'feel' features very

differently in, for example, 'feeling a pain' and 'feeling sick', not to mention 'feel this fabric'.

Is simulation theory really a rival for TT?

The idea behind TT is that, as very small children, we confront a generic problem, which is that we do not – yet – understand other people. At some point in childhood we solve this problem by contriving a method for understanding other people which, according to Theory-Theory, is a matter of devising a theory about how other people's mental states cause their behaviour. We will now turn to an influential alternative to Theory-Theory, and examine whether this approach avoids the problems we have identified. According to simulation theory (ST), interpersonal comprehension involves creating simulations of other people's mental states and processes to introspectively track (or unconsciously enact) how those mental states will figure in reasoning processes that would eventually produce behavioural precipitants on one's own part. These behavioural outputs are not themselves realized, the reasoning sequence is aborted when the behavioural outcome is specified, but before it is implemented. These sequences run 'off line' and therefore provide an output that is used to conclude about what, in comparable circumstances, the other person is (*ceteris paribus*) likely to do. This kind of understanding is often treated as being affiliated to 'empathy'.

ST may hold that it is scenarios rather than theories that are involved in the capacity to interpret and predict what others will do, but it provides the same fundamental picture as TT. This is that adults do (purportedly) understand other people, but they can only do so because, in childhood, they solved the problem of understanding, finding it necessary and useful to credit other people with inner mental states. These states are 'inner' ones and therefore cannot be themselves 'directly' identified – they can only be 'postulated' – but it is seemingly functional to postulate these as 'underlying' whatever of others' behaviour we can observe. The child must not only contrive the machinery of attribution – a theory or a simulation – but must also determine the content of mental state attributions, with which kinds of mental states to populate the mind of self and other, not to mention fixing their precise explanatory function in theoretically subsuming or predictively simulating behaviour. For TT and ST the problem of understanding others has a fundamental one-off solution devised in childhood, and an adult's comprehension of his or her fellows is a matter of applying, according to the doctrine preferred, either their theoretical schemes or their simulation processes.

We have suggested above, that a 'Theory of Mind' is superfluous because there is no genuine problem to be solved by the individual's postulation of a theory of mind. In that respect, we differ profoundly from those who criticize TT as though there is a genuine problem – that of how it is possible that we understand other people – complaining that TT does not solve it. Whilst such a rival, in the inward-looking, narrow framework that dominates modern philosophical psychology, may seem – in flatly rejecting the idea that any such theory is involved – fundamentally opposed to TT, it seems to us very close kin to TT, accepting the same starting assumptions.

Both TT and ST are popular enough to have sufficient adopters amongst whom there can be disagreement about the intricacies of the respective schemes. Neither TT nor ST are entirely uniform doctrines, but one cannot review all the variations within their respective camps in a brief assessment. As with TT, we will focus on central tendencies within ST although the relevant doctrines may not be common to all ST adopters.[15]

Like TT, ST *generally* begins with the idea that there is an asymmetry between my own case and that of others, the 'generally' registering the fact that complications can attend the question of how the asymmetry works out. Deep within the cognitivist tradition is the strong assumption that I genuinely (or directly) know things that are immediate to me. The problematic for ST is the same as for TT: how can I understand that and what other people understand when I am not in direct contact with their understanding? There can be strong temptation to suppose that such understanding as I can have of others is a function of the understanding I have of my own case. According to ST, I determine the other's understanding through a scenario that plays out my own likely response to the situation the other confronts.[16] Having determined what I would do as far as identifying the appropriate next action, I now have a basis for anticipating what another person would do in those same circumstances. Note that 'understanding' other people is commonly tied to *predicting* what other people would do in TT and ST, which adds attraction to the simulation as an alternative to a theory of mind: both are understood to have predictive capacity.

Postulation of simulations is not necessitated by empirical evidence that these take place in anyone's experience on the scale required for ST to be a general account or how could there be any disagreement about whether simulations, if there are any, run consciously or not? – we would surely be only too aware that we were constantly simulating if we were doing so consciously.[17] The question is not whether we run simulations unconsciously, but whether we run them in the required sense at all? No one is denying that we can sometimes imaginatively simulate a situation and our reaction to it, but ST is advanced as a generalized account of how we understand others and requires, therefore, that we be simulating pretty much all the time.

The postulation of simulation is necessitated by the framework problematic, which is to explain how, knowing what one would do, one is also able to understand what someone else would do in the same circumstances even though one does not have – cannot have – 'direct' access to *their* understanding. Where can one come up with any understanding of what would be done in these circumstances save from one's own existing resources? These are understandings of what one would do. Seemingly, however, the only way of knowing how one would respond to some circumstances is to work through a scenario representing one's reaction to those circumstances, hence the nature of one's pre-existing understanding is established (for oneself) by a review of the transformation over one's mental representations. *Ceteris Paribus,* what one would do is a good representation of what someone else would do, and one can now anticipate their response to the situation – it will be the same.

Does this really provide a scientific description of a set of evidentially determined empirical processes, or simply a cumbersome redescription of otherwise commonplace affairs? Consider this from Stich and Nichols in which they simulate one of Paul Harris's arguments:

> Suppose, for example, that someone were asked to predict what one of our Rutger's colleagues would say when asked: who is the President of Rutger's University? Or suppose we were asked to predict what our wives would say when asked: 'Who was the third President of the United States?' In both cases, we suspect, we would proceed by first answering the question for ourselves – recalling who *we* think is the President of Rutgers or who we think was the third president of the US. Then, since we assume that our colleagues (in the first place) and our wives (in the second case) believe the same things we do on questions like this, we would predict that they would say the same thing as we would. In all of these cases, it would be perfectly natural to say that a sort of 'simulation' is being exploited.
>
> (Stich and Nichols, 1995, p. 92)

Even if it was 'perfectly natural' to say that 'simulation' is involved, it seems that it is, even in Stich and Nichols' view, only a simulation of an attenuated kind, and the examples seem quite unnatural. The invitation to 'predict' what one's colleagues would say seems to be a rather roundabout way of asking 'Do your Rutger's colleagues know the college President's name?,' a question which might be answered on the basis of having heard them speak of the President by name. The fact that the request to 'predict' what people will say can sometimes be treated as if it posed two separate questions, as with 'what is the President's name?' and 'do these people know it?' leads on to a theoretical specification of a two-stage psychological process. Further, it seems as if being asked a question by someone else itself involves a two-stage process, so that in response to their question, do my colleagues know the name of the University President?, one *first* asks oneself: do I know the name of the University President?, then initiates a process to ascertain that one does. Having done that, one can then ask: do my colleagues know that that is the name of the President?[18]

Another superficially appealing illustration is that of being asked to predict what the outcome of someone else's addition will be. One can do the sum oneself, thus identifying the total which, if the addition is done correctly, the other will arrive at. As so often, the notion of 'simulation' is a theory-imposed surplus on otherwise plain facts. It is true that *my* understanding of arithmetic is indispensable if I am to do the same sum as someone else. It is not, however, the case that my understanding of arithmetic itself comes from simulation – I imagine myself confronted with the symbols '2 + 2 =' and then run a simulation to see what one would do in such an event. One can only 'run the simulation' if one already knows what to do, that is, to write down '4' and, of course, one does not understand this by virtue of having originally determined it oneself, but by having learned it from others. Thus, whilst the replication of the same calculation might seem a supportive example, in fact it only highlights the need to appreciate how much understanding *goes into* being able to run a simulation in the first place. The understanding that goes into doing a calculation does determine what I would do in this case, but it does so because what one does is determined by what the rules of calculation are, which determine what *anyone* should do in this case. One's own effort to determine what the other will do by a replication of the calculation is itself premised not in an understanding of oneself, but of the other, namely that he or she understands basic arithmetic, and it is that fact that gives one confidence in the relevance of undertaking the calculation oneself.

The notion of simulation of course does not need to be tied to the idea that understanding other people is a matter of 'predicting' what they will do. We suspect it is done because such association of understanding with prediction contributes to the persuasiveness of the simulation picture. If we are trying to predict what someone will do, it can seem as if we are anticipating the outcome of a process, which we cannot observe, but can only imagine, that results in the occurrence. Since we want to predict how the other's thoughts turn out, our imaginings must aspire to identify the processes that they are following, if we are to arrive at the same outcome as they will reach. Hence, whether they are enactments of my own presumably parallel processes or envisaging on behalf of the other, they are essays in simulation. The imagery of 'predicting', however, misdirects the attention, pointing it toward a very partial aspect of understanding, obscuring the patent fact that even in cases where we do predict what others are doing, this does not require a speculative recreation of unobservable psychic processes, but often only the identification and comprehension of the course of action in which the other is currently observably engaged. We can often predict where someone's course of action will come out precisely because we can 'track' that course of action's sequence to *prescribed* outcomes – the car in front is signalling a left turn, so we can 'predict' – we are entitled to *expect* – that it will turn left, the convention of signalling turns being precisely a facilitator of our capacity to anticipate what the others will be doing.

The point is that simulation is supposed to be a means for understanding what other people are doing, but were simulating to be *the* means of understanding, then to be an effective technique it would be wholly dependent upon what we already understand about other people and what they do. It seems easy enough to imagine that, confronted with the question 'what would someone else do in a certain situation?', it can be effectively answered on the basis of considering what *I* would do in that case? But how do I know what *I* would do in such a situation? The cognitivist picture is of us treating the actual or imagined situation as input to a causally sequenced succession of mental states which eventually specify a response to the situation. But what provides the content of this supposed causal sequence? Where does that come from? 'What would someone else do if they lost their credit card?' in ST precipitates the simulative question, 'What would I do if I lost my credit card?' The answer to the second question is, however, the same as the first, in that the thing to do in the event of losing a credit card is to contact the issuing organization. The two questions are only functional equivalents to 'What does (any)one do if (any)one loses their credit card?', where the common sense understanding is: what action is *appropriate* to prevent financial loss and replace the lost card? But all this derives from an understanding of what a credit card is, and that understanding is a prerequisite to understanding the nature of the situation in which someone who has lost their credit card finds themselves – there is an organizationally supplied answer to this question. It would be very different if one was asking 'what would someone do if they lost their credit card?' in a context where this was an unprecedented occurrence unattended by standardized solutions. That the understanding can be stated impersonally – what does *one* do when one loses one's credit card? – shows that there is no asymmetry between myself and another in respect of determining the appropriate next thing to do *in such a case*,[19] and my capacity to determine what that situation would be for me (one of financial loss and inconvenience) comes from the same source as does my capacity to determine what (*ceteris paribus*) it would be for someone else (namely the understanding of what a credit card is).

We are doubtful, with respect to TT and ST, whether there is any *general task* of 'understanding how others' minds work', and therefore any correspondingly general method for doing this. In many – not, we concede, all – cases, 'understanding how the other's mind works' cashes out as 'understanding how activities work': 'predicting' the outcome of someone else's calculation involves nothing other, nothing more, than understanding how to calculate, requiring neither theoretical generalities about their minds nor simulations of any mental processes but simply resort to the rules of arithmetic. The capacity to understand any other individual's current activity commonly presupposes either: (a) that we already understand a great deal about what they are doing, such as to be able to recognize what their situation is, and to be able to track and even anticipate how courses of activity typically or appropriately go, or (b) being assisted by others in recognition and comprehension of the otherwise unfamiliar activity that they are about (being given instruction, explanation, information).

In sum, we have tried to show that the root difficulties with ST are the same as those with TT, namely the set of traditional philosophical assumptions that they share with the mentalist tradition more generally, and with post-Cartesian philosophy of mind even more generally. It seems that ST fails on a specific and basic point, which is that of circularity – as Gallagher puts it, it seems that 'the simulator already has some knowledge of what is going on with the other person. The question is where does such knowledge come from and why isn't that already the very thing we are trying to explain?' (Gallagher, 2007, p. 64).

Understanding other situations

It is sometimes suggested that ST has affinity with the vernacular request to put ourselves in another person's shoes, though ST itself is rather more a case of putting other people in our shoes. There are occasions on which we are invited to put ourselves in someone else's shoes, but these are usually ones in which we are being encouraged to be *more* imaginative about someone else's situation, often as a means of challenging our own assumptions – complacency, even – about what we would do in their situation, an inclination to suppose that we would act differently than they have done in such a situation. Condemning people who lived compliantly under a totalitarian regime can give rise to such an invitation – think rather more about how their situation differs from yours; don't be so confident that you would behave any differently. It is easy to imagine oneself as a bold resister until one thinks more deeply about how terrifying such regimes can be, appreciates the difference between being a comfortable dissenter against non-threatening authorities at home and defying a regime that extensively terrorizes and liquidates its own population abroad. Accept that in important ways you do not know what you would do in such situations, and would have to be put in one to really tell whether you would be so boldly defiant as you like to think or would turn out to be just another cautious individual: perhaps you would be boldly defiant, but do not *assume* this.

There is another case where putting on the other's shoes troubles social, more than psychological, studies, and this has to do with the perennial question of understanding other cultures. This supposed problem, like those of TT and ST, arises more from a nest of philosophical assumptions than it does from genuine difficulties in actual cases.

It is only *practically* problematic to understand what people in some alien culture are doing (i.e., there is no principled, metaphysical obstacle to this).

The notorious cases are those in which people make use of magical practices, such as those of witchcraft. It should be noted that *absolutely no one in this prolonged debate* has complained of difficulties in comprehending what returning anthropologists report to us. No one has difficulties in following the anthropologists' accounts of how the aliens consult their oracles, solicit the help of witchdoctors or what may be at stake in these practices. The difficulty that many have found in understanding this 'other culture' is that of grasping how people can go about doing these things while keeping a straight face – how can they possibly accept this way of doing things as a plausible, practical practice?

Here again, though, the 'problem' may be much less of one than it is made to seem. It does not represent, first of all, a general problem in 'understanding other cultures' but only one of understanding practices that are substantially at odds with our own, and only perhaps at odds with ours in certain quite specific ways, and the demands for understanding may, again, lie with the need to be less complacent, even self-congratulatory, in our own assumptions, to recognize that it is *these* that are getting in our way, obstructing our ability to realize that both we and they are equally unreflecting in and unquestioning of ways of acting in which, since childhood, we have respectively been immersed. It is no more a logical impossibility to understand how aliens can consult the oracle with a straight face than it is to understand how so many of us devotionally pursue the convoluted routines of subservience to monarchical authority (or the ludicrously exaggerated attachment to football teams), though it may require some strenuous effort on our part, depending on just how unsympathetic we are to the view in question.

Our persistent theme is, then, that the 'problem of understanding minds' is a philosophical artefact, one whose credibility is sustained by the dissociation of 'the understanding of the mind' from the lives that actual people actually lead, making it seem as though all issues are to be posed and resolved in terms of the difficulties involved in accessing and tracking the mechanics of a brain-based operating system. As is widespread throughout the human, social and psychological 'sciences', contemporary mentalism is afflicted by an obsession with explanation that is so intense that it operates in near complete indifference toward that which is supposedly the object of explanation.

Cognitivism is intended to explain what people do (in terms of the brain-based cognitive system regulating the movement of the body), but it takes only a perfunctory interest in the things that people do outside of artificially constructed 'experimental' situations, of the ways in which their activities work, and of the extent to which an understanding of these is indispensable to the very identification of what it is that people are doing. We can perhaps reinforce this general point by drawing attention to a couple of arguments from Gilbert Ryle's pioneering attempt to explain where mentalism goes wrong.

Reviewing Vendler's (1972) Chomsky-like account of language acquisition, Ryle (1974) emphasized the oddity of its picture of childhood, one from which interaction with other people is completely absent, as are the innumerable ways in which adults assist children's learning. Chomsky himself motivates such exclusion by supposing that anything to be called teaching must effectively take the form of classroom instruction, and it is obvious that there is little teaching of that kind to be found in the very earliest years of a child's encounters with language, but it is a mere idiosyncrasy to think of teaching in that way, leaving out all the ways in which example, demonstration, rehearsal, practice in, and application of, language provides teaching and the multifarious forms participation in those matters may take, as many and varied as the activities adults engage in with growing children. By stripping away the child's environing human relations it is possible to make it seem as if the child, in the process of learning, faces an immensely difficult lonely intellectual task (one so difficult that the child is actually incapable of it, hence the resort to 'nativism') of figuring out even the most basic things. This, however, is to misrepresent the nature of relations between children and others as one between a distant spectacle of human activity and its remote observer, leaving out the innumerable mutual participatory transactions that run extensively and intensively between the child and others.

On yet another point, Ryle reminds us of the difference between language as the stock of expressions that we use to say things, and of what we say making use of those expressions (1971, pp. 407–8). Our capacity to use the language for real, to say intelligible, appropriate, effective things in it, requires learning much more than the stock of expressions. It calls for understanding of the activities within which the language is to be deployed – for example, 'Energy is mass times the speed of light squared' is made up of from the stock of recognizable English expressions, though what is says does not belong to English but to physics, and it is an understanding of the latter that is required to understand what this expression says.

What is the bearing of this on ST? It makes relevant some otherwise obvious points. One is that children's learning is very much a matter of learning *from* others and learning things that those others can already do. Another is that the growing child is progressively enabled to understand other people in increasingly numerous and assorted ways, because those others provide the child with the means to understand them and equip it with a grasp on the language and on how activities are done. In short, they enculturate newcomers. Enculturation should not be thought of as something one-off and confined to childhood, for it can arise at any of very many points over the life course. Equally, with respect to the 'problem of other cultures', it need only be recognized that the 'other culture' is the obstacle to but also the means of our understanding.

A final word on ToMism

As a result of their underlying philosophical commitments, TT and ST are both inclined drastically to marginalize the fact that human beings are cultural creatures (McDonough, 1992) and the extent to which 'the solution' to 'the problem' of understanding other people – of 'understanding that other people have mental states' – does not require the ingenious one-off contrivance (or innate activation) of some psychological mechanism, but is the accumulating product of the *progressive* enculturation of the individual. Through enculturation the individual acquires a large and heterogeneous array of (culturally constituted) skills enabling participation in a range of diversified activities, and it is the appropriate application of those skills *in participation* with others that determines in actual instances what will count as someone successfully understanding someone else or their failing to do so. 'Understanding other people' is no unitary task, accomplished in any one way, by any single 'mechanism', but is a multifarious one, and it is perhaps the tendency to think of this in an almost wholly abstract way which creates the false impression that it is a single, well-defined affair.

Notes

1   These terms can be treated as interchangeable for the purposes of this chapter.
2   On some versions of TT, even our own minds are not directly available to us.
3   A set of rules and a deductive theory are quite different things, and our question is, in a way, how much of the work supposedly done by the theory is done by rules of usage?
4   If children did operate on an independent and individual basis as theorists, why should some of them not conclude that, for example, breathing was subject to mental states, or alternatively adopt a 'behaviourist' view of the mental concepts – how would a child who did this be disadvantaged relative to others? Or, to put it another way, the question we are repeatedly asking is: what is the *linguistic* difference between our existing language construed in 'behaviourist' and 'mentalist' terms respectively, such that the child's supposed theorizing could find any purchase? Or, again, why do children not make up *their own* terminologies?
5   In respect to sociology, we should have to moderate Wittgenstein's comment to indicate that it is beset by conceptual confusions and related empirical methods and studies rather than experiments.
6   A good example of this may be found in the recent exchanges between one of us, Jeff Coulter (1999, and 2004), and Jonathan Potter and Derek Edwards (2003).
7   There is extensive illustration of this point in Chapter 11 of this volume.
8   Directly unobservable here functions as an equivalent to 'unobservable'.
9   'Informal logic' is Ryle's equivalent to 'grammar'.
10   Dribble's first law of sociology reads: some do and some don't.
11   See, e.g., Fodor (1983) on modularity of mind.
12   On this, see Bennett and Hacker (2003).
13   We are not suggesting that visual capacities are also verbal ones, but that the capacity to exercise one's visual capacities is extensively tied up with mastering

practices that involve use of the language – being able to read for obvious example.

14 To respond in more detail to Gopnik's position would be to enter the very terms of the discourse which we have hitherto been concerned to reject. If we *were* to become entangled in these essentially 'in-house' disputes, we would risk losing sight of our major objective, which is to disparage all theorizing of this peculiar sort. The foundational point of disagreement concerns the notion of 'folk psychology'. This idea metamorphosed into the idea that lay people depend upon, and employ, in their everyday lives, a 'theory' of mentality, and not just a practical command of the grammar of predicates of personal attributes and features. This is claimed as a precondition for making sense of others' and their own speech and conduct *vis-à-vis* what Cartesians would refer to as the 'mental'. All of us, lay as well as professional 'folk', supposedly *rely upon*, use and even on occasion articulate one or another sort of *version* of what *mentality* is or consists in. There is even postulated to be an *evolutionary* dimension at work here, namely that our 'folk' psychological theory or theories are precursors to what became 'scientific psychology' insofar as the latter gets its inspiration from, or is thought to be an 'extension' or 'modification' of – or, yes, even a principled 'rejection' of – the former. A major impediment to this view of things is simply this: lay people can vary enormously in their explicit versions or accounts of what 'mind' is, but they continue nonetheless to get along very well using the so-called 'mental' concepts/predicates in their unreflective moments in their everyday lives in grammatically standard ways.

15 The idea that simulation is an unconscious process is often an assumed, rather than required, supposition (Gordon, 1992, pp. 12–13), and there are disagreements about whether the simulation of another person's beliefs, rather than their behaviour, is to be subsumed under ST (Harris, 1992; Stich and Nichols, 1995). Some of these differences would require more discriminating argument than can be given here.

16 The supposition that I work from my own case is not essential here, for if I can take the other's point of view, then I base my simulations on that, but this then dilutes the idea that I am simulating their behaviour in order to understand it.

17 Of course, someone may occasionally make imaginative scenarios of someone else's behaviour.

18 Mentalistic jargon avoids use of the word 'know' since the question of whether someone knows the University President's name asks whether they can *correctly* identify the President. Mentalism programmatically prefers the word 'belief' to maintain the impression that it is 'mental states' that are under consideration, rather than the determination of matters of fact.

19 Bear in mind that the argument here is not that 'simulations' are never used, only that simulation theory distorts their role and overstates their significance amongst the *diversity* of ways in which individuals are enabled to understand others, *insofar* as, in any given case, they are able to do so (cf. Overgaard, 2006, p. 66).

Part 2
Applications

5
Participants Don't Need Theories: Knowing Minds in Engagement

Vasudevi Reddy and Paul Morris

In *Persons in Relation* John Macmurray draws a powerful distinction (one not usually recognized in modern studies of the development of this process in children) between spectators and participants in the process of knowing other minds:

> In reflection we isolate ourselves from dynamic relations with the Other; we withdraw into ourselves, adopting the attitude of spectators, not of participants. We are then out of touch with the world, and for touch we must substitute vision; for a real contact with the Other an imagined contact; and for real activity an activity of imagination.
>
> (Macmurray, 1991, p. 16)

It is difficult to write today about understanding people without reference to the words 'Theory of Mind'. Google Scholar yields an incredible 36,000 publications using the term, 13,000 of which also refer to infants or children. And the manner in which the term is used is awesomely matter-of-fact – with a taken-for-grantedness hitherto reserved for those other staples of psychology such as 'growth spurt', 'toilet training', 'short-term memory' and 'secure attachment'. Despite this, the 'Theory-Theory'[1], as it is called, stands on shaky grounds. The main empirical challenges are from the everyday actions of infants and toddlers, particularly those involving communication and deception, which occur well before the theory argues that they can (see also Astington, 2003; Dunn, 1988, 1991). In order to deal with these challenges the Theory-Theory has had either to implausibly dismiss them as 'mere behaviour' or to violate its own coherence by various revisions involving modules, auxiliary hypotheses, implicit theories, precursors and interactions with 'executive factors' (Bretherton, McNew and Beeghly-Smith, 1981; Hala, Chandler and Fritz, 1991; Gopnik, 1993; Clements and Perner, 1994; Baron-Cohen, 1995; Leslie, 1995; Cadinu and Kiesner, 2000; Hala and Russell, 2001).

We review key behaviour in infants and toddlers which theory of mind research has often had to 'explain away', and explore the reasons for its discomfort with what infants and young children actually *do* with other minds in everyday life. We argue that the problem lies in psychology's commitment to epistemic detachment (see Costall and Leudar, Chapter 3 this volume), which, we think, stems from thinking of the knower as fundamentally isolated, thus requiring some mediation – an idea, a theory, a revelation, a concept – to bridge the gap from Self to Other, or, in the case of the 'Theory-Theory', to bridge the gap from behaviour to mind. Through this insistence on mediation, Theory-Theory distances itself from action both in its explanation of social development and in the evidence it draws upon. As an alternative (both for the psychologist and for the infant) we propose a 'second-person' stance to knowing minds, in which the 'Other' is a 'You' rather than a 'He' or a 'She'. This stance emphasizes action and engagement, not only as the route to knowing minds without the mediation of intellectual bridges, but also as the way in which minds develop to be known.

Doing what they didn't ought'er

The Theory-Theory makes some key predictions about social actions that should not be occurring in infants and toddlers. There are different versions of the 'theory' view even within the group of theorists that Astington (1995) describes as constituting its core. Amongst other things, the differences concern what precedes a 'full' Theory of Mind (see, e.g., Perner, 1991 vs. Gopnik and Wellman, 1992).[2] Amongst all the Theory-Theorists, however, the focus is on the possibilities for action and explanation that emerge from understanding the representational capacities of minds. The central idea is that minds represent, and that interacting with minds requires, and is therefore constrained by, an understanding of representation. Such understanding is therefore seen as a prerequisite for appropriate engagement with other minds.

In order to test for an understanding of representation (and of how representation leads to action) the Theory-Theory has typically used situations of mismatch between representation and reality (because such tests cannot be passed through simple matching with reality). Most of the Theory-Theory's predictions concern, therefore, the failure by infants and toddlers to explain, predict or act upon actions that stem from misrepresentations of the world. If children cannot really understand representations, they should not (according to the Theory-Theory) be able to act appropriately in some situations: essentially, Theory-Theorists argue that telling lies, understanding intentions contrary to actual actions, understanding lack of knowledge and understanding misunderstandings are all dependent on complex representational skills which do not develop until about four years. As David Olson (1988) put it in an early paper, it is the acquisition of a Theory of Mind in the preschool years that allows the development of tricks, secrets, lies – all of those things that make children appealing:

> It is at this third stage [i.e. at age four with the development of a Theory of Mind], I suggest, that children become deliberate and self-conscious; they come not only to think of themselves and others as holders of belief states, they also become capable of separating intentions from action, intentions from utterance, beliefs from reality and the like. Tricks, secrets and lies become possible.
>
> (Olson, 1988, p. 424)

However, all of these predictions are problematic. Children do lie, they do repair misunderstandings, they do tell people things they don't know, they do tease people and manipulate their intentions, well before the age of four. Furthermore, they are treated by those around them at the time, even parents who are developmental psychologists, as really doing these things. Dismissals of data such as early deception, teasing, communication and referencing, for example, on the grounds that such actions are rote-learned routines (Perner, 1991), or indicative of superficial knowledge of behaviour (Camaioni, 1992) are becoming implausible. In the following sections we describe some of these behaviours and the key predictions that they embarrass.

Deception and false-beliefs

The claim that children cannot lie until they pass the false-belief task was made partly on the logic of the theory, and partly on the evidence that children with autism and children under the age of four both fail the false-belief task and are reported not to lie (Stouthamer-Loeber, 1986). However, this prediction ran into problems from the start. An early challenge came from Chandler, Fritz and Hala (1989), who showed that children under three can deceive in a laboratory task, although this finding was generally dismissed on the grounds that the children were trained to achieve this (Sodian, 1994). There have been more recent laboratory studies, however, which show that children do pass deception tasks even when they fail false-belief tasks (Celani, Battistelli, Marco and Battacchi, 1998).

The most serious challenge to the prediction, however, comes from studies which have seriously explored naturalistic deceptions and have challenged the Theory-Theory's reliance on a study showing that parents believe lying to begin at about four years (Stouthammer-Loeber, 1986).[3] Parental judgements about when lying begins differ when they are asked in a general way about the past than when they are asked to judge actual examples in young children (Newton, 1992), and parents often underestimate children's lying (Wilson, Smith and Ross, 2003). Using mothers as observers, Newton,

Reddy and Bull (2000) found no relationship between the prevalence of different types of lying and performance on false-belief and deception tasks in three-year-olds. This was so when comparing groups of passers and failers and when comparing the same children over time. Even the lies of a two-and-a-half year old were not limited to punishment-avoiding or reward obtaining: they involved a variety of motives such as face-saving, trickery and fun, and were sometimes complex and creative. These findings were confirmed and extended in an observational study of two-year-olds (Wilson, Smith and Ross, 2003): not only were two-year-olds telling a variety of lies, but also, quite contrary to previous assumptions, their lies were no more implausible than those of four-year-olds. What was found to increase with age instead was the frequency and the verbal fluency of the lies. Skills at deceiving continue to develop through (at least) the middle childhood years (Talwar and Lee, 2002). These data cannot be explained away as formulaic verbal strategies, given the variety and complexity of lies in children who should not, according to the theory, be able to lie at all. Nor can they be dismissed as resulting from straightforward reinforcement, given that parental punishment does not relate to the frequency of lying at this age, when parents are far more likely to challenge than to accept the false information and far more likely to punish the transgressing child than, for example, the accused sibling (Wilson, Smith and Ross, 2003). The reinforcement argument is, moreover, a red herring, implying, illogically, that anything learned from reinforcement cannot constitute genuine knowledge.

The ability to deceive seems in fact to start in the first year: as any parent knows, children attempt to conceal forbidden actions much earlier than two years and deliberately tease with false requests and false offers even before the end of the first year (Reddy, 1991). Applying the non-verbal category scheme for tactical deception developed for non-human primates by Andy Whiten and Dick Byrne to human infants (Whiten and Byrne, 1988, Byrne and Whiten, 1990), a recent analysis of the available naturalistic data has shown that several categories of tactical deception are present from well within the first year of infancy (Reddy, 2007). Such early deceptions involve attempts to deflect attention from ongoing actions as well as attempts to attract attention through the instrumental use of expressions, displaying more dyadic and 'close-range' (Byrne and Whiten, 1990) forms of deception than distal and triadic. These continuities suggest that tactical deception is not easily explained by the Theory-Theory. Deceptive communication, like any other form of communication, seems to be an early ability, developing in skill at managing information from the start rather than emerging belatedly at four years.

The recent experimental success with non-verbal false-belief tasks with infants of 14 and 15 months of age (Onishi and Baillargeon, 2005) raises a completely different set of questions and theoretical challenges. The false-belief 'watershed' appears to have shifted now to a pre-verbal age (albeit some six months after the age when the early tactical deceptions can be detected). This early experimental test-passing could be interpreted as validating and being validated by the naturalistic data, and providing a new watershed for the development of false-belief understanding. In other words, the naturalistic data and the new experiments could be seen as coming together to simply lower the critical age for false-belief understanding to just after 12 months, and as providing new and dramatic evidence for the reality of a (now non-verbal) 'Theory of Mind'. Alternatively, however, the early passing of a non-verbal 'false-belief' test could be seen as a fundamental challenge to the idea of false-belief understanding itself. It is not plausible to suggest that the 'same' understanding of false belief present at four years is now evident at 15 months. If we accept that the success at 15 months must involve partial or a different form of false-belief understanding – perhaps constituting a new mini-watershed – we still have the problem of explaining its relation to the naturalistic data. First, the naturally occurring deceptions occur from about six months earlier than the new watershed. And second, there appear to be developments in the naturally occurring deceptive communication, requiring, implausibly, the invention of several new mini-watersheds, perhaps one every month between 8 and 15 months. Positing a non-verbal Theory of Mind as leading to deceptive communication seems just as inconsistent with the naturalistic data.

Correcting ignorance and understanding knowledge

Another related Theory-Theory prediction is that because children under four cannot understand that not perceiving something leads to ignorance about it, they should not be able to correct ignorance caused by lack of perceptual access by giving information appropriately. Standard tests supported this prediction (Pillow, 1989; Pratt and Bryant, 1990; Robinson, Thomas, Parton and Nye, 1997; Wimmer, Hogrefe and Perner, 1988), as did young children's inability to take account of people watching while they hide. This was interpreted by Perner (1991) to mean that while getting out of sight was not a problem for children under three, getting out of knowledge was. However, several studies suggest that this conclusion is problematic. O'Neill (1996) found that at three and even at two-and-a-half years, children appropriately used information about whether or not their mothers had been present when a currently hidden toy had been introduced to them. Those whose mothers had not been present used additional location information while requesting their mothers to give them the toy, suggesting clear awareness of a link between perceptual access and knowledge. In two other studies, using non-verbal measures of 'information-giving' such as pointing and showing, even 18-month-old children were found to discriminate between people who had already witnessed an event or toy, and people who had not witnessed it (Reddy and Simone, 1995; Simone and Reddy, 1997).

The children selectively reported or showed things to the latter, and when reporting anything to people who already knew about it, did so about specific features of the object or event. Clearly, from the middle of the second year, infants act on people's knowledge and ignorance through selecting both people and information. Poulin-Dubois and colleagues have shown, similarly, that by the middle of the second year, infants are able to connect objects with others' visual experience even when the objects are no longer visible (Poulin-Dubois, Sodian, Metz, Tilden and Schoeppner, 2007). That this awareness may be present even at the end of the first year is suggested by a more recent experimental study (Tomasello and Haberl, 2003) showing that even 12-month-olds successfully selectively give a 'surprised' adult the toy which is novel to them rather than the one which they have seen before. Dismissal of these data in terms of physical associations or learned strategies is hard to maintain in the face of the subtlety of these selective acts. It could be argued that the infants may have simply associated someone's physical presence with the target object, or have learned formulae for 'telling' such as 'when someone comes in who has not already been in the room when something interesting has happened, say something about it', or 'when telling somebody about something they have already seen, only tell them specific details', or 'when asking for an object which you saw when the other was not in the room, tell them where it is'. However, such mechanistic explanations may in fact demand considerably greater skill and cognitive complexity than the mentalist explanations they are meant to replace (Whiten, 1994). Further, such explanations would leave very obscure the motivation for the children's selective 'telling'. They make a serious mystery of *why* children would want to communicate about things.

Repairing miscommunication and understanding understanding

Similarly, according to Theory-Theory logic, until children understand misrepresentation they should not be able to understand that others have misunderstood or misperceived information and therefore cannot repair these errors. However, children as young as 14 months consistently and sensibly correct others' misunderstandings of their communicative attempts (Golinkoff, 1986, 1993). The response from the proponents of the Theory-Theory has been, once again, that these corrections could be strategies for achieving instrumental ends or learned conventions of discourse rather than reflecting any awareness of misunderstanding (Shatz and O'Reilly, 1990). Not even the finding that children repaired about as many conversational utterances as they did instrumental imperatives has convinced the critics that these were true repairs. This dismissal seems motivated by a theoretical opposition to the possibility of early communication, an opposition neatly contained in the somewhat theoretically biased definition of true communication as being that 'in which both participants have equal access to interpretive procedures that entail sophisticated theories of mind' (ibid., p. 142). Other studies too have shown that two-and-a-half year olds persist in attempts to repair misunderstandings even when a requested object is already obtained (Shwe and Markman, 2001), and that even 12-month-olds show active message repair when interested adults get the referent wrong – for example, by pointing again to the correct target (Liszkowski, Carpenter and Tomasello, 2007).

Declarative pointing and multiple representations

A theory-based definition of communication not only invites infinite circularities, but also turns many acts which would normally be seen as a communication of information into 'merely behavioural' strategies for the obtaining of behavioural goals. Another example of the problem that the Theory-Theory faces in explaining early communication concerns the claim that when infants (at the end of the first year) engage in 'communicative' pointing, they are indeed communicating something about the world to the other person (e.g., Bates, 1979; Trevarthen and Hubley, 1978). Within the perspective of the Theory-Theory view, however, this interpretation of infant pointing is unacceptable: such communication would require that the infant should have a grasp of the other person as capable of attending to something, that is, that the infant is capable of representing that the other person can mentally represent something about the world. And such multiple representations of reality are disallowed in Perner's (1991) version of the Theory-Theory until about 18 months of age. From this perspective, infant pointing at the end of the first year could not really be communication or sharing of the world with another person, but must be simply experimentation upon the other's physical reactions (ibid., 1991). Given that infants (perhaps innately) find their mother's eyes and gaze so fascinating, we think it equally plausible that infants engage in 'protodeclarative' pointing and check their effect on their mother's eyes because they enjoy their mastery over her eyes. And there is a boost in these mastery activities at around one year because at this age, as Piaget (1953) observed in his children's interactions with inanimate objects, they are able to combine sensorimotor schemes and start to systematically explore novel effects (tertiary circular reactions). One way of testing the contradiction between these different interpretations would be to consider what children point at in natural circumstances. If Perner is correct and if the motive for pointing is not to communicate about the target, then there should be little significance in the selection of the targets. However, infants do not generally point to things with a primarily experimental motive. In one study of a 14-month-old infant (Reddy, 1992) the majority of proto-declaratives involved the infant having just seen or heard the target, often with positive affect and excitement. Nor, in fact, did gaze to face always accompany the pointing (especially when communication and a common body orientation with the recipient had already been established). Perner's mechanistic explanation becomes very hard to envision. Several recent studies have suggested that by the end of the first year infants are genuinely attempting to direct others' attention to 'sights' in the environment, engaging in declarative pointing to people, but not to inanimate objects such as a contingently responsive toy dog (Legerstee and Barillas, 2003). That this pointing is aimed solely at sharing the 'sights' with others is suggested by a study in which infants repeated their pointing when adults deliberately responded with a positive look either to the infant or to the object. Only positive looks by the adult (back and forth between the 'sight' and the infant) served to satisfy the infant (Liszkowski et al., 2007). Furthermore, 12 month-olds also seem to point things out to adults to 'inform' them even when they themselves are not interested in the object (Liszkowski, Carpenter, Striano and Tomasello, 2006).

Other challenges to the communication interpretation have sought evidence of conditioning in the emergence of gaze following (Corkum and Moore, 1995, 1998) and of specific facial stimuli eliciting communicative behaviour (Johnson, Booth and O'Hearn, 2001), and the debate continues in both empirical and theoretical terms (Legerstee and Barillas, 2003; Reddy, 2003). Communication presents a major problem for the Theory-Theory and for all cognitive-developmental views, which see it, first, as a primarily mental activity, divorced from (or only incidentally related to) the body and its actions, and, second, as the activity of one individual subject towards another rather than as something that emerges between them. For example, intentional communication has been described in the developmental psycholinguistic literature as the intentional transfer of information by an agent who is aware of the information she wishes to send and aware of the receiving agent's ability to receive it and understand it and understand the intention to send it (Camaioni, 1993). Such definitions presume the existence of a prior script, the isolation of the communicator from the receiver, and a separation of the act of communication from its content, and make the loneliness of the subject almost insurmountable (see Reddy, 1995, for a discussion of other views of intentional communication). From such presumptions, minds become impossible to know and persons become impossible to communicate with. Many theorists who accept that 12-month-olds do communicate, nonetheless hold on to the same sort of intellectualist explanation of communication. For example, Tomasello (1999) talks of a socio-cognitive revolution at 9–12 months where the same sort of representational understanding is supposed to do the same sort of work, only slightly earlier than Perner (1991) suggested. The problem of communication cannot be solved by simply lowering the age at which a theoretical grasp of minds is possible; it needs a solution which avoids the presupposition of initial egocentrism or 'mindblindness'.

The theory problem

The essence of the problem with Theory-Theory is its paradoxical and fundamental exclusion of action from the domain of knowing. Despite its commitment to predictions and hypothesis-testing, the Theory-Theory has emerged, and survives, independently of the evidence of what people actually do in everyday action and interaction. This exclusion of action is paradoxical because the *raison d'être* of the Theory-Theory is supposed to be precisely about its consequences for social interaction. But the Theory-Theory's links to action as evidence, and as test of its claims, are genuinely suspect. The exclusion of action from the accounts of understanding is fundamental because it is unavoidable, given Theory-Theory's premise of the inaccessibility of mind to anything but thought. As Macmurray puts it:

> this is the 'egocentric predicament', in which the subject, portrayed as thinker, is necessarily withdrawn from action and relation: The act of thinking is constituted by a purely theoretical intention. It involves a withdrawal from action, and so from all positive, practical relations with the Other. When we think, we shut ourselves within the circles of our own ideas and establish, as it were, a methodological solipsism. We behave as though we were 'pure subjects', observers only, un-implicated in the dynamic relatedness of real existence. Our activity, we assume, makes no difference to the things we think about, but only to our ideas of them, upon which alone we are operative. [...] when, for philosophical purposes, we adopt a theoretical standpoint, and so define our own being as that of a thinker or subject, then, whether we are aware of it or not, we transform this methodological solipsism into an existential one. We exist as thinkers. We are imprisoned in an 'egocentric predicament' and there is no way out. *We are committed to explaining knowledge without reference to action.*
>
> (Macmurray, 1991, pp. 20–1; emphasis added)

To seek to explain how children come to know other minds through explanations of their thinking about minds leads the Theory-Theorists to a merry-go-round from which they cannot jump off. This is the same merry-go-round that psychology finds itself on when it tries to explain its *own* scientific knowledge of minds through its theories and inferences.

Theory without power?

Theories are supposed to help us literally to 'get ahead' (Karmiloff-Smith and Inhelder, 1974) by predicting events in the world and changing our actions accordingly. The Theory-Theory, like any other, predicted serious transformations in children's actions, each of which was supposed to lead to improved manipulation of people. However, as we have seen, passing the false-belief test does not give the child the ability to tell lies; passing the knowledge and ignorance test does not give the child the ability to tell others what they need to know; developing multiple representations does not give the child the ability to tell others about the world, or to correct others' mis-understandings about the world. All these predicted benefits of possessing a Theory of Mind have been shown to happen well before the development of the theory supposed to enable them. Why is it so hard to detect in everyday action the transformations which are supposed to follow the achievement of a Theory of Mind? A defence suggesting that the predicted transformations were not actually critical for the theory would vitiate the Theory-Theory's central claims. There is a further 'defence' that its experimental meth-odology is not yet sufficiently ecologically and socio-emotionally valid (Astington, 2003). But this leaves us asking why the Theory-Theory doesn't, then, directly use everyday action rather than experimental data as a more valid source of evidence of knowing minds! Other counter-explanations, through predicting more graded levels of transformation, also leave the central problem untouched: they would predict a series of smaller trans-formations, each led by a prior representational advance, and each subject to the same problems.

Redefining phenomena to accord with theory

Having an independent measure of the transformations that it predicts is vital for any theory. However, there is a peculiar redefinitional tendency in the process of building a scientific paradigm, in which the theory not only defines its own investigative remit but also usurps common meanings and thus redefines its evidence. An interesting behaviour, seen as evidence *of* a theoretical claim, soon becomes defined *by* that claim. For example, deceptive behaviour was believed to emerge at four years and was used as evidence for the emergence of the understanding of false beliefs at that age. Soon, however, the understanding of false beliefs became the criterion for the acceptance of deceptive behaviour as true evidence; consequently, examples of deception without collateral proof of false-belief understanding came to be dismissed as inconclusive. For example, Perner has argued that lying in three year-olds *must* be 'pseudo-lies' since they cannot (according to his theory) be the intentional manipulation of another person's beliefs (Perner, 1991). Only by challenging this redefinition can the development of deception actually be explored. Wilson and colleagues did just this in their study, by defining deception in functional terms as 'any false state-ment whose function required that others believe the lie or, at least, act as if they did' (Wilson, Smith and Ross, 2003, p. 42). Similar shifts can be seen in relation to pretend play and communication. Explained as symbolic play by Piaget (1972), pretence began to require evidence of other symbolic skills in order to be accepted as genuine pretence. Pretence was later explained as meta-representation, and its absence, in contrast to the apparently simpler 'functional play', was seen as an important diagnostic criterion in autism (Baron-Cohen, Leslie and Frith, 1985; Leslie, 1987; however, see Williams, Reddy and Costall, 2001). Soon, pretence came to be defined within the Theory-Theory as that which is not functional play. Similarly, some recent definitions of communication derived from the premises of the Theory-Theory rule out what would otherwise be accepted as communication. Shatz and O'Reilly, for example, define communication as requiring 'interpretive procedures that entail sophisticated theories of mind' (1990, p. 142), and Camaioni (1993) defines it as the intentional transfer of information with an awareness of the recipient's ability to receive and understand the information and the intention to send it. Other-directed acts that do not involve such transfer of information or such theories of mind are deemed pseudo-communication. Given such redefinitions, the club of pseudo-phenomena cannot but grow, adding 'pseudo-repairs' (Shatz and O'Reilly, 1990) to 'pseudo-lies' (Piaget, 1972) and 'pseudoconversation' (Kaye, 1982), and probably, although Perner didn't put it this way, 'pseudo-pointing'!

Untestability of behaviourist vs. mentalist explanations

The point has often been made, although not often accepted, that the Theory-Theory is neo-Cartesian in its acceptance of mental substance as essentially different (in terms of observability) from physical substance (Coulter, 1979; Leudar and Costall, 2004b; Sharrock and Coulter, 2004). The Theory-Theory has not only re-created the problem of other minds, but has also built the mind–behaviour dualism into a developmental scheme, which is possibly dependent on folk-theory. Despite some views about a starting-state mentalism giving way to representationalism (Gopnik and Wellman, 1992), it is widely presumed that a behaviourist phase of development precedes a mentalist phase. Olson (1988) argues that an essentially behaviouristic infant develops into an intentionalist toddler and then into a mentalist child.[4] Similarly, Perner (1991) argues that a 'situational theory of behaviour' at two years gives way to a mentalistic theory of behaviour at three and then to a representational Theory of Mind at four. The sequence has also been adopted in relation to evolution, with monkeys being described as good ethologists (reading behaviour but not minds) but poor psychologists (i.e., bad at reading minds!) (Cheney and Seyfarth, 1990). In this way, mentality is conceptualized as a gradually emerging intervening variable in the understanding of behaviour, paralleling the emergence of the O in S–O–R (stimulus–organism–response) relationships (Whiten, 1994).

The belief in the difficulty in perceiving mentality is still current. Gergely (2003), for instance, is keen to denounce the 'myth of primary intersubjectivity' by arguing that the only qualities the infant at two months can be argued to perceive in others are behavioural contingencies and not psychological qualities.[5] The Theory-Theory's dismissals of the 'reality' of everyday actions which would appear to challenge its predictions have usually been based on this dualism. The 'challenging' behaviours are simply dismissed as 'mere' behaviour. However, the basis of this dismissal cannot itself be tested and neither, therefore, can the Theory-Theory's developmental claim that a behaviourist phase in understanding others gives way to a mentalist one. The reason for this is clear: the Theory-Theory assumes that in order to 'prove' a mentalist explanation we need to rule out a behaviourist one. Behavioural associations, in this view, become 'contaminating' factors in the search for evidence of mind knowledge. However, since behavioural explanations of an associationistic kind can never be ruled out, and, furthermore, claims about mind can never be divorced from claims about behaviour (unless we are talking about telepathy), we are faced with an untestable developmental hypothesis and the theory is shielded by another circularity. Take for example, Perner's dismissal of proto-declarative pointing at 12 months as being merely due to a behavioural association. This explanation could never be disproved since any pointing, however complex, and even if performed by adults, could always be seen to have prior associations with people's reactions and reinforcements of some kind.[6] The challenge we offered in terms of complex and systematic patterns of what infants point to is therefore not ultimately a challenge to Perner's dismissal at all. However, by the same token, neither is Perner's dismissal a challenge to a mentalist interpretation of these infant actions. If a behaviourist explanation cannot be tested and rejected, then neither can a mentalist one be tested and accepted. The solution to this dilemma can only come from avoiding this dualist trap and taking action seriously by envisaging it as embodied mind.

In summary, the Theory-Theory has entered into a peculiar relationship with everyday action. The original excitement of the Theory-Theory lay in the transformational power that a Theory of Mind was believed to have over the everyday actions of typically developing children and perhaps some apes, and to fail to have on the everyday actions of children and adults with some disorders. The representational structures of a Theory of Mind should, according to the Theory-Theory, show up as serious transformations in everyday life. From the standpoint of this claim, therefore, the Theory-Theory cannot simply dismiss evidence relating to everyday actions as irrelevant and misleading. However, this is precisely what the Theory-Theory has done with the challenging evidence of everyday actions in young children. It has done this by invoking the Cartesian gulf between mind and behaviour (without its first-person privilege) and therefore between the understanding of mind and the understanding of behaviour. This gulf allows the Theory-Theory to make its claims about its representational structures radically transforming everyday actions and yet hide from tests of these claims by being able to dismiss everyday actions as mere behaviour.

Towards an approach from engagement

Most of the empirical challenges to Theory-Theory predictions that we have described have come from actual engagement outside the laboratory between infants and adults. We suggest that it is in engagement with other people rather than in thought that people normally and fundamentally know other people as intentional beings (see also Hobson, 2002). Engagement gives you access to information that is otherwise much less obvious. As normal adult humans, we are enormously sensitive in our interactions with others to the subtleties of contingency and responsiveness, of emotional attentiveness, of responsive or emotion-filled pauses, of the coordination of different aspects of the other's expressions – widening of the eyes, partial opening of the mouth, sudden stilling of the limbs, the quality of the attention directed to us – in invitation or response to us. This information can still be gained from watching someone else interact, but with more difficulty and often only convincingly if presented with detailed statistical analyses. For example, at a conference in 1993, the late Professor Liz Bates commented in response to another speaker's paper on neonatal imitation that she had not believed it existed until she had tried it herself in engagement with her newborn daughter. Now her scepticism was about its significance not about its existence. The challenges to the Theory-Theory, many of which come from psychologists' own engagement in the first instance with their infants, further support this point.

There is a deeper dimension to engagement than simply being closer to the 'action': one is also 'inside' the action in a different way. Macmurray (1991) argues that we can know other people as people only by relating to them as intentional beings. As he puts it, 'I can know another person as a person only by entering into personal relation with him. Without this I can know him only by observation and inference; only objectively' (ibid., p. 28). In a personal relation we do not see the other just as an object making sounds and movements (although we also see these): 'what we apprehend through these are the intentions, the feelings, the thoughts of another person who is in communication with ourselves' (ibid., p. 34). In contrast, in an impersonal way of relating to people, we see them as objects (even if objects of interest), perhaps focusing deliberately on the movements and sounds they make, treating them as phenomena to be reflected upon and understood. Martin Buber (1958) made a similar point when he talked of the primacy of the *I–Thou* relation, a way of relating (whether to a person or a tree) that involves openness and complete presence in the engagement. In contrast, the *I–It* mode of relating involves distance between the self and the other, seeing the other as an *It* to be reflected upon. When we enter into engagement with an infant, we naturally, even if for short times, treat the infant, and are treated by the infant, as a person, a *Thou*, not an object or *It*. What difference does this make to how we know them and how they know us?

An example of a beautiful, but disengaged, observation from Piaget (1972) might throw some light on this question:

> OBS 63. At O;10(3) J. put her nose close to her mother's cheek and then pressed against it, which forced her to breathe much more loudly. This phenomenon at once interested her, but instead of merely repeating it or varying it so as to investigate it, she quickly complicated it for the fun of it; she drew back an inch or two, screwed up her nose, sniffed and breathed out alternately very hard (as if she were blowing her nose), then again thrust her nose against her mother's cheek, laughing heartily. These actions were repeated at least once a day for more than a month, as a ritual.
>
> (Piaget, 1972, p. 94)

Piaget's observation focuses on the individual actions and sensory interests of Jacqueline. They do not include reactions from others or from himself. In this particular instance, however, it is hard to believe that the mother, whose cheek was being rubbed and breathed into, and whose ears were filled with a 10-month-old daughter's hearty laughter, did not react at all. Or that on subsequent occasions, there were either no reactions from other people or that they had no impact on Jacqueline's actions and interests. His observation of Jacqueline, although containing some acute perceptions of her intentionality, curiosity and playfulness, nonetheless portrays her as separated from, and unengaged with, himself.

There is something different about relating to the other person as a *Thou*, in the second person, rather than as a *He* or a *She*, in the third person; or to use Macmurray's terminology, as a person rather than as object. Within such a relation there is always emotional engagement, however mild and indifferent, and this emotionality is the medium within which people (self or others) are known. Although emotional engagement can exist, even to a person with whom we are not in direct engagement, as when we are watching a film, or watching two people argue on the street, it is often the case that our engagement as observers, especially if it is intense, involves some sort of identification with one of the people we are observing, making the other into a sort of *Thou*. The emotionality in an *I–Thou* exchange informs the 'observation' in fundamental ways. Consider the following examples: a baby laughs at something you have said; a student looks hurt when you laugh; a colleague moves aside as you pass by; a neighbour smiles when your eyes meet. And consider in contrast: a baby laughs at her mother; a student looks hurt when someone laughs; a colleague steps aside as someone passes by; a neighbour smiles at someone. Although even as an observer, you might appreciate the laugh, the look of hurt, the avoidance and the smile, the emotion they arouse in you is likely to be different when they are directed at you (or at someone you are identifying with). Your feeling of pride when you have made the baby laugh, your feeling of guilt at hurting the student, bewilderment when the colleague avoids you or pleasure when your neighbour smiles at you are constitutive of your perception of the person. It cannot be otherwise. And the same is true of infants' perceptions of us in their engagement with us. In engagement they are not confronted with objects whose movements they need to match with (or interpret through) something else in order to understand what they mean. This is the way in which the problem of other minds is sometimes expressed – that is, as the need for a bridge between third-person perceptions and first-person experience (Barresi and Moore, 1996). In engagement, however, the infant is not observing others as objects, from a third-person perspective, but rather is experiencing them as intentional beings in relation with their own intentionality, as second persons (Reddy, 1996). The fact of engagement necessitates that the other is included in some sort of 'field of the personal'. If this were not the case, we would have very odd engagements indeed, engagements worthy of the label 'autistic', which some authors use to characterize the period of awareness before the development of intellectual bridges between minds (Barresi and Moore, 1996; famously Mahler, Pine and Bergman, 1975; but see Williams, 2004, and this volume, Chapter 8).

There is a third and vital aspect of engaging with persons as persons: genuine engagement actually creates the minds that are there to be known. Take, for instance, the specific observation described above of Jacqueline by Piaget. It is common practice, and one that we have often been guilty of, to deliberately refrain from intervening or engaging with the observed person in order not to influence some curious behaviour one is observing. If Piaget had been always, rather than temporarily, emotionally disengaged from Jacqueline's action, there is little doubt that its meaning – both for her and for him – would change. It would involve a major disengagement from Jacqueline as a person. The theory of the individual infant would, in this case, in fact be creating an individual infant given to solitary explorations. The way in which we allow ourselves to engage with others circumscribes the way in which we can know them. You might say, the more we engage with others, the more there is to engage with. So what does happen in infant–adult interaction according to the story depicted by the Theory-Theory? The answer is profoundly puzzling: a series of prior mutual misunderstandings would have to give rise somehow to 'correct' mutual understanding (see also Leudar, 1991). The mother of an infant at 2, or 12 or even 14 months would, in this view, have to misinterpret her baby's acts as being conversational or informative or corrective, misattributing to the baby a knowledge of minds that they do not have. On the other side of the engagement, the baby in interacting with the mother must misinterpret the mother's reactions as having a mindlessness that they do not have. And, somehow, these two sets of misunderstandings of each other's mentality must conclude in a situation where both partners reach a more mutually acceptable or veridical understanding of each other's intentionality. Given that the Theory-Theory does not accept that infants can have genuine engagement with other people as intentional beings, it is indeed a mystery how this series of mutual misinterpretations could ever allow the infant to have anything other than 'pseudo'-awareness leading to pseudo-theories of mind.

Theorizing *presupposes* the knowledge of others that is evident in engagement. Reflections upon, and theories about, other people's intentions and motivations do enter into everyday discourse, but these are developmentally and experientially secondary to actual engagement with these intentions and motivations. The Theory-Theory has simply not taken early development and engagement seriously enough.

Notes

1 In recent writings in psychology, the usage of the term 'Theory of Mind' has shifted from referring to a theory about *how* the child develops social understanding, to a seemingly a-theoretical description of the *domain* of enquiry. The latter usage presupposes, however, the 'theoretical' nature of such understanding. The term 'Theory-Theory' is used to refer to one or both variants of the original 'theory view' and is often used as distinct from 'simulation' and 'innate' or 'modularity' theories (see Carpendale and Lewis, 2006, for a detailed discussion of variants of these terms). Many of the criticisms in this chapter that apply to the Theory-Theory also apply to other approaches within the theory of mind umbrella such as simulation and modularity views.

2 One key difference between their positions appears to be that while Gopnik and Wellman (1992) view the transition from infancy to childhood as one of an increasing understanding of representations – 'children seem to start out as mentalists though they learn to be representationalists' (p. 150) – many others, such as Perner (1991) and possibly Astington (1995), see the development as a transition from a behaviourist understanding to a mentalist one.

3 Their own judgements do tend to be forgotten, however, or even replaced by more complex experiences, as the children grow and become more skilful. This might also explain persistent theoretical differences between psychologists whose experience is mainly that of older children and those who work mainly with infants, that is, the difference between 'scoffers' and 'boosters' noted by Chandler (Chandler, Fritz and Hala, 1989; see also Zeedyk, 1997, for a similar finding regarding shifts in parental perceptions of infant intentionality).

4 '[T]he structure of one's meta-representations, that is one's theory of mind, may depend on the folk theory into which one is socialised. The developmental scheme we end up with, then, has at least three distinct stages. The first is essentially behaviouristic: Behaviour is to be explained without recourse or appeal to intentional states. Ascriptions by observers of such states as "Baby think that mother

is going to leave" are entirely for the convenience and pleasure of the ascriber; they are not literally true. The second stage, we may say, is intentional. Children who have learned to talk, to make assertions and requests, may be credited with the corresponding intentional state. [...] And finally, at the third stage, children acquire a theory of mind, a folk psychology that permits them to think of their own and others' talk and actions in terms of mental states' (Olson, 1988, p. 422).

5 Gergely, interestingly, portrays the intersubjectivity position as neo-Cartesian and his own as anti-Cartesian since it rejects the privileged access of the first person. However, Gergely's position, along with many others, is better described as a Cartesian one (continuing its separation of mental and physical qualities) which gives privileged access to the third person. Our position, on the contrary, seeks to give privileged access to the second person, and, by so doing, necessarily accepts the transparency of mind in engagement.

6 A common feature of this paradigm has been to see the ability to speak about mental states as clear evidence of a mentalist conception. However, speaking about mental states is itself a 'behaviour' (see also Sharrock and Coulter, 2004) and therefore also subject to the same associations that the Theory-Theory sees as undermining the mentalistic significance of non-verbal actions such as pointing and so on.

6
Specifying Interactional Markers of Schizophrenia in Clinical Consultations

Rosemarie McCabe

Introduction

Schizophrenia is a serious mental illness affecting approximately one per cent of the population. Despite major advances in brain-imaging techniques since the naming of schizophrenia more than a hundred years ago, the basic character of the illness remains poorly understood. An influential theory of schizophrenia proposes that it can be explained by an inability to understand and reason about the mental states of others. In particular, an inability to correctly infer the mental states of others is believed to give rise to delusions and other psychotic symptoms. Our recent research has, however, shown that, in general, patients with schizophrenia adequately represent their own and others' mental states and use this competence to communicate successfully in social interaction. In talk with delusional content, patients recognize that others do not agree with their delusional claims and are not persuaded by the justification they provide for these claims. Importantly, they recognize their own and others' discomfort at the disagreement this causes. However, they do not revise their claims and the tenacity with which delusional claims are held can be striking. This is all the more interesting given their ability to appreciate and respond appropriately to others' mental states and their evident discomfort in the face of others' disagreement. The questions are: (1) Is this incorrigibility specific to talking about delusions and other psychotic symptoms or is it a general problem? And (2) Why are patients so tenacious in disregarding others' accounts of their problems?

'Theory of Mind' and schizophrenia

A unitary theory of schizophrenia has been proposed by Frith (1987, 1992, 1995). Given the elusiveness of a unitary theory to explain the heterogeneity of symptoms displayed by people diagnosed with schizophrenia, this theory has been met with considerable interest. Frith proposed that, as in autism, an impairment in 'Theory of Mind' (ToM) explains schizophrenia.

Having a theory of mind, in Frith's terms, means that one knows that other people have minds different from one's own and one can infer the beliefs, wishes, intentions and so on of others in order to predict their behaviour. It is helpful to know something about the symptoms of schizophrenia and how they might be linked with impaired theory of mind. The symptoms are generally classified as either positive or negative: positive symptoms are abnormal by their presence and involve an excess or distortion of normal functions, whereas negative symptoms are abnormal by their absence and involve a diminution or loss of normal functions.

The positive or so-called 'psychotic' symptoms, which involve a loss of touch with 'reality', tend to be of principal importance diagnostically (e.g., American Psychiatric Association, 1994) and occur mainly in the form of hallucinations, delusions and formal thought disorder. Hallucinations are perceptual experiences that occur in the absence of external stimuli. They may occur in any sensory modality but the most common are auditory hallucinations, usually heard as voices, for example, a single voice making a running commentary on one's behaviour or two or more voices talking about the patient in the third person. Other forms of hallucinations are visual, tactile, olfactory or gustatory. Delusions are false beliefs held with conviction and despite contrary evidence. Delusions can also take many forms: the most common are delusions of persecution (e.g., being followed by the security service), delusions of control where one experiences one's own actions as being controlled by an external force outside of the person's control (e.g., by the TV, aliens or the army) and delusions of grandeur (one is somehow special or has special powers not held by others, e.g., being Jesus). Formal thought disorder or disorganized thinking is described when the person's thinking, manifested in their speech, is illogical, tangential and incoherent, all taken to indicate a loosening or fragmentation of association in the patient's thought processes. Negative symptoms are marked by a loss of normal functioning: 'affective flattening' or a lack of emotional expressiveness; 'avolition-apathy' or a loss of energy and ability to initiate activities; 'alogia' or poverty in the amount and content of speech; and anhedonia or a loss of interest and pleasure in social activities.

Frith (1992) proposed that the range of symptoms seen in schizophrenia can be explained by impaired meta-representation, that is, knowledge about representations. He suggested that two specific deficits explain the positive symptoms of schizophrenia. First, problems monitoring one's own intention to act result in passivity symptoms such as delusions of control, thought insertion, thought withdrawal and auditory hallucinations (e.g., Corcoran, 2000, 2001). Second, the inability to infer correctly the mental states of others gives rise to delusions, such as paranoid delusions and delusions of reference (Frith, 1992; Frith and Corcoran, 1996). Meanwhile, negative symptoms are thought to be due to an inability to represent one's own and others' intentional mental states (Corcoran, 2001). While the precise explanatory pathway is not clear in relation to negative symptoms, it is suggested that the patient's difficulty working out others' mental states means that they cannot cope with and respond appropriately in the social world causing them to withdraw from and lose interest in social life (Corcoran, 2001). Hence, the ToM framework proposes that the mechanisms underlying positive and negative symptoms are overlapping.

If the putative underlying impairment, that is, faulty theory of mind, is thought to be the same in schizophrenia and autism, are they similar in their clinical presentation? Frith (1992) notes that social withdrawal, stereotyped behaviour and lack of communication are all features of childhood autism and 'negative' schizophrenia. However, there are also notable differences. The positive symptoms described above do not typically feature in autism. Frith (1992) accounts for the different symptoms in autism and schizophrenia by reference to the differing age of onset. Autism is a childhood disorder whereas schizophrenia typically develops in early adulthood. While most autistic children fail to develop mentalizing skills, people with schizophrenia develop these skills in the normal way, but they subsequently break down with the onset of the disorder. Before the onset of schizophrenia, people who develop the disorder in adulthood have known about the existence of others' mental states and managed ToM effectively. As a result, distortions in how the patient interprets their own and others' mental states are possible. In Frith's words:

> The schizophrenic knows well that other people have minds, but has lost the ability to infer the contents of these minds: their beliefs and intentions. They may even lose the ability to reflect on the contents of their own mind.
>
> (Frith, 1992, p. 121)

Previous knowledge of mental states, coupled with a breakdown in the mechanism that manages them effectively, create the possibility for symptoms such as delusions and hallucinations. According to Frith, people with schizophrenia continue to make inferences about others' mental states even though this ability has broken down. For example, they will believe that others are lying to them and are out to do them harm, an inference that, in this framework, an autistic child could not make because s/he has never known about others' intentions towards her/him.

Empirical studies

Following Frith's proposal, there has been a rush of experimental studies investigating mentalizing in schizophrenia. As Frith proposes that different mentalizing deficits produce different symptoms, these studies have focused on how particular deficits are related to symptoms. Frith distinguished between first- and second-order ToM deficits. First-order representations are concerned with a person's belief about the world (e.g., 'My sister thinks I am not ill.'), while second-order representations (the meta-representations) are concerned with a person's belief about the belief of another person (e.g., 'My parents think that my sister is wrong.').

While some experimental studies involving patients with schizophrenia found evidence of impaired performance on both first- and second-order ToM tasks (e.g., Corcoran, Mercer and Frith, 1995; Frith and Corcoran, 1996), some found more evidence of first-order deficits (Mazza, de Risio, Surian, Roncone and Casacchia, 2001) and yet others more evidence of second-order deficits (Doody, Gàtz, Johnstone, Frith and Cunningham Owens, 1998; Drury, Robinson and Birchwood, 1998; Pickup and Frith, 2001). Apart from these studies which used the classic false-belief test, there has been a cluster of related studies reporting deficits in how people with schizophrenia understand indirect speech acts, irony and other verbal humour (e.g., Mitchley, Barber, Gray, Brooks and Livingston, 1998; Winner, Brownwell, Happé, Blum and Pincus, 1998; Herold, Tenyi, Lenard and Trixler, 2002; Langdon, Davies, and Coulthart, 2002). Conflicting findings have been reported on how these deficits are related to specific symptoms. While it is not possible to consider this issue in detail here, it appears that patients with more severe symptoms and patients with negative symptoms rather than positive symptoms perform more poorly on ToM tasks.

Most of the aforementioned studies were conducted with patients when they were acutely ill, that is, experiencing an increase or worsening of positive symptoms. Of two studies that investigated ToM skills outside of the acute episode, one found that ToM deficits present during an acute episode were no longer present at recovery (Drury et al., 1998) while the other (Herold et al., 2002) did find evidence of impairment in chronic patients.

Although the evidence is somewhat confusing, it may be summarized as follows:

1. People with schizophrenia perform more poorly than psychiatric or healthy controls on experimental tasks that hinge on an appreciation of others' mental states during an acute episode of psychosis and possibly when they are in remission.
2. A differential association between different ToM deficits and specific symptoms of schizophrenia has not been established.

It is important to point out that schizophrenia is a heterogeneous disorder, varying widely in its symptom presentation and course. Its symptoms vary as do its subtypes (see APA, 1994), so much so that two people with the diagnosis may not have any symptoms in common. Indeed, Bentall (1992, 2003) has questioned the validity of the diagnosis of schizophrenia and argued that it should be abandoned in favour of symptom-based classifications. Hence, any attempt to provide a unitary theory of schizophrenia is of significant appeal and also an ambitious undertaking. While one of the strengths of Frith's approach is that it is a unitary theory that is symptom based, the heterogeneity of symptoms seen in schizophrenia makes it difficult to account for such varying symptoms with the aforementioned deficits. A related problem, in experimental studies, is the difficulty classifying individuals into distinct symptom categories and investigating their performance on ToM tasks as they typically present with multiple and overlapping symptoms (cf. Mazza et al., 2001).

Proponents of the impaired theory of mind model of schizophrenia, and others, predict that, as in autism, individuals who have problems representing their own and others' intentionality should have great problems communicating. Indeed, both clinical accounts and empirical studies concur that disordered language and discourse are central to schizophrenia (e.g., Bleuler, 1911/1950; Rochester, 1979; Thomas and Leudar, 1995; Thomas, Leudar et al., 1996). If, as the ToM model predicts, people with schizophrenia have problems understanding others' mental states, specific interactional difficulties should be evident (Frith, 1992; Doody et al., 1998; Corcoran, 2001; Langdon et al., 2002). Frith predicts that:

> they will still have available ritual and behavioural routines for interacting with people, which do not require inferences about mental states.
>
> (Frith, 1992, p. 121)

It is clear from detailed conversation analytic studies of interaction that talk is constructed moment-by-moment and is designed for that particular recipient at that particular point in a given interaction (see, e.g., Heritage, 1984). The sequential organization of talk is such that if an individual had only ritual behavioural routines at their disposal, they would fail quickly in interaction. Even if one were to accept counterfactually that interaction could be successful if it relied on behavioural routines, the issue is an empirical one – how do people with schizophrenia manage in interaction and do they rely on behavioural routines where others follow rules? Studying interaction directly has distinct advantages, perhaps most importantly in this context predicting how a particular skill as operationalized and tested in experimental situations can be generalized to everyday interaction. Moreover, it facilitates an analysis of where exactly in conversational 'mentalizing' individuals with schizophrenia fail, or, conversely, how they manage their own and other peoples' intentionality adequately.

One such study has analysed how people with schizophrenia manage their own and others' mental states in naturalistic social interaction (McCabe, Leudar and Antaki, 2004). Conversation analytic techniques were used to analyse routine encounters between people with a diagnosis of schizophrenia and their psychiatrists and cognitive behaviour therapists. Conversation analysis is concerned with identifying the structural organization of ordinary social activities, with implications for the social competencies of those who participate in them. Hence, it is particularly suited to identifying competence and, if relevant, incompetence in routine interaction. Using this analytic approach, we found that schizophrenics with ongoing positive and negative symptoms appropriately reported first- and second-order mental states of others and designed their contributions to conversations on the basis of what they thought their communicative partners knew and intended.

The following extract comes from a routine outpatient psychiatric consultation.[1] The psychiatrist has no problem using the patient as a source of information about his girlfriend's thoughts (about medication) (line 2) and the patient has no problem responding, in this case saying that he has no direct knowledge of what she thinks (lines 3–4). See Appendix for transcription symbols.

Extract 1: Co35: 52

(Dr = psychiatrist, P = patient)

1.   P   .hhh I live at (.) in (place) with my girlfriend at the moment
2.   Dr   .hhh and what does she think about the medication
3.   P   =she sort of ah (0.2) <I don't know (0.2) she (0.1) she I donno she she's > the
4.   <u>negative</u> side of it a lot of the time
5.   Dr   =what's the negative side of it
6.   P   =I donno .hhh (.) she always thinks I have a bad memory you know (.) it makes
7.   me s:orta slow down an stuff <but it>

Interestingly, the patient does not stop there, but continues to infer for the psychiatrist what his partner is likely to think, reasoning on the basis of her experience with himself (or more precisely 'the negative side of it', lines 3–4). It is on this basis that he represents her likely thoughts to the psychiatrist (lines 6–7). So the patient can anticipate other people's beliefs about himself, and relate these to their social experiences. Moreover, reporting what others believe of him involves the patient in considering his own beliefs reflexively. The following extract is from the same consultation.

Extract 2: Co35: 57

1.   Dr   .hhh <ye:s she has known yo:u quite a long time> =
2.   P   =yes <she is totally fin:e with it to the point where she> (.) you know she
3.   recently did some re:search on the internet of <schizophrenia> (.) .hhh and er
4.   <you know she just I mean read a thing about Risperidone> about a woman who
5.   had writt:en <written a> page on some website you know she said .hhh that this
6.   wom:an didn't (.) under:stand why other people were not given Risperidone it
7.   was sort of <it (.) it> such such a good medicine. .hhh (.) so I me:an <it's a good
8.   goo:d she knows it's a good pill> and that it do:es does the do. (0.2) .hhh <But I
9.   mean> she s:een me i:ll on pill:s <but she never (...) >You know I know what I
10.   was like when I wasn't taking (0.1) any:thing and that was not pleasant sort of
11.   thing

P represents his girlfriend's knowledge of risperidone to the psychiatrist (lines 4–5), tying that knowledge (evidentially) to her research. He proceeds to do meta-representation of increasing complexity. P is being reflexive: he is commenting on himself as he was before and what he is like now *and* evaluating this from the point of view of his partner as she didn't see him when he was more ill when he wasn't taking any tablets (lines 9–11). Moreover, he is saying this to the doctor, for a purpose. The psychiatrist has no problem accepting his reasoning and uses it as grounds for a proposed action (he proposes to involve the girlfriend in the consultation). In other words, P clearly demonstrates sensitivity to the knowledge and feelings of others and uses this appropriately to resolve a problem. He is able to reflect on his own knowledge and contrast it with another person's knowledge.

The following example comes from a different consultation in which a psychiatrist asks a patient to explain why he attends the psychiatric clinic, for the benefit of a medical student who is also present. The patient speaks about his beliefs in some detail and in particular his delusional belief that he was called upon by God to deal with Satan.

Extract 3: Co23: 59

```
 1.  Dr   I was ↑wondering if you might <be able to:> (.) for Sarah's benefit to just explain
 2.       to her a little bit about why (.hh) you come to see us
 3.       (0.2)
 4.  P    You £mean my ↑sto:ry£?
 5.  Dr   £A little bit yeah£.
 6.  P    oh[khhhay.
 7.  Dr     [(if you could/good).
 8.  P    £.hhh my story is£ continually deve:loping. (.) I think I've reached the point now
 9.       where I've em:: (.) .hh got the whole pictu:re. (0.4) emm (1.0) .smt (cough)
10.  P    about 10 years ag:o almo:st <to the the> month <Augu:st
11.       Augu:st> 10 years ago .hhh (.) I was um (.) mind:ing my own business a::nd
12.       <er>.hhh (.) I was <suddenly call:ed upon by God> (.) to er (.) um.hhh (0.3)
13.       <get> in:volved with the .hhh (.) dealing with <Satan> (0.3) .hhh an::d u::m
14.       ((sniff)) (0.2) what I've discover::ed <over time was that Satan> (.) .hhh is an is
15.       <art::ifi:cial intelligen:ce (.) as is Jesus (.) anoth:er artificial intelligence (.)
16.       <he's not a man at a↑ll> .hhh An::d these two artificial intelligences to::gether
17.       (.).hhh when they were together were causing havoc in the world (.) er (.)
18.       death (.) disease (.) and (0.3) er <mayhem and so on> and drugs and <so on
19.       and so forth> (0.2) .hhh so (.) ((coughs)) my re:mit was to to (.) contact <these
20.       these intelligences> and to <get them in touch with God (.) and bas:: basically
21.       scare them a way .hhh er I have DONE tha:t (.)an::d (.) er <the world is now a
22.       better place> .hh and u- ultimately in the short order .hhh eh: (.) we will have em:::
23.       eternal life p- in para:dise .hhh now th- now that we've solved the problems of jesus
24.       and satan.
```

The patient clearly has delusional beliefs, one of them being that he is immortal, a delusion that is not related to a ToM problem. His account of this immortality is, however, inconsistent.

The psychiatrist asks him if there is eternal life now and he replies 'not yet' in the following excerpt (lines 1–3). Yet, when the psychiatrist asks if he himself has eternal life, the patient responds in the affirmative (lines 5–8).

Extract 4: Co23: 115

```
1.   Dr   =so is there (.) is there eternal life now
2.   P    (.).hhh not yet (.) until God <says says>(0.2) until Go:d can make the
3.        decision to go forward with it
4.   Dr   [right]
5.   Dr   =have y:ou got <eternal> life
6.   P    yes (.)
7.   Dr   .hhh so how long will you live for
8.   P    forever
```

Note, however, that despite this inconsistency in his own expressed beliefs, in the following excerpt he is not failing to appreciate the psychiatrist's concerns about the beliefs and how they may influence his actions.

Extract 5: Co23: 124

```
1.   Dr   = <right> .hhh does that mean you don't need to take care or yourself o:r
2.   P    no not at all .hhh theoretically I could die=
3.   Dr   =yeah=
4.   P    =but in practi::ce er (.) in practi::ce er (.) er (.).hhh the um (0.3) .hhh eternal life
5.        will be he:re before <I (.) I> reach the point at which (.) which <my my> natural
6.        life will expir:e
7.   Dr   so if you got hit by a car or a bus or something like that <what would (.) what
8.        would> happen to you
9.   P    I'd probably die but I'd come back again
10.  Dr   right (.) does that mean <you (.) you> are vigilant when you cross roads or
11.  P    of course I am <I don't want (.) I don't want> to test the thesis
12.  Dr   you don't want to test it out!
13.  P    no!
```

After eliciting information from the patient about his thoughts, the psychiatrist makes relevant his prior questioning of the patient 'It's always concerning when people have thoughts about, about, sort of [...]' (lines 1–2). This utterance is completed by the patient with "What, thinking they're immortal?" (lines 3–4).

Extract 6: Co23: 97:142

```
1.   Dr   right (.) right m (.) right its always conce:rning when people have (.).hhh
2.        thou:ghts about <about> sort of
3.   P    what thinking they're immortal? right (.) <obviously (.) obviously> that's just a
4.        thought .hhh I don't go ar::ound thinking I'm immortal
5.   Dr   no=
6.   P    =I'm just thinking about a theoretical issue
7.   Dr   okay alright
```

The patient clearly represents the psychiatrist's representation of his (i.e., the patient's) thoughts; in other words, he successfully displays second-order theory of mind skills. He deals appropriately with the pragmatics of the exchange. The psychiatrist begins to formulate his concern cautiously and delicately, that is, as a general one about 'people' having thoughts, rather than directing it specifically to the patient. He hesitates in selecting the next words and the patient continues with this general formulation about people 'thinking they're immortal'. In this collaborative completion, the patient offers a candidate understanding of what the psychiatrist is concerned about, which is not rejected by the psychiatrist. He responds to this concern – it is just a thought, he does not go around thinking he is immortal – and successfully allays the psychiatrist's concern, as indicated by his acceptance 'okay, alright'.

We found that patients coped successfully with the requirements of social interaction. They successfully expressed beliefs about others' states of mind, as well as about their own. They also provided justifications for attributions about their own and others' mental states when this was indicated. They designed their turns in conversation on the basis of their authors' communicative intentions and initiated and completed complex conversational sequences that hinged on an anticipation of their interlocutor's beliefs. Further evidence of their capacity to appreciate others' states of mind was clear in how they reflected on their own beliefs, and contrasted these with beliefs of different people. Moreover, the clinicians, without exception, treated the patients as intentional and able to reflect on complex representations of mental states.

There were, nevertheless, communicative problems. In order to investigate these in more detail, we identified and analysed sequences of talk that were the most problematic interactionally. These sequences were marked by explicit disagreement between the patient and clinician when patients raised the 'reality' or 'validity' of certain experiences and beliefs for discussion. Patients recognized that others did not share their delusions and attempted to reconcile others' beliefs with their own, but problems arose when they tried to warrant their delusional claims. They did not make the justification for their claim understandable for their interlocutor. Nevertheless, they did not fail to recognize that the justification for their claim was unconvincing. Yet, the ensuing disagreement did not lead them to modify their beliefs. Interestingly, the patient who claims to have eternal life presents his 'story' as truth rather than belief and the interactional criteria for these are different (Stich, 1983; and see Wes Sharrock's Chapter 10 in this volume). This area warrants further research, in particular detailed attention to patients' presentation of their experiences in talk as facts or beliefs. Psychotic beliefs persisted despite the realization they are not shared, but not because patients could not reflect on them and compare them with what others believe.

Although these patients were not acutely ill, they had 'active' symptoms which required ongoing medication and monitoring, for example, one patient believed that he was God and that other people were spitting on the ground to insult him (a grandiose and persecutory delusion), another that he was called upon by Jesus to deal with Satan and was immortal (a grandiose delusion), and another that people were drilling holes in her head (a hallucination) and were after her (a persecutory or paranoid delusion). While these patients specifically talked about this phenomenology, they were competent in talking about and responding to their own and others' (e.g., clinicians, carers and others) thoughts, beliefs and feelings.

This study showed that contrary to the findings from experimental studies, people with schizophrenia can use knowledge of their own and others' beliefs, wishes, intentions and so on to interact effectively with others. (This parallels the finding in developmental psychology that children who fail false-belief tasks, nevertheless, communicate effectively in everyday life – see Reddy and Morris, Chapter 5 in this volume). The problem that patients displayed is not a ToM deficit proper. It stands in contrast to ToM deficits described in autism, in particular that if an autistic child knows something, s/he assumes that others know it too. This was not the case in the above study. Patients who had bizarre beliefs or experiences did not assume that others would know about them. They specifically highlighted the differences between their own and others' beliefs, and attempted to reconcile others' disbelief with their own beliefs by considering why these differences existed.

We have, of course, no way of knowing whether these participants with schizophrenia would have failed or successfully completed the 'false-belief task'. If they failed it, they would exhibit the contradiction we aim to explain – the formal assessment indicates ToM deficiency, everyday communication does not. If, however, they succeeded in the task, their symptoms would not be explicable in terms of ToM deficits.

Accounting for discrepant findings in experiments and conversations

So how do we account for the discrepant findings of ToM deficits in experimental studies, but not in our naturalistic study? There are some issues specific to research in the field of schizophrenia and other conceptual issues relevant to ToM research in general to consider.

Research in schizophrenia

Some researchers, including Frith, have suggested that ToM deficits might be state-related (present only when patients are acutely ill) rather than trait characteristics of schizophrenia (present all of the time whether patients are acutely ill or in remission). In other words, ToM deficits may disappear when the patient is in remission. Our naturalistic study analysed talk of chronic patients, whereas most of the experimental studies were conducted with acute patients (with the exception of Brüne, 2003).

Hence, it might be suggested that we did not find ToM problems because the patients were not acutely ill. In practice, however, acute and chronic states exist on a continuum. Patients classified as acute are typically in-patients in hospital, but who gets admitted to hospital is not simply a matter of symptom severity (i.e., acuteness) because practical factors (e.g., availability of accommodation, location) influence who is admitted and when (cf. Weaver, Tyrer, Ritchie and Renton, 2003). However, of over-riding importance in countering this suggestion was our finding that patients were, in the ToM framework, 'mentalizing', with various degrees of complexity in talk which would be classified as psychotic – in fact 'mentalizing' with respect to positive symptoms. They understood others and responded to them as people with experiences and beliefs distinct from their own.

The second specific issue relates to the way in which ToM is typically assessed. Most ToM studies to date have used the classic 'false-belief' task, designed to test the ability to infer a character's appreciation of the mental states of another character. For example, in a story where Sally and Ann play with a toy, Sally goes out of the room, Ann hides the toy and Sally comes back. The respondent (person with schizophrenia) is asked where Sally will look to find the toy or where she thinks the object is. The plaus-ible answer is that she will go first to where she last saw it, not knowing that Ann has relocated it. So if the respondent answers that Sally will first look in the new hiding place, which she could not have known about, then s/he is failing to appreciate her mental state. Even if one counterfactually accepts the theory of ToM, there is more to passing the false-belief test than 'Theory of Mind' (Bloom and German, 2000). To solve the task, the person must follow the actions of two characters in a story, remember that one character could not have seen the switching of the object's location, remember where the object was and where it is at the time of the test, and understand the precise meaning of the question (Sharrock and Coulter, 2004). These task demands may be quite problematic for people with schizo-phrenia when they are psychotic as their attention and concentration is significantly diminished. In fact, poor attention is rated on most symptom scales for schizophrenia. Indeed, even within the ToM framework, a num-ber of authors (e.g., Drury et al., 1998; Mazza et al., 2001; Brüne, 2003) have concluded that it remains to be seen whether ToM deficits found in experimental studies are genuine primary deficits or a result of information processing overload, compromised attention and concentration, IQ, work-ing memory or executive dysfunction (e.g., Drury et al., 1998; Mazza et al., 2001; Langdon et al., 2002). In general, the more psychotic a person is, the more poorly they will perform on any task. Garety and Freeman (1999) question whether the reports of ToM deficits are simply a replication of the finding that people with schizophrenia perform poorly on a wide range of cognitive tasks.

Some studies have attempted to tease out this issue. For example, Doody and colleagues (1998) and Langdon and colleagues (2002) found mentalizing deficits when IQ had been taken into account and in the Langdon and colleagues study, this was also the case when executive functioning (compromised in some patients with schizophrenia) was controlled for. On the other hand, when Brüne (2003) took IQ deficits into account, ToM deficits disappeared. Drury and colleagues (1998) used memory and feedback aids in an attempt to reduce the confounding influence of memory impairment and still found ToM deficits. However, it would be difficult to design an experimental test of ToM that would control for the influence of poor attention.

It is worth reflecting here on the ecological validity of the methods used to investigate 'mentalizing'. In experimental tasks, the support structures available in natural everyday interaction are removed. In the latter, people provide information in interactional sequences so that formal inferences about thoughts, beliefs, etc. are not necessary. Antaki (2004) has shown through interactional analysis that 'mind-reading' does not have to involve theorizing about another's inner mental state. In practice, an interlocutor makes certain resources publicly available in their talk in the context of a particular action (e.g., reporting one's feelings). Wootton's (1997) study of the development of request sequences in two- to three-year-olds also reports this phenomenon. Although requests are logically contingent on their addressee having certain knowledge, beliefs and so on, he found that psychological inferences about the nature of this knowledge were not necessary as this information tended to be displayed either before the relevant sequence or in the request sequence itself. Hence, the kind of skills tested in ToM experiments are, most likely, quite different to the practices used to manage 'intentions', beliefs' and the like, in everyday interaction. So-called 'mental states' are, in practice, displayed for co-participants so that they do not need to make inferences about them.

There are clearly conceptual problems with using ToM experiments to test whether people understand and appreciate others' perspectives and relying on them to understand what is required to communicate successfully with others. Notwithstanding these problems, why might people with schizophrenia perform poorly on experimental ToM tasks? Recent work, primarily in the field of cognitive psychology, has shed some light on the cognitive and affective processes that might play a role in the production and maintenance of psychotic symptoms. This research has focused more on delusions (e.g., Dudley, John, Young and Over, 1997; Freeman, Garety and Kuipers, 2001; Colbert and Peters, 2002; Bell, Halligan and Ellis, 2003; Freeman and Garety, 2003) than hallucinations (e.g., Leudar and Thomas, 2000). With respect to delusions, there is increasing evidence that people with delusions display a specific reasoning bias in decision-making, that is, they tend to jump to conclusions more hastily than healthy controls, and use less evidence in making a decision when the decision involves both neutral and emotionally salient material (e.g., Huq, Garety and Hemsley, 1988; Dudley et al., 1997). In the Huq and colleagues study, patients were also overconfident relative to healthy and psychiatric controls in their judgments. More recently, Bentall and Swarbrick (2003) reported that currently ill and remitted patients with paranoid delusions are highly intolerant of ambiguity. Interestingly, in their experimental ToM studies, Sarfati and colleagues (1997) observed that schizophrenia patients' interpretation of intention and false beliefs was based specifically on a socially familiar experience rather than the context of the story, and Drury and colleagues found that patients were distracted by the relations between the story characters and their own personal experiences. It may be that patients make overly hasty decisions on experimental tasks (including test of a ToM), which Dudley and colleagues (1997) suggest may be compensating for other deficits (e.g., impaired working memory) by reducing cognitive demand.

Conceptual issues

Perhaps more importantly, there are considerable conceptual problems associated with the theory of 'Theory of Mind'. These are more extensively discussed in other chapters so a brief synopsis of key points will suffice here. Leudar and Costall trace the historical roots of 'Theory of Mind' from its Cartesian origin, which views the body and mind as distinct entities. Within this tradition, the body is public and observable while the mind is private and unobservable. It follows that if minds are essentially private, we need to speculate about or infer their contents along the lines of 'I think that John is angry'. However, detailed attention to the language we use and how we use it suggests that theorizing about others' mental states is not an accurate reflection of what happens when we communicate with each other. Sharrock and Coulter (2004), after Ryle, argue persuasively that how we speak ordinarily does not embody Cartesian suppositions.

Hence, empirical studies suggest that inference is typically not needed to identify others' thoughts, feelings, beliefs and the like (Wootton, 1997; Antaki, 2004). Rather, talk is designed so that communicative intentions are, at least some of the time, obvious. In other words, they have public criteria, following Wittgenstein's position that the 'mind' is not internal and that internal events of the 'mind' need outward public criteria (Sharrock and Coulter, 2004). Inferences are of course necessary sometimes – such as when deception is suspected or one participates in an unfamiliar language game. However, experimental studies would need to test the ability of people with schizophrenia to make pertinent inferences in an ecologically valid way: that is, by incorporating scenarios where drawing inferences about another's intentionality is typically required in experimental tasks.

The patients in McCabe, Leudar and Antaki's (2004) study did not show failures in appreciating and responding to their interlocutor's thoughts, feelings, intentions, et cetera. Sources of interactional trouble arose because of a different problem, that is, anomalies in how patients used evidence to justify their beliefs and, following on from this, how they were confused about why others did not accept their evidence and therefore believe their contentious claims. With respect to how people use evidence in normal belief formation and maintenance, Garety (1998) notes that relevant evidence is not treated in a consistent manner. Strong beliefs are held with little evidential support and a 'confirmation bias' has been identified, whereby confirmatory evidence is preferentially sought out and attended to, and contradictory evidence ignored. This tendency seems to be even stronger in the context of abnormal beliefs. People with delusions perform abnormally when evaluating evidence (Bentall, 2001) and psychotic patients are less inclined to modify their judgments in probabilistic reasoning tasks when confronted with potentially disconfirmatory data (Brankovic and Paunovic, 1999). Jones (1999) has also found that delusional beliefs are arrived at rapidly and do not involve the rational weighing of data. Hence, it appears that the confirmation bias that is characteristic of normal beliefs may be exaggerated in delusional beliefs.

In an attempt to redefine delusions more accurately than they are defined in diagnostic manuals, Spitzer (1990) has argued that it is not falsity of a belief that makes it delusional. Rather, it is the unjustified claim for intersubjective validity that makes a belief delusional. He notes that in clinical practice, the emphasis in diagnosis is on how a delusional person talks, gives reasons, or fails or refuses to do so in relation to their claims. He observes that the patient typically presents his delusion as a statement of fact and that, in practice, the clinician attends to the way a person claims statements or argues about his/her views. Spitzer's emphasis on how a person argues about his or her views rather than the truth of falsity of the belief is consistent with our findings.

Spitzer also suggests that delusional patients' way of talking about their claims, that is, with conviction and subjective certainty, are more consistent with the experience of knowing than of believing. This does appear to hold in the case of the patient above who has eternal life. Spitzer distinguishes between our differential entitlements to make claims about 'internal' mental states versus external events. According to Spitzer, as we have privileged access to our mental states, and because our mental states are coextensive with our experience of them, we are entitled to claim a proprietary relationship to them and insist that our knowledge of them is irrefutable: patients misappropriate the certainty and incorrigibility reserved for claims about private mental states to their (delusional) assertions about external reality. Delusions are thus redefined by Spitzer as statements about external reality, which are uttered like statements about a mental state, that is, with subjective certainty and as incorrigible by others.

In light of the previous discussion about how internal events require outward public criteria, Spitzer's distinction between the ways in which we can make claims about internal and external events is problematic. Indeed, our analysis highlighted just how claims about one's experience do stand in need of certain criteria that are accessible to others.

There is a further problem with Spitzer's account of delusions. Patients, in our naturalistic study, had problems providing justifications for their delusional claims and, even though others disagreed with them, did not modify their claims. However, while Spitzer suggests that schizophrenic patients are not concerned with 'intersubjective feedback' or reasoning about anything pertaining to these claims, we found that patients were concerned with others' beliefs and attempted to reason about and provide evidence for their claims. Where they failed was in recognizing why others found their evidence unconvincing.

There is of course a caveat, which is that our work to date is not representative of all psychotic symptoms. Although our analysis was of talk about various types of delusions and hallucinations (McCabe, Leudar and Antaki, 2004), there is a wide range of psychotic phenomenology. Moreover, the very nature of these symptoms is poorly understood. For example, with respect to delusions alone, there is ongoing debate about how delusions should be defined, what it means to say someone is delusional and the role of different delusional subtypes (e.g., Spitzer, 1990; Sedler, 1995; David, 1999; Jones, 1999; Freeman and Garety, 2000). It remains to be investigated whether the same anomaly in patients' reasoning is characteristic of all psychotic symptoms or whether there are different deficits underlying different symptoms. The interactional analysis, described herein, would need to be applied to all of these symptoms along with each symptom subtype on a case-by-case basis.

Conclusion

This chapter presented the impaired ToM account of schizophrenia, briefly reviewed the conflicting experimental evidence, and summarized an alternative methodological approach, that of conversation analysis, to analysing the putative problem. This showed that actively psychotic patients had no problem appreciating, talking about and warranting their own and others' mental states. However, it documented: (a) that patients failed to provide convincing evidence to warrant their claims; (b) were puzzled by their failure to convince others of their claims; and (c) maintained their claims despite repeated exposure to competing formulations from others. Although patients were concerned with what Spitzer referred to as 'intersubjective feedback' (they displayed discomfort in the face of others' disagreement), repeated disagreement with others in the form of competing accounts did not lead them to modify their claims. It is their resistance to revision of their beliefs, not their failure to recognize that their beliefs are different and problematic, which appears to be the striking feature of delusions. A question for further research is whether this resistance is specific to delusional phenomena or applies to other psychotic symptoms or is even a more general reasoning bias characteristic of the condition.

We have demonstrated a strong *prima facie* case against the hypothesis that ToM deficits generate psychotic symptoms of schizophrenia (McCabe, Leudar and Antaki, 2004). While the contrast between the experimental evidence for ToM and the evidence from natural interactions demonstrates the power of the conversation analytic approach, the latter does not unravel the character of the condition. The patients are procedurally competent in conversation, for example, in making requests, in disagreeing, in warranting claims. It is the contents of their beliefs that are problematic. To use the Wittgensteinian metaphor, there are certain language games that these patients will not play, but conversation analysis does not (and indeed cannot) say anything about why this is so. An adequate account will need to address why they have experiences that they themselves identify as anomalous, why their accounts are so resistant to competing formulations, and why they find others' accounts somehow incommensurate with the phenomena they are attempting to explain.[2]

Appendix: Transcription notation

(.)	Just noticeable pause
(.3), (2.6)	Examples of timed pauses
[word [word	Square brackets aligned across adjacent lines denote the start of overlapping talk
.hh, hh	In-breath (note the preceding fullstop) and out-breath respectively
wo(h)rd	(h) is a try at showing that the word has 'laughter' bubbling within it
wor-	A dash shows a sharp cut-off
wo:rd	Colons show that the speaker has stretched the preceding sound
(words)	A guess at what might have been said if unclear
( )	Unclear talk. Some transcribers like to represent each syllable of unclear talk with a dash
word= =word	The equals sign shows that there is no discernible pause between two speakers' turns or, if put between two sounds within a single speaker's turn, shows that they run together
<u>word</u>, WORD	Underlined sounds are louder, capitals louder still
°word°	Material between 'degree signs' is quiet
>word word< <word word>	Inwards arrows show faster speech, outward slower
→	Analyst's signal of a significant line
((*crying*))	Transcriber's representation of something hard, or impossible, to write phonetically
£ talk £	The talk pronounced in smiling voice
!	Animated talk

Notes

1   Some of the data extracts and accompanying description originally appeared in McCabe, Leudar and Antaki (2004). The data has been transcribed according to conversation analytic conventions and an explanation of these is provided in the Appendix.
2   I would like to thank Phil Thomas, Ivan Leudar, Alan Costall and Pat Healey, and hope that this chapter does justice to their constructive comments.

7
The Roots of Mindblindness

Stuart Shanker[1] and Jim Stieben

Introduction: the significance of selective impairments

This chapter challenges the hypothesis that the type of social impairment observed in children with autism is evidence of a specific underlying malfunction in a 'theory of mind mechanism', resulting in 'mindblindness'. To establish this point, the chapter takes up two interesting ideas in the 'Theory of Mind' literature, but purged of their Cartesianism: first that the study of autism does indeed provide us with critical insights into the development of social understanding and empathy. And second, that no meaningful distinction can be drawn between a child's interpersonal and intrapersonal development. The chapter seeks to show how the ability to understand someone else's thoughts and emotions is a product of countless co-regulated interactions with a caregiver in which develop the child's own emotions and sense of self, as well as her understanding of what others are thinking and feeling, what they believe or intend to do. One of the reasons why children with autism so frequently exhibit impaired social relatedness is because basic biological challenges – such as sensory over- and under-reactivity, social motivation and attentional failures – inhibit their ability to engage in these co-regulated interactive experiences across the developmental landscape.

* * *

Like geologists who scour the landscape in search of tell-tale signs of topographical anomalies that might signify a rich mineral deposit underneath, modularity theorists have taken to scouring the landscape of developmental disorders in search of tell-tale signs of specific processing malfunctions. Some of the richest veins mined in recent years have been based on stroke-victims whose aphasias are so precise that their only language impairment might be that they cannot remember the names of vegetables; or children who have normal intelligence, are socially outgoing, and have no hearing problems, but cannot use grammatical morphemes; or children who have trouble communicating the simplest of needs, yet can master foreign languages; or children with normal visual acuity who can't recognize other people's faces (in some rare cases, even their own) yet can recognize other people by their voice, gestures, gait, clothes and so on; or children who can solve the most intricate calculation problems but can't grasp the simplest of 'knock knock' jokes.

In all these cases, modularity theorists have sought to discover the dedicated mechanisms involved in the normal processing of these different kinds of information, and perhaps, at an even deeper level, the genes that contain the blueprints for these processing mechanisms (see Baron-Cohen, 1995; Pinker, 1997). And in all these cases, closer investigation has uncovered a much more complex ecological terrain. The stroke victim's capacities are seen to vary according to the subject's state and/or the context in which stimuli are presented (see Goodglass, 1993). The morphological deficits of the child with Specific Language Impairment are seen to vary according to the child's capacity to attend to and process auditory stimuli (see Leonard, 1998; Shanker, 2002). The linguistic savant's communication deficits are seen to vary according to their internal state and social context, while their mastery of foreign languages is similar to the eidetic feats that autistic savants display in other 'isles of expertise' (see Howe, 1989). The neurological patterns associated with prosopagnosia turn out to be vastly more complex than an isolated malfunction in the fusiform gyrus, and to add further to the complexity, the performance of such subjects improves when shown faces that are upside down; and when asked which name goes with which face (for familiar contacts), they consistently make the right connection even while insisting they cannot recognize either face. But for the purposes of the present chapter, our interest lies in the last of the above 'selective impairments': the child who has so much difficulty understanding human behaviour but may be remarkably adept at solving logical or mathematical problems.

Consider the following anomaly: four-year-old children with autism have considerable difficulty with the Sally-Anne task, in which they are asked to predict where another child will look for a doll that unbeknownst to them has been moved to a different location (see Wimmer and Perner, 1983; Baron-Cohen, 2000a, b), yet have very little difficulty with what is known as the 'false photograph' task. In the latter, an experimenter explains how a Polaroid camera works, takes a photo of a toy cat sitting on a chair and places the photo upside down. While the photo is developing the experimenter moves the cat from the chair to a bed and then asks the child where the cat will be sitting when they look at the photo (see Leslie and Thaiss, 1992). Why is it that children with autism have so little difficulty with this task, yet so much trouble with the Sally-Anne? Why is it that they have no trouble 'finding Waldo', yet have so much difficulty identifying facial expressions of basic emotions (see Hobson, 1986, 1989)?

According to the modularity view of 'Theory of Mind' (ToM), the answer to this question lies in the fact that, for reasons still to be determined, children with autism suffer from a damaged ToM mechanism (see Perner, Frith, Leslie and Leekam, 1989). Perhaps this is due to a genetic defect in a dedicated ToM module, or to a malfunctioning core module that provides the necessary social information for a ToMM to process (see Baron-Cohen, 1995). For in addition to their markedly poor performance on false-belief tasks, children with autism characteristically display a number of more basic deficits suggestive of a lower-order malfunction, such as problems with joint attention, or being unable to read facial expressions of emotion and other nonverbal affect cues. Thus, autism is seen by modularity theorists as potentially holding the key to figuring out which centres in the brain were shaped, some time in the Pleistocene, to represent other agents' mental states.

As we have argued elsewhere, and several philosophers have shown in much greater detail, the epistemological picture on which this view of ToM is based is grounded in a Cartesian theory of cognition (see Savage-Rumbaugh, Shanker and Taylor, 1998; McGeer, 2002; Thomson, 2002; Zahavi, 2002; Sharrock and Coulter, 2004). The picture of the child as a miniature scientist, actively constructing her sense of reality, has emerged as a powerful means of drawing attention to the sorts of trial-and-error thinking and hypothesis-testing that can be observed in remarkably young children (Gopnik, Meltzoff and Kuhl, 1999). But the cognitivist version of this thesis goes a step further and argues that, in order to make sense of the categorial difference between physical and social reality, the child formulates what is in essence a Cartesian theory about the nature of the mind and its contents.

The idea that the child can be seen as a miniature Cartesian has been subjected to intensive scrutiny from within the ranks of psychology as well, ranging from the attacks launched by 'simulation theorists', who are wary of an overly cognitivist interpretation of a child's capacity to understand what other agents are thinking or feeling (see Gordon, 1996); to questions about the reliability and validity of the findings (see Reed and Peterson, 1990); to investigations into whether ToM tasks are actually tapping into language abilities (see Eisenmajer and Prior, 1991; Leekam and Perner, 1991; de Villiers, 1999); and most recently, attempts to account for the deficit in terms of an executive dysfunction (Pennington and Ozonoff, 1996; Pennington et al., 1997).

Philosophical critiques have largely focused on the question of whether a child's knowledge of other minds is legitimately described as 'theoretical' (see Zahavi, 2003), and more fundamentally, on the Cartesian view that the mind constructs concepts such as desire, intention and belief in order to explain and predict human behaviour as a unique realm of experience (see Shanker, 2004a). As Sharrock and Coulter (2004) point out, such an argument renders it a mystery how all children should chance on the same mental concepts in order to explain and predict human behaviour. It is only by appealing to the fortuitous notion of *inner constraints* that the cognitivist version of ToM can hope to circumvent this problem (see Shanker, 2001). But then, this is a consequence that some advocates of ToM are more than willing to embrace, seeing in autism yet another vehicle for the evolutionary psychological argument that key human attributes were naturally selected at the dawn of our species (see Carruthers, 1996).

Indeed, even the charge of Cartesianism may not carry nearly the weight that is assumed; for the advocate of a ToM module might feel that, far from signifying that ToM is *merely* a consequence of the Cartesian picture of social cognition, the similarity between the theory of mind presented in *Discourse on Method* and the theory that four-year-olds are normally said to construct can be seen as a testament to Descartes' remarkable insight into how the human mind was designed. That is not to commit one to the extreme ToM hypothesis that Descartes discovered that mental states are 'invisible and weightless' (Pinker, 1997, p. 329; see Tooby and Cosmides, 1995) but only, to the idea that human beings are programmed to construct the notion of mental states in order to explain human behaviour.

The importance of autism for the ToM modularity hypothesis lies in this very point; for given that a child with autism is said to suffer from a selective impairment in the ability to categorize human thoughts and feelings, this must be because of a defect in the processes involved in the framing of the theoretic constructs needed to explain and predict human behaviour. Indeed, some advocates of a ToM module will insist that the hypothesis actually marks a significant advance over the epistemological asymmetry Descartes postulated between first-person and third-person knowledge of mental states. For there is an influential contingent within the ranks of ToM theorists who would argue that *both* types of judgment are inferences grounded in a theory of mind, as is reflected in the fact that so many subjects with autism have as much difficulty with first-person as with third-person judgments (Carruthers and Smith, 1996).

The advocate of a ToM module can thus claim that the hypothesis avoids the sceptical problems entailed by Descartes' theory of 'privileged access' while providing a coherent explanation of the fundamental problem that has bedevilled western thinkers from at least the time of Descartes to the present: the question of how a child comes to recognize other human beings *as human beings*. Furthermore, the advocate of a ToM module can insist that, despite the weight of the myriad critiques to which it has been subjected by psychologists and philosophers alike, the onus is on these critics to provide an alternative, non-Cartesian explanation of the anomaly seen in children with autism. Moreover, such an explanation must account for the considerable amount of data amassed over the past decade that seems to point to a highly specific impairment in the child with autism's capacity to read facial expressions of emotion and other nonverbal affect cues (Or and Yirmiya, 1993; Happé, 1995; Yirmiya, Erel, Shaked and Solomonica-Levi, 1998; Grant, Grayson and Boucher, 2001).

Our goal in this chapter is to address precisely this challenge, and to do so by taking up two very interesting ideas in ToM – purged of any Cartesian bias: first, that autism may provide us with critical insights into the development of social understanding and empathy. And, second, that no meaningful distinction can be drawn between a child's interpersonal and intrapersonal development. Both of these themes are critical to the functional/emotional model of intelligence that we develop in *The First Idea* (Greenspan and Shanker, 2004). The basic principle of this model is that affects play a pivotal role in the development of the mind, facilitating the integration of the different sensory-motor processing capacities and serving as the foundation for communicative and linguistic abilities, social understanding, and empathy. We argue that the ToM deficits seen in autism are the result of a series of complex developmental failures in the dynamic interplay between ontogenetically early brain systems (hardwired upstream deficits) and those experience-expectant/dependant systems requiring specialized inputs from experience and the environment. Before we look at this model, however, it will be illuminating to probe more deeply into the historical background to ToM.

From sign-reading to mind-reading

If nothing else, ToM attests to a perennial fascination with autism, dating back at least to the Renaissance. To be sure, autism wasn't baptized as a developmental disorder until 1943 (Kanner, 1943); but western thinkers have long been captivated by this unique population of human beings characterized by their sometimes quite advanced cognitive abilities coupled with impaired social relatedness. As Uta Frith and Rab Houston show in their study of the eighteenth-century Scottish laird Hugh Blair (Houston and Frith, 2000), there are strong grounds to suspect that many of those individuals who were then labelled 'natural fools' may have had autism. But, then, if this is the case it indicates a striking shift in our attitudes towards autism. For from the Renaissance on, the natural fool was regarded as having almost preternatural powers of social perception. Time and again Shakespeare uses the figure of the natural Fool to express insights that the audience is meant to share but which evade the characters in the drama[2]: a far cry from our modern understanding of autism.

The reason why the Fool could serve as a touchstone was because he was oblivious of the artifices that people use to conceal their true feelings or intentions (see Welsford, 1966).[3] He thus acts as a reminder of how important it is to study human behaviour carefully. This was the whole point of the manuals that began to appear in the seventeenth century on how to read the 'passions of the soul' that are expressed in the face, and particularly, the eyes (see Wright, 1604/1971). As Descartes was to warn:

> the soul is able to change facial expressions, as well as expressions of the eyes, by vividly feigning a passion which is contrary to one it wishes to conceal. Thus we may use such expressions to hide our passions as well as reveal them [...]
>
> (Descartes, 1649/1970, p. 368)

In an age in which merchants were starting to have more and more dealings with complete strangers, it was becoming imperative that individuals be taught how to read these 'signs' (see Harrison, 1998). Herein is one of the main reasons why Descartes' mechanist theory of emotions was to have such a powerful influence on his contemporaries. For according to Descartes, the basic emotions are *complex reflexes* that are triggered by internal and/or external stimuli (Descartes, 1649/1970; Shanker and Reygadas, 2002). What makes them unique, *qua* species of reflex, is that they are accompanied by characteristic facial expressions, which, like other bodily phenomena, could be precisely measured (*à la* contemporary coding systems like FACS; see Ekman, 1972).

Why was it that the Fool was thought to possess the capacity to read men's souls whereas the rest of us have to study philosophy in order to master its secrets? The answer is because the Fool was seen as 'blessed'[4]: a creature of nature who, like the original Adam, could literally see their internal states in the eyes and faces of both animals and men. After the Fall, however, humans lost this innate ability and, in its stead, had to *learn* how to infer the significance of these signs. One of the major changes that Descartes helped to usher in was the belief that, by painstakingly acquiring this knowledge, we could take the first step of returning to the state of innocence in which humans had control over their passions: and indeed, over nature. Thus, one of the main purposes of Descartes' *Passions of the Soul* was to serve as an instructional text for reading their 'signs' in order to acquire control over one's own or other people's passions (see Schmitter, 1994).

What is so interesting about the transition from seventeenth-century views of *sign-reading*[5] to the ToM view of *mind-reading* is how, placed in a secular context, Descartes' carefully worked out philosophical theory becomes something that the normal four-year-old is said to acquire on her own (see Astington, 1994).[6] In this inversion of the original seventeenth-century picture, the child with autism becomes the one who does not possess this innate capacity and can acquire this ability only through painstaking instruction. What remains constant, however, is the archetypal theme that post-lapsarian humans must infer what someone is thinking or feeling from the signs that are carried on their face and in their eyes.

That is, at the heart of the seventeenth-century picture of sign-reading is the dualist picture of emotions as inner phenomena that are indexed by 'natural signs' (gestures, physical changes, facial expressions, eyes, body movements, posture). These emotions can be observed, singly, in different animals, but occur all together in humans, which is why reading human emotions was thought to be such a complex task (see Harrison, 1998). But the scientist is able to learn, by carefully studying animals as well as humans, which 'facial expressions as well as expressions of the eyes' index which emotions (Descartes, 1649/1970). And it is this dualist picture that has carried through to ToM, albeit it is now young children who are the ones that are said to 'learn like scientists', very much along the lines spelled out in Descartes' *The Passions of the Soul*.

Descartes' views were systematized by the late seventeenth-century French painter, Charles Le Brun. Le Brun set out to codify the general laws of facial expressions. His *Conférence sur l'expression générale et particulière des passions* was to serve as the standard manual for depicting facial expressions of emotion for the next hundred years (see Montagu, 1994). In his paintings, Le Brun went to some pains to depict these characteristic facial expressions as physiological reactions. In a recent chapter on 'Painting the passions: The *Passions de l'Âme* as a basis for pictorial expression', Christopher Allen vividly illustrates the effects achieved by this method by contrasting Le Brun's paintings with those of the great French baroque painter, Nicholas Poussin. Allen describes how Le Brun's paintings are:

> surprisingly bland. Perhaps this is in fact because the action-reaction model is primarily physiological, primarily concerned with what is not much more than an elaboration of the reflex of flinching. [...] Poussin's figures are not merely reacting to some stimulus which has impinged upon their sense of self-preservation. They are responding, that is to say, reaching out beyond their sphere of self-interest, extending themselves in sympathy towards the experience of another. After all, they are human beings, not machines. [...] and the same capacity for involvement with other contributes to that mutuality and that collective aspect which [...] is inherent in Poussin's treatment of expression, and which Le Brun is incapable of apprehending or emulating. [...] In short, Poussin's approach to expression begins with the sense of an event's moral, metaphysical and poetic significance, and is based on *the active, mutually involved response of the participants in that event*. Le Brun starts from the opposite point of view – from passions considered as immediate corporeal reactions to outside stimuli; as atomistic states; as the reactions of isolated individuals – and from that he must build up the whole. [...] *Poussin thinks of the meaning, and he finds his expressions; Le Brun is obsessed with the mechanics of expression and he misses the meaning* [...]
>
> (Allen, 1998, pp. 83–9; our emphasis)

Not only is this a wonderful description of the problems inherent in the Cartesian view of emotions, but it serves as an invaluable introduction to our discussion of autism. For the subject for whom Le Brun's model best applies is actually the child with autism! What the child with autism is unable to experience are precisely those meaningful encounters that Poussin depicts. What we need to understand, then, are the reasons why a child with autism is unable to be an active partner in social events, and thereby learn by experiencing the meaning of facial expressions, gestures, looks of the eye and so on, and is forced, in Temple Grandin's words, 'to learn by trial and error what certain gestures and facial expressions mean' (Grandin, 1995, p. 135).

Autism and mental development

The reason why researchers have focused on impaired social relatedness as the core feature of autism is because this deficit cuts across varying levels of cognitive and linguistic abilities seen in autistic spectrum disorders and persists into adulthood. In particular, the child with autism has trouble reading facial expressions of emotion, which is critical for making sense of human actions and emotions.[7] We now know that this deficit is part of a much more pervasive complex of emotional problems. Recent research has established that children with autism express less emotion overall (Yirmiya, Erel, Shaked and Solomonica-Levi, 1989); less positive emotion (Snow et al., 1987; Kasari, Sigman, Mundy and Yirmiya, 1990); more negative and neutral emotion (Bieberich and Morgan, 1998; Krzeminska, 2001); and that they display atypical facial expressions of positive emotion, marked by asymmetry, reduced movements in the eye and mouth regions, shorter duration, highly labile and less intensity (Loveland, Tunali-Kotoski, Pearson et al., 1994).

Even more important is the growing body of evidence of a developmental trajectory leading to these deficits (Greenspan, 1997; Greenspan and Wieder, 1998b). Lewy and Dawson showed that co-regulated interactions between infants at risk of developing autism and their caregivers are jeopardized because children withdraw in order to reduce arousal created by social interaction (Lewy and Dawson, 1992). Hobson has shown that deficits in facial expressions of affect may further exacerbate problems in social interactions and the development of intersubjectivity (Hobson, 1986, 1989). Deficits in facial expressions of affect may also impair a caregiver's responsiveness to the child, thereby further undermining co-regulated affective interactions (Dawson, Hill, Spencer and Galpert, 1990), and may interfere with opportunities for the caregiver to imitate and enhance an infant's facial expressions, which may further impair the infant's affective development (Malatesta and Izard, 1984). Finally, deficits in facial expressions of affect may impair the shared gaze interactions needed for affective development (Mundy and Sigman, 1989).

Most important of all, for the purposes of constructing a functional/emotional model of social and emotional intelligence, is the growing body of research showing that an infant's emotions and emotional understanding develop in the context of co-regulated and shared emotional experiences (i.e., interactions in which partners are continuously active, continually adjusting their behaviours to each other), including the capacity to recognize the significance of, or respond automatically to, facial expressions of emotion (for a review, see Shanker, 2004a). Far from being pre-determined phenomena, the emotions and emotional depth that a child experiences, and the capacity to understand the emotions that another person is experiencing, *are two aspects of one and the same phenomenon*, both shaped by the nurturing relationships that a child experiences with her primary caregivers. From very early on, there is endless variation in emotional experience, and the only way we can understand this variation is as part of a co-regulated interactional system. The universality of certain features in the basic emotions may therefore lie not only in primitive emotion circuits (Panksepp, 1998), but also, in common early nurturing patterns that have developed over many eons and are typically present in all human cultures (see Greenspan and Shanker, 2004).

The study of autism has indeed played a critical role in the development of this thesis; for the problems that children with autism experience in the differentiation and depth of their emotions, their ability to regulate their emotions, and their problems in understanding other people's emotions, stem from biological deficits that impede their ability to engage in co-regulated affective interactions with their caregivers early in life. One of the most basic kinds of challenge that can impair or constrict a child's development – which is highly prevalent in children with autism – is that the child's senses may be under-reactive or over-reactive to different kinds of stimuli. For example, the sound of a vacuum cleaner can be unbearable for a child who is over-reactive to auditory stimuli, while the intonation changes of motherese might come across as indistinguishable murmurs to a child who is under-reactive. An ordinary T-shirt can feel like sandpaper rubbing against their skin for a child who is over-reactive to touch, while a hug might leave a child who is under-reactive to touch feeling deeply insecure. Even something as innocuous as a colourful mobile can overwhelm a child who is over-reactive to visual stimuli or fail to elicit the slightest interest from a child who is under-reactive.

To see how such basic deficits can impair a child's emotional and social development, consider how a child who is over-reactive to visual stimuli may resort to tuning out the world as much as possible in order to cope with this incessant assault. Simply looking into his mother's eyes when *en face* may be more than he can bear. But then, the more he avoids interactions with his caregivers the more he is depriving the various systems that comprise the 'social brain network' (the neuronal networks responsible for emotion decoding, regulation and action) of those very experiences that are critical for their development (Johnson, Griffin, Csibra, Halit et al., 2005). These impoverished systems in turn will constrain the range of 'developmental possibilities' open to the child, resulting in the child becoming more and more likely to adopt behaviours that will further exacerbate his communicational problems.

Indeed, recent research on this theme helps explain why gaze-aversion is such a prominent feature of autism. Subjects with autism typically demonstrate diminished activity in their right fusiform gyrus (the so-called 'face-processing area') when viewing photographs of faces, which lends support to the ToM 'biological malfunction' hypothesis (see Peirce, Muller, Ambrose, Allen and Courschene, 2001). In a recent study, however, Gernsbacher and colleagues (2003) revealed a more complex picture. Adults with autism were shown photographs of actors displaying happiness, anger or fear, half of them with their eyes looking straight ahead and half with their eyes averted. There was indeed a significant diminishment in the activation of their right fusiform gyrus along with a significant increase in the activation of centres involved in conflict monitoring and the detection of threat when these subjects viewed the eyes-straight-ahead photographs, but not when they viewed the eyes-averted photograph. Thus, what the Gernsbacher and colleagues' study seems to be telling us is that participants with autism avert their gaze in order to reduce their stress. But the explanation for this behaviour would appear to lie in sensory over-reactivity to visual stimuli, not in the malfunction of a dedicated 'face-processing' system. For, as we know from many earlier studies, the eyes are the most stimulus-rich part of the face: in the case of the subject with autism, overwhelmingly so (see Schore, 1994).

The key point here, as far as concerns the development of a child who experiences such sensory over-reactivities, is that such a child will have much more difficulty engaging in ordinary interactions with his parents and the people in his immediate environment. He may perplex, confuse, frustrate and undermine purposeful, interactive communication with even very competent parents. Without such experience, he may not be able to absorb the rules of complex social interactions or develop a sense of self. The child may not develop an intimate relationship with his caregivers, which develops at an especially rapid rate between 12 and 24 months of age.[8] By the time such a child receives professional attention his stunted interaction patterns may have excluded him from important learning experiences and may be intensifying his difficulties. The loss of engagement and relatedness to key caregivers may cause him to withdraw more idiosyncratically into his own world and become even more aimless and/or repetitive. What later looks like a 'mind-reading' deficit that was present from the start, therefore, is the result of a dynamic process in which the child's lack of emotional interactions has intensified specific, early, sensory and processing challenges and derailed the development of critical social, emotional, communicative and cognitive capacities.

The dynamic developmental view of ToM

Recent advances in affective neuroscience lend support to the dynamic developmental approach to ToM sketched above. According to this approach, the 'mindblindness' seen in autism can be traced back to biological deficits that appear much earlier than is generally specified by a modularity view of ToM. These low-level biological challenges put the child at risk of a developmental trajectory leading to autism. In addition, it is difficult for the modularity view of ToM to explain the massive heterogeneity of symptoms and symptom severity commonly observed with autism. Most importantly, the modularity view neglects the very experiences which promote the growth and integration of the brain systems currently believed to be at the root of the social, emotional and communicative deficits seen in autism.

The construction of this 'social brain network' takes place over development and is integrated through co-regulated nurturing interactions. It is through these nurturing interactions that the child develops the capacity to understand – unconsciously or automatically – what someone else is thinking, feeling, et cetera. That is, it is through these countless interactions that the child learns, by experiencing, the meaning of the 'affect signals' which reveal what is going on in the minds of those around him.

We are not simply referring here to a subjective phenomenon; for recent research on the development of the social brain suggests that, through these early interactions, the limbic system becomes primed to resonate with other brains. Much of this activity is automatic: a 'low road' in social interactions that operates beneath the threshold of consciousness (LeDoux, 1996; Goleman, 2006).

The amygdala in particular appears to play an influential role in the modulation of neural systems underlying cognitive and social behaviours in response to emotional cues. Animal models have demonstrated how the amygdala is critical for the formation of both conditioned and observational fear learning. Developmental neuroscientists are beginning to investigate the extent to which the responsiveness of the amygdala to social stimuli is itself a result of this confluence of biological and experiential factors, and not simply a hard-wired phenomenon.

As far as the development of ToM abilities is concerned, the important point here would appear to be that a child's unconscious processing of the nonverbal affect signals of those around her, and thence her basic capacity to understand what others are thinking and feeling, is forged in the earliest years of development, when the brain is going through its massive growth spurt and subsequent pruning. These connections formed between the amygdala and paralimbic and prefrontal neural systems influence how an individual responds to certain kinds of social stimuli, not only in infancy, but for their entire life.

Thus, failures in 'mind-reading' seen at four years are not the product of a defect in some ToMM, or in a lower-level system feeding into a 'ToMM', but rather, the by-product of compromises in the social brain network brought about by a series of *cascading developmental deficits*, often beginning with structural abnormalities in systems sub-serving perception, affect and emotion appraisal, sensory regulation and integration, reward anticipation in the social domain, kinaesthetic awareness and motor coordination. The early deficits that can set a child on the developmental pathway leading to autism include sensory perceptual deficits (unimodal vs. amodal perception) and over-activation of amygdala-orbitofrontal systems of emotion circuits (Bachevalier and Loveland, 2006; and many others) and therefore a reduced reward salience for the social experience. This circuit, including the ACC, is critical for recording viscerally significant motives and the somatic output (marker) of interactions, and is used as a 'reward salience-reward expectation-action output' circuit.

Intervention outcomes

Over the past 20 years, Stanley Greenspan has developed a comprehensive therapeutic programme for children with developmental disorders based on the model outlined in the preceding section.[9] The basic principle of this Developmental Individual Relationship (DIR) programme is to tailor interactions with children according to their motor, sensory and language processing strengths and weaknesses, with the goal of enhancing their ability to engage in long, sustained bouts of co-regulated emotional interactions. A recent study of 200 children diagnosed with autism that underwent this programme bears out the significance of this approach (see Greenspan and Wieder, 1998a; Greenspan, Degangi and Wieder, 2001).

Outcomes were divided into three broad groups: a 'good to outstanding' group that included children who, after two or more years of intervention, evidenced joyful relating, with a variety of emotional gestures. These children were able to engage in purposeful, organized and sustained interactions and share attention in various social, cognitive and motor-based tasks. They could use language creatively and imaginatively and engage in coherent conversations. They no longer showed self-absorption, avoidance, self-stimulation or perseveration. On the CARS, a standard test for autism, all the children in this group had shifted into the non-autistic range.[10] These children no longer had any trouble with ToM tasks.

A second group made significant gains in their ability to relate and communicate. They became much more attached to their parents, often seeking them out in a joyful and pleasurable manner. They could enter into long sequences of purposeful emotional interactions. They could share attention and engage in social, cognitive and motor problem solving. In this group, however, the children were still having significant problems developing their language abilities. Many could express simple desires, but were not yet able to engage in conversations or elaborate play sequences. This group, like the first group, no longer evidenced self-absorption, avoidance of relating, self-stimulation or perseveration. And this group, like the first, no longer had trouble with ToM tasks.

A third group continued to have significant difficulty in attention and pre-symbolic affect gesturing. They continued to demonstrate a significant degree of self-absorption, avoidance, self-stimulation and perseveration. Many in this group were making slow progress in their basic ability to relate with warmth to others, but some alternated between progress and regression. And not surprisingly, many continued to have difficulty with ToM tasks.

Of the 200 children studied, 58 per cent were in the 'good to outstanding' outcome group, 25 per cent were in the 'medium' outcome group, and 17 per cent continued to have significant difficulties. For a full review of the emotional, social, cognitive and linguistic gains that the children in the first two groups made, and the sequence in which these gains were observed, see Greenspan, Degangi and Wieder (2001). For the purposes of the present chapter, the point we wish to highlight is that in the 83 per cent of the children who showed significant improvement, there was a marked advance in the range and depth of their engagement and their pleasure and emotions. Within the first three to four months these children would begin to demonstrate greater joy and positive emotions in their interactions. Even children who had been extremely avoidant and self-absorbed would begin going over to their parents to seek out interaction. Perhaps most striking of all is how, contrary to the ToM stereotype of autism, these children appeared eager for emotional contact and were visibly grateful when their caregivers helped them find ways to engage in greater social interaction.

If such results could be replicated, it would require us to rethink, not just the aetiology of so-called 'mind-reading' deficits, but more fundamentally, the reasons why emotional experience should have been excluded *ab initio* in the ToM paradigm. No doubt it will require future historians of ideas who are as distanced from these debates as we are from the seventeenth century's concern with reading the passions to explain just why ToM has exercised such a strong appeal on contemporary thought. But one is tempted to argue that, apart from the fact that Cartesian epistemology continues to exert such a strong pull on cognitivist thinking, one large reason why the field has been so drawn to ToM is because it seems to offer such an economical explanation of the results consistently obtained in false-belief tasks. The problem is, however, that ToM may represent the costs of striving for too economical a model of child development.

The richness of complexity

The crux of the functional/emotional model sketched in this chapter is that a child's emotional capacity, social understanding and empathy cannot be separated from the child's emotional/interactional experiences. That is, the ability to understand someone else's thoughts and emotions at the level of unconscious processing requires endless co-regulated interactions, in which the child's own emotions and sense of self develop. One of the primary lessons we learn from studying children with autism is how their catastrophic emotions tend to disrupt this developmental trajectory. For example, it is common for a toddler with sensory hypersensitivities to fly into a fearful panic or a rage attack, which allows for very little if any co-regulated emotional interaction. Because catastrophic reactions tend to lead to immobilizing panic or withdrawal, they undermine the ability to experience sustained affective interaction patterns. They do not form a basis for grasping a pattern of emotional interaction. The intensity of the emotions is often so severe that even the experience and awareness of a simple pattern, such as 'I get angry and he gets angrier' may fail to develop.

When one observes infants and toddlers locked into these catastrophic emotional experiences one tends to see fragmented behaviour along with aggressive outbursts, withdrawal, and/or panic. One rarely, if ever, sees long chains of affective interchange. As these children become older, if their circumstances remain the same, one tends to observe a continuation of these patterns of fragmented, withdrawn or fearful/panicky behaviour. To the degree that cognitive and language skills emerge, they often also have these characteristics. It is not unusual, for example, for such a child to jump quickly from one piece of frenetic play to another or to become self-absorbed and escape into an inner dialogue of fragmented thoughts and words. One also observes fragmented thinking in children who at older ages become dominated by intense catastrophic emotions rather than co-regulated emotional interaction patterns. These are often the same children who treat their parents like a piece of the furniture, or who are oblivious of the effect of their behaviour on others, or impervious to someone else's distress.

To be sure, such behaviours represent a fairly extreme polarity in the spectrum of social impairments; but then, that is not so much a reason for postulating specific processing malfunctions as grounds for looking much more closely at the continuum of impaired social relatedness. For there are infinite variations in the interactional patterns that children experience, which would lead to subtle individual differences in the manner in which children perform on varying ToM tasks, if only these paradigms were varied. But the fact is that the same paradigms are repeated over and over with very little variation, which only serves to disguise the real complexity that confronts us here.

Perhaps the problem is that ToM is seen as an autonomous cognitive capacity, as opposed to being part of a more general ability for reflective thinking and empathy. What is often not fully appreciated is that there are different levels and variations in a child's capacity for reflective and empathetic thinking. For example, a child with very good visual-spatial abilities may readily identify how another person perceives a physical object from their vantage-point on the other side of the room, but be unable to anticipate how another person would feel in a given situation. The opposite also holds true. Some children who are very social and are able to intuit how other people feel are unable to intuit how they might perceive physical objects from another vantage-point.

The same holds true for understanding different emotions. For example, one child might have no difficulty in the Sally Ann task yet have considerable difficulty in recognizing that the little boy is angry when he discovers that his chocolate is missing. Another child might have no trouble recognizing his anger but considerable trouble empathizing with love; and so on. And this is only a fragment of the complexity with which we are dealing. For in order to assess a child's capacity for social relatedness we have to observe that child over a considerable length of time in varying contexts with varying partners. And to understand the reasons for whatever the constrictions we observe, we not only need to identify the child's various processing strengths and weaknesses but also capture a sense of the child's developmental history.

Finally, the same point applies to the basic Sally-Ann paradigm; for children vary in their capacity to disengage attention from a focal object (Hughes and Russell, 1993), and, as we have shown elsewhere (Bialystok, Sherry, Shanker and Codd, 2003), in their ability to inhibit or screen out non-salient information. The fact that young children or children with autism have so much trouble on tasks that require both conceptual and response inhibition is entirely what one would expect on the above developmental model; for the ability to attend to salient information and adapt to the rapid shifts that characterize social communication is one of the main effects of experiencing countless sustained affective interactions (see Greenspan and Shanker, 2004, ch. 2).

By no means does such an argument diminish the significance of the sorts of anomalies with which we began this chapter. But they cease to appear as signs of simple system malfunctions, and come rather to be seen as extreme conditions in a continuum of constrictions characteristic of human functioning in general. Once we understand their history, these anomalies not only lose their appeal as a potential key to discovering genetic modules, but much more importantly, they guide us in our efforts to help children with severe deficits to overcome their challenges.

Such an argument may also account for the phenomenon of 'mirror neurons'. It has been suggested that failures in 'mirror neuron' systems – neurons which selectively fire to both execution and observation of actions – are responsible for the theory of mind deficits seen in autism (see Oberman and Ramachandran, 2007, for a review). The problem is that, even if it should be established that a 'mirror neuron' deficit places a child at risk of being on a developmental pathway leading to autism, the seriousness of this deficit will be mediated by the child's developmental history.

It must always be born in mind that what the qualifier 'at risk' really means is that between a biological deficit and a downstream outcome are the countless interactions that enhance or inhibit the development of those neural systems that, in adults suffering from some disorder, are seen to be underdeveloped or hypo-functioning. What the study of typical development has taught us is that learned experiences are critical for laying down additional pathways in the infant's developing brain, which enable higher and higher levels of experiential organization. What the study of autism has taught us is that children robbed of these critical learning experiences – for whatever reason – not only do not develop 'mind-reading' skills, but do not develop the underlying central nervous system capacity for higher and higher levels of organization (see Greenspan and Shanker, 2004).

Thus, a child's capacity to regulate and differentiate their emotions is literally bound up, neurophysiologically, with their ability to know what others are thinking and feeling. What Gallese has discovered is that our motor system 'resonates' when we observe another agent performing an action (as if we ourselves were performing that very action). Gallese has further speculated that the same principle may apply to our abilities to engage in social communication (Gallese, 2000) and to empathize with other agents (Gallese, 2001). And indeed, it has recently been reported that our motor system 'resonates' when another person is speaking (Watkins, Strafella and Paus, 2003). According to the model sketched in this chapter, these 'mirroring' processes begin very early, and are enhanced by the child's earliest co-regulated interactions with her caregivers. Future research should establish the same sorts of 'resonance' for all the other forms of nonverbal communication involved in understanding other minds, and for the development of empathy. One of the most interesting questions that will need to be addressed here, however, is whether these 'mirroring processes' are the basis for these various forms of 'resonance', as some have speculated, or in fact the consequence of the co-regulated interactions that take place between infant and caregiver, which are guided by various forms of affect signalling (Greenspan and Shanker, 2004).

The scientific exploration of developmental pathways

We suggested at the start of this chapter that modularity theorists can be likened to geologists scouring the landscape of developmental disorders for signs of processing malfunctions. To take this analogy a step further; like geologists, they seek to infer developmental processes from the settled land-forms they can examine. That is, the modularity view of the neural systems involved in a psychological disorder is almost entirely derived from neural imaging performed on adult subjects with the disorder.

There are clearly regularities in the systems affected in adults with a specific disorder, although these can be extremely complex and subtle. Modularity theorists quickly jumped to the conclusion that what we learn from studying these neural regularities in adults is how evolutionary pressures produced genetically encoded neural systems for specific tasks (Barkow, Cosmides and Tooby, 1992; Pinker, 1997). But in recent years neuroconstructivists have begun to document how the structural regularities seen in the adult brain are the result of psychological experiences and the fact that the different kinds of cells in different neural systems turn out to be better suited for specific kinds of tasks (e.g., the fusiform gyrus for processing facial expressions of emotion; see Karmiloff-Smith 1998). Hence the topographical regularities seen in the adult brain are very much the result of a fundamental synthesis between experiential and neurological factors.

Furthermore, one can never exclude, *a priori* as it were, the possibility of altering a child's neurobiological developmental trajectory. In studying the effect of 'cascading constraints' (Lewis, 2005), one is looking at how changes in the cortex and subcortex involve a narrowing of developmental freedom. But while a neurological deficit constrains the scope of future developmental possibilities, this does not entail that the child's developmental trajectory is fixed. What is missing in any linear account of how biological deficits impinge on developmental interactions is precisely this question of how one might change a developmental trajectory through therapy, early intervention and so on.

Indeed, what is missing in the sort of mechanistic account entailed by modularity theory is the powerful effect that positive affect can have on a child's developmental trajectory. At any given point of development, the child's brain may constrain what is possible in her 'zone of proximal development', but the child's motivation, interest, curiosity, pleasure, desire and the like may enable her to exert the effort required to make the leap required for that next step in development, which in turn may force her brain to develop the connections needed for the task at hand.

Herein lies the most fruitful metaphor for understanding the direction in which developmental science is heading: it is not seeking to discover a set of 'genetic blueprints' that were 'formed down during the Pleistocene', but rather exploring what developmental possibilities for children might be opened up in the future. That is, the goal today is to understand the pathways that lead to a child's cognitive, communicative, social, emotional and physical well-being; the factors that impede or cause deviations from these pathways; and the experiences that can mitigate the developmental consequences of these deviations.

Notes

1 This chapter is suffused with the ideas, insights and writings of Stanley Greenspan, with whom I have worked on these problems for the past few years. In *The First Idea* Greenspan and I develop the thesis presented in this chapter in much greater detail (see Greenspan and Shanker, 2004). I am also deeply indebted to Barbara King, and to Ljiljana Radenovic, who first brought to my attention the fascinating parallels between current views of mind-reading and the seventeenth-century doctrine of sign-reading.

2 This is a fascinating reversal of the penetrating example with which Victoria McGeer begins her highly insightful paper on autism and ToM (see McGeer, 2002).

3 Interestingly, we can see a residue of these earlier beliefs in the initial attitudes towards facilitated communication.

4 Recall the original meaning of *silly*.

5 For more on the doctrine of 'signatures', see Foucault (1989, pp. 25–30).

6 The theory in question is said to be that: the mind is private; mind is distinct from body; the mind represents reality; minds are possessed by others; and thoughts are different from things (see Baron-Cohen, 1989, 1995; Frith 1989; Perner, Frith, Leslie and Leekam, 1989; Wellman 1990).

7 As Uta Frith explains in *Autism: Explaining the Enigma*: 'The failure of many of the autistic children [in Hobson's classic face-reading studies, see Hobson, 1986] [...] are proof of some specific difficulty in emotion recognition which is independent of general intellectual ability. The question is whether these results point to an irreducible deficit in the innate ability to understand expressions of emotions. There is much evidence that there is such an innate ability in all higher animals and it could be argued that this ability in people is closely related to an innate mechanism that permits affect relationships between people' (Frith 1989, p. 148).

8 See Bell (1970); Emde, Biringen, Clyman and Openheim (1991); Greenspan (1979 and 1997).

9 See Greenspan (1992) and Greenspan and Wieder (1998b).

10 Most of the children in this group, even the ones with precocious reading or math skills, continued to demonstrate some degree of either gross or fine motor challenges.

8

Who *Really* Needs a 'Theory' of Mind?: Insights into the Development of Social Understanding Drawn from the Autobiographical Writings of High-Functioning Individuals with an Autism Spectrum Disorder

Emma Williams

Introduction

According to the original Theory-Theory account of social cognition, children develop a succession of theories of mind that, just like scientific theories, postulate abstract coherent mental entities and laws, and provide predictions, interpretations and explanations. These, in turn, enable them to interact successfully with other people. Individuals with autism or Asperger's syndrome are said to be unable to do this.

This chapter presents evidence from personal accounts, written by individuals diagnosed with either high-functioning autism or Asperger's syndrome, that turn the Theory-Theory explanation on its head. These autobiographical writings suggest that it is individuals with autism, *not* typical children or adults, whose approach to understanding other people can best be characterized as scientific and rule-based. Moreover, the adoption of a logical, rule-based approach to understanding other people by those with a high-functioning Autism Spectrum Disorder leads not to successful social relationships, as the Theory-Theory account would predict, but instead to inflexibility and frequent social breakdown. I will argue that we do not usually have to *theorize* that other people have minds in order to understand and relate to them. Our ability to make sense of other people develops gradually from the earliest months of life in the course of our active, affectively patterned engagement with those around us in many different situational contexts. It is this, not any 'theory', which underpins our skill in negotiating day-to-day social interactions.

For the past two decades autism has provided a model for exploring the development of our understanding of other people as mental beings: a model which, according to some, has profoundly shaped conceptual thinking in this field (Frith and Happé, 1999). The ability to make sense of other people is said to require the capacity to reflect on mental states, and it is widely accepted that autism is characterized by a specific difficulty in this area (Baron-Cohen, 1995).

Autism is a devastating developmental disorder, which affects around one in 100 people if you include all diagnoses that fall within the autism spectrum (Baird, Simonoff, Pickles, Chandler et al., 2006). It was first identified as a distinct entity in the 1940s, almost simultaneously, by Leo Kanner (1943) in Baltimore, and Hans Asperger (1944) in Vienna, who both cited 'aloneness' as its cardinal feature (Sacks, 1995). At the present time no biological marker has been found, and diagnosis is made on the basis of the co-occurrence of certain patterns of behaviour, which onset before 36 months. These include abnormalities in the areas of social development, communicative development and imagination, together with marked repetitive or obsessional behaviour or unusual, narrow interests (American Psychiatric Association (APA), 1994; World Health Organization (ICD-10), 1993).

The predominant view in the developmental literature is that it is the apparent inability of individuals with autism to think about *thought* that explains their impairments in social relations, communication and imagination, all behaviours which are central to the diagnosis. More specifically, they are said to lack a 'Theory of Mind' (Baron-Cohen, Leslie and Frith, 1985). The term 'Theory of Mind' (ToM) refers to the ability to attribute independent mental states (such as beliefs, desires, intentions, imagination, and emotions) to the self and other people in order to explain and predict their behaviour (Premack and Woodruff, 1978). According to Baron-Cohen (2000a) the capacity to reflect on the content of one's own and other minds, in turn, enables us to interact successfully with those around us. The cognitive processes underlying the development of a theory of mind are still a matter of heated debate (Gopnik, Capps and Meltzoff, 2000; Leslie, 2000). However two positions have dominated the field. Whilst both argue for the development of a theory of mind, they disagree as regards the extent to which this is hard-wired or genetically programmed to mature over time. The first explanation, the modular view, is that evolution has equipped the brain with a theory of mind mechanism (ToMM), that helps the child to attend to the invisible states of other people, and which may be underpinned by a separate brain system (Leslie, 1987; Baron-Cohen, 1995; Frith and Happé, 1999). In the second, 'Theory Theory of Mind (TToM)', a young child is said to use their general intellectual capacities to develop a common-sense theory of mental states, in the same way that the scientist does by examining evidence and testing hypotheses (Wellman, 1990; Perner, 1991). It is this second approach which will be primarily addressed in this chapter.

Theory Theory of Mind

The Theory Theory of Mind approach draws close analogies between scientific theory and children's folk psychology (Astington and Gopnik, 1991; Perner, 1991; Gopnik and Wellman, 1994). Our ordinary understanding of the mind is said to proceed by the formation, revision and replacement of successive theories of the mind (Gopnik and Wellman, 1992; Gopnik, 1999; Gopnik, Capps and Meltzoff, 2000). Children are said to understand the world by constructing coherent views of it and changing those views in light of the evidence they encounter in their daily lives. Indeed, it is argued that they are better theorists than adult scientists!: 'we would say not that children are little scientists but that scientists are big, and relatively slow, children' (Gopnik and Wellman, 1992, p. 168).

Theories are abstract; they postulate hypothetical entities, such as gravity, that provide a separate causal-explanatory level of analysis to account for the things that we actually observe, like bodies moving in a particular way in relationship to each other. They also consist of theoretical constructs, which do not work independently from each other, but in systems characterized by interrelated laws or structures. Likewise, children are claimed to postulate abstract, coherent mental entities (e.g., beliefs and desires) and laws (e.g., 'if an agent desires X, and sees it exists, he will do things to get it'), which together enable the child to make predictions, interpretations and explanations about their own behaviour and that of other people (Gopnik, 1999).

It is not only in terms of their content, though, that children's understanding of mind is likened to a scientific theory. An interaction between theory formation and theory-testing is said to drive the development of knowledge in children, just as it drives the historical development of knowledge in science. Theories develop and undergo change as a result of both internal structural factors within the theory, a drive for simplicity for example, and external factors such as the accumulation of evidence which confirms or runs counter to it. In the same way children's views of the world are said to change in light of their active accumulation of counter-evidence, the gathering of new data, and performing of experiments.

Theory Theorists do not, however, argue that children construct their theories simply from 'raw', incoherent, data. Rather, they suggest, the infant begins life with an innate 'starting state' theory (Gopnik and Wellman, 1992). In support of this hypothesis Gopnik, Capps and Meltzoff (2000) cite evidence of infants' abilities to imitate facial gestures and their tendency to pay special attention to stimuli relating to people (e.g., voice, attentional gestures), arguing that these are indicative of the existence of some sort of beliefs about the relationship between self and other already being in place at birth. Such beliefs are said to provide an initial conception of the mind, which undergoes radical revision and reconstruction as the infant learns more about their own experiences and behaviours and those of other people. Gopnik and Wellman (1992) contrast this with the ToMM account proposed by Leslie (1987) where a maturational mechanism is said to set limits on what a ToM might be like.

Theory Theory and autism

According to the Theory-Theory approach, three things are required for the normal development of an understanding of mind: an innate starting theory, an innate general theory-forming capacity, and data from the environment. Proponents of this approach suggest that autism may involve a deficit in one, or both, of the two innate structures posited (Gopnik, Capps and Meltzoff, 2000). It could be, and this is said to be the most likely possibility, that infants with autism have no initial theory of persons, or if they do, that this starts from a different place than that of the typically developing infant, with cascading negative consequences for subsequent development. Gopnik and colleagues (2000) contend that the comparative inability of young children with autism to copy gestures (both facial and manual) and their failure to pay special attention to stimuli relating to other people (Dawson, Meltzoff, Osterling, Rinaldi and Brown, 1998) suggests a basic deficit in responding to and making links between themselves and those around them. An alternative possibility put forward is that individuals with autism may have a more general difficulty with theoretical thinking itself, rather than a more specific problem with Theory of Mind. In other words, individuals with autism may never come to understand the mind in a genuinely theoretical way, even though they acquire a great deal of knowledge about human behaviour. Gopnik and colleagues (2000) substantiate this argument by referring to the findings from their recent study, examining the deeper understanding of 'folk biology' in a group of high-functioning children with autism. They found that the children with autism were more often incorrect in their classification of animacy/inanimacy, compared to typical children matched for verbal IQ, and showed a less sophisticated understanding of biological concepts in their reasoning about why things were inanimate or animate.

Insights from high-functioning people with an ASD

Argument of this chapter

According to the Theory-Theory approach, the great majority of us successfully *develop* a theory, or more accurately theories, about minds in a way that is akin to scientists, with the exception of those with autism who are simply unable to do so. As I have already indicated, my aim is to turn this argument on its head. I contend that it is misleading to present the task of achieving social understanding as a logical one, similar to that of a detached scientist observing behaviour and working out what is going on. I suggest that typical children do not have to *theorize* that there are minds as they have an intuitive grasp arising initially from mutual, co-regulated, interaction with other people. The problem is not how children develop more and more sophisticated and appropriate ToMs but how they enter into more and more enriched, intricate, and coordinated interactions with those around them. However, I argue that high-functioning individuals with autism *do need* to engage in such theorizing about other minds, in the sense of explicit intellectualizing and inferring if-then rules from close observations of everyday behaviour, if they are to bridge the gap that exists between themselves and other people. Failure to do this would leave them unable to explain and predict human behaviour well enough to function, with at least some success, in social situations.

In support of this proposal, this chapter presents findings from an interpretative phenomenological analysis (IPA) (Smith, 1996; Smith, Flowers, and Osborn, 1997; Smith, Jarman and Osborn, 1999) of ten published autobiographical accounts written by high-functioning individuals, diagnosed with an Autism Spectrum Disorder.

IPA study

Autism is a complex and heterogeneous disorder. As such, its manifestations cover a wide spectrum and individuals may have an IQ at any level (Happé, 1999; Wing, 1981). Whilst some of those falling within this diagnostic category may be silent and aloof, have a low IQ, and be locked into stereotypical rocking and hand flapping, others are relatively high-functioning, with intact speech and language skills (albeit pedantic and verbose), along with rarefied special interests. Such individuals may have a desire to interact with other people, but be awkward and odd in the way they make their approach (Happé, 1999). By diagnostic convention, if an individual has an IQ in the normal range (or above), they are said to have high-functioning autism (HFA). If they meet all of the criteria for HFA apart from the one specifying a history of clinically significant language delay and/or communicative difficulties, they are said to have Asperger's syndrome (AS) (Baron-Cohen, 2002).

Analytic strategy

The ten autobiographical accounts of individuals diagnosed with either high-functioning autism (HFA) or Asperger's syndrome (AS) were analysed for recurrent themes relating to the individual's understanding of, and relationships with, other people using IPA (see Table 1). Themes emerged both within and across the individual narratives. The process of identifying these themes involved several steps. The first step comprised repeated reading of Temple Grandin's (1996) autobiography. Anything significant or interesting relating to her personal experiences of trying to understand and interact

Table 1   Diagnosis, gender and occupation of authors

Case	Diagnosis	Gender	Occupation
TG	HFA	F	Animal Scientist
ES	HFA	M	Former computer programmer
LH-W	AS	F	Academic (Education) and researcher
DP-H	AS	F	Professor of Anthropology
D	AS	M	Psychology student
J	HFA	M	Anthropology student
GB	AS	M	Unemployed
WL	AS	F	Social worker and adult educator
JS	AS	M	Counsellor and adult educator
TMcK	HFA	M	Writer and Poet

with other people was noted in the left margin. These comments included summaries of the content, associations, connections and preliminary inter-pretations. Grandin's narrative was chosen as the initial one to work from for a number of reasons. Her work inspired the project, it was the most extensive and detailed, and Grandin herself is probably the best known individual diagnosed with HFA. In the next step the text was reread and any emergent themes identified, recorded in the right margin and tentatively organized. These were checked back with the data to ensure that any interpretations made were consistent with the written account. Attention was then focused on the themes themselves to define them in more detail and establish how they interlinked with each other. Following this, the same process was repeated with the personal narratives of the remaining ten individuals, with the initial theme list being edited, added to and modified accordingly. The themes were then ordered so as to produce a coherent research narrative.

Analysis of the autobiographies

Analysis of the ten autobiographical accounts revealed four themes, which emerged as recurrent understandings across all accounts. These were con-cerned specifically with the difficulties the writers experienced in trying to relate to other people, and the coping strategies they devised to try and address these. They include the sense of a wide, unbridgeable, gap between themselves and other people, an awareness of the existence of social and emotional experiences of others that were inaccessible to them, the coping strategies adopted to help negotiate social situations, and the limitations of those strategies in guiding successful interaction.

Distance between self and other people

Most of the authors wrote about the great distance that they felt existed between themselves and other people. However, whilst this was a recurrent theme, there were differences in terms of how the individual authors conceptualized this gap. These are detailed below under the sub-themes: detached scientist, alien and onlooker.

Detached scientist.   Temple describes herself as a detached scientist, recording observational data. She comments that this is not how she thinks things should be, but that it is a position she has adopted as a result of not knowing how to relate to other people:

> When other students swooned over the Beatles, I called this an ISP – an interesting sociological phenomenon. I was a scientist trying to figure out the ways of the natives. I wanted to participate, but I didn't know how. In my high school diary I wrote: 'One should not always be a watcher, the cold impersonal observer – but instead should participate.' Even today, my thinking is from the vantage point of an observer.
>
> (Temple Grandin, 1996, p. 132)

Liane also likens herself to a scientist collecting observational data but, unlike Temple, conveys a sense of fascination, rather than discomfort:

> I was captivated with the way their hands moved when they spoke, how they would bend them into shapes that looked like little buildings or twirl them about as if the hands were the message. I watched people like a scientist watches an experiment. Never did I feel like I was looking in a mirror. Always did I feel that I was here and they were there.
>
> (Liane Holliday Willey, 1999, p. 42)

Jim[1] describes how, after reading a number of anthropologists' studies of 'strange cultures and far-away lands' (Prince-Hughes, 2002, p. 67), he decided to deal with his autism by becoming an 'anthropologist' and adopting the same methodology to study the 'normal' culture he lived in:

> I can remember thinking that the worlds they [anthropologists] studied were as strange to them as the world around was to me – so the same methodology should teach me about my world.
>
> (Jim, in Prince-Hughes, 2002, p. 68)

Alien from outer space.   In his autobiography Edgar argues that Temple Grandin's description of herself to Oliver Sacks (1995) as 'an anthropologist on Mars' (p. 233), should be amended to read 'an anthropologist *from* Mars' (Edgar Schneider, 1999, p. 99) if it is to fully capture the extent of the gulf he feels exists between himself and other people. Jim Sinclair describes himself as an extraterrestrial in need of an 'orientation manual' (in Schopler and Mesibov, 1992, p. 302) and Dawn comments that likening herself to an alien helped her make sense of her predicament:

> I was an alien from outer space. It solved so many problems and explained so much about me, both to myself and my peers. I [...] prayed for my *real* people to come and get me in a flying saucer and take me home where I could no longer be laughed at, seriously assaulted, confused and awkward and odd.
>
> (Dawn, in Prince-Hughes, 2002, p. 113)

The Onlooker.   A number of writers describe themselves as onlookers to the human interaction that they observe going on around them. Both Wendy's and Garry's personal narratives convey a sense of an individual left standing still, whilst the rest of the world moves on:

> One of the best ways of understanding what autism is like is to imagine yourself as a perpetual onlooker. Much of the time life is like a video, a moving film I can observe but cannot reach. The world passes in front of me shielded by glass.
>
> (Wendy Lawson, 2001, p. 1)

> It was as if I was a seed frozen in time. The other seeds were growing and developing and I was getting further and further out of step and never looked like catching up.
>
> (Garry Burge, in Prince-Hughes, 2002, pp. 2–3)

In both accounts there is a sense that the gap between themselves and other people is unbridgeable. Wendy describes herself as being behind a sheet of glass, which she cannot reach through, and Garry sees himself as a seed that is 'frozen', whilst the other 'seeds' continue to grow and develop, so that the gulf between them and him continues to widen. Other writers share this sense of being an onlooker, but present it as more of a positive choice in the sense that it is a situation that they clearly enjoy, or feel more comfortable with than actually participating in interaction:

> In the tree I could watch everything around me without having to interact [...] I was an avid observer. I was enthralled with the nuances of people's actions.
>
> (Liane Holliday Willey, 1999, p. 26)

> A [computer] system with multiple lines, it provides an ideal atmosphere to observe social interaction without leaving the home. I have found the situation that I am most comfortable in is one where I am with others and alone at the same time.
>
> (Thomas McKlean, 1994, p. 49)

Social and emotional cues are 'hidden' or inaccessible

Most of the personal accounts revealed difficulties in picking up both the nonverbal and verbal social and affective cues that help mediate human interaction, such as particular gestures, physical changes, facial expressions and tone of voice. This theme encompasses the following sub-themes: the mysterious/enigmatic nature of social interaction; difficulty in picking up cues that are 'hidden' or uninterpretable; an inability to pick up social and emotional cues due to sensory problems; and development of the ability to 'pick up' social and emotional cues.

The enigmatic nature of social interaction

Some of the writers describe human interaction as completely mysterious to them: 'Humanity is basically nothing but an enigma to me' (Thomas McKlean, 1994, p. 50); 'For me, the ordinary interactions of my daily social experiences have always been a great mystery.' (Wendy Lawson, 2001, p. 8). Liane's discussion of the difficulties she faced in the arena of intimate relationships echoes this sense of something mysterious and hidden, but she adds the point that she deliberately chose not to look too closely at it as this caused anxiety:

> The men I had been dating were nice men who shared some of my interests and hobbies, but with each of them there was always an unspoken and unseen something that stood between us – like the curtain that kept the truth of the Wizard from the people of Oz. I never gave a thought to what the curtain was hiding because when I did, it led me to distraction.
>
> (Liane Holliday Willey, 1999, p. 78)

Difficulty in accessing 'hidden' social and emotional cues

Some of the other writers talk of being aware that 'something' is going on, but that they are unable to interpret it: 'I sometimes notice the cues but I don't know what they mean' (Jim, in Prince-Hughes, 2002, p. 300). Both Temple and Edgar use metaphors relating to music in their efforts to try to explain to the reader their feeling of being unable to 'tune into' the emotional resonance that they see as characterizing social interactions:

> Real-life emotions appear to me to consist of things felt in an unexpressed manner, and with another person also feeling them, almost in the manner of sympathetic vibrations at a resonant frequency.
>
> (Edgar Schneider, 1999, p. 52)

> During the last couple of years I have become more aware of a kind of electricity that goes on between people, which is much subtler that overt anger, happiness, or fear. I have observed that when several people are

together and having a good time, then speech, and laughter follow a rhythm [...] The problem is that I can't follow this rhythm.

(Temple Grandin, 1996, p. 91)

It is not only cues relating to body language that are said to be difficult to pick up. Liane describes the difficulties she had in accessing the sub-text of verbal conversations:

> I understood their language, knew if they had made grammatical errors in their speech, and I was able to make replies to anything that was spoken to me; but I never came to hear what they were really saying [...] Suffice to say that, at this point, I was unable to read between the lines. Subtext and innuendo may as well have been birds flying by my window.

(Liane Holliday Willey, 1999, p. 56)

Inability to pick up social and emotional cues due to sensory problems

Most writers comment on the disruptive effect their sensory problems have on sustaining social engagement. Not only do they report that they are hyper- or hypo-sensitive to everyday sounds, smells, tastes, lights and textures easily tolerated by us (see Shanker and Stieben, Chapter 7 this volume), they also comment that they actually perceive things, including the social cues that mediate interaction, differently, and have difficulty switching their attention between visual and auditory senses:

> Since people with autism require much more time than others to shift their attention between auditory and visual stimuli, they find it more difficult to follow rapidly changing, complex social interactions.

(Temple Grandin, 1996, p. 138)

> I still have problems in groups where there is too much information going on, or where the informational flow is too fast. I simply can't shift my attentional focus quickly enough to the relevant part of the inter-action process. Consequently, I miss a lot of vital information needed to interpret social messages. There is no such thing as adequate delayed social interaction. One either is quick enough to keep up, or one is weird and socially disabled.

(Darius, in Prince-Hughes, 2002, p. 25)

Jim Sinclair attributes his inability to pick up social signals to the fact that in a sensory sense he interacts differently with the world as compared to other people: 'Sometimes I'm not aware of social cues because of the same perceptual problems that affect my understanding of other aspects of the environment' (Jim Sinclair, in Schopler and Mesibov, 1992, p. 300).

Development of the ability to 'read' emotional cues

It is clear from a number of accounts that the reported lack of awareness of and inability to pick-up on the subtle social and emotional signals that oil the wheels of human interaction are not necessarily unchangeable. For example, whilst Liane had difficulty in her college days in tuning into emotional signals, she improved over time in the context of a stable relationship:

> I could not intrinsically or intuitively fathom what lay in the shadows, things I can now identify as the cornerstones for patience, flexibility, empathy and objectiveness. Before I came to terms with myself, these emotions were held at bay, nearly in my vision but just beyond my reach. It took years with my husband before I could swim into each one.
>
> (Liane Holliday Willey, 1999, p. 78)

Wendy reports that careful study of the body language of other people has enabled her to distinguish between different emotions:

> I have learnt to recognise the subtle differences between anger, frustration and disappointment, and understand why I feel these things. By studying an individual's posture, actions, voice tone, and expression, I can now usually work out what they are feeling. The hard work of studying the reactions of others and recognizing that people respond differently to different emotions has been very beneficial to me.
>
> (Wendy Lawson, 2001, pp. 8–9)

Coping strategies

Most of the writers comment on the fact that they had consciously set about devising explicit strategies designed to help them negotiate social situations in the absence of social intuition that we take for granted: 'Most people take the routines of life and day-to-day connections for granted. The fact that they can see, hear, smell, touch and relate to others is "normal"' (Wendy Lawson, 2001, pp. 2–3). These strategies are detailed below under the sub-themes: studying other people's behaviour, the imposition of rules, and the use of a 'visual library'.

Studying other people's behaviour

Linking back to Wendy's comments, cited earlier, regarding the fact that her close study of people's body language had enabled her to differentiate certain emotions from each other, a number of writers made similar allusions to using their study of other people's behaviour to guide their own actions:

> I had no insight into social conventions which regular people take for granted [...] I find myself studying young people to see how they work, talk to one another, what interests them and how they dress.
>
> (Garry Burge, in Prince-Hughes, 2002, pp. 2–3)

Sometimes, though, the help of someone else was required to 'interpret' these 'findings':

> What can I do better to fit in with mainstream society? I think I have found a possible solution. I have been lately very careful to observe society and interaction. There are many ways that people communicate and many things that they do while they are together that simply make no sense to me. Sometimes I make a note of these things I see, and then I contact someone who knows me well enough to answer my question about it in a way that I can understand.
>
> (Thomas McKlean, 1994, p. 50)

The imposition of rules

As a result of their lack of social intuition several of the writers reported that they had devised their own system of rules to help them to manage social situations:

> Since I don't have any social intuition, I rely on pure logic, like an expert computer program to guide my behaviour. I categorise rules according to logical importance. It is a complex algorithmic decision-making tree [...] I constructed a decision-making program for whether rules could be broken, by classifying wrongdoing into 3 categories: 'really bad', 'sins of the system', and 'illegal but not bad'. Rules classified as 'really bad' (e.g. stealing, injuring another person [...]) should never be broken. The 'illegal but not bad' rules can often be broken with little consequence, e.g. speeding. The 'sins of the system' covers rules that have very stiff penalties for seemingly illogical reasons. Using my system has helped me negotiate every new situation I enter.
>
> (Temple Grandin, 1996, p. 103)

> I have had to develop, in order to function in society, a bit of thou-shalt-not and thou-must (what mathematicians call the 'cookbook approach').
>
> (Edgar Schneider, 1999, p. 95)

Jim talks about using 'task analysis' to deal with social 'tasks':

> While I was busy trying to institute permanent changes in my behaviour, I developed an interest in lithic technology – stone tools. Writers spoke

of 'tool kits'; it seemed they were combining the physical technology and the cognitive skills under this single heading. I began to consider adapting this to my needs. Such a 'tool kit' would consist for my purposes, of a package of cognitive skills and behaviours to meet the needs of the situation. This led me to task analysis. For example in order to make coffee I need to: fill the reservoir on the coffee maker, put a filter in the basket, measure the coffee grounds [...] In situations calling for social interaction, a similar package or 'module of behaviour' would allow me to carry out social 'tasks'.

(Jim, in Prince-Hughes, 2002, p. 70)

Both Temple and Edgar recognize that such rule-based strategies are very different from those generally used. They suggest that the major difference lies in the fact that the coping strategies they have developed are based on logic, rather than emotion:

There is a process of using my intellect and logical decision making for every social decision. Emotion doesn't guide my decision; it is pure computing.

(Temple Grandin, 1996, p. 103)

My thought processes [...] have been mathematically logical. I have been told, by more than one person and on more than one occasion, that I put too high a premium on logic and rationality, giving short shrift to the emotions.

(Edgar Schneider, 1999, p. 20)

Jim Sinclair echoes these thoughts, adding the point that these are adopted as a result of the lack of what he calls 'basic instinct': 'I have to use cognitive strategies to make up for basic instincts I don't have' (Jim Sinclair, in Schopler and Mesibov, 1992, p. 302).

Not all of the writers who reported using rules to guide their behaviour said that they had devised their *own* rules. Dawn describes how she adopted and became obsessed with the already extant rules at school, in conjunction with watching how her fellow schoolmates behaved:

In first grade I became increasingly obsessed with rules. I studied people's behaviours and actions and read written rules carefully to try to make sense of my school community and fellow human beings.

(Dawn Prince-Hughes, 2002, p. 110)

The use of a 'visual library'

Both Temple and Liane report making use of their superior visual memories to keep a 'record' of past social situations which they could access at a later date in order to search for solutions to new situations that they had encountered. Liane likens this to having a photo album which she searches to find a 'reliable picture to guide me along' (Liane Holliday Willey, 1999, p. 85). Temple describes herself as having a library of video 'clips' which she can mentally 'play-back':

> Over time I have built up a tremendous library of memories of past experiences, TV, movies, and newspapers to spare me the social embarrassment caused by my autism, and I use these to guide the decision process in a totally logical way [...] Earlier in my life, my logical decisions were often wrong because they were based on insufficient data. Today they are much better, because my memory contains more information.
>
> (Temple Grandin, 1996, p. 137)

Limited success of alternative strategies

A recurrent theme throughout the writings is the inadequacy of the cognitive strategies devised by the writer's in helping them deal successfully with the variety and complexity of the social situations that they encounter daily. Jim reports on the failure of his 'module of behaviour' when he applied it for the first time in a basketball game. In this game, he knocked another player over and did not realize why this upset the other players. His response was to make revisions to his initial module, with the help of a 'neurotypical' friend, to deal with ethics:

> we classified things that most would consider 'manners'. None of it made sense to me, despite her attempts to explain, so we set some tentative rules and some default modes. If I'm unsure how to behave I can follow these rules.
>
> (Jim, in Prince-Hughes, 2002, pp. 70–1)

Temple reports how, despite being equipped with both rules and her visual library, her responses to very unfamiliar or unexpected situations are still too slow, and she is left with feelings of fear and panic:

> I still have problems with rapid responses to unexpected social situations [...] I have no problems if I mentally rehearse every scenario, but I still panic if I'm not prepared for a new situation, especially where I travel to a foreign country where I am unable to communicate. Since I can't rely on my library of social cues, I feel very helpless when I can't speak the language. Often I withdraw.
>
> (Temple Grandin, 1996, p. 60)

Liane describes how her 'photo album' of past situation was unable to guide her behaviour in new situations:

> For some reason I cannot recall how to act as easily as I can recall how I did act. It is as if when I look backwards I see a photo album filled with vivid images and shapes, but when I try to look forward I cannot call to mind one reliable picture to guide me along.
>
> (Liane Holliday Willey, 1999, p. 85)

She reports that when this strategy failed she ended up rehearsing every possible scenario that she could think of. Reflecting on this, she comments:

> Of course things rarely turn out exactly as I had rehearsed and so I suppose it will never be possible for me to always know how to act. The human saga is just not reliable enough for me to predict.
>
> (Liane Holliday Willey, 1999, p. 85)

Liane goes on to highlight the fact that sometimes social situations appear to be so complex that they are not easily dealt with by the use of a few rules:

> Do I really have to talk on the phone to anyone if I think the conversation is boring or a waste of my time? If there is a lapse in the conversation, am I supposed to hang up or tell a joke or just sit there? What if I like the person well enough, but I decide I can't stand one of their behaviours or habits? Can I tell them right away or do I have to wait a while, and if so, how long, and if not, what am I supposed to do to keep from focussing on their annoying habit? The questions are endless, and the concerns mountain high. This is why human relationships usually take me beyond my limits.
>
> (Liane Holliday Willey, 1999, pp. 68–9)

Both Dawn and Wendy describe how the fixed rules they tried to impose on the behaviour of other children proved socially disastrous:

> Often what they said or recorded as the rules were, in fact, not standard human practice. I began policing the playground to make sure students did not break the rules [...] Needless to say this did not go over well with my peers.
>
> (Dawn Prince-Hughes, 2002, p. 110)

> [I lacked] the know-how of friendship building. Most people felt uncomfortable with my egocentric and eccentric behaviour. I wanted things to go by the rules – and my rules at that! My clumsy efforts usually ended in trauma.
>
> (Wendy Lawson, 2001, p. 16)

Wendy later goes on to report a difficulty in understanding the more flexible rules written by people who do not have an Autism Spectrum Disorder:

> There are days when just trying to make sense of the rules for social inter-action is too difficult. It is especially so when we take into account that individuals often write their own rules! For example it's fine to take your clothes off to have a bath, but only a model takes her clothes off for the photographer; or you can laugh at that story, even though it's about a fat lady, because it's a joke.
>
> (Wendy Lawson, 2001, p. 98)

Difficulties in generalizing

One of the most common themes which emerged from the different per-sonal narratives was the difficulty each of these people had in generalizing their learning, and their rules, from one situation to another. Wendy, for example, says of those with AS: 'they may learn the rules for a particu-lar situation but will not know how to translate that into other situations' (Wendy Lawson, 2001, p. 100). Liane discusses the problem of generaliza-tion in the context of the difficulties she faces being a parent with AS:

> One of my parenting problems is grounded in my inability to generalise information to specific situations. I am only a good problem solver under two circumstances: if there is no real right or wrong answer, for instance when I am writing a creative fiction story; and if there are very clear-cut answers, for example the kind that can be found when I design and con-duct research studies. When flexible variables affect the situation, things like human emotions, social mores, hidden agendas, and personal biases, I am left without a clue [...] I approach each new obstacle we come to as if I have never met anything like it before.
>
> (Liane Holliday Willey, 1999, p. 102)

Jim Sinclair and Darius both report on their difficulty in generalizing from one person to another:

> I don't have much sense of people-in-general as things to be involved with. And I don't know how to have prefabricated relationships; if I happen to be involved with some person-in-particular, I practically have to learn to talk all over again to develop a common language with that person.
>
> (Jim Sinclair, in Schopler and Mesibov, 1992, p. 300)

> I have to learn everything from the start again [if the environment changes] and the same is true if I meet someone new. Social learning does not transfer to different people or situations.
>
> (Darius, in Prince-Hughes, 2002, pp. 24–5)

Thus it appears that the general cognitive strategies employed by the writers in their heroic efforts to make some sense of their daily social encounters are not 'fit for purpose', leaving them inadequately equipped to deal with new and unexpected situations. Such strategies, some observe, do not appear to do the 'work' done by the subtle social and emotional cues they believe other people use to help them navigate the intricate complexities and nuances of social situations; signals and resonances which they report they are unable to pick up on or 'feel'.

Discussion

The nature of AS/HFA 'theorizing'

The writers with AS/HFA describe the problem they are faced with in trying to understand human interaction as one of striving to make sense of something that appears to them to be essentially mysterious and inaccessible. In their efforts to somehow get beyond and behind this enigma the approach they take is a logical one, similar to that of a detached scientist making close observations of phenomena of interest and drawing inferences from these about what is 'really' going on. Whilst the excerpts reveal that they are able to reflect on their own mental states and attribute mental states to those around them (see also Frith and Happé, 1999), a close study of the autobiographical accounts suggests that these individuals do not regularly try and make sense of other people by theorizing about mind in particular. Instead, they proceed through the systematic collection and classification of numerous examples of everyday social behaviour. Inferences are drawn from this collection of observations in the form of laws or 'if-then' rules, which they then try to apply more generally to help them understand and predict people's behaviour in any new situations they might encounter. In some cases these rules appear to be open to amendment in the face of contradictory evidence (cf. Jim's discussion of revisions made to his 'module of behaviour' when he encountered problems applying it in a basketball game, in Prince-Hughes, 2002, pp. 70–1). It is reasonable to ask whether such a scientific approach is unique to those individuals with AS/HFA who write reflective and insightful autobiographies or who are in academic/scientific occupations (as half of the sample are), and therefore is unrepresentative of the group as a whole. This does not appear to be the case. In a recent book Simon Baron-Cohen reports that, in a clinic run for adults with AS, he regularly encounters individuals who appear to be struggling to work out a huge set of rules, detailing how they should behave in each and every particular social situation: 'It is as if they were trying to write a manual for social interaction based on if-then rules, or as if they are trying to systemize social behaviour [...]' (2004, p. 141).

Both the personal accounts presented here and the observations made by Baron-Cohen (2004) based on his extensive experience of working with those who have AS/HFA, reveal how distressingly prone to failure this scientific, systemic, approach adopted by these individuals in their efforts to make sense of human interaction can be. The autobiographical narratives testify to the huge amount of effort invested, which is repaid more often than not by social breakdown rather than successful engagement. These individuals encounter a number of problems in trying to generalize from specific cases to help them deal more effectively with new social situations. A number of them apply their rules too rigidly, irrespective of context, resulting in wholesale rejection by other people. For them, the fact that other people break rules, adapt them, or even sometimes make up their own, does not make logical sense and frustrates them. Sometimes the application of a particular rule makes them pay attention to one aspect of a social situation at the expense of another, with disastrous consequences (as in the case of Jim and his first attempt to apply his 'behaviour module' to a basketball game). Whilst they find that a set of rules or visual 'cues' can often help them cope with clear-cut situations, they break down when 'flexible' human variables such as emotions are involved. Even when they have amassed a large number of these in their memory, some writers report that they still find themselves unequipped to cope with unexpected social situations. Moreover, this can itself lead to an individual being overwhelmed by the sheer number of rules that appear to be required to engage effectively with other people. As Liane argues, such strategies are not able to deal with the unpredictability, variety, creativity and complexity inherent in human interactions (Holliday Willey, 1999). This is not to say, though, that specific interactions are themselves unstructured and unpredictable, otherwise how could we explain the apparent ease with which we typically negotiate them? Rather, what it does mean is that there is no desituated, abstract, structure that informs our dealings with other people. What there is, however, is plenty of locally produced information available in the interaction itself which helps us understand other people well enough to act effectively most of the time. As Louch (1966) powerfully puts it, making sense of what people are doing and saying is a question of the local, *ad hoc*, putting of behaviour into context, not a question of inference to something hidden behind those actions: 'human conduct is a response to an incalculable variety of situations. What is important is the detail, not the general features which afford grounds for general laws' (p. 207).

This has implications for the 'Theory-Theory' view, since it follows that the postulation of a set of theoretical constructs and laws, however extensive and coherent, would not, on its own, be sufficient to allow us to cope successfully with the unpredictability and complexity of interactions with other people. There is no 'right' theory that individuals with HFA or AS could potentially arrive at which would help them out of their difficulties. Moreover, the autobiographical accounts reveal that the difficulties encountered are not so much in the learning of the rules, but in their application.

Therefore, I would suggest that even if the individuals with HFA or AS could learn all the theoretical constructs and laws precisely as specified by the Theory Theorists they would need a wisdom beyond these to be able to apply them effectively to particular social situations. To the extent that proponents of the ToMM approach to ToM (Leslie, 1987) pose the problem in the same way, suggesting that certain modules are automatically going through the moves of theorizing, but not drawing upon any wisdom apart from that theory, they are subject to this same criticism.

The expert versus the beginner

Some of the writers report that they are forced into taking a logical, empirical approach as a result of their lack of 'social intuition', and write about the frustration they experience at having to engage in such hard work when other people around them appear to interact so effortlessly. They draw a striking contrast between their own method of relating to other people and that of those who do not have AS/HFA. They view other people as being emotionally engaged with the people they are interacting with, rather than adopting a position of logical detachment. They also make a distinction between their own position of having to infer what is going on due to their sense of separation from those around them, and other people's apparently effortless ability to directly pick up on cues apparently available in the interaction they are involved in.

The comparison that Dreyfus and Dreyfus (1991) make between how an expert in a particular skill and a beginner go about their business, captures some of this distinction in social understanding and interaction between typical individuals and those with AS or HFA. In their paper, Dreyfus and Dreyfus counter the traditional view that expertise necessarily involves inference (which is the general view of those in AI and proponents of ToM). They propose instead that someone who is expert in a particular skill, who has talent and a great deal of involved experience, intuitively sees what to do without applying rules. Whilst their performance may break down in unusual circumstances, typically the expert understands, acts and learns from his or her results without any conscious awareness of that process: 'An expert's skill has become so much a part of him that he need be no more aware of it than he is of his own body' (ibid., p. 27). Dreyfus and Dreyfus (1991) go on to suggest that, in contrast to the expert, someone who is new to a skill relies more on the use of rules and facts to guide their actions (just like a pre-programmed computer), as a result of their lack of extensive situated experience.

The typical individual can be compared to the expert in terms of their ability to interact effectively and effortlessly with other people. An increasing body of researchers contend that our ability to understand the thoughts and feelings of other people, as well as our own, develops in the course of our mutual everyday, affectively patterned, interactions with other people beginning in the earliest months of life. As such our understanding is sensitive to subtle social nuances, and flexible enough to be transferred across different situations (Hobson, 1993, 2007a, b; Reddy, 2003; Reddy and Morris, 2004; Shanker, 2004a; Costall and Leudar, 2007). It is not theoretical in nature, either in the sense that we postulate and test out implicit abstract entities and laws, or in the sense of being encapsulated in a module which automatically does that theoretical work for us. However, in the absence of the kind of sustained situated empathic interaction with other people that underpins our own social 'expertise', the writers with HFA or AS are forced to engage in explicit theorizing to try and make sense of social situations.

Alternative conceptions of the development of social understanding

As we have seen, those who advocate the 'Theory-Theory' approach describe the task of achieving social understanding as a logical one, similar to that of a detached scientist observing behaviour and working out what is going on. I argue that in using scientists and what they do as a metaphor for the development of social cognition, proponents of this theory have unwittingly presented us with an 'autistic' mode of how we might come to understand other people. The position they ascribe to the young child bears a striking resemblance to the situation the writers with AS/HFA assign to themselves. The lone child is charged with the task of making an inferential leap beyond what they can actually experience of another person if they are ever to come to truly understand and relate to those around them. Since I first published this argument (Williams, 2004), Zahavi and Parnas have arrived at a similar conclusion: 'to put it somewhat ironically, the evidence suggests that autists (providing they possess a sufficiently high IQ) might be more characterized by an excessive reliance on a theory of mind (in the proper sense of the word) than by a lack of such a theory' (2005, p. 68).

In portraying the child as a 'thinker' rather than a 'doer' those advocating this position pass over what the writers with AS/HFA themselves recognize as fundamental to normal human interaction, that they are primarily characterized by emotional engagement rather than reflective detachment, and are situated not context independent. It is, as Reddy and Morris contend, 'in engagement with other people rather than in thought that people normally and fundamentally come to know other people as intentional beings' (this volume, Chapter 5, p. 103).

Proponents of both the 'Theory-Theory' and modular approaches to ToM assume that social understanding can only ever exist in the individual in the form of representations and conceptual schemas. However, another possible location is in the interaction *between* people. Reddy (1996, 2003, 2007) offers an alternative explanation for the development of self–other awareness that emphasizes continuity and the importance of active affective engagement in early second-person reciprocal interactions (see Reddy and Morris, this volume for more on this argument). Rather than the ability to share attention to a third object and capacity to understand and practise deception indicating a sudden theoretical shift or the onset of a specialist module, they are said to emerge gradually in the course of the infant's engagement in increasingly intricate and coordinated affect-ive relations with those around them, particularly familiar adults. These mutual exchanges are said to shape and inform, rather than derive from, conceptual representations of the self and other. For example, Reddy (2003) argues that there is a gradual expansion in the infant's understanding of objects to which attention can be directed, beginning with awareness of attention to the self, which is extended to actions produced by the self, fol-lowed by objects held in the hand, then objects distal to self and eventually to those that are out of sight. As such, infants are slowly drawn into more complex attentional relations with other people. Awareness of the inten-tional relations of other people towards external objects is seen to emerge from prior understanding of other people's intentional relations with the self. Reddy (2003, 2007) suggests that if the self is the object of attention, then the relations between the 'looker' and the object can be directly expe-rienced without needing to be inferred. Aspects of intentionality can be perceived that are not possible outside this relationship, with the second person acting as an 'embodied bridge' (Reddy, 2003, p. 401) between the infant and themselves. According to this account what is needed for social development is simply a motivation to engage and reciprocal emotional responsiveness rather than any innate theories, general theory-forming capacity, or specialist cognitive modules.

Hobson (1993, 2007) and Shanker (2004a; Shanker and Stieben, this vol-ume, Chapter 7) both propose that many of the behavioural disorders asso-ciated with the syndrome of autism can be understood as the cascading, detrimental, consequences of a congenital disturbance in the children's abil-ity to enter fully into affectively patterned engagement with other people. Shanker (2004a) suggests this is further compounded by their tendency to over- or under-react to different stimuli, which serves to further disrupt their ability to relate affectively to other people. For example, a child who is so over-stimulated by a parent's face to the extent that they avoid looking at it misses out on information vital to the development of normal social rela-tions. The limited available evidence regarding infants with autism (from pre-diagnostic home video tapes and retrospective parental reports) sup-ports the argument that they may have difficulties entering into the kind of early, affective relationships involving reciprocal turn-taking with their primary caregivers which are central to the development of social under-standing (Di Lavore, Lord and Rutter, 1995; Bernebei, Camaioni and Levi, 1998). Analysis of home video recordings suggests that children with an autism spectrum disorder in the first two years of life behave in a number of unusual ways that would disrupt the mutuality that typically character-izes early parent–infant interactions. These include a failure to look at faces, abnormal eye-to-eye gaze patterns, limited facial expressions, problems in imitating gestures/body movements, and difficulties in initiating inter-actions (Adrien, Faure, Perrot, Hameury et al., 1991; Sparling, 1991; Adrien, Perrot, Sauvage, Leddet et al., 1992; Osterling and Dawson, 1994; Bernebei, Camaioni and Levi, 1998; Mars et al., 1998). Wimpory, Hobson, Williams and Nash (2000) interviewed parents of children aged between two and four about the first two years of their child's life. Not one of the children subse-quently diagnosed with autism was reported to show frequent and intense eye contact, or to engage in turn-taking with adults.

Conclusion

In summary, I argue that we do not typically employ a theory in order to make sense of and relate to other people. Conversely, the evidence presented in this chapter from writers with high-functioning autism or Asperger's syndrome suggest that they do resort to an intellectual theory-driven approach in their efforts to make some sense of what are to them confus-ing and unpredictable social encounters. However, their autobiographical accounts clearly reveal the pitfalls of taking too 'cognitive' an approach to guide interactions with other people. In the absence of sustained experience of mutual empathic engagement with other people, and their difficulty in reading social and affective signals, these individuals find themselves in a position where they *have* to intellectualize social interactions. They devise cognitive strategies, based on rules and past examples, to help them negoti-ate their way around the social world. However, such strategies are inflexible and often fail to take account of all the most relevant aspects of a social situ-ation. The distinction that Dreyfus and Dreyfus (1991) draw between the expert and the beginner suggests that following any kind of theory would not lead to practical expertise in the field of social interactions. Even if we were to follow such a theory, we would still depend for its successful appli-cation on a wisdom that goes beyond the theory itself. This criticism can be applied to any account, which proposes that our understanding of other people is essentially theoretical in nature.

Proponents of Theory Theory of Mind, in trying to formulate a set of the-oretical concepts and laws to explain how we successfully deal with other people in our everyday lives, might be engaged in as futile a task as was Socrates in Plato's *The Euthyphro* (Dreyfus and Dreyfus, 1991). *Euthyphro*, a known expert in pious behaviour, resists Socrates' efforts to extract from him a set of abstract rules for determining piety, making it clear that his expertise is based on his own extensive, situated, experience, and not on any mechanical rule-following. Even if Socrates (perhaps through torture!) had eventually managed to wrench an extensive, coherent, set of rules from *Euthyphro*, this still does not change the fact that these are *not* what *Euthyprho* himself uses to recognize pious behaviour.

Note

1   Jim's account formed part of a collection of autobiographical writings from individuals diagnosed with Asperger's syndrome, which were published together in a book edited by Dawn Prince-Hughes (1992). Some of the writers did not give their surname or used a pseudonym. The name used in this chapter is that used for identification by the individual concerned.

9
Do Animals Need a 'Theory of Mind'?

Michael Bavidge and Ian Ground

Introduction

How should we regard the Theory 'Theory of Mind' (hereafter TToM[1]) in relation to animals? Is it a brave attempt, long overdue, to embrace the view that the animal world is mindful?

One might think so. After all, the term 'theory of mind' in this sense, was coined by Premack and Woodruff (1978) in the context of animal studies. They reached the conclusion that the ability of primates to predict the actions of their conspecifics could only be explained by ascribing to them the possession of a 'Theory of Mind' (ToM). From animal studies, TToM migrated into explanations of human development and, in particular, into aberrations of child development, such as autism (Sodian and Frith, 1992). As a result it has become the subject of general controversy (Davies and Stone, 1995) in the philosophy of mind where it confronts rivals such as Simulationism or empathic accounts. In this more general form, the aim of TToM is to explain how any psychological subject can arrive at psychological judgements about others: to track 'the heuristic route by which we arrive at our views about what is going on in other people's minds' (Heal, 2003, p. 5). We might conclude that if an approach which started life as an account of how animals conceive of the psychological lives of their conspecifics also proves fruitful in the human case, where, presumably, our minded nature is not in doubt, it is time to abandon scepticism about animal minds and to welcome TToM as their champion.

Despite this initial impression however, we shall argue that, at a deeper level, TToM is inimical to the notion of animal minds and should be treated with suspicion by those who want to change the climate of thinking about the character of minds other than our own. We provide some sketches of an alternative approach, rooted in the methodologies of Ethology and we confront both TToM and our positive account with serious arguments in the philosophy of mind which contend that animals cannot be mindful in any genuine sense. As a result of these encounters, we conclude that TToM must be rejected, and the alternative ethological approach embraced, if we are ever to take seriously the reality of other minds in a shared world.

Why a theory?

A first question to ask is this: why are proponents of TToM so keen to impute the possession of a *theory*? Why a *theory* theory? Why not just say that the ascribing agent, human or animal, must have *beliefs* about the mental states of others? Human beings, after all, have many beliefs and not many of them hang together so systematically as to merit the term 'theory'.

Some reasons for this are quite general and have nothing in particular to do with minds, human or animal.

First of all there may be harmless cultural reasons why it is a common tendency of cognitive scientists to call any set of beliefs, rules, principles or procedures which is under their scientific scrutiny, a 'theory'. It may seem natural enough that for theorists of cognition, 'theory' possession should seem the paradigm of cognitive activity. Perhaps we should just regard over-use of the term 'theory' and the dangers attendant on that, as an occupational hazard for cognitive scientists and try our best to read, charitably, between the lines.

A second general, if rather more dangerous reason, perhaps implicit in the very idea of scientific explanation, is the temptation to project the character of our *explanans* into the character of our *explanadum*. Thus a typical scientific explanation rightly models causal connections in the phenomenon under examination in terms of logical connections in our explanation of that phenomenon. There is nothing wrong with this: to do so belongs to the nature of giving intelligible explanation. But, in certain circumstances, it becomes curiously compelling to project those logical connections back into the phenomenon itself as if the complex causal phenomenon were really a rational phenomenon all along, as if indeed, the causal connections were just an empirical shadow thrown by the real and rational connections beneath. In the current context, though we are dealing with cognitive capacities, not mindless causal systems, there is an analogous danger. It is tempting to think that because we can theorize a capacity, and produce, in our theory, the same output from the same input as the normal exercise of the capacity, it must be that the capacity itself consists in the exercise of that very same theory. The point is not that this move is always fallacious: it may sometimes be the right thing to do. But whether it is so is an empirical matter and we should guard against the unconscious or unthinking extension from the realm of explanation to that of phenomenon. Thus, other considerations aside, it may be that if we can model our ordinary predictive judgments about others, then that model itself is what we actually use in our ordinary predictive judgments. But we should be very wary of thinking that it must, as a matter of course, be so.[2]

These general considerations aside, however, there are more particular and practical reasons why advocates of TToM wish to talk of a *'theory'* of mind. The acquisition and deployment of a theory allows for development and different levels of competence. One can have a more or less secure grip on a theory and, presumably, one can be more or less skilful in deploying it. One's grip or skill might be compromised, disrupted or disabled by any number of extraneous causes. TToM thus appeals to clinical scientists who are interested in explaining and curing dysfunction in our ability to understand others.

Related to this is the need to explain our ability to understand others as part of a developmental process. In some experiments (Wimmer, Hogrefe and Sodian, 1988), three-year-old children were prone to deny that other children know the hidden contents of a box even though they had seen them looking inside the box or being told about the box if the others had not themselves said what was in the box. Stich comments:

A very natural way to describe the situation is that while the younger children know that people who say that p typically believe or know that p, these children have not yet learned that people will come to know that p by seeing or being told that p. The younger children have acquired a fragment of folk psychology, while the older children have acquired a more substantial piece of the theory.

(Stich and Nichols, 1992, p. 64)

The role of 'theory' here is to allow for the possibility of gradation and augmentation, necessary in a developmental process.

Another kind of reason for *'theory'* is a matter of philosophical strategy. If we can represent the way in which we think of ourselves and others as a theory, then we can represent it as a theory which could be false and which could be replaced by a better one. Thus TToM makes it possible to claim that our ordinary beliefs about the minds and the concepts in which they are framed form a Folk Psychology – and could be mistaken. Our ordinary beliefs are just one competing theory alongside innatism, materialism or functionalism and have no particular primacy. It follows that our ordinary beliefs about our own and other minds are not part of what 'Theories of Mind' are called upon to explain. Thus TToM is welcomed by those who champion philosophies of mind which appear counter-intuitive when compared to our ordinary thinking about each other. When we can fully specify the content of Folk Psychology through TToM, we can force a Copernican moment in human psychology: we finally realize that our intuitions even about our own minds are wrong and that we only have those intuitions because that is how we look from here.

For these sorts of reasons then, our fundamental abilities to relate to others are held by advocates of TToM to be founded on the skills of hypothesis formation, in which scientists are acknowledged to excel.

A final reason offered to justify the use of the term 'theory' betrays more of the philosophical assumptions of TToM. The general premise, derived from accepted scientific methodology, is that the appropriate way to conceive the explanatory move from an observable to an unobservable must be in terms of a theory. The second premise is that behaviour is observable, but mental states are unobservable. It follows that anything that attributes mental states to anything else must do so via a theory.

Since, moreover, a ToM is used by an organism to *predict* the behaviour of others, the thought is: what else could justify the inductive move from past to future behaviour other than a theory? And now mental states feature as postulates in this theory. It is in the context of prediction that a ToM, precisely as a theory, is supposed to trounce its rivals. The recognition that it has to be a theory is a response to the problem which its empirical rivals, behaviourism, associationism and connectionism, are forced eventually to deny: the gap between observable behaviour and psychological states which the agent is constantly trying to bridge. If we really think that what is to be explained are the predictions that an agent makes about others and that agent is in the position of having to constantly bridge a gap between observable behaviour and hidden psychological states, it looks like only something with the deductive shape of a theory will do the job.

The use of 'theory' brings additional bonuses. Since theories are in principle revisable, we are not locked into the fixed pattern of response that rationalist innatism would require. Since theories must, in principle, have a structure, we can articulate that structure in our scientific theories of the theories of mind being employed by agents. Since in theorizing about the agent, we have to be using precisely the same set of skills as the agent uses in theorizing about others, we will feel able to claim that 'the theory theory [...] is both a theory of cognitive development and a scientific, naturalistic, psychological, account of scientific knowledge' (Gopnik, 2003, p. 241). It will seem especially advantageous to some that our ordinary thinking about people should in this way be able to segue into scientific psychology which in turn should meld into brain sciences (Heal, 2003). Why? Because we want to be 'realists about the psychological [...] in a way obviously compatible with the natural sciences' (ibid., p. 5). Simply by casting ordinary thinking into what looks like a proto-scientific theory, TToM seems able to underwrite that realism.

We have been discussing the putative attractions of TToM but do these attractions survive a journey across the species barrier? In regard to animal minds, TToM can be thought to be the answer to two different questions. The first concerns human knowledge of brute animals' mental states. The second concerns animals' knowledge of each other's mental states. We will look at these in turn. In the course of doing so, we will be preparing to examine the presumption, upon which the supposed advantages of TToM depend, that, in our knowledge of others, there is an epistemic gap to be bridged.

Human knowledge of animals

How can we humans know the minds of animals? Answers to this question are shot through with tensions. Thus when Descartes writes:

> But though I regard it as established that we cannot prove there is any thought in animals, I do not think it is thereby proved that there is not, since the human mind does not reach into their hearts.
>
> (Descartes, 1649/1970, p. 244)

he expresses scepticism about the existence of animal minds whilst at the same time leaving it open that such scepticism is only a consequence of our cognitive limitations.

When Lorenz writes:

> From many excellent photographs it can be seen that the lion, in the dramatic moment before he springs, is in no way angry.
>
> (Lorenz, 2002, p. 19)

he evinces a confidence that we can see the lion's psychological states, together with a warning about how easy it is for us to misread the behaviour of other animals.

Is TToM an explanation of the means we use to arrive at our beliefs about what animals think or feel? When we attribute mental states to animals are we relying on the ToM that we more habitually use for other humans?

It should be noted that it is possible to reject TToM in the human case but think it necessary in relation to animals. ToM may seem too rational, too scientific and too objective to be the way in which humans achieve personal knowledge of each other. An alternative empathy-based methodology may seem closer to how we actually relate to each other. However, it may seem that the differences between brutes and humans perhaps make any empathetic methodology a perilous and inherently anthropocentric exercise. An objective, theory-based approach to other species may appear to be the only one available because of the distance between us and them. Our approach to alien minds has to be one of observation, experiment and theorizing. TToM appears to offer an objective methodology which avoids what is seen as the principal threat to achieving genuine knowledge of non-human minds: anthropomorphism. If TToM does not produce interesting results, it may not have failed; rather it may reflect the actual situation we are in. More or less deep scepticism about animal minds may be the intellectually honest position for us to adopt.

In regard to our knowledge of animal minds, TToM may possess a further explanatory advantage. TToM seems to allow the possibility that we humans have a ToM which functions successfully in our own case and which we spontaneously extend out to cover other animals. TToM will then success-fully anticipate the lack of success of our ToM when we apply it to animals. TToM may even claim that since there is no selective disadvantage in our overestimating the cognitive abilities of sabre-toothed tigers, our habitual anthropomorphism may be a trait favoured by natural selection and there-fore quite to be expected (Kennedy, 1992). Whichever way we tell this story, it looks as if TToM will be welcomed by evolutionary psychologists thinking about our relation to other animals.

To generalize this point, those who welcome TToM in relation to our knowledge of other animals, should remember that TToM is not commit-ted to the truth of any particular ToM. Someone can hold TToM to be true and yet be a behaviourist in regard to animals. The behaviourist can hold that human beings possess a ToM normally applicable to other humans but that we systematically over-extend it in the case of animals. Or, the claim might be that we have a specific theory of animal minds but that it is systematically false. We may habitually say, for example, that the dog sees the cat up the tree or that the lion is trying to avoid being noticed by the gazelle. But the behaviourist can maintain that the postulated mental states in animals do not actually exist nor are required to explain animal behaviour. This echoes the claims made about 'Folk Psychology' in the human case. The whole point of talking about ToM may be, not to make sense of our talk about animal minds, but to show that to talk of animals in this way is false.

Animals' knowledge of each other

The second question about TToM in relation to animals concerns not our knowledge of their minds, but their own knowledge of each other's mental states. This is the substantive question. Do animals rely on a ToM in their interactions with each other? Because TToM gives a positive answer to this question, it appears to be a welcome recognition of the psychological real-ity of other animals. Despite the possibility outlined above, it appears to be a rejection of behaviourism's claim that mental states could not feature in such explanations.

Of course, it is moot whether TToM will be able to say what the con-tent of any animal ToM is. If it is able to successfully identify, say, beliefs and desires as postulates in animal ToMs, then we have the makings of a non-species-specific ontology of mental states. There may be all sorts of differences between brutes and humans, but at the most general level there are kinds of mental states in common. Alternatively, we may say that other animals must be using a ToM, but be unable to say anything about the ontology of that theory. Still, then, we have committed to the claim that, in regard to our respective conspecifics, humans and animals are in pre-cisely the same cognitive predicament, namely that we both are in need of a theory to bridge a gap between behaviour and mind. Either way, TToM seems not just to be compatible with evolutionary theory but to provide the threads of a seamless robe of Nature. This will be welcomed by anyone who resists the idea that human beings transcend the natural order. Ethologists, like Francis de Waal (de Waal, Macedo and Ober, 2006), welcome TToM primarily because they see it in this light.

But we would urge ethologists to be wary. It is noticeable that de Waal himself has only a vanishingly weak sense of what, in TToM, the term *'theory'* means:

> [TToM] refers to the ability to recognise the mental states of others [...] If you and I meet at a party, and I believe that you believe that we have never met before (even though we did meet), I have a theory about what is going on in your head [...].
>
> (de Waal, Macedo and Ober, 2006, p. 69)

De Waal is convinced that other apes can 'take one another's perspective', and he believes that TToM provides support for this view. But his own view is that possession of a ToM only makes sense as the outer layer of a system in which 'hard-wired' empathy is at the core and indeed he thinks that it is that empathy which is doing most of the work. There is not much more weight to 'theory' in my 'theory about what is going on in your head' than beliefs about you.

This is not what the champions of TToM have in mind. Thus Gopnik argues that TToM attributes ToM in the strongest possible sense of theory. Her view is that there are 'deep similarities between scientific theory formation and cognitive development' (Gopnik, 2003, p. 240). She is prepared to maintain this position even though the theorizing she attributes to infants manifests some obvious differences from scientific thinking. It is, for example, unconscious and it does not depend on the social and intellectual context that makes scientific theorizing possible.

If we now apply this strong sense of theory to animals, what are the results? The complexity of the situation immediately becomes evident. A whole range of questions under different headings present themselves:

1. Analogy

Does the evidential base for the animal's ToM rely on the animal's understanding of its own experience, and proceed by analogy, or does it depend only on direct observation of the other?

2. Abstractability

Are there complex inferential links in the animal's use of ToM? Do the inferred outcomes available as abstractable content allow for further inferences? Or are the outcomes of the animal's use of ToM directly wired into the animal's subsequent behaviour?

3. Normativity

Are the outcomes of the animal's use of the ToM quasi-normative reasons for action or more like causal triggers to behavioural change? Does the ToM provide the animal with reasons to flee the predator or does it just bring about flight?

4. Range

Is the animal's ToM restricted to conspecifics or does it range over non-conspecifics including, at the limit, any other animal?

5. Revisibility

Is the animal's ToM autonomously generated by the animal itself and revisable in the light of the individual animal's experience or is it a fixed neurological inheritance?

6. Meta-theory

Is the relation between input to the ToM (observed behaviour of others) and output from the ToM (predicted behaviour of others) one of empirical inference to 'unobservable mental states' or generalizations over 'observable behaviour' or something else? That is, is the meta-theory underlying the animal's ToM conceived in quasi-Cartesian terms or behaviourist terms or some alternative ontology?

7. Reflexivity

Can the animal be said to be aware of the ToM as a theory?

How we answer these questions will determine what kind of ToM we ascribe to animals. Possible positions include:

1. Animals inherit a fixed system of thoughts in which the psychological states of conspecifics and non-conspecifics feature as postulates.
2. Individual animals inherit a relatively large (or small) system of thoughts in which the psychological states of other conspecifics and non-conspecifics feature as postulates but which is, to a relatively small (or large) degree, revised and enlarged in the light of the animal's specific experiences.
3. Individual animals develop, *ex nihilo*, their own systematic theories in which the psychological states of conspecifics and non-conspecifics feature as postulates and which is revised and enlarged in the light of the animal's specific experiences.
4. Animals are sensitive to, and directly aware of, the expressive repertoires of other animals, complete with the immanent psychological significance

of those repertoires. They can have thoughts whose content we must characterize in terms of the use of psychological concepts and this capacity exhibits gradation, across the species world and, within those worlds, differentially between conspecifics and non-conspecifics and may vary greatly even for individuals.

Of course, TToM proponents will regard these questions and positions as possible research projects. That they can be asked is testament to the scientific fertility of the approach.

If someone believes something like 4, but, for cultural reasons in their discipline, wants to call it 'holding a theory', then perhaps one should just be charitable about this. But the evidence is that a great deal more is being smuggled across the species barrier disguised as 'theory' than first appears.

Why should we be suspicious? It is because 'theory', invoking a contrast between observed evidence and hypothesized unobservables, is the cover for sneaking a closet-Cartesianism into the minds of other animals as the meta-theory underlying their putative use of a ToM.

TToM, behaviourism and closet-Cartesianism

Behaviourism in the philosophy of mind, it is often supposed, has been exposed both as an incoherent theory and as an unproductive methodology. Unfortunately, here, at the species barrier, it retains its force both as a methodology and as a substantial theory of animal minds. The resilience of behaviourism is due in part just to this vacillation between method and theory. Griffin describes the shift:

> When the behavioristic position is stated at its scholarly best [...] it is essentially agnostic. It does not deny the existence of mental states, but argues that they are one and the same as neuro-physiological processes, and that it is unprofitable to attempt any sort of scientific analysis based on introspective reports. Half a century of behavioral science has progressed on this basis, along with many discoveries in neurobiology in the broadest sense, including Ethology. But what was originally an agnostic position tended to drift implicitly into a sort of de facto denial that mental states or consciousness exist outside our own species.
>
> (Griffin, 1981, pp. 111–12)

The alternation between method and theory at the heart of behaviourism becomes even harder to pin down when the alternation itself is made to hop to and fro across the species barrier. Behaviourism began its career as a strategy for avoiding the supposed privacy and subjectivism that characterizes introspective reports of human inner life. When, as in the case of other animals, there are no such reports and hence no dangers to be avoided, to escape redundancy it retrains as a theory centred on the denial of such a life. Should an unfriendly critic claim that 'such a theory has no real function', it can always fall back on its methodological origins, but now defending us not from the unscientific method of introspection, but from anthropomorphism, which is seen as a sort of collective subjectivism.

One of the curious things that happens on the far side of the species barrier is that behaviourism and Cartesian theories of mind coincide. Both deny that our ascriptions of psychological states to animals are ever justified. The Cartesian is prepared to be behaviourist in his attitude to non-human animals perhaps merely as a consequence of the theological dogma that God gave souls only to us. But as Wittgenstein[3] argued, behaviourism is deeply Cartesian in its presuppositions and in many of its epistemic commitments. It is illuminating in the present context to follow the twists and turns in behaviourism's reaction to Cartesian privacy.

As a methodology, behaviourism at first accepts the quasi-perceptual account of introspection given by the Cartesian and, in doing so, internalizes the whole Cartesian metaphysical picture. This picture embodies the analogy between a mental and a physical process. Our primary model of a real process is that of a real physical process. In order to save the status of mental processes, then, we must model their reality on that of physical processes. We take the reality of a physical process to consist just in its being approachable from more than one point of view. This threatens the analogy between the physical and mental process because the mental is not accessible in this way. But we hang on to it anyway and think of self-ascriptions of psychological states as a peculiarly private and incorrigible form of observation report – the same kind of report we make about physical processes.

Now the behaviourist objects. In the absence of objective controls, introspective reports must be ruled out of the scientific court. The trouble is that, at least currently, objective, neurological accounts of mental states are unavailable. Here is a dilemma. Introspection is universally available, but constitutionally subjective. Neurophysiology is objective, but cannot yet provide the crucial data. Now the restriction of the inquiry to behaviour seems justified, for it is the only approach which is both objective and available.

As the behaviourist inquiry proceeds, and appears to be delivering results, methodological scruple becomes metaphysical denial. At this stage the internalization of the Cartesian picture proves disastrous. For since the behaviourist has only the Cartesian model of mental states at his disposal, he takes himself to be forced to deny that there are any mental states at all.

In short, behaviourism is the conclusion of the doomed attempt to combine Cartesian theory of mind with a scientific commitment which takes reality to consist only in whatever is objectively accessible. Cartesianism is committed both to privacy of access and to the objective status of mind. It insists on the distinctive nature of the mental and yet sees the mind as a thing in itself alongside physical things in the world. In correctly cashing out the latter in scientific terms, behaviourism reveals how the two aspects of Cartesianism militate against each other. It reacts to the failure of the Cartesian synthesis by dropping the intended target of the inquiry.[4]

As an illustration of closet-Cartesianism in the discussion of TToM consider the controversy over mirror experiments on chimps. Julian Jaynes writes:

> that a mirror-educated chimpanzee immediately rubs off a spot on his forehead when he sees it in a mirror is not [...] clear evidence for self-awareness, at least in its usual sense [...] Our conscious selves are not our bodies [...] we do not see our conscious selves in mirrors. Gallup's chimpanzee has learnt a point to point relation between a mirror image and his body, wonderful as that is.
>
> (Jaynes, 1978, quoted in Kennedy, 1992, p. 108)

Here straightforwardly dualist thoughts – that 'our conscious selves are not our bodies' and 'we do not see our conscious selves in mirrors' – are used to object to the claim that chimps might have a concept of self.

Of course, viewed in a different light, Jaynes' objection can be given a sense. As Hume pointed out, conscious selves could never appear in anything like a mirror:

> For my part, when I enter most intimately into what I call myself, I always stumble on some particular perception or other, of heat or cold, light or shade, love or hatred, pain or pleasure. I never can catch myself at any time without a perception, and never can observe any thing but the perception.
>
> (Hume, 2004, Book I, Part 4, Section 6)[5]

That is, the self, chimp or human, conceived as the conscious owner of experience, could never be data at all, not even in a inner 'mirror of introspection'. More likely, however, Jaynes simply thinks that selves just are the sort of things that could only appear in inner mirrors: this is Cartesianism disguised as stringent scientific methodology.

Similarly, C. M. Heyes, in a critical review of the literature, seeks to show that:

> A survey of empirical studies of imitation, self-recognition, social relationships, deception, role-taking and perspective-taking suggests that in every case where nonhuman primate behaviour has been interpreted as a sign of theory of mind, it could instead have occurred by chance or as a product of nonmentalistic processes such as associative learning or inferences based on nonmental categories.
>
> (Heyes, 1998, p. 101)

Heyes spells out what, in her opinion, a theory of mind involves and what it excludes:

> The theory of mind hypothesis (or, more accurately, hypotheses) [...] assert that primates categorise and think about themselves and others in terms of mental states. Consequently, the distinctive, unifying feature of nonmentalistic alternative hypotheses is that they do not assume that primates represent mental states. They assume instead that primates respond to or categorise and think about themselves and others in terms of observable properties of appearance and behaviour.
>
> (Heyes, 1998, p. 102)

After questioning the reliability of the evidence in the chimp mirror experiments (Gallup, 1970) Heyes complains that 'even if there were [reliable evidence], such a capacity would not indicate the possession of a self-concept or any other component of a theory of mind' (Heyes, 1998, p. 104). This is because it would only show that the animal possesses what she calls, in a question-begging phrase, a 'body concept', which is a necessary condition of even simple 'collision free locomotion' and that, 'a "body concept" does not relate to a mental category' (Heyes, 1998, p. 105). But what kind of 'body concept' is it that does not 'relate to' a 'mental category'? It can only be one that depends on a fundamental contrast between body and mind. The animal, we are told, has only a 'body concept'. The real issue is what is contained in the concept of a mere body. If 'body' is taken to mean a mere physical object, we have straight behaviourism. The notion of a 'self' has therefore been ruled out by stipulation. If, on the other hand, body is taken in its normal sense, to signify the body of a living creature, then it is perfectly possible to have reason to believe that an animal that can have a 'body concept' also has a sense of itself as a living creature.

Heyes recommends that:

> We should stop asking Premack and Woodruff's question and considering the implications of a positive answer until we have designed procedures that have the potential to yield evidence favouring a theory of mind interpretation over other current candidates.
>
> (Heyes, 1998, p. 102)

However, it is clear that if the debate is to be conducted on all sides in terms of a Cartesian account of the nature of mind, there cannot be empirical data that would settle the matter either way. Trapped within a Cartesian model of mind, data, however assiduously collected, will never amount to knowledge of other minds under the aegis of any theory.

Heyes and Jaynes share the fundamental philosophical assumption of the original experimenters, namely in order to be able to understand others as intentional agents, one must be possessed of a theory in which the other's 'invisible' psychological states feature as postulates. Animals either think about other animals in terms of mental concepts referencing non-observable entities or they are reacting to conspecifics and non-conspecifics on the basis of observable behavioural evidence. The fundamental assumption here is that mental states are invisible whereas behaviour is visible: ' "Folk" and cognitive psychology both regard the reception and processing of information as internal events which may be inferred from behaviour but not observed directly' (Heyes, 1996, p. 470).

Insofar as these criticisms affect what we say about the 'Self' of an animal, we may not feel too worried. The 'Self' looks like a philosopher's invention anyway. What is more worrying is that this avenue of criticism runs to all aspects of any creature's subjective take on the world, even in what is for many, its most obvious manifestation: the social life of the animal. Thus Heyes:

> It has been said [of studies of the social behaviour of primates], in addition, to show that primates have knowledge of social relationships, and this seems entirely appropriate when the term knowledge is used in a very general sense, and social relationships are understood to be observable properties. If, on the other hand, knowledge of social relationships is taken to involve the attribution to conspecifics of knowledge about their social interactants, or dispositional mental states such as loyalty, dislike or affection, and to be acquired by a means other than associative learning, then the evidence to date does not support the conclusion that primates know about social relationships.
>
> (Heyes, 1998, p. 105)

Heyes's claim is that we can only think of primates as having knowledge of social relationships in the sense that they can respond to the behaviour of conspecifics as a human behaviourist scientist would describe their behaviour: that is, in terms which are free of psychological attributions. Similarly, the primate could be said really to have knowledge of social relationships only if that knowledge is of the same kind as that which a human cognitive scientist would have, which is to say, at the minimum, that it is knowledge not acquired associatively. She holds that it is conceivable but not proven that primates could have the kind of genuine knowledge which cognitive scientists have about something other than behaviour as the human behaviourist scientist would describe it.

What is critical here is the option that appears to be not even conceivable for Heyes, namely that the primate has a kind of knowledge which (a) is not modelled on the kind of knowledge a cognitive scientist has and (b) is about the behaviour of conspecifics, where that behaviour is not conceived as a human behaviourist scientist would describe it. In other words, the primate has something like the kind of knowledge of its conspecifics that you and

I may have of each other and which is about the sorts of entities that make up social relationships: namely the actions, reactions, and interactions of psychological beings.

What excludes this possibility is a set of tactical moves:

- genuine knowledge is identified with 'scientific knowledge'
- 'behaviour' is emptied of any psychological content
- what counts as 'observable' is restricted to what a mind-blind information processor would record

Under the self-denying ordinance that Heyes proposes, it is simply not possible to raise, in a way that admits of a meaningful answer, questions about the existence and nature of animal minds. The fundamental problem is that within cognitive science, the debate surrounding TToM amounts to asking whether or not non-human animals have interiorized one or other of the false pictures of intentional agency that have so bedevilled our account of the human mind. We simply cannot expect meaningful results either way, nor, we suggest, is it even scientific, to ask: 'If animals can be said to think at all, are they behaviourists or Cartesians?'

Is there an alternative picture? Is it possible to ask questions about animal minds, free of false pictures of the nature of mind, without ceasing to be scientific? In our own view, the key philosophical concept is that of expression and the genuinely scientific methodology which emerges from it is Ethology. Together they make TToM redundant.

Expression

Why is expression, without any theoretical scaffolding, able to support psychological ascriptions? Is expression a special kind of evidence – a kind of magic super-evidence that allows us to close the gap between overt behaviour and inner psychological states? No, the claim is more radical: understanding expression involves realizing the gap is an illusion.

Expressive behaviour is not data waiting to be theoretically interpreted. It manifests in the world a point of view on the world. For this reason it resists being reconceptualized to suit the beliefs of any detached observer. It consists of interventions in meaningful interactions within a community. Expressive behaviour is interactive. Expression is directed at others. It requires agency – organisms with their own agendas. It directly impinges on others and makes demands on them. It elicits not speculation or theorizing, but direct response.

This claim that expression is the heuristic route to direct knowledge of the mental states of others cuts deep. It questions the connections between knowledge, theory and realism. There is an interesting parallel between these remarks about knowledge of other minds and what Gopnik, who is an enthusiastic Theory Theorist, says about syntactical knowledge. She allows the possibility that syntactical knowledge is not acquired through theory formation: perhaps 'syntax is simply not the sort of thing you can have a theory about' (Gopnik, 2003, p. 251). The reason she finds this an acceptable possibility is that 'theory formation depends on a kind of realism, it depends on the idea that there is something out there that you can have a theory about'. And 'interestingly syntactic development is not like this. There is nothing out there that syntactic representations are representations of, knowing a syntactic structure and having a syntactic structure are just the same thing'. This line of thought leads to the conclusion that 'the same arguments that say that syntactic knowledge is not a kind of theory, call into question whether it is really a kind of knowledge either' (ibid.).

Thinking about sociality can lead to a similar sequence of thoughts. Sociality is simply not the sort of thing you can have a theory about. Our basic sociality cannot be built out of interpretations of information.[6] But this need not lead to a denial of the reality of experience or the possibility of knowledge of experience, our own or others'. The denials run in the opposite direction: knowledge is not to be equated with processing objectively available data and objectively available data is not coextensive with the real.

Experience becomes manifest through the expressive actions of the animal whose experience it is. Expression is recognized in being, like a threat or a kiss, communicated. This is important not just from an epistemic point of view; it says something about the nature of experience. Experience is not constituted out of inner states that are first objects of knowledge. Experience is not data, not even for the subject of the experience. This is true even for enlanguaged creatures like ourselves. In expressive language, we speak out of our experience before we speak about it. Subjective experience is so close up and personal it can only be manifested as subjective through being expressed.

This explains why the significance of expression is only visible from within relationships. It is not a tiresome peculiarity of subjective experience that it can only become patent through communication. The significance of expressive lives is manifest only inside the relationships which they constitute and regulate. This does not mean that the significance of an expressive exchange is unavailable to objective study. But it does mean that it is understandable only to the extent that the observer can make sense of the inside of that exchange. One may hear a couple argue without hearing the words that are said. But one can still hear and see, directly, the tensions, regrets, resentments and resolutions. This is not a matter of inference to some unobservable mysteries going on in their heads. But it does require the observer at least to have the idea that there is an inside to this exchange – that the couple are interacting with each other. And of course, this is an idea that we acquire through having been on the inside of all manner of expressive exchanges ourselves.

As regards our understanding of other species, the challenge is to acquire the capacity to see these exchanges in their other-directness. This is the central methodological principle of Ethology. The task of Ethologists is to find ways to discover how the species-specific behaviour – and not the behaviourist 'behaviour' – of animals is significant for themselves and their conspecifics in the contexts in which they live. This means gradually acquiring the ability to read the behaviour as expressive. In the case of many animals, we have a good start since there is a deal of shared expressive repertoire. In other cases, it will be much more difficult. In both cases, the possibility of error is real: the fact that the reading of behaviour as expressive requires us to be immediately open to its significance does not commit us to infallibility about it, any more than the immediacy of perceptual judgements commits us to infallibility about physical objects.

But, however near or remote the animals are to us, error is not systemic to the whole enterprise. And whatever difficulties we encounter, they do not arise because we can never be sure that we have inferred the right invisible mental state on the basis of observable behaviour. Nor, if we weaken the objectivity of the 'data' on which we base our understanding of animal behaviour, will there be anything to prevent us from sliding into subjective anecdote – and 'the plural of anecdote is not data' (Bernstein, 1998, pp. 247–8; see also Heyes, 1996, pp. 470–3). Where there are errors it will be because we have failed to adequately position ourselves to be receptive to the significance of the expressive behaviour. That is not a single philosophical mistake but a messy set of empirical mistakes. Avoiding these errors requires habituation and imagination, both of which are principal virtues of good science. It also requires scientific discipline about facts. But the discipline is not to restrict oneself to an artificially curtailed set of 'facts' as they are for us and then to make only justified inferences from them. It depends on an ability to sustain a position where one can see into the facts of animal lives as they really are for the animals.

What we suggest, then, is that, freed from Cartesian and behaviourist strictures, an ethological concept of expression provides the basis of a methodology for investigating the reality and character of animal minds which is genuinely scientific. By contrast, TToM is the sublimate of closet-Cartesian philosophy of mind in the form of scientific methodology. Neither we nor other animals need the theory of mind that it postulates.

At this point our discussion must take a new turn. For even if the importance of expression is conceded and the objections to its epistemic role are abandoned, there is still a major obstacle to understanding how it can found a genuinely scientific conception of the possibility of animal minds.

The problem is this: there is no attributing significance to expressive behaviour without also attributing content to specific exercises of the animal's expressive repertoire. If we can recognize a piece of behaviour as expressive, we must be able to say what is being expressed. But how can the expressive behaviour of non-linguistic animals entitle us to attribute content to their expressions? We think ourselves entitled to say of the lioness that she has noticed the antelope. But how can we fix what it is that the lioness has noticed unless we are able to attribute the use of a concept, namely 'antelope' to the lioness? One line of argument – which has become a standard theme of contemporary philosophical thought about mind – appears to imply that we cannot attribute concepts to animals. We need now to turn to consider this objection. Doing so will bring a deeper understanding of why TToM is inimical to the understanding of animal minds.

Conceptualized experience

The principal objection to which we will now turn is that we cannot attribute content to expressive behaviour because to do so is to attribute concept-use to animals and concept-use cannot be attributed to non-enlanguaged animals.

One influential version of this argument has its roots in the philosophy of Kant. A key thought for John McDowell (1994), is that the primary use of concepts is their employment in judgments, that is, at the minimum, in assertions and denials of what is the case about the world. And such judgments are simply not possible if the very same concepts used in these judgments do not also structure our experience of that world. Unless experience and judgments meet, as it were, on the same ground, judgments could not be about our experience of the world (and there is nothing else they could be about) and experience could not answer, to confirm or deny, our judgments. As the Kantian dictum has it: 'concepts without intuitions [perceptions] are empty: intuitions without concepts are blind' (Kant, 2004, A51–B75). Thus, if we seriously say that the lion sees the antelope, we are committing ourselves to the view that the lion's experience is structured by the concept 'antelope'. It is central to this kind of view that we cannot say that the lion sees some indescribable, unconceptualized patch of something, and then makes the leonine judgment that, 'yes, that kind of patch normally means an antelope'. Rather concepts are *always already* operative in experience. If we want to say that the lion has noticed the antelope, then it really has to be antelopes and not patches of unconceptualized data that the lion sees. From this neo-Kantian perspective, it is not even right to talk about the lion seeing data that are, as it were, waiting to be conceptualized. For even the idea of pre-conceptualized data fails to capture the neo-Kantian insistence on the idea that 'antelope' is not some internal representation of lions but a way that the world comes at the leonine life. The lion must be conceived as living in a world, not in a self-contained box of representations. If we want to say that the noticing of the antelope is part of the explanation of the lion's subsequent behaviour, then only *seeing antelopes* will do.

We should note here that this move in itself strikes at the heart of TToM in its most general form. If conceptualization is not applied to, but operative in, experience, then, at the fundamental level at which we are aware of and responsive to others, the distinction between data and hypothesis, which TToM must employ to secure even the least substantive sense of 'theory', will be unavailable. For the contemporary neo-Kantian, others cannot first strike us as undifferentiated data, about which we then need a theory so that we can conceptualize those neutral data into other *agents*. That makes TToM untenable though it leaves open the question of what it is about an experience that makes it an experience of another agent. As we hope will now be evident, our own view is that our experience of others as expressive beings precisely is the conceptualization of them as other agents: behaviour without expression is blind: expression without behaviour is empty.

However for neo-Kantians like McDowell, and many other contemporary philosophers, another route is more attractive. The claim is that nothing can have concepts unless it also has language. For only language, or something very like it, can supply sufficient determinacy to distinguish the use or attribution of one concept from another. If we are to say, meaningfully, that the lion notices the antelope we need that to be a different attribution from other possible ones, say, that the lion has noticed the elephant. But differences between the concepts 'antelopes' and 'elephants' can only be embedded in a structure with sufficient complexity to distinguish them. For many philosophers, this can only be a language. The position, then, is that language must go all the way down. It is language that delivers determinacy of sense. In turn, determinacy of sense delivers the possibility of a subjective track through an objective world. And there, and only there, is where the notion of 'mind' gets a grip. Sense, mind and world run together.

This has drastic results for our thinking about animal minds. The implication is that we can attribute mental states, which can be about the world, only to language-using beings. Thus for McDowell, we enlanguaged creatures are able to live in a *world*, one we are able to regard as independent of us. Language allows us, as subjective beings, to find our way through an objective world.

But non-linguistic creatures cannot do so. They live in 'mere' environments which consist of sets of opportunities and obstacles. However the bad news does not end there. It would seem to follow that the animal's notion of another animal is equally impoverished relative to the conception of another person used by language users. Notions of self, others and world stand or fall together too.

This position strikes a double blow against TToM. First of all, if the claims about the necessity of a complex structure to embed concept use are true for attributions of even minimal *judgments* to animals, the argument will be much more damaging for attributions of *theories* to animals. This is because theories require more complex structures within which they are articulated than judgements. Moreover, it is hard to see how it is even intelligible to talk of theory use without the use of that theory issuing in at least minimal judgments.

Second, the animal does not need a theory of mind if the very notion of another minded being cannot be a reality for it. TToM simply cannot be given a useful job to do across the species barrier. For human beings, other humans are rich, deep, psychological sources, which are problematic to predict and so our ability to do so seems to require explanation. But if animals live only in mere environments, in which the notion of an objective order is not operative, it is far from clear that they can have any genuine sensitivity to other animals *as others*. Perhaps other animals can appear only as particularly mobile pieces of environment or familiar and recurrent patterns of opportunity.

The implied accusation from this neo-Kantian quarter of contemporary philosophy is that TToM, if applied to animals, amounts to a form of what we might call logomorphism: a fallacious attempt to project onto non-linguistic creatures the means of concept formation and deployment that are operative only in the case of linguistic creatures like ourselves. On this view, TToM, oblivious to the profound implications of what living in an enlanguaged world means, is a Dolittlian fantasy written up as cognitive science.

But if this kind of position is a problem for TToM, it may be thought no less a problem for the alternative ethological view we have outlined. For, how, it might be asked, can the expressive repertoire of an animal play the role of delivering up determinacy of sense that language plays for us? What is there in what the non-linguistic lion can do that can give sense to a distinction between noticing the 'antelope' and noticing the 'elephant'. If we can't make that distinction, ethological thinking can get us no further than the Dolittlian TToM. Faced with this profound difficulty aren't we better to abandon the thought that animals have anything worth calling minds?

There are two challenges to this move both of which also help to explain further the significance of the ethological perspective. First of all, we suggest, the neo-Kantian critique, though it accuses TToM of logomorphism, is itself logomorphic and more profoundly so. It assumes that only the kind of determinacy of sense delivered up by language can deliver up a world and hence deliver up the mind of an agent.

In our own lives, questions about what we mean are normally raised and answered in language. Our capacity to specify more and more exactly what we mean suggests that language provides us with a set of perfectly focused photographs of the world which brings clarity and precision to what would otherwise be vague and misty impressions of the world. Perhaps we and the dog both see the cat run up the tree, but only we see the ginger tom run up the silver birch. But of course if there is a problem about 'ginger tom' and 'silver birch', there is an equal problem with 'cat' and 'tree'. Now we seem to condemn the dog to living in a vague and misty world. This line of thought has gone wrong at both ends: the animal's experience has all the precision it needs; the dog barking at the foot of the tree gives no sign of confusion or vagueness in its behaviour, anymore than we do when we call the sky blue. We don't think ourselves hopelessly vague for not distinguishing cobalt from azure. We can make those further distinctions, and sometimes do. But the sense of the concept 'blue' is not waiting on us to do so. It does its job when we talk to our neighbour about the pleasant weather. Linguistic specificity is rooted in our forms of life; and, as Wittgenstein puts it, 'to imagine a language is to imagine a form of life' (Wittgenstein, 1972, §19). Language is the vehicle for the determinacy of sense that makes specifically human concept-use possible. But still, in the end, it is the myriad shapes of human life that fix sense and not some linguistic medium floating above life and running parallel to it. That it is the shapes of lives that fixes significance is an ethological principle and one that applies equally to our enlanguaged selves and to non-linguistic animals.

A consequence of rooting meaning in forms of life is that the idea of 'critical experiments' becomes suspect in an ethological context. For example, there is nothing wrong with investigating what chimpanzees make of mirrors. But it could not constitute a critical experiment to determine whether chimpanzees are 'self-aware'. Self-awareness is not the sort of thing that can appear as a discrete phenomenon. The disputes about the mirror experience are carried on as if self-awareness may or may not have been sighted on this or that occasion, like the Loch Ness monster. But the significance of whatever a chimpanzee does with strange artefacts like mirrors can only be understood in the context of the animal life. And it is to the whole of the animal life that we must look.

Our claim, then, is that contemporary neo-Kantianism is right to insist that conceptualization is not an operation carried out on experience. Rather concepts should be thought of in terms of the ways in which the world comes at living beings. Thus the whole idea of conceptualization is only really separable from that of experience as a philosophical convenience, and one fraught with danger at that. But neo-Kantianism is wrong to claim that only a language can deliver the necessary articulation that enables experience to be of a differentiated world. Instead, we suggest, it is the specificities of particular forms of life, modulated through expression, which deliver up the contrasts between self, other and world that are the minimum conditions of having a mind.

Conclusion

It may seem to the unwary that the purpose of the account offered in this discussion is to narrow the gap between what we can say about the minds of other humans and what we can say about the minds of other animals. It will then seem puzzling that we should do this in the context of an attack on TToM. For after all, it will be said, what is TToM if not an attempt to narrow precisely that gap by arguing for a shared cognitive structure between ourselves and animals in terms of a shared theory? But this is to misunderstand what is wrong with TToM.

TToM only appears to hold out the promise of the recognition of other animal minds. For even when we have put aside its closet Cartesianism and its logomorphism, we have still not got to the root problem that bedevils our understanding of other animal minds. The root error, we contend, is to continue conceiving of animal minds as just versions of our own. In TToM, animals are modelled on human beings as rational theory-makers, though in comparison to us they prove to be more or less incomplete, inadequate or dysfunctional theorists.

This is not what we need. The challenge is to recognize both the reality and the otherness of other kinds of mind: to see other animals as mindful and to recognize the differences, and the nature of those differences, between the species.

We can make a start by at least thinking correctly about our own case and how it is that our kinds of mind differ from others. Language changes everything. We do not share exactly the same set of capacities as (some) other species, as it were, up to a certain line and then after that line, language takes over and the distinctive differences between us and other species kick in. Language does not just make a linear difference, as it were, forwards or upwards. Rather its effects wash back over activities and capacities that are not themselves in origin or nature intrinsically linguistic.

Of course we share primitive pain behaviour with our mammalian cousins. But once we have language, even the cradling and protection of the wounded body part takes place in a new world of meaning and value. We share a repertoire of cries and grimaces with other animals but, once language is on the scene, these expressions acquire whole new worlds of nuance and consequence. We, like other creatures, see and hear, taste and touch. But language transforms what it is to do these things and thus transforms the shape of the world in which we live.

Being enlanguaged is therefore a profound difference between one species on this planet and, as it appears, all of the others. It is profound in the sense that it reaches back down through our species nature, so transforming it that we worry whether it still makes sense to say that we *share* the *same* capacities as other animals so that the commonalities between us and other species are recast. We share a common evolutionary inheritance with other species, but in our expression of that inheritance, the character of the differences between us and other species is radically transformed.

What needs to be grasped is the necessity of generalizing this lesson beyond the human. Being enlanguaged is not the only such profound difference between the species of this planet. Other kinds of difference between other species, in the possibilities of movement, in perceptual modes, in the relation of perceptual mode to movement and action or in the relation of the animal to its conspecifics which TToM seeks to explain, may be equally profound. These differences also wash backwards over the rest of an animal's shared inheritance, affecting what it makes sense to say of its commonalities with other species. It is these profound differences which come to constitute a distinct set of ways in which the world is present to, and trapped by, a particular species nature. These distinct ways in which the world is present to different species natures give the sense to the thought that the world is shared.

So to have a genuine sense of the world as shared, we have to come to see that other animals do not live in private worlds of their own. Nor do they live in impoverished, deranged or fantastical versions of ours. The world is present to them as a world and not as data for theorizing. There is one objective world and it is so just insofar as it makes sense to think of it as hospitable and present to radically different kinds of mind. The human mind, even in all its radical complexity, is one amongst others, and the world is shared.[7]

Notes

1 We use TToM to refer to the theory that agents, animals or organisms must possess a 'Theory of Mind' and ToM to refer to the putative 'Theory of Mind' itself held by the agent, animal or organism.
2 Wittgenstein (1972) offers a penetrating critique of this move in his discussion of the machine-as-symbol (§193–7).
3 'How does the philosophical problem about mental processes and states and about behaviourism arise? – The first step is the one that altogether escapes notice. We talk of processes and states and leave their nature undecided. Sometime perhaps we shall know more about them – we think. But that is just what commits us to a particular way of looking at the matter. For we have a definite concept of what it means to learn to know a process better. (The decisive movement in the conjuring trick has been made, and it was the very one that we thought quite innocent.) – And now the analogy which was to make us understand our thoughts falls to pieces. So we have to deny the yet uncomprehended process in the yet unexplored medium. And now it looks as if we had denied mental processes. And naturally we don't want to deny them' (Wittgenstein, 1972, §308).
4 'Suppose everyone had a box with something in it: we call it a "beetle". No one can ever look into anyone else's box, and everyone knows what a beetle is only by looking at his beetle. – Here it would be quite possible for everyone to have something different in his box. One might even imagine such a thing constantly changing. – But suppose the word "beetle" had a use in these people's language? – If so it would not be used as the name of a thing. The thing in the box has no place in the language-game at all; not even as a *something*: for the box might even be empty. – No, one can "divide through" by the thing in the box; it cancels out, whatever it is. That is to say: if we construe the grammar of the expression of sensation on the model of "object and designation" the object drops out of consideration as irrelevant' (Wittgenstein, 1972, §293).
5 Essentially the same insight is a consequence of Kant's distinction between 'empirical self-consciousness' and 'transcendental apperception' (cf. Kant, 2004, B155).
6 '[S]ociality cannot have the same structure as knowledge' (Lévinas, 1985, p. 60).
7 A more extensive discussion of these themes can be found in Bavidge and Ground (1994).

Part 3
Alternatives

10
Closet Cartesianism in Discursive Psychology

Wes Sharrock

Discursive psychology (DP) may not be as established in psychology as the theory of mind paradigm yet it does have some influential proponents and a fair number of followers. This chapter considers Discursive Psychology's capacity to address and resolve the problems created by the idea of theory of mind and to provide a viable alternative. Through a detailed analysis of an argument between two discursive psychologists (Derek Edwards and Jonathan Potter) and an ethnomethodologist (Jeff Coulter) we show how DP is caught up in some of the same confusions as ToMism and that it fails to provide an original alternative to it distinct from ethnomethodology and conversation analysis.

The case against 'Theory of Mind' (ToM) made in several chapters in this book is that the capacity for understanding other human beings that is supposedly acquired through speculative theory construction is in fact acquired with the language. In Chapter 4 we argued that the construction of a personalized 'theory of mind' was redundant, supernumerary to learning to use language. As for ToM's 'rival', Simulation Theory (ST), the argument was modestly elaborated to show that first language learning is not a distinct and isolated activity, but something that is done in and through given social practices and their constituent doings, and integral to learning to participate in these. The capacity for understanding others comes *through* that kind of learning, is expanded, elaborated and diversified by engagement in and mastery of the numerous and diverse practices of life, rather than being a generic precondition for relating to others.

The argument that the problem ToM and ST propose is not one to be solved, but one to be eliminated by attention to the geography of the ordinary language *in use,* can be a hard one to make stick. There are some long-standing, rather standard objections to this line of argument, and, as this chapter will consider, there are even sympathetic contemporaries who, nonetheless, think that this idea is significantly misconceived, that its application in relentless deconstruction of mentalist doctrines eventually goes too far. The opportunity to respond to this worry of discursive psychologists may enable further clarification of what the line taken in Chapter 4 involves.

The disagreement with mentalists is often misunderstood as a disagreement between psychological theories, where the mentalists maintain one theory and their opponents (such as myself) advance a different – behaviourist – one. This pitches the issues at the wrong level – such supposedly theoretical disagreements are only superficial manifestations of a much deeper divergence. Mentalists think that their problems are to be solved by empirical research and theorizing, whilst my argument against them is both that this is not what they are really engaged in at all, and that the crucial division is in terms of the respective understanding of how the natural language works when put to everyday use in practical affairs.

Since mentalists suppose that their task is to theorize about a natural phenomenon, mind, they do not pay too much attention to how the language of mind works, and tend, therefore, to hold rather unelaborated assumptions about certain features of it. As the issue of 'folk psychology' shows, the default assumption tends to be that the terms making up the everyday 'mentalistic vocabulary' are to a significant extent theoretical ones, or at least manifestations of an amateurish lay theorizing about what goes on 'inside' the cranium. Mentalists tend also to presuppose that our use of language depends upon an accompanying 'picture' or preconception about the nature of the things that we talk about. Deeply rooted in that tradition, and carrying right through to its contemporary offshoots in arguments about folk psychology, is the supposition that the ordinary language intrinsically carries with it a dualist ontology, one demarcating mind from body in a dualistic pairing. Thus, the classic Cartesian picture supposedly captures, right at the start of this continuing controversy, what all of us as speakers of the language naturally, seemingly intuitively, suppose about 'body' and 'mind' on the basis that this is the conception that comes with the language.

It makes a great deal of difference to the argument if it is recognized that it is these latter suppositions about language that are being questioned. The idea that the meaning of words depends upon accompanying – mentally held – conceptions is no neutral assumption upon which mentalism can begin to build its case, for it is itself to be counted amongst mentalism's assumptions, and, as such, is contestable.

If the use of words in the language does not *depend* upon the possession of attendant quasi-theoretical conceptions of the nature of things, then the assumption that a Cartesian picture of the nature and relations of 'body' and 'mind' is built into the language does not hold. Though it has long and often been made, this counter-argument rarely gets much of a hearing outside its own circles, and seldom one that comprehends the terms of its argument: it is not understood as relocating the dispute onto different territory, that of the forms and applications of language *in use*, but simply as the – perhaps not direct but implicit – adoption of one side, the behaviourist, in an ontological argument. This is why criticism from one branch of Discursive Psychology can provide a useful opportunity for clarification of this line of thought, since, as will be shortly seen, it is an important element in DP's position formally to concur with 'grammatical' analyses in the tradition of Wittgenstein and Ryle that are pursued here, whilst nonetheless insisting that its mentalist views of language use have *some* validity.

'Discursive Psychology' is an attempt to provide an alternative to mentalism within psychology. Its doctrinal content is largely derived from other theories, purportedly adapting them to psychology's specific problems as a means to bring psychology into closer contact with two general movements that have spanned the humanities and social sciences in the past half-century and more – 'the linguistic turn' and 'the turn to the social'. Those practising under the title 'Discursive Psychology' are not by any means unified in their views, and are quick to recognize that they make up at least two schools, one dominated by Rom Harré and his associates, the other in the hands of Derek Edwards, Jonathan Potter and their colleagues. As the name implies, 'Discursive Psychology' (hereafter DP) proposes that psychology can be – at least partly – converted into the analysis of discourse and, either additionally or alternatively, that 'the nature of the mind' is to be understood through examination of discourse that involves 'mental' matters. Examination of 'discourse' surely invokes the fact that the 'discursive' expression of these matters will be irreducibly involved in particular oral exchanges between individuals. Considering 'the psychological' in the context of discursive transactions, relations between people, avoids the excessive 'individualism' of which mentalist psychology is often accused, and directly connects with the 'turn to the social'.

DP's own exercise, at least in the form we shall be concerned with here, is meant to be a compromise and synthesis between two ostensibly opposed views. It seeks to resolve the issues through examining language in use, but casting doubt on the supposition that language use *per se* is entirely independent of mentalist conceptions. The compromise is between the grammatical and mentalist lines: if not *all* uses of language in its practical applications conform to the mentalist picture, at least *some of them* demonstrably do. There are, that is, some everyday Cartesians who can be found, and they are recognizable by virtue of *the way they speak*.

McHoul and Rapley (2003, pp. 507–22) argue just this: their central contention is that Wittgenstein denied that psychological terms were names standing for 'internal' referents. They then proceeded to attack a doctrine they call 'Coulterism' (after one of my collaborators, Jeff Coulter) which asserts that if such predicates are used to identify inner mental states in everyday talk, then their users are 'misguided' (p. 519). Suffice to say that neither Coulter nor myself has ever made any such proposal. What we have argued is that lay people's *substantive versions* of 'psychology' can be just as misguided as those of professionals. It is amusing to read McHoul and Rapley use almost the same quotations from the work of Harvey Sacks as did one of us (Coulter, 1983, pp. 136–40) 20 years ago in a discussion of these issues to avert just the kind of misinterpretation that they make of our position. The issue is not to be resolved by reference to empirical examples in which, for example, someone speaks of hearing voices 'in my head' or musicians sing of going to Carolina in their mind since these instances represent rather than do anything to resolve the problem. The question, then, is what people mean when they say such things, what kind of 'grammar' governs the use of 'in' in expressions like 'in the head'?

McHoul and Rapley assume that 'in' operates as an expression of spatial location. There is, however, no more reason to suppose that 'in' has that kind of application in these supposedly referential cases, any more than it does in expressions like 'in time', 'in accord with the law', 'in the story' and 'in principle', and there are good reasons to suppose that it does not. This is, and always has been, the point: that expressions like 'in my head' are entirely acceptable idiomatic expressions within the language, and that they are not, as such, the bearers of any kind of proto- or full-blown Cartesian conceptions.

Consider persons who hear voices 'in their head'. How do they determine that these voices are 'in their head'? This cannot be done *in general* by the acoustic character of the voices that are heard, in the first instance at least. More often the voices are understood to be the voices of an actual speaker in the ambient environment, and it is *in the absence* of any such discoverable speaker that the individual concludes that the voices must be 'in their head' (cf. Leudar and Thomas, 2000, ch. 9). 'Voices in my head' equates in meaning to 'voices that I alone seem to hear'. And, someone who goes to Carolina 'in their mind' hasn't gone anywhere or identified any spatial relocations – all they have said is that they have imagined themselves in Carolina. No one is opposed, either, to the examination of empirical examples, but the point is, and always has been, that many would-be 'social scientists' are subject to misconceptions about what that examination can deliver.

The Edwards and Potter branch of DP is also in a very ambiguous position relative to mentalism, one in which, without themselves endorsing the mentalist position, they nonetheless perpetuate mentalist ideas, mainly by projecting them into their examples, unilaterally assigning them as tacit understandings of those whose activities they examine. Their doing so only begs the questions against mentalism.

Edwards and Potter (EP) want to differentiate three positions on 'what is going on when someone says how they feel, what they think, want or believe'. The first, mentalist, position (P1) is that 'the expression and communication of thoughts is basically what talk does' which is certainly a position that would be rejected by most contributors to this volume, though it is not quite the same position that this chapter and its predecessor have argued against. Their second position (P2) is 'recommended by linguistic philosophers such as Ryle and Wittgenstein':

> Here, the notion that words such as 'think' or 'feel' express or refer to mental states is rejected in favour of analysis of how those words are properly used, in publicly ratifiable ways. Anyone, whether philosopher or lay persons, who claims to be using such words to refer to an essentially private mental experience is making a conceptual error.
>
> (Edwards and Potter, 2005, p. 255)

Whilst acknowledging these arguments, there is yet a third position (P3). This is EP's own which

> recognizes that there is some substance to the idea of referring to private mental states, *though not as the analyst's favoured theory of language and mind.* [...] In this third approach, the status of reference to internal mental states is not something to be refuted, even though it is conceptually refutable, but rather, studied as a practice within a public form of life. People may sometimes talk as if, or on the *proposed and oriented-to basis*, their words are expressing inner thoughts and feelings.
>
> (Edwards and Potter, 2005, p. 256; emphasis added)[1]

Responding to EP's formulation of positions enables a clarification not merely of the immediate issues of interpretation, but of two deep, persistent and related issues: those of (a) the relation between 'the inner' and 'the outer' (which EP transmute into that of the possibility of 'public' and 'private' thoughts), and (b) the idea that a critique of 'the inner' *cannot avoid* ending up in behaviourism (which they direct at proponents of P2).

Note that, for EP, mentalism is not 'the analyst's favoured theory', and that they are not therefore called upon to justify their own reliance on mentalism, but instead aim to establish the intelligibility and practicality of some mentalist preconceptions in some social contexts, such as – their chosen examples – telephone counselling and police interrogation. EP use these examples as a kind of test case between the unrefined Position 2 and their own, supposedly more discriminating, Position 3. There are two ways in which these illustrations are invoked: (a) specific ways of speaking are singled out as being directly associated with mentalist presuppositions, and (b) both cases are taken to instantiate people – *at least* these individuals – who are speaking as if inner states really exist.

The specifics of the two cases and problems with EP's interpretation of them will be detailed, but, as in all such purportedly crucial confrontations, a great deal depends upon the way in which the sides have been set up. Everything depends upon the way in which Position 2 has been specified and on whether EP's formulation is less than generous to P2 whilst indulgent to P3. In other words, are the genuine differences between the two positions fairly set out, or do they entail misunderstanding and misrepresentation?

There is surely a difference between (a) a critique of the possibility of *any* 'inner' phenomena', and (b) the critique of mentalist doctrines about the inner. It is a common fallacy in the social and human sciences for critiques of theoretical interpretations to be wrongly taken as critiques of the phenomenon's ontological status, and to mistake a denial that there is any such thing as 'the inner' *in the mentalist sense* for a denial of 'the inner' *tout court*.

Denying that there is an 'inner theatre' (or its functional equivalent) of the sort conceived in the classic Cartesian tradition is not casting doubt on whether people, for example, ever feel pains – it is just, if the doubts are accepted, that 'feeling a pain' will no longer be conceived after the fashion of something making its appearance in the display apparatus of an inner theatre (or its functional equivalent in, e.g., the tokening of inner representational forms). Many of 'the phenomena' over which *philosophical disagreements* (or their social science equivalents) arise are *seriously* indubitable (systematic scepticism does not count as serious doubt), but attention to their occurrence is often theoretically top heavy. Much theoretical spin needs to be added to the fact that I have a pain in my arm to bring it within the terms of mentalist conceptions of sensation. To reduce matters to their crudest and simplest terms, it would be one thing to find people ordinarily making reference to 'pains' or speaking of their pain sensations as 'inner' ones (Task 1), and quite another to show that when they use these expressions they have anything like the 'inner theatre' (or its functional equivalent) in mind (Task 2). Succeeding in the first task does not even start on the second one.

EP set it up so that P2 seems to propose an *a priori* adjudication of everyday expressions, deciding that, for example, all references to 'inner sensation' or to 'private thoughts' should be placed under a ban (as conceptual confusions and consequently unintelligible). Such a policy would fundamentally conflict with something else of which P2 is often accused, namely that of sanctifying the ways of ordinary uses of the language that would effectively prohibit all possibility of practical and scientific revisions of language. *Neither* of these are P2's actual policies, which, as just explained, simply cannot presuppose that commonplace ways of speaking must be dependent, for their practical deployments, on mentalist presuppositions. That they actually are so dependent is not to be taken as a wholesale assumption about our 'folk psychological' vocabulary. Putting 'folk psychology' in inverted commas does not deny that words like 'mind', 'thought', 'intention' and the rest are parts of daily language, but only questions whether these words at all resemble theoretical terms, to be thought of as part of as an – hitherto unsubstantiated – theory about the functional relations amongst a set of discriminable inner states.

EP therefore burdens P2 with a methodology[2] it would foreswear, and, moreover, they treat it as if it amounted to the behaviourism that mentalists insist is the only conceivable alternative to mentalism. P2 is, however, not a rival to mentalism in that way at all – mentalists and behaviourists function as a kind of cartel, cooperating to obscure the fact that there is a different order of objection to the very terms of their disagreement that can be made to their shared dichotomization of 'inner' and 'outer'.

What was the private language argument about?

Wittgenstein's 'private language argument' is notorious for featuring references to 'pain behaviour'. If construed superficially this may not only strongly suggest behaviourism, but also give an effective illustration of behaviourism's supreme folly. Suppose that 'pain behaviour', which involves such things as crying out, gasping, writhing and the like, is understood by Wittgenstein as the referent of the word 'pain', making pain into something entirely external. If Wittgenstein was not denying that there is any such thing as pain, was he denying that the word 'pain' has anything to do with what each of us can unquestionably feel when we are in pain? This would be a behaviourist-type idea, and also clearly absurd.

But if, instead, Wittgenstein is trying to persuade us that the word 'pain' is often, in first-person uses, not a referring term at all, then it cannot have either sensation *or* behaviour as its referent. In Wittgenstein's view, the word 'pain' in its first-person use is much more of a socially sanctioned equivalent to and substitute for pain behaviour, such as crying out. If he is not trying to persuade us that pain refers to pain behaviour rather than to the sensation (since it refers to neither) what is he trying to persuade us of? 'Pain behaviour' functions not as the referent of the word 'pain' but as criteria enabling (third-person) identification of that sensation. One can tell (defeasibly) from the fact that someone is holding a swollen cheek and moaning that they are in pain – indeed, that they have toothache. Wittgenstein is trying to establish that there is no insuperable *logical* disjunction between 'the inner' and 'the outer' by drawing our attention back to the natural, *organic* connection between them, that pain behaviours are packaged natural reactions of organisms such as humans that are integrated with the sensation of pain.

The logic of the private language argument is of course about the way language works, and the invocation of pain behaviour is part of an attempt to undermine the view that the meaning of words depends upon their association with some idea (considered as an inner mental occurrence) – this view is essential to the 'privacy of the inner' line that Wittgenstein *does* attack. It is a tempting (but misguided) idea that I know what I mean by the words I use because I associate an idea with each word. Does it not then follow that if I know what my words mean because I match them with ideas of my own contriving, it is possible that others may not be able to comprehend the meaning of my words for, after all, only I have access to the ideas that give those words their meaning? Thus, with respect to 'pain': only I can know what pain means in my mouth because only I know what the sensation I associate with it actually feels like. Perhaps that feeling is different to the feeling that others associate with their use of this word. I surely know what 'pain' is like from my own case, and the same goes for everyone else: they know what they mean by 'pain', but how can I know that they mean the same as I do – since that surely involves comparing the sensations themselves, not our use of words?

The private language argument is against an idea of how words acquire their meanings, namely as each individual's private affair, a consequence of the underlying conception that grasping the meaning of a word consists in associating it with an idea. The 'private language' argument itself is designed to show that an individual cannot *identify* his or her sensations entirely and independently from his or her own case, from immediate experiences. Sure enough, the individual is the one who has the sensations, but they have no personal criteria for connecting these sensations with words in the rule-like way that is an essential for something's being a word in a language. Learning the language of sensations is not a matter of two distinct tasks, learning the words and learning to apply them to cases. This is because words function criterially and learning to use them is learning where they apply and where they do not. The 'public' prevails over 'the private' in this sense (only): individuals learn to identify their inner states from the public language, on the basis of the natural, organic connection between *what is experienced* and the *manifest reactions* (i.e., the 'pain behaviour') that function as criteria for the character of the former. This doesn't mean, I hasten to point out, that, having learned the words, one then goes on to determine whether one is in pain by checking to see if one is moaning, gasping and so on. Learning the language enables discriminating identification of one's own feelings by learning (*inter alia*) from how others respond to certain situations. Learning to use a language is not a matter of figuring out how to operate it according to one's own rules, but of recognizing and adopting the pattern of application manifest in other people's *language use* (cf. McGinn, 1997, pp. 171–5).

Notice that the private language argument is about the relationship between sensations, reactions and the meaning of words, and the way in which publicly manifest reactions can – at least for sensation words – function as criteria for the identification of sensations. When Wittgenstein remarked that '"an inner process" stands in need of "outward criteria"' (1953/1958, §580) he did not mean that 'inner processes have been displaced by external public reactions'. The private language argument's thesis does not yield the unqualified assertion that 'there are no inner sensations, there are no such things as private thoughts' – but only a much more restricted claim: there are no inner sensations (or private thoughts) *in the sense in which* mentalists conceive of these. Equally, it would be seriously misleading to take refutation of the argument that 'it is logically impossible ever to tell whether someone else is in pain' as licensing affirmation of 'it must *always be* possible to tell whether someone else is in pain', as though there could be no pain in the absence of manifest pain behaviours. The argument is, many pain behaviours are replaced by the verbalizations of the fact that one has a pain in the arm, has toothache. Since such verbalizations are not mandatorily associated with the occurrence of pain sensations, it is clear that people can experience pains, without notifying others that they are, just as they can affirm that they have a pain when they feel no such thing.

The possibility of private thoughts

A second strand of thought needs connecting to this first one, if the Wittgenstein/Ryle line of thought is not to be crassly simplified and drastically distorted. Wittgenstein's quote about 'inner processes' standing in need of 'outer criteria' should not be taken as providing a general statement of his position on the relation between 'the inner' and 'the outer'. In the case of 'pain' and 'pain behaviour' there is an association between an inner occurrence – the sensation of pain – and an outward reaction, but 'in the case of' needs to be emphasized. The mentalist temptation is to take those cases where talk of 'the mental' features related inner and outer occurrences as though they instantiated a general pattern for the whole mentalistic vocabulary, as though all identifications of instances of public activities carried with them postulations of an inner accompaniment.[3] P2 resists absorbing all the varied patterns of use found within the 'mentalist vocabulary', a heterogeneous collection of 'mental terms', to one overall paradigm, since it is this that both Wittgenstein (1953/1958) and Ryle (1949) regard as a compelling source of philosophical confusion. Ryle's *The Concept of Mind* is an attempt to catalogue some from amongst the very varied range of linguistic forms that are involved in application of 'mental terms', many of which just do not fit the picture of outward occurrences and inward counterparts *at all*. Ryle argumentatively emphasizes the example of dispositions as a corrective, pointing out that ascribing mental characteristics such as, say, duplicity, is more like attributing a disposition than reporting an occurrence or a state, and ascribing a disposition is more like making a prediction about behaviour than describing a presently happening episode. Because of the emphasis on dispositions, Ryle is apt to be seen as reducing 'the mind' to dispositions, thus essentially reinstating allegations of behaviourism – his own strictures on adopting any single grammatical form as generically modelling the mind notwithstanding. It is misleading to treat either 'There is no "inner", there is only "the outer"' or 'The application of mental terms is always to both an observable outer and an accompanying, criterially connected, inner' as *the general* position of P2. The nearest P2 comes to a general position is: there are many and very different cases. Bear in mind, too, that 'the inner' and 'the outer' are both being stripped of association to mentalist or behaviourist associations, and invoked only for cases which *by anyone's standards* are ordinarily called, for example, 'inner', as with 'inner life', 'inner determination', et cetera. EP's test cases would only cut ice if P2 was understood as making the *unqualified* denial 'There are no such things as private thoughts', rather than the *qualified* denial – 'There are no such things as private thoughts *in the sense that* the private language argument envisages these'.

EP pitch their argument as follows: some people talk and act as if they believed that there *are* private thoughts. Leave the sense of such 'private thoughts' out of the equation for a moment, for the first query is whether people who invoke private thoughts conceive of *all* thoughts as private. That is, are those who attribute private thoughts to others in a position where attributing thought and attributing private thoughts is just one and the same thing – 'private thought' as a pleonasm? Or is it that those who are attributing private thoughts to another (or to themselves) make a contrast between 'private thoughts' and 'non-private ones'? The two assumptions differ, and the differences would presumably have far-reaching practical consequences – *depending* on which assumption one assigns to the speaker, the attribution of 'private thoughts' is either simply a redundancy or it is not.

If there is a contrast, what is its content? EPs conception of 'private thoughts' apparently cashes out in practice as a quite everyday commonplace one, but that is not the conception of 'privacy' that P2 shows is incoherent. Going by EP's examples, private thoughts are simply those that people have so far kept to themselves, thoughts that occurred to them *but* that have not yet been publicized. These are not thoughts that are private of necessity, impossible to publicise, or by their nature incommunicable. Their 'privacy' is merely a matter of exigent circumstance: someone has a thought, but is not sharing it. Far from privacy being a logically imposed state, it is a contingent and circumstantial one. The circumstances of the two examples will be seen to reveal plain reasons for keeping some thoughts temporarily private: these are potentially incriminating in the first example, only metaphorically so, in the second more literally so. The expression 'private thoughts' in its ordinary usages often subsumes thoughts whose admission is problematical, best kept from at least some other people: the thoughts entered in teenagers' diaries are not for parents to read. However, not all thoughts that are kept to oneself are private in that same sense; there are many thoughts one keeps to oneself because they don't deserve repeating, and in the length of a single day one may have a good many of these.

The first half of an argument should not be taken for its whole: acknowledging 'private thoughts' in this everyday sense should not encourage taking the occurrence of private thoughts as the model for all thoughts, as though all thoughts start off with a private life with only some of them then making their way into the full glare of publicity. 'Privacy' with respect to everyday thoughts does not parallel the mentalist's 'inner'/'outer' separation (though EP seem to be treating it as though it does) – as with the teenager's diaries, private thoughts can be set out on paper.

Having cast doubt on EPs general strategy, whether their examples are cogent to the issues they aim to be addressing, consideration of the way they employ their examples is needed. The difference between P2 and P3 is not in whether the parties to the recordings say certain things, but what kind of understanding attaches to what they say. There is what might be called 'a plain English understanding' and then there is the question of whether theoretical topspin modifies that understanding in any way.

Two test cases

Case 1

The first example is taken from a telephone helpline for reporting child abuse. The caller has been describing to a counsellor problems with her male partner that may relate to events in his childhood. Despite the length of the transcript,[4] all the real interest is concentrated on the turn in lines 18/19.

Excerpt 1: NSPCC BN 15

```
 1.   Caller:...I said to him y'know is – is it is it thi:s.
 2.   (.)hh and he said I was not to ever mention
 3.   that aga:in...hhh W(h)elhhhh=
 4.   CPO: =It's extraordinary.
 5.   Caller: Very extraordinary.= I've just .h ih he got
 6.   very very an:ngry when [I mentioned that. ]=
 7.   CPO:                     [Defensive?        ]
 8.   Caller: = An I did- hhv:very. Yes
 9.   (0.8)
10.   A-and that bothered me too:.
11.   CPO: um
12.   (0.6)
13.   Caller: I mean- I I don't rea:lly know what we're
14.   dealing with here.
15.   CPO: pt [hhhhhh      ]
16.   Caller:   [ I really don't ]
17.   (0.5)
18.   CP{O: .hhhh In the- very back of your mi:nd were you
19.   sort of toying with the idea that somehow your
20.   husband may have had (.)
21.   Caller: I don't know.
22.   (0.5)
23.   Caller: I don't know
24.   CPO: No you don't know but are [you playing with
25.   the idea: ]
26.                                  [(((coughs)) I
27.   possibly ] I possibly am. =I possibly am.
28.   (0.3)
```

'At the back of your mind' (line 18) keys the potentially offending assertion (Potter and Edwards, 2003, p. 177). It doesn't matter because of its potential to be taken as the outcropping of a topographically regionalized conception of 'the mind', but because of its role in imputing 'unspoken thoughts'. For EP this case shows that 'the mentalistic appeal to unspoken thoughts in the head is one practical and intelligible means available for doing this' (ibid.), enabling the counsellor to make a delicate transition of topic. Note, though, that the expressions 'mentalistic' and 'in the head' are neither essential to the claim and are introduced by EP, not found in or derived from consideration of what the telephone counsellor says. The telephone counsellor is responding to a caller over concerns about spousal participation in child abuse. The counsellor counters the caller's denial of prior suspicion that the husband might be involved in some such activity. Though the caller denies considering such a possibility, the counsellor replies with 'surely this thought must have occurred to you'? EP see the counsellor's formulation of this counter as a delicate one – it does not directly confront the caller, suggesting that the caller – despite denials – has considered this possibility. Rather, the challenge is moderated. Though the caller is not entirely unaware of this possibility, it is not one that has been seriously entertained, it is a possibility of which the caller might have only a sneaking suspicion, rather than full-blown realization or, perhaps, it may even be intimated as a thought that the caller cannot easily face up to, and does not perhaps find easy to admit even to herself. Although the counsellor does not flatly challenge the caller, the counsellor does counter the caller's claim about what she knows, suggests that the caller has been entertaining thoughts of this kind, even if she is reluctant to speak about them to others (and the caller concedes 'possibly').

The expression 'at the back of your mind' itself is a piece of English idiom, that often has to do with either (a) the partially developed nature of some thought – that the thought is not full blown, but partial, unclear, only faintly apprehended, or (b) it is a thought that has been entertained for some time but has not had sufficient priority or opportunity to be acted on – 'I've had it in the back of my mind' is often of a piece with 'I've finally got around to this' asking or telling someone. It is more likely the former in the counselling case than the latter, but, in either case, it refers only to thoughts that have previously been had, but were previously neither announced nor acted upon. In other words, 'private' is a matter of merely or advisedly kept to oneself or both. P2 is not involved in offering *its own* account of the nature of thought, but of tracing out some of the grammar of the word 'thought', so why would it adopt a conception of a sort of Tourette-like relation between thinking and announcing – someone can only have had a thought if they have blurted it out?[5] P2 is not putting up any doctrine about the relationship between two phenomena, thought and language, but is tracing only the way in which the expression 'thought' (amongst related others) features in the language. That thoughts can occur independently of being mentioned and can be kept to oneself is just an unexceptionable part of that grammar, not something that depends for its viability or intelligibility upon endorsement from one or other philosophical point of view.

Case 2

EP suggest that the concept of private mental states, and their reports, are rhetorically useful.[6] We can ask how and when, and in the performance of what kinds of actions, do people talk 'as if they were in possession of a privately available mental life, which their words may either truthfully or falsely express' (Edwards and Potter, 2005, p. 247).

EP's second example demonstrating such talk is more complicated. Private thoughts, rather than being imputed by another, are supposedly being self-assigned. The example is taken from a police interrogation of someone accused of assault against a woman shopkeeper by virtue of having pushed her. The person, W, admits theft but denies assault – he made no physical contact with the woman shopkeeper.

Excerpt 2

```
 1.   W:   I didn't push the woman or nothin' (0.5)
 2.          I really did not do that. I'm not that type of person
 3.          y'know what I mean. .h Fair enough
 4.          I stole the ciggies, (0.5) I wouldn' hurt an
 5.          old lady
 6.          (0.5)
 7.   Pl:  [Right  ]
 8.   W:   [No.    ]
 9.          (.)
10.   W:   Not a chance
11.   Pl:  =What I'm saying is this (0.5)
12.   W:   I hope there's a Ceer – a camera at the shop=
```

As far as EP are concerned, W is speaking as if he has privileged access to his inner mental states. He is speaking as if he knows what these are because he can inspect them directly, whilst those to whom he is speaking cannot inspect them and therefore cannot know with the same certainty whether W is reporting those inner states faithfully or not. In substantive terms, this involves W in making a public claim about a private state that he is in, namely one of 'hoping', the claim being such that it is invulnerable to refutation at that moment – only W can know if he is in that state, for only he can inspect the conclusive evidence, namely his personally held privately experienced mental state.

Accept, for the moment, that W is well understood as speaking in this way, but then ask, how are we to understand his adoption of this Cartesian speech mode? Are we to understand that he speaks generally, naturally and unreflectively in this manner? Or does he have only an instrumental relationship to this mode, electing it because it may be rhetorically effective in this situation (and how are we to tell that difference?). This ambiguity leaves two very different possibilities: (a) W is either telling the truth or lying about his inner state – he is saying that he hopes for something when – having examined his inner state – he knows very well that he hopes for no such thing, or (b) W is as much misleading about his possession of inner states as he is about the specific state he is in, he isn't basing his expression on any actual inspection of an inner state, but is only speaking as if he was in such a state because it will contribute to the invulnerability of his suggestion that objective evidence would vindicate him (though this can only be rhetorically effective if appeal to 'inner states' is believed in by the interrogators).

Is this rhetorical advantage a plausible one? It sounds as if W's claim is made credible by the fact that only W can know if it is true or not. However, the issue for W's interrogators would not be whether W knows what state he is in, but whether he is reporting this honestly – it is presumably a commonplace of police work that people may tell untruths about things to which they have privileged access. For W's example to gain traction against P2 would seemingly require P2 to suppose that lying is unintelligible, at least with respect to 'inner' or 'mental' states. That is, if expressions such as the avowal of a hope are accepted as advancing descriptions of inner and private mental states, but the existence of any such states is denied, there is nothing that these descriptions could be wrong about. Buying into this should not mean: since they can't be wrong, therefore they must be right. Instead, it means: since they can't be wrong, they can't be right, either.

P2 has no need to put itself in the perverse position of denying that, for example, W cannot possibly be lying about what his hopes are. Instead, it casts doubt on whether such expressions as ones of hope are best understood as descriptions of inner mental states. If they are not descriptions of inner mental states, then they cannot be either correct or incorrect descriptions of them.

Recognizing that EP are not themselves endorsing the mentalist story – it is 'not the analyst's preferred story' – they are, nonetheless, putting the mentalist's ideas into W's mouth. If W's expression of hope is not a description of an inner mental state, then what sort of description is it? Not one that W might further describe for us, presumably. If W was genuinely describing an inner state of, for example, hoping, then it would seem reasonable to assume that W can identify this state when he experiences it, so it would be reasonable to call for further description: what is the state like, how does W identify it, tell the difference between it and other states? Descriptive answers to such questions, most readers presumably realize, would be unlikely to be forthcoming, not out of secrecy but because one – including W – would be at a loss for something to say. The fact that it would be unlikely is reflected in the status attributed to folk psychology as theoretical: it purportedly postulates inner mental states corresponding to, for example, thinking, hoping, imagining and so forth, but carries no specification of the empirically determinable properties of such states. Hence, even if one did treat W's expression of hope as a self-assignment of a determinate inner state of 'hoping' (whatever that might empirically look like), such a postulation could play no part in the practical intelligibility of W's attribution since no corresponding determinate properties are identifiable by EP, their readers, by W or by his interrogators. Wittgenstein ironically remarked that a nothing is as good as a something about which nothing can be said, and this applies well to the 'discernible mental states' which putatively accompany expressions of the kind that W offers.

Insofar as what W offers *is* a description, what does it describe? It describes a possible state of affairs – that a CCTV camera is found to have been recording the events in the shop, and indicates an attitude toward the realization of that possibility: W would be pleased if it came to pass. Taking 'hope' as descriptive of a mental state, one might suppose that W could, alternatively, have been in a mental state of *expectation*, expecting *that* there would be a camera. Asking about how, in a 'world of private experience', being in a state of hoping differs from one of expecting would turn out to be something that can be decided by the difference between the grammars of the words 'hope' and 'expect', for example, in respect of how these words signal different degrees of confidence and certainty that can be invested, and in the way that 'hope' evaluates the possibility of occurrence whilst 'expect' does not necessarily do so. Thus, if W expected there to be a camera, one might ask for justification – what led him to expect there was one? One can hope there is a camera without having any basis to expect there is one. An expression of 'hope' characteristically features a description of what it is that is hoped for, not one of any internal state. Further, expressing a hope may not involve so much a report on a feeling one currently has – is there a 'feeling of hope' that anyone can put their finger on? – but has a predictive aspect, making claims about how one *would* feel in the event that what is hoped for came to pass: W would unquestionably be pleased.

The persuasive force of W's expressed hope depends upon its acceptance as an authentic expression: he is sincere in his claim. In the immediate interview situation, his sincerity is invulnerable in this way; his interrogators have no *evidential* basis to attack his claim. However, W's claim is not invulnerable because of its connection to a private inner state that only W could ever examine. It is not, that is, that W's interrogators are poorly placed relative to introspectively discriminable states of W's mind/brain, but only poorly placed relative to W's informational status. Whether or not W is sincere in his claims depends upon what W already knows. W knows whether he made contact with the shopkeeper because he was there, whilst his interrogators were not and must depend on contested testimony to reach their own conclusion. W may already know that there is no camera in the shop, for he has been briefed by his solicitor, and that briefing may have included the shopkeeper's testimony, including the fact that there is no such camera. The 'privacy' which secures the – perhaps spurious – sincerity of W's expressed hope is that of the legally entitled privacy of the solicitor-client encounter, not that of privileged access to some configuration of mental states. If we *knew*, for sure, that W had been briefed that there was no CCTV camera, then we would also know equally surely that W's hope for one was just fake, made purely for its potentially persuasive effect. If W is insincere, then his dishonesty is with respect to the facts of the case rather than about what his introspections scrutinize. Possession of the *relevant* facts could definitively overrule W's first person expression entirely, based on the detailing and appraising of W's various *circumstances*. Any uncertainty attached to W's hope is unrelated to any constitutional inaccessibility of concurrent inner mental states, but to a possibly transient uncertainty as to what, for example, W did in the store and what he has been told. At no point does the construal of this incident depend upon *anyone* hypothesizing a determinately specified inner state, and so saying that W is describing a private mental state adds nothing to observing that W says that he hopes, and that it is possible he may be lying about this.

So there is no way of extracting, from either of the two exchanges, any idea of what sorts of *inner states* would count as, for example, hoping for something or having something at the back of one's mind. This in turn implies that thinking of the attribution of 'inner mental states' as an integral element of doing so-called folk-psychology is otiose. It is bereft of content, and so it cannot play any consequential role in the transactions between the parties to these occasions or in our understanding of them. It seems as if the actual users of folk psychology find that the access they have to information about situations and circumstances can be sufficient for them to make definite attributions to others, ones which sometimes categorically overrule first-person declarations, and which, where they are indeterminate and uncertain (as in both cases considered), are so because less than conclusive information about relevant circumstances is all that is available, not because there is no possibility of direct examination of the content of the cranium (or need for indirect inferences about this).

The two examples were introduced by EP as cases in which P2 should condemn the speakers, W and the Counsellor, for conceptual confusion, but, as I have tried to make plain, there is absolutely no reason why P2 should regard what the Counsellor has to say as involving conceptual confusion at all. There is nothing *in the words* of either of these speakers that requires the introduction of mentalistic conceptions of 'the inner' in order for them to make sense. The mentalistic construal of those words is volunteered by EP, but even if that construal were other than gratuitous, it would make EP's argumentative strategy no more effective, since it is grounded on misconceptions about the philosophical problems with 'the inner' and 'the private', reflecting, perhaps, other confusions about the relationship between conceptual and empirical problems.

The mentalist/behaviourist cartel again

The above case studies provide an opportunity to illustrate the fact that P2 does not fall on either side of the line – that between the body and the mind, the inner and the outer, the public and the private – that mentalism and behaviourism draw to divide themselves. It does not, like behaviourism, dispute the occurrence of 'inner' experiences, but it is vastly less indiscriminate than mentalism in treating all mental terms as invoking the occurrence of inner phenomena because it does not treat the grammar of our 'mental vocabulary' as at all uniform. It therefore declines the general view of the relation between the inner and the outer – as that between mental events and bodily movements – that behaviourists and mentalists both hold, but not because of the lack of uniformity amongst 'mental terms' without offering any alternative statement of a general relationship. As I have stressed, P2 sees the real differences as coming down to conceptions of language.

Mentalists differentiate themselves from behaviourists because of the need, as they see it, to postulate a rich and complex inner structure since only such a structure can adequately explain the transformation of behavioural inputs into behavioural outputs. From my point of view (P2), the mentalists disregard the rich and complex requirements on language use that derives from the part language plays *in* the intricate lives and activities of individual human beings and their associations. Far from encouraging a reductionist view of mental terms as referring only to behaviour (in the narrow behaviourist sense of that word), it altogether redirects attention to diverse connections that different 'mental terms' have with the various things that, in the complicated contexts of our human lives together, human beings want to know about and do with (and against) each other. That they have been able to conduct those lives for so long without any knowledge of what goes on inside the skull suggests that carrying on the lives in which 'mental terms' play their part has not, and does not, depend on consideration of inner states in the mentalist sense, even hypothetically.

I have questioned whether EP are successful in the immediate task of providing examples of people who speak in a specifically 'mentalist' or 'Cartesian' way, and thus doubt their success in their strategic objective of showing that DP encompasses phenomena that are occluded both by mentalists and their 'grammatical' critics (it is like a Venn diagram, picking out phenomena that purportedly infringe Wittgenstein/Ryle-style grammatical strictures, conform to mentalist preconceptions, and yet are to be examined by non-mentalist methods). Success in this venture is crucial to the claim that DP deserves the name of a distinctive venture, rather than being identified as no more than the application of ethnomethodology's and conversation analysis' methods to instances in which the sort of thing that psychologists like to talk about happen to turn up (there being nothing analytically distinctive from an ethnomethodological or conversation analytic point of view about the use of 'mentalistic' vocabulary). As so often with attempts to establish proprietary brand names in the social and human sciences, any appearance of success in establishing an independent remit for DP is produced through reliance on uncharitable interpretations of other approaches, in this case, the grammatical approach.

Notes

1 Jeff Coulter (1999, 2004) provided a critique in which he doubts whether 'Discursive Psychology', as a composite of existing elements, has any distinctive identity. Hence, the importance for EP of maintaining that there is a real difference between positions 2 and 3.
2 That of evaluating the practical applications of this vocabulary.
3 Mentalists don't, of course, accept that the connection is criterial: they are resolute that it is proto-theoretical.
4 Transcription conventions for this transcript and those below are provided in Chapter 6, p. 124).
5 The position EP aim to oppose is perhaps taken seriously in the other wing of DP, endorsed by Rom Harré (e.g., Harré and Secord, 1972) that individuals are constituted only by their appearances to others. Such a view would be a long way from anything Wittgenstein or Ryle would support.
6 They clearly are meaningful ideas, if only to allow us to call it 'cognitivism' and oppose it!

11
A Dialogical Approach in Psychology: An Alternative to the Dualism of ToM

Ivana Marková

Many psychologists adopt a dogma they never question: if you want to learn something about the human mind, you must start with the cognition of the individual. Only then can you ask how that single mind comes to realize that there are other minds and how, sooner or later, it starts imputing intentions to others and interacting with them. Considering the dominant belief in the rationality of the individual and the cognitive power of the mind/brain, such dogma is of course *à la mode*. But dogmas, whether religious, ideological or scientific are not permanent and in the end they give rise to alternative perspectives. And the Theory of Mind is not an exception (cf. special issue in *Theory & Psychology*, guest editors Leudar and Costall, 2004a).

One alternative to rationalist approaches based on the cognition of the individual, including the 'Theory of Mind', are dialogical approaches to the study of the human mind. In contrast to the former, the point of departure of the latter is that human minds produce themselves in and through interaction.

There are, today, a number of dialogical approaches in the studies of language and in human and social sciences, like 'the dialogical self', 'the dialogical turn', 'dialogism(s)' and so on. These approaches have a long list of predecessors. Their beginnings can be traced to Vico's 'New Science' in the seventeenth century, through Hamann, Herder, Humboldt and Hegel, to the neo-Kantians, Bakhtin's Circle, and up to the present. All these scholars have in common the idea that the mind, knowledge and language are products of social interaction rather than of the individual's cognition. Naturally, the perspectives of these scholars do not form a homogeneous bloc; they conceive social interaction and the interdependence of human minds in a variety of ways, bringing into their theories the work of history and culture, relative stability and dynamics, emotions, the unconscious and the depth of consciousness. These perspectives do not paint a black-and-white picture of the human mind but inspire alternative ways of thinking.

It is within this tradition of thought that I have been developing the concept of 'dialogicality' to characterize the fundamental capacity of the Ego to conceive, create and communicate about social realities in terms of the Alter. I am assuming that this capacity is such a basic condition of human existence that we can talk about it as the *ontology* of the human mind. What the human individual has become through the work of the past and what his/her prospects are for the future is due to this capacity (Marková, 2003). Knowledge, symbolic thought and language are all products of dialogicality. In other words, there can be no single mind without other minds: they dialogically co-constitute one another. The concept of interaction between the 'Ego–Alter' which I conceive as the ontology of the human mind is abstract and theoretical. In concrete and contextualized dialogical situations it is always expressed as a specific Ego–Alter or Self–Other(s); for example, 'I–you', 'minority–majority', 'I–group', 'group–another group', 'I–culture', and so on. Indeed, these specific Ego and Alter rarely exist in a vacuum but are embedded in yet other Ego–Alter interactions. For example, mother–child interaction is contextualized in a specific culture, or is part of a special social group and so on. Or a conversation between two individuals is not just an exchange of words between me and you that takes place in a specific here-and-now. Instead, conversations have their past, present and future, in which various Alters, for example, parents, leaders of political groups, friends, 'generalized other' et cetera, may speak through the mouth of each Ego. Such embedded Ego–Alter interdependencies may form complex conversational patterns, in which implicit and explicit meanings mingle together and affect the discourse as well as contributing to the formation of knowledge in all dialogical participants. In other words, the Ego and Alter co-constitute one another in a dynamic figure-ground set-up, both transforming in and through dialogical communication and symbolic interactions.

The assumption that the Ego and Alter are ontologically co-constituted implies a dialogical theory of knowledge. Let me explain. Theories of knowledge – including the 'Theory of Mind' – by definition presuppose some kind of a relation between the knower and an object to be known. For example, some theories of knowledge are concerned with the question how the individual (the knower) processes information coming to the individual's brain from external objects like rocks, plants, stars, or even nations or systems of democracy. Other theories attempt to find out how the mind (the knower) gets to know other minds (as objects of knowledge). Still other theories of knowledge presuppose that the knower is a collective (rather than a single individual). The collective knower (society, a social group, etc.) is in possession of knowledge accumulated through the history of mankind, for example in the form of collective representations in a Durkheimian manner; collective representations, for example, beliefs, images or symbols arise directly from social structures. They are external to the individual who does not contribute towards their formation, but they impose irresistible pressure on individuals who yield to their coercion and internalize them and so perpetuate these social forms of acting, thinking and feeling.

In contrast to theories based on the relation between the knower (whether individual or collective) and the object of knowledge, the dialogical theory of knowledge requires not a single knower, but two interdependent knowers in each instance of knowing: the Ego and the Alter (Marková, 2003). The theory presupposes that each individual lives in the world of others, interacts with them, influences others and is influenced by them. Bakhtin expressed this idea pertinently in his analysis of Dostoyevsky's novels. Consciousness must be in interaction with another consciousness in order to achieve its proper existence:

> justification cannot be *self*-justification, recognition cannot be *self*-recognition. I receive my name from others, and it exists for others (self-nomination is imposture).
>
> (Bakhtin, 1984, pp. 287–8)

Dostoyevsky, Bakhtin points out, was hostile to world-views, which see the final goal in merging, in dissolution of consciousnesses into one consciousness and in the removal of individuation: 'No Nirvana is possible for a single consciousness. A single consciousness is *contradiction in adjecto*' (ibid., p. 288). Consciousness, therefore, is only social: one consciousness always stands in relation to another one. Even looking at oneself in the mirror in not a sole activity: 'I look at myself simultaneously with the eyes or myself and of the others, so we have here an intersection of different world views, an intersection of two consciousnesses. Human life is an open-ended dialogue' (ibid., p. 293), in which the model of the world based on individual cognition is being replaced by a dialogical one.

If knowledge is generated neither by the Ego nor by the Alter on their own, but by the Ego–Alter, then the minimum unit of knowledge cannot be expressed as a relation between the Ego–Object, but as a triadic relation Ego–Alter–Object (Moscovici, 1972a, 1984). However, the triadic relation composed of the Ego–Alter–Object is an abstract unit of knowledge. In practice, and as already indicated, different embedded Ego and Alter form complex patterns of interdependencies, even with respect to a single object. Moreover, such embedded triadic relations are dynamic and in tension in multiple ways. But what role is playing the object of knowledge in this triadic relation?

Some objects of knowledge may appear relatively stable over eons of time, for example, natural and physical objects. In contrast, objects of social knowledge, for example, money, democracy or institutions, are usually fluid and transient: they are phenomena in a relative stability and in change. The changing nature of objects of knowledge gives rise to scientific and public disputes. The object of knowledge may constrain the process of knowing by being linked to implicitly shared, but hardly ever spelled out routines and habits. In contrast, it may facilitate the process of knowing by breaking down such routines and habits.

The changing nature of an object may lead to yet another kind of dynamic – to the change in interaction and relations between the Ego and Alter. For example, the changing knowledge of an illness like AIDS is not just an accumulation of neutral facts, but is something that affects stigmatization of individuals and groups and the ways individuals' and groups' actions and interactions are perceived. We could say that the more 'social' the object of knowledge, the more fluid it is; its fluidity has, in turn, an effect on the Ego–Alter construction of social knowledge.

Although in the dialogical theory of knowledge these dynamic triadic relations apply to all kinds of objects of knowledge, I shall narrow down my discussion in this chapter to knowing 'other minds'. Using examples from various areas of social psychology (e.g., influence, identity, social representations, trust), I shall discuss the Ego–Alter–Object interdependence in terms of four dialogical concepts: the two tendencies in the Ego–Alter interaction; asymmetries and dialogical tension; unconsciousness and implicitness in social knowledge and communication; and cognitive polyphasia and heterogeneity in thinking and dialogue. However, this does not mean that this account exhausts all forms of dialogical interaction between the Ego–Alter–Object. It is meant as a selective, yet not a fully comprehensive perspective.

The two tendencies in the Ego–Alter interaction

There are two fundamental dynamic tendencies in the Ego–Alter interaction. We could characterize one of them as a tendency of the Ego towards unification with the Alter, for example, the search for intersubjectivity and mutuality; and the second tendency, in contrast, as a desire of the self to be an independent agent, and to separate itself from the Alter.

The first tendency has been of a significant interest in social-developmental psychology which, probably more often than other kinds of psychology, starts from the concept of the primary interdependence between the Ego–Alter. Taking just one example, Erikson argues that the starting point of the Ego–Alter interdependence is a sense of 'primary or ontological trust' or 'the ontological source of faith and hope' (1968, p. 82). For him, 'basic trust' is the first mark of the mental life of a baby; it is openness towards others that exists prior to any feelings of autonomy and initiative. Trust develops through 'unmistakable communication'; and equally, basic distrust signifies the failure in balancing and integrating the child's experiences with others. Just as the self develops through otherness, so learning to trust the other means learning to trust oneself; and in turn, Erikson claims, trusting oneself implies trusting the trust of the other. Trust is therefore vital for communication and is transmitted by communication. Both the Ego and Alter seek visibility and recognition of one another, each actualizing their potentials through interaction and communication: they understand and create meanings of their world in and through communication with others. The child, equipped with an innate capacity for intersubjectivity, also learns through action, experience and communication to differentiate between the mental states of others, between feelings, and between trustworthy and untrustworthy relations. Learning to trust and distrust others *reflectively* is part of the process of socialization in which the Ego–Alter interaction acquires complex communicative strategies.

But this desire of the self for intersubjectivity, and even for merging with the other, is balanced by the second tendency with which it is dialogically interdependent. The self is an agent who, in and through interaction, tends to establish his/her own independent position. It is the desire to be socially recognized that is another basic tendency of the self directed towards others. Through social recognition, human history can be conceived as a history of desired desires (Kojève, 1969, p. 9). This is why quite insignificant physical objects, for example, a piece of paper or metal, can become symbols of social recognition. Once they acquire symbolic value, they become objects of human desire: they now carry the meaning of social recognition. And so we see how the symbolic social reality is created. The striving for social recognition is not a peaceful process, but takes place in and through tension and negotiation of goals between the self and others. And if this strife is not successful and the self is deprived of the feeling of social recognition, it also means that he or she is unable to satisfactorily function with respect to things which matter to humans, for example, partaking in democratic decisions or having the feeling of justice.

In social psychology, the search for social recognition is fundamental to Moscovici's (1979) theory of minority–majority interaction and to his genetic model of social change. Dialogically speaking, minorities and majorities arise together; there could be no minority prior to a majority and vice versa. Minorities are defined in terms of majorities and a group could become the majority only with respect to that specific minority. One cannot define their characteristics as being *a priori* important. Instead, they define a particular majority–minority, say, Estonians *versus* Russian minorities, and these characteristics could be totally irrelevant in relation to another pair of majority–minority, for example, Estonians *versus* European immigrants. It is a total misunderstanding of the dialogical approach to ask the question that is so often posed, as to whether minorities are more influential then majorities and vice versa. Such a question implies that minorities and majorities are treated as independent of one another and that therefore influence of one group versus the other one can be measured using some external criteria. This question, moreover, ignores the fact that the effect of specific minorities and majorities is mutual and can be evaluated only against the specific social context in which it takes place; in addition, some aspects of influence are implicit and unconscious and their effect may reveal itself in future interactions.

Asymmetries and dialogical tension

The two tendencies in the Ego–Alter interaction discussed above express themselves in dialogical situations as a tendency towards symmetry and asymmetry. Let me explain. In mundane language the phrase 'to be in dialogue' usually means having 'a good dialogue', referring to a discussion or a conversation in which the participants maximize their effort to establish intersubjective understanding and increase symmetry and reciprocity. In contrast to this meaning, in a dialogical approach 'to be in dialogue' takes on a larger perspective. While it does not exclude features of 'a good dialogue', dialogue in the dialogical approach is characterized, above all, by asymmetries, by the power of ambivalence and by the struggle between dyadic oppositions. When I use the notion of 'dialogue', I mean not only a personal interaction but also dialogues in group phenomena, 'dialogues of ideas' and even 'dialogues between cultures and historical epochs'.

The Ego and Alter are partners in reciprocal communication even if communication is highly asymmetric. An example of a highly asymmetric relation could be communication between an expert and novice; the Ego may not question, at least temporarily, the expert knowledge of the Alter. For example, it is hardly ever acknowledged by those who do not have speech and communication problems that people with impaired speech are experts or have a certain kind of knowledge (Collins and Marková, 1999). Another example of high asymmetries could be communication of certain societal habits which are so deeply established that they are not negotiated in interaction, but are automatically assumed; or orders given by a representative in a totalitarian regime; and so on. On other occasions, however, communication is less asymmetric and the Ego and Alter negotiate the meaning of the object of knowledge, for example, they discuss social representations of democracy, argue about a particular disability, defend an ethnic minority and so on.

The idea of asymmetry and oppositions has a broad significance in various dynamic systems. For example, it is often argued that some changes in physical and biological systems take place through movement from symmetric to asymmetric states. This idea can also be applied to social systems, and it can be suggested that asymmetries and tension between dialogical components (or participants) keep dialogue moving (cf. Galam and Moscovici, 1991, 1994, 1995). Moscovici and Galam explain this point with respect to group activities. Group activities involve two kinds of opposite tendencies. One is concerned with an effort for consensus, in which individuals conform to one another, make compromises between their opinions and choices and, in general, shift towards convergence in order to reduce conflicts. The opposite tendency in group activities favours change rather than stability: it works through tension, divergence and differentiation between people, and even through conflict. Group dynamics is a product of these two oppositional tendencies that operate simultaneously. Galam and Moscovici point out that a dynamics within a group prevents interactions from becoming uniform for all individuals: 'The breakdown of symmetry', in contrast, implies that each individual has a capacity 'to switch from dissensus to consensus, from conformity to innovation and *vice versa*' (1994, p. 485). Such processes keep a dynamic flux yet, at the same time, they avoid a total breakdown of interactions and their directions.

Equally, for Bakhtin, dialogical relations are not engaged solely in the search for intersubjectivity and in peaceful contemplation. Instead, cognitions and affects are in tension; they clash, judge and evaluate one another. Bakhtin foregrounds dialogue as a strife of divergent perspectives: 'one point of view is opposed to another, one evaluation opposed to another [...] this dialogic tension [...] permits authorial intentions to be realized' (1981, p. 314) in a heterogeneity of languages and of ideas. Understanding, precisely because it is active, is always evaluative.

And so dialogue usually presents the interplay of opposing tendencies. For example, trust with respect to others could be intermingled with an effort to surmount the unknown and the strangeness of others. Bakhtin's notion of strangeness between dialoguing participants is tied up with a constant negotiation of tension and with the attempt to appropriate the thoughts and speech of others. There could be no dialogue if participants were not opposed to one another through mutually experienced strangeness. Strangeness creates tension between them and opens up a possibility for discourse. The tension is not bound to either of the two participants, but it actually exists between them; it is ever present, whether participants strive for intersubjectivity, for dominance or for any kind of dialogical mutuality. Even if participants in dialogue are in a close intersubjective relation and share a great deal of knowledge, it is a tension between different kinds of mutual interdependencies that keeps their dialogue going. Therefore, the strangeness of the thoughts and speech of other people, just like trust, both facilitate communication and give credit to it.

Let us conclude this section by saying with Bakhtin that ambivalence between mutualities and strangeness between Ego and Alter never changes into monovalence. Instead, these two tendencies coincide in the world of becoming, in which there are no hard boundaries between objects, words or cultures. Boundaries always change because, as Bakhtin assumed, 'a tense dialogic struggle takes place on the boundaries' (Bakhtin, 1979/1986, p. 143).

Unconsciousness and implicitness in knowledge and communication

The existence of unconscious and implicit processes of the human mind has been well acknowledged for several centuries. Surprisingly, however, contemporary social psychology emphasizes the pre-eminence of conscious thought, largely ignoring unconsciousness, and it has not examined unconsciousness in any systematic manner. Instead, our discipline finds the unconscious disturbing. Referring to Freud's concept of the unconscious, and to McDougall, Le Bon and Durkheim, Moscovici suggests that the reason why the study of unconscious processes has been excluded from social psychology could be related to fear that our discipline might be in danger of becoming associated with madness and the crowd mind (1993, p. 39). Such associations would be harmful to the 'respectable' models of rationality that social psychology is attempting to construct in a variety of topics that it examines.

Let us take as an example a very popular theory in contemporary social psychology that attempts to solve intergroup conflicts using a contact hypothesis, based on a rational model. The hypothesis claims that intergroup peace can be achieved if groups have more contact and better understand one another. Many experimental and field studies devote a great deal of effort in order to substantiate this hypothesis in the hope that social psychologists will be able to come up with a recipe for how to reduce intergroup prejudice and discrimination. Social identity theory, specifically, is attempting to provide a theoretical insight into how, by bringing together members from in-groups and out-groups, conflict and discrimination can be diminished (Allport, 1954; Hewstone, Cairns, Voci, Hamberger and Niens, 2006). Yet for anyone who takes a broader perspective upon social life and human history, it could be surprising that it has taken such a long time to come up with this easy solution. How is it possible that throughout the long past of the humankind that has been filled with conflicts and wars, the idea that bringing people together alleviates conflicts has had to wait for experimental social psychologists of the twentieth and twenty-first centuries? Have not such proposals been made by religions all over the world throughout centuries even if not with such precise social scientific criteria that are postulated by the contact hypothesis? But what is contact? It is one thing for members of in-groups and out-groups to mix together in public, to sit next to each other on a train, or in a café, or to play games together. It is quite another matter to mix privately and have intimate physical contact, like touching the other person, drinking from the same cup or having sex, or even more importantly, destroying unconscious barriers between the self and others. While some kinds of contact can be examined using experiments, attitude scales and opinion surveys, other kinds of contact can hardly be accessed in this way at all. The contact hypothesis ignores the fact that subjects may be only partly conscious or even totally unconscious of symbolic and subtle taboos that are transmitted in and through interactions and communications; these have established themselves through culture, collective memories and implicit and explicit prohibitions of contact (e.g., Douglas, 1966; Moscovici, 1972b; Brandt, 1985).

My example of such a taboo of contact comes from our studies of social representations of haemophilia, a genetic disorder affecting blood clotting. People with haemophilia do not form a homogeneous group. There are different types of haemophilia of which the commonest is a sex-linked recessive disorder; haemophilia affects the male and the gene is passed on by the female. The patient with haemophilia may bleed excessively either externally or into internal organs after a physical or an emotional trauma. The blood mysticism, prevalent in religions and in mythologies, implicit fears of blood impurity as well as the actuality of the disease, all these factors contribute to the formation of social representations of haemophilia in the general public. There is a widespread belief among the general public that haemophiliacs would bleed to death from superficial cuts of the skin and that, therefore, haemophiliacs are untouchable. Equally, haemophiliacs have representations of others' representations. Analysing views of people with haemophilia about their employment prospects, we have found that because of fears of rejection, adult men attempt to conceal haemophilia from their potential or actual employers as well as from their sexual partners (e.g., Forbes, Marková, Stuart and Jones, 1982; Marková, Wilkie, Naji and Forbes, 1990; Marková, 1997). And so while people with haemophilia live in society like anybody else and have contact with others, in some ways they are separated by an invisible screen. In his autobiography *Touch me who dares*, Shelley (1985), himself affected by haemophilia, describes how, from his childhood, he had to cope with the ignorance of other people and with their fear that he would bleed to death from superficial injuries. Another author, Robert Massie (1985), too, in an account of his childhood describes an unforgettable event when his schoolmaster announced that no one was to touch Bobby Massie under threat of punishment. He states that his sudden transformation into an untouchable, although the headmaster did that with good intentions, filled him with a sense of powerlessness and stinging humiliation.

This example shows that although people with haemophilia take part in daily life, social representations of haemophilia impose control upon the kinds of contact and interaction that may and may not take place. More generally, if the taboo of contact guides interactions between groups, control as to what is permitted and what is forbidden can be imposed in and through behaviour, language and communication, through the rules of politeness not allowing trespassing into the private space. Control in communication, in particular, can be very powerful: the speaker says something to the other, but he or she may not communicate. Words are used, but they are no more than labels or signals; they do not carry proper meaning and are not part of any trustworthy relations. They may be 'politically correct' expressions, safe kinds of messages that are expected to be said in a given situation, but they leave the common space empty, and so they isolate interlocutors, placing the addressees into a ghetto. And so despite being in contact, controlled non-communicative words and gestures appear as the only forms of 'communication'.

It has often been presupposed in the history of humankind that progress in society can be achieved through education, enlightenment and through the pursuit of knowledge. Like rationalistic models in social psychology, believers in progress in society assume that, through working towards better knowledge of others, barriers between groups will eventually break down. For example, political and anti-racist campaigns are based on an effort to change 'the mind' of the general public through education. They assume that if we transform belief-based social representations that engender discrimination and prejudice into knowledge-based social representations, and if we promote more contact between groups, we will challenge discrimination and improve intergroup relations. This is also why people with haemophilia often make considerable educational efforts to change belief-based social representations of the general public, which are based on wrong ideas, into knowledge-based social representations, based on the truth about the illness. And this is why governments, in order to eliminate the spread of AIDS, run educational campaigns under slogans like 'Don't die of ignorance'.

These attempts to transform beliefs into knowledge, whatever good intentions they have, usually fail to take into account that the resistance of a belief lies in its attachment to other beliefs. For example, the belief that people with haemophilia are 'untouchable' may be connected with another belief, for example, that a person with haemophilia will bleed to death from a needle-prick, or even with an unexpressed belief that has something to do with impurity of blood or, in contrast, with the saintly nature of blood and so on. People who hold convictions or belief-based social representations do not try to find proofs for their beliefs. Beliefs live in the community and may be transmitted unconsciously from generation to generation through collective memory and through common-sense knowledge. They may not even be activated for generations and they rely primarily on consensus with others, exerting an irresistible pressure to conform. This is why our contemporary ideas are loaded with meanings of the past, with affects and myths. Through language, the unconscious past finds access to the present and since we are unaware of its existence, the pressure that it imposes is very powerful, and it perpetuates and reinforces itself in and through discourse with others. It is brought to awareness during periods of tension and conflict when unconscious ideas come to the surface and become problematized and thematized. In this way the dialogical approach opens up psychology to further examination.

Cognitive polyphasia and heterogeneity in thinking and dialogue

In contrast to rigorous rational thought that would follow an identical logical route from one moment to the next, different cognitive and emotional goals employ heterogeneous modes of thinking and communicating. To think means to take diversions and to pursue diverse mental routes. These may range from the scientific to the religious, from literal meanings to metaphoric interpretations, from jokes to formal expressions, and so on. Common-sense thinking and common-sense knowledge display themselves in cognitive polyphasia, that is, in 'diverse and even opposite ways of thinking' (Moscovici and Marková, 2000, p. 245), which are suited to and articulated in the different contexts of which they are part. These diverse and multifaceted ways of thinking and communicating are often in conflict, one confronting the other. Speakers create links to others' communications, anticipating their responses, reactions and feelings. Moreover, the speakers' dialogues are filled with ideas of absent others (third parties) who speak through their mouths, with their commitments and loyalties; speakers contest the opinions and world-views of others.

Let us remind ourselves once again that the notion of 'trust', which exists in different languages, cultures and socio-political systems, is a highly polysemic term. Individuals acquire meanings of 'trust' through the process of socialization and communication and through locally relevant systems of social knowledge. Trusting God, parents, friends, institutions, professionals or the future takes a variety of forms, different kinds of interaction, relationships and communication. In daily language the word 'trust' may hide specificities of different interactions and communication. Quite often, 'trust' can be substituted by other words like confidence, reliance, expectation, solidarity and so on. Some scholars might restrict the meaning of trust to immediate apprehension of the Ego–Alter relations, while others take a broader perspective and include trust as reflected obligations, morals and contracts. Trust, like many other social phenomena, has ontogenetic, historical, cultural and socio-political characteristics; these keep changing throughout history. For example, interaction with a therapist or a doctor is based on different social representations of trust than those involving an accountant in the bank. While the former is concerned with trusting (or distrusting) the professional capacity of the therapist, the latter is based on rational decision-making of the accountant's self-interests. This could involve knowledge, and/or the calculation of costs and benefits as well as other contexts, for example, institutions, rules or established guidelines requiring different forms of trust, including both explicit and hidden agendas. These different social representations of trust involve not only different interpersonal and institutional relations of trust, but also different forms of thought, different communicative genres and language.

Thus, when one uses the word 'language' in the dialogical approach, it always means speaking about languages and heteroglossia (or multivoicedness). Heteroglossia takes on different forms. Not only are there different ways of speaking through dialects, professional languages, social classes and ethnic groups which have specific ways of marking differences and accents in speaking, but equally important, dialogues are saturated with hidden and open polemics, parody, irony, hidden dialogicality, open and hidden rejoinders, collisions and quarrelling. All of these ridden with tension, leaving always a loophole, thus exposing dialogue to the openness of different interpretations – and therefore to novelty. Thinking and speaking are rarely fully determined; there can always be new interpretations of meanings depending on *who* the other *is*. New interpretations involve tension and negotiation of conflict. And as already remarked, yet another aspect of heteroglossia arises from the implicit dialogue involving third parties or the inner Alter, which express their presence through speakers' voices.

Conclusion

There is no doubt something attractive about believing that human rationality expresses itself through the power of a single cognition enabling the individual to control and predict the world in which he or she lives. Yet these flattering beliefs of humankind, nurtured by psychology in general and by Theory of Mind specifically, may even cause disservice to our discipline, if they ignore knowledge of the social nature of the human mind that has been accumulated by other social and human sciences, and especially, perhaps, history and anthropology. Such beliefs about the power of a single cognition may be doing no more than scratching the surface of complex social phenomena.

The dialogical approach outlined in this chapter offers an alternative theory of social knowledge in the study of the human mind. Its point of departure is the Ego–Alter interdependence in generating knowledge and discourse. A range of dialogically conceived concepts broaden the scope of phenomena considered to be relevant to that study, like past social beliefs and future anticipations, heterogeneities, tension and asymmetries in thinking and communication, unconscious and implicit collective ideas hidden in thought and language. And above all, these phenomena that contribute to the richness of social knowledge have their basis in the ontological relation between the Ego and the Alter. This is why a dialogical approach, by examining the basis of the psychology of the individual and presenting an alternative to the Ego–Alter interdependence in its irreducible multiplicity, offers a new agenda for social psychology.

12
ToM Rules, but It Is Not OK!

Daniel D. Hutto

> It is difficult to write today about understanding people without reference to the words 'Theory of Mind'. Google Scholar yields an incredible 36,000 publications using the term, 13,000 of which also refer to infants or children. And the manner in which the term is used is awesomely matter-of-fact – with a taken-for-grantedness hitherto reserved for those other staples of psychology such as 'growth spurt', 'toilet training', 'short-term memory' and 'secure attachment'.
>
> (Reddy and Morris, this volume, Chapter 5, p. 91)

Introduction

A distinctive part of our everyday adult way of making sense of one another involves making sense of actions performed for reasons. This practice, which has been the focus of intense scrutiny, frequently dons the somewhat unfortunate label 'Folk Psychology' (or FP) in the philosophical literature.[1] It travels under many other names too: common-sense psychology; naïve psychology; *Homo sapiens* psychology; the person theory of humans; belief/desire psychology – to name but a few.[2]

FP explanations proceed by calling upon a common stock of familiar mental terms, deploying these in systematic ways. In line with this, mentalistic vocabulary is generally regarded to be a kind of well-regimented and clearly demarcated rule-governed domain, at the heart of which we find intentional attitude psychology, and – crucially – belief/desire psychology. Intentional attitudes are psychological attitudes – such as hoping, recognizing, noticing and so on. They are described in this way because, when in such states of mind, people are related to or directed at objects or states of affairs in a special way. Familiarly, adopting the attitude of fear with respect to a particular thing or type of thing – as when one fears a specific snake or fears snakes quite generally – is a clear instance of having an intentional attitude. Sometimes the objects of intentional attitudes are more complex: we can adopt attitudes to situations or states of affairs too. Such states of mind are known as propositional attitudes – where propositions can be understood, crudely, to be that which is expressed by or follows a *that*-clause. Belief is the paradigmatic example of a propositional attitude, because to have a belief is to think *that* some state of affairs or other obtains; where the proposition in question is captured by a sentence that expresses the relevant content.

It is a commonplace in some circles in philosophy that explaining your friend Y's going-to-the-pub-behaviour by relating that he did so because 'He thought that the pub was open and he wanted a pint' is to engage in a bit of FP. This sort of explanation works because the cognitive element (the belief) in Y's psychological mindset conjoins with the conative element (the desire or, more precisely, the pro-attitude) – and this is so in virtue of these attitudes sharing some semantic elements of their intentional contents. Of course, for the explanation in question to work there are many other background factors that must hold too, but these typically go unmentioned. For example, Y must not be irrational (in any very strong sense), he must not harbour any stronger countervailing desires, and so on.

It would be difficult to deny that adults, in many cultures, systematically make sense of actions using this familiar intentional attitude idiom and schema. Not only do they explain themselves by regularly producing accounts highlighting their relevant 'states of mind' (such as beliefs, desires and hopes), they also quite readily digest the accounts supplied by others with ease. This is so even when such explanations are abbreviated in the extreme. If so then FP is a sophisticated, structured, interpretive practice.

To avoid possible confusion, the shorthand FP should be taken to indicate 'folk psychology' *sensu stricto* – that is, the practice of giving and receiving reason explanations for actions that minimally, if only implicitly, involve beliefs and desires at root (though this might represent only a small subsection of our reason-giving practice). Even amongst those who take FP to be an interesting and important *explanandum* there are philosophical disagreements about the precise scope, character and basis of this practice. The most popular of which – and perhaps now the most contentious (as this volume makes clear) – construes our FP abilities as sponsored or constituted by the having of a 'Theory of Mind' (or ToM). Accordingly, engaging in FP involves the deployment of the relevant mentalistic concepts, by making use of a distinctive set of principles – a network of laws or propositions about intentional attitudes and their relations to other states of mind. This 'system of inferences' allegedly constitutes the core framework for making sense of actions in terms of reasons. It is thought to be the engine of the kind of everyday interpersonal understanding, prediction and explanation that is FP, even though it must be supported by further auxiliary generalizations about what people typically do in a range of circumstances. This proposal has been named the 'Theory Theory' (or TT) by philosophers (however, given its long reach and resilience, it might be more aptly named the 'theory research programme or framework').

Since the mid-1980s its primary contender has been the simulation theory (or ST), of which there are many varieties. Simulation theorists take it for granted that we regularly engage in FP, but they hold this does not involve utilizing a set of principles or a structured theory. Rather, given that our minds are already populated with the relevant mental states (which can be systematically manipulated in precisely the sorts of ways the Theory Theorist's principles aim to describe), it is possible to make the relevant mental ascriptions to other minds by using our own minds as direct models for them. Although this is a structured activity involving the use of mental concepts (at least in the ascription phase), no principles would actively be consulted or used in the process. ST theorists propose to explain how we can make mentalistic ascriptions without recourse to any 'theory' after all.

After years of marshalling philosophical considerations and evidence from psychology, few TT/ST purists remain; most researchers working on everyday psychology accept that the best hope of providing an adequate account of the relevant abilities will draw on resources from both camps. Negotiations continue about how precisely to divide the labour. Everyone admits that there are still many unresolved questions about just how we acquire and carry off our mentalistic feats.[3] Yet the kind of TT/ST union just mentioned is possible only because TT and ST theorists agree on several big issues.

First, proponents of these theories simply assume that the primary function of FP is to predict and explain actions in third personal contexts through the attribution of causally efficacious inner mental states. Crucially, both camps recognize that FP has two undeniable features: 'coherence and mentalism' (Wellman, Cross and Watson, 2001, p. 655). All variants of TT and ST acknowledge these two features *at least* – and they attempt to accommodate them in their own specific ways (as briefly described above). A common characteristic of nearly all of the offerings of the major players is that they posit the existence of complex mechanisms (usually inherited) that manipulate structured mental representations *in one way or another*. It is typically held that this is a base-line requirement for being a credible candidate theory in the game of trying to explain this most sophisticated aspect of our everyday psychology (whether or not one accepts that it involves any kind of theory or theory-like process). The reason why this matters so much is that it fosters general agreement about the nature of the *explanandum* even in the teeth of uncertainty about its *explanans*. If what we are interested in is the coherent, structured activity of making mentalistic attributions for the purpose of causal prediction and explanation – that is, the exercise of FP – then even ST theories can be reasonably enough characterized as aiming to explain our 'Theory or Mind' (or ToM) abilities. Such a characterization is regarded as being neutral between the various rival theories. In making the spectatorial assumption about FP, both TT and ST are interested in explaining our capacity to engage in FP, which they take to be equivalent to ToM 'mentalizing' and 'mind-reading' abilities (the latter labels being very much in vogue).

In what follows, I give reasons for avoiding this all too common way of understanding FP, which is far from philosophically innocent. My intention is to persuade the reader that it would be best to free ourselves completely from ToM-based thinking. To start the process we must ask if the ToM characterization of FP practice can be justified, notwithstanding its popularity. If ToM rules, does it do so by right?

What do the scientists say?

A major reason that ToM rules is that its labels have become a staple part of the *lingua franca* that allows for intellectual trade across a range of disciplines when discussing social cognition (broadly conceived). In this respect ToM talk parallels the way in which talk of 'inner representations' has become integral to those research constituencies that comprise the cognitive sciences. What should we make of such facts? Focusing on the second case, and seemingly forgetting his own key part in initiating the intellectual revolution that made theorizing about mental representations respectable again, Fodor attempts to justify such usage by bidding us, in his usual tongue-in-cheek fashion, to observe an apparently salient fact.[4]

> Philosophical attention is hereby directed to the logical form of such theories. They certainly look to be quantifying over a specified class of mental objects [...] The usual apparatus of ontological commitment – existential quantifiers, bound variables, and such – is abundantly in evidence [...] If, therefore, psychologists say that there are mental representations, then I suppose that there probably are.
>
> (Fodor, 1987, p. 144)

This rhetoric, at best, only thinly disguises the logical howler. Unless we ignore the rule that we can't derive 'ought from is', we should remain unmoved by such facts. And the same verdict applies to the observation that there is a pervasive use of the ToM label that Reddy and Morris describe in this chapter's headline quotation.

That nothing of real importance hangs on this is easily seen if we consider that the reason for such widespread use is that the ToM brand has become closely associated with the empirically robust and highly testable 'phenomenon' of false-belief understanding in children. The false-belief test (or FB test) was first used by Perner and Wimmer in 1983 and it now comes in many subtly different variants. Its popularity derives from the fact that it supplies psychologists with a well-constructed, portable and modifiable experimental paradigm that can be applied (again and again) on countless different populations (including humans, young and old, and, with adjustments, many other animals) in hundreds of conditions. In their 2001 meta-analysis focusing on experiments conducted prior to 1998, Wellman, Cross and Watson reviewed 178 such studies, involving 591 conditions. The number of FB experiments has increased considerably since then. FB tests have become a veritable industry in psychology. Hence, given the mere fact that such tests are often called ToM tests, no one could seriously doubt that the ToM framework has been associated with probably the fastest-growing body of empirical research in psychology over the last 25 years (Leudar, Costall and Francis, 2004, p. 572).

Associations apart, we must ask: What is the true relation between FB tests and the ToM labelling? There has been a clear political advantage to strengthening the association. The burst of experimental activity surrounding such tests has surely been aided by the fact that it apparently tells us something very important about a central (and perhaps even species typical) cognitive competency – one that marks the utterly pivotal moment in the developmental schedule of human children. For it looks to be the point at which they attain the last and most important piece in their set of core mentalistic concepts – the concept of belief – and it is only with their explicit mastery of this concept that they satisfy the necessary conditions for making full-fledged FP attributions (other refinements to their FP ability that come further down the line are taken to be just that, mere refinements). So construed, FB experiments not only get at a psychological phenomenon of some interest, they target one that is a crowning, culminating achievement in human understanding. That this is the default view of many psychologists suggests that they have been influenced by the philosophical framework described in the first section; a framework that looks to have made them aspect-blind to other possible descriptions of the same phenomenon.

Neutrally presented, false-belief findings do not automatically lend themselves to ToM interpretations. Those interpretations are sponsored by reinforcing and framing assumptions about the nature of our basic modes of relatedness to others. What FB data show is that before a certain age (which varies considerably in line with individual differences) children are unable to make correct belief attributions or to correctly answer questions about belief-related actions when this requires them to specify the content of the divergent cognitive points of view of others. It is vital to observe, however, that all such tests confront children with a task that *inherently demands* that they adopt a spectatorial stance. Consequently, the experimental data provide no genuine insight into the true range of children's false-belief understanding and fail to say what role such understanding might play in children's ability to make sense of others in more natural and less restricted interactional settings. Moreover, since FB tests do not probe deeply into the child's understanding and since they are only conducted in spectatorial conditions, they leave us none the wiser as to how frequently or centrally such FB understanding is used; how the children come by it; what enables its acquisition; which other tasks it might be used for; and so on. At most, such tests tell us something about the onset of children's, still fairly basic, third-personal mentalizing abilities. This might be very important if the ToM interpretation was the correct one, but that would have to be independently established. And, of course, FB experiments say nothing at all about whether such abilities are rightly classed as 'ToM' abilities in the first place, nor could they.

To suppose that third-personal speculation about the content of other minds is the base-line way in which children encounter, respond to, and make sense of, others is clearly an unwarranted imposition – it is not even an extrapolation from existing data. This is the crux. Filtered through particular philosophical lenses, the tendency has been to treat a special case of third-personal attribution as if it adequately models the modes of understanding that informs everyday social encounters in all other, more ecologically valid settings. What we have here is a case in which 'a particular skill as operationalized and tested in experimental situations [is being] generalized to everyday reasoning and interaction' (McCabe, this volume, Chapter 6). My suggestion is that certain questionable philosophical assumptions are ultimately the true sponsors of this activity.

In a precisely similar way the so-called mirror-test aspires to serve as a 'critical experiment' offering an appropriate litmus test for the presence or absence of self-awareness. It fails in this because those who hope to use it in this way wrongly assume that self-awareness is a simple kind of psychological competence that can reveal itself through success in a readily assessable, repeatable task. To permit of such testing by means of controlled experimentation, the competences in question *must* manifest themselves in fairly straightforward ways. Or so the standard thinking goes. The root trouble is that in order to conduct such experiments, participants are required to use unusual objects in strange settings. More worrying still is the fact that how they fare in such cases is – deliberately – examined in isolation from the sort of behaviour normally associated with the named phenomenon under investigation, behaviour that is woven into wider patterns of activity that constitute the normal course of human and animal lives. Given its express agenda, such experimentation is self-defeating; for it is only by giving appropriate attention to the context of the relevant behaviours that we are able, confidently, to recognize them as being instances of self-awareness at all. This applies across the board to humans and other species. Bavidge and Ground make exactly this point in their contribution. For this reason, they stress: 'Self-awareness is not the sort of thing that can appear as a discrete phenomenon' (Bavidge and Ground, this volume, Chapter 9). The moral is clear and it generalizes: treating isolated behaviours (such as success or failure on specific tasks) as reliable indicators of important underlying psychological phenomena is an unwarranted de-contextualization.

With respect to FB testing, we have, in a similar way, allowed 'a single task [to] become the marker for complex development' (Astington, 2001, p. 687). This has certainly impeded our understanding of false-belief understanding. For in adopting the ToM framework, many vital questions have not been actively investigated (presumably because their answers are implicitly taken for granted). Consequently, we urgently need to inquire into precisely what goods FB understanding yields for those who attain it; what new skills it engenders; how and when it is used; and so on. Also, we must better understand the roles played by language (the mastery of both its syntax and semantic aspects) and by social scaffolding in bringing on and shaping this particular competence. Such work has been forced out of the limelight by the dominance of certain theoretical tendencies and assumptions which, collectively, can be rightly characterized as constituting a kind of dogma (see Marková, Chapter 11, this volume).

This observation fuels the headline worry, much voiced of late, that far from providing a neutral way of studying natural cognitive development in humans, FB tests have systematically promoted a profound misrepresentation of the character of children's early forms of interpersonal understanding. Several psychologists and philosophers have emphasized the artificiality of these experiments and the contrived third-personal kinds of social situation in which they are conducted. They have independently reached the conclusion that while FB tests allow for the focused collection of data, these data in fact tell us precious little about the nature of normal human social engagements, that is, those we find 'in the wild' and 'in the streets' (Gallagher, 2001; Leudar, Costall and Francis, 2004; Ratcliffe, 2007a). Ultimately, the reason for this is that the standard assumptions about what such tests are uncovering is almost always presented under the aegis of certain larger-scale philosophical pictures of the nature and character of our ordinary practice. That these pictures *are pictures* and that they operate in this way is not generally mentioned and hence their legitimacy is rarely questioned. This is in large part why the ToM framework rules. Likely it will continue to do so until there is a sustained and successful attempt to properly contextualize false-belief understanding of children, so that its role and place in our lives and practices is clarified.

Without doubt something important happens in normal child development somewhere between the ages of three to five, when false-belief understanding is acquired (see Nelson, 2003, 2007). Certainly FB tests do highlight 'a real change in children's competence' (Astington, 2001, p. 686). It would be foolish to deny this, but it would be still more foolish to jump to the conclusion that the relevant change (when it occurs) *necessarily indicates* the pinnacle achievement of ToM mastery. Rather, what has to be accepted is that, despite their robustness, FB tests have a quite different value than is commonly supposed. Here it is important to be clear that the 'Empirical results need not be disputed in order to challenge the theoretical framework through which those results are routinely interpreted' (Ratcliffe, 2007a, p. 55).

It should be clear by now that the relationship between FB tests and the ToM framework is anything but simple. A major knock-on effect of the incredible energy and investment that has been put into such experimental activity is that it has been quietly feeding this particular philosophical monster. By way of return, the ToM interpretation has encouraged yet more experimental work of the FB kind because under its auspices such tests appear to have a special importance. The FB experimental paradigm and standard ToM interpretation are in these respects mutually supporting.

For many years the fact that psychologists have been complicit in the manufacture of the ToM industry has typically gone unreported. But it seems safe to say that the cat is now, well and truly, out of the bag. It has been recognized that:

> The 'theory of a theory of mind' (ToM) [...] is little more than a compound of philosophical misconceptions and inappropriate experiments.
>> (Sharrock and Coulter, 2004, p. 580;
>> see also Sharrock and Coulter, this volume, Chapter 4)

That the ToM interpretation of FB tasks is simply not justified by the available evidence has become a primary target for a growing resistance movement. In a now common refrain, it is repeatedly complained that those who promote ToM thinking, 'illicitly project the character of our *explanans* into the character of our *explanandum*' (Bavidge and Ground, this volume, Chapter 9). Many voices have joined the chorus:

> The experiment, far from being exploratory, has become stipulative.
>> (Costall and Leudar, 2004, p. 628; see also p. 631)

> An interesting behaviour, seen as evidence of a theoretical claim, soon becomes defined by that claim.
>> (Reddy and Morris, 2004, p. 655)

> the experiments do not just 'test' the theory, but themselves reproduce the unnoticed assumptions of the theory.
>> (Leudar, Costall and Francis, 2004, p. 574)

It turns out, *pace* certain advertisements, that 'treating children and adults as theoreticians is not actually an empirical discovery at all, but a background assumption' (Leudar, Costall and Francis, 2004, p. 572).

Clearly, if so, this undercuts any attempt that might be made to appeal to the extensive scientific graft in order to justify the conclusion that *third-personal mentalizing* has been *shown* to play a vital and central role in human social cognition. Any attempt to appeal to the evidence for this purpose must be examined with a critical eye. The mere fact that so many respectable studies have been and are still being conducted using an allegedly ToM methodology lends exactly *no* support to the claim that the framework is itself the correct one to adopt. That our everyday understanding of intentional action takes the form of 'theory of mind abilities' has not been vindicated by any hard data.[5]

The preceding analysis highlights a desperate need for a philosophical reassessment of the ToM framework in the context of our understanding of FB-testing, but that framework has other noteworthy pernicious effects. As noted in the first section, most theorists hold that we operate with a set of platitudes that are so tightly meshed as to constitute a distinctive network of laws or principles governing our everyday understanding of intentional action. This interpretation of how we make sense of other people is problematic enough but confusion is not restricted to the high-level phenomena of making sense of a person's reasons for action or Folk Psychology (FP) *sensu stricto*, the ToM framework also infects the way researchers conceptualize a much wider range of related phenomena, including quite basic forms of social interaction.

Adoption of the ToM framework interferes with our understanding of primary modes of intersubjective engagement and understanding by casting a long shadow. Thus it is typical for everything that precedes the alleged attainment of full-fledged ToM capacities to be understood as simply paving the way for their arrival. There is a general acceptance that direct interpersonal engagements matter crucially to our ability to make sense of others and that undeniably, 'even very small infants are capable of teasing, comforting, deceiving, helping, joking – behaviours which [loosely put] all presuppose understanding psychological states of other people' (Leudar, Costall and Francis, 2004, p. 574). Social understanding is complex; it has many facets and forms, and anyone hoping to account for its basis must adopt both high-road and low-road strategies, if they are to succeed.

Those who endorse the ToM framework recognize this – for example, it is now common to distinguish between low-level and high-level forms of mind-reading (Goldman, 2006). Nevertheless the early, participatory interactions are regularly regarded as being 'implicit', 'proto' or 'pseudo' ToM abilities – and, as such, they are thought to be driven by the very same or similar mechanisms that underwrite more mature modes of explaining action.

For many years the dominant view has been 'not that young children know nothing about mental states but that they fail to understand representational mental states' (Wellman, Cross and Watson, 2001, p. 656).[6] Interpreted through a ToM filter it can therefore appear as if we are faced with a false choice: animals and children are either weak mentalists or adept behaviourists. The choice is a false one because, as Bavidge and Ground, stress: 'Expressive behaviour is not data […it] is interactive […] It elicits not speculation or theorizing, but direct response' (Bavidge and Ground, this volume, Chapter 9).[7] Accordingly, in studying the expressive behaviour of animals (including human behaviour) ethologically we are not studying 'behaviourist behaviour' (Bavidge and Ground, this volume, p. 19; cf. Leudar and Costall, 2004b, pp. 602–3).

To accept this requires rejecting the well-entrenched view that takes 'behaviour to be just bodily movement and so strips it of intentionality, relocating all that is alive and intelligent in the hidden mind' (Leudar and Costall, 2004b, p. 603). The resultant concept of 'behaviour' is mechanical – one devoid of meaning or purpose. This is why it needs to be somehow 'informed' by mindful processes that lurk behind the scenes. This is the Cartesianism inherent in the system.[8] In contrast to this understanding of behaviour and mind, there are ways of making sense of end-directed organismic activity that is infused with intentionality but which is not reliant on cognitivist stories about mental representations *of any kind* (see Hutto, 2006, 2008).

Another clear example of how ToM thinking intrudes is evidenced in the controversy that has broken out over the recent discovery that even 15-month-old infants look significantly longer when agents do not act upon their false beliefs (in a celebrated experiment these beliefs were about a toy's hiding place). Using the non-verbal 'violation of expectation' paradigm, it has been claimed that these infants are capable of passing at least one type of false-belief task – the so-called implicit false-belief task (Onishi and Baillargeon, 2005; Onishi, Baillargeon and Leslie, 2007). This has promoted the idea that perhaps children are fully qualified mentalists, having mastery of FP much earlier on than the FB tests have hitherto suggested but that this fact is masked by the fact that other factors (e.g., executive control, processing problems, etc.) interfere with their performance.

Yet again, this is not the only possible explanation. Infants might have a means of re-identifying and tracking intentional attitudes of others even though they have no conceptual understanding of what they are tracking. This might be the true basis of their expectations (see Hutto, 2008, ch. 6). If so, something quite different is happening between ages three and four, when an explicit understanding of false belief is acquired.

The problems do not end there. Once in the grip of the ToM way of thinking, it is natural to try to explain certain prominent mental disorders as if they involved a relatively straightforward failure of ToM mechanisms – mechanisms that we have inherited from our ancient ancestors and which were forged at the 'dawn of our species' (Shanker, 2004; McCabe, Leudar and Antaki, 2004; McCabe, this volume, Chapter 6). This is a familiar story of what lies behind various mental disorders, such as autism and schizophrenia. For if normal development leads naturally to mentalistic ToM abilities (of the FP variety), and if these are sponsored by ToM mechanisms of some kind (whether of the TT or ST sort [or some combination]), then it is natural to suppose that the failure of said mechanisms is the source of the trouble when things go wrong. FB tests have been conducted in order to make the relevant comparisons with normally developing children and other control groups with this thought in mind.

By now the story should be familiar. For, yet again, we find that a proper understanding of the real roots of these complex disorders is obscured. For example, with respect to the autistic population, Shanker (and others) suggest that the situation is much more complex and that 'sensory challenges' play a critical role in preventing children from engaging with others in ways that eventuate in adult forms of folk psychological understanding (Shanker 2004b, pp. 693–5; see also Belmonte, 2007).[9] This would also explain, more directly, why such individuals are not able to interact with others socially – emotionally and imaginatively – in the way other children do (Gallagher, 2004; Gallese, 2006; Hobson, 2007a). In acknowledging this, new possibilities emerge for intervention, therapy and treatment (see Shanker 2004b, p. 698).

We can conclude from this analysis that ToM talk is not justified by the empirical evidence, and that the underlying reason why ToM talk is so prevalent is that there is a widespread, uncritical acceptance of the standard philosophical characterization of FP steeped in its terms and assumptions.

Reaction and over-reaction

It is natural to want to put something in the place of the discredited ToM interpretation as a straightforward alternative. But what might take its place? A growing number of thinkers have been attracted to the following sorts of claim:

> The alternative […] is to take situated social actions as the object of psychology, whose intentionality is directly graspable, without the benefit of an inference or a mediating theory.
>
> (Leudar, Costall and Francis 2004, p. 574)

> Social understanding […] is a form of what is often called 'situated', 'embodied', 'embedded' or 'extended' cognition. Social understanding is *inextricable from interaction* with the social world.
>
> (Ratcliffe, 2007b, p. 86; emphasis added; see also p. 107)

This kind of situated, embedded approach is a welcome and long-overdue challenge to the kind of cognitivist and mentalistic thinking that has dominated philosophy and psychology since at least the late 1960s. There is great merit in focusing on the non-representational and unprincipled character of the impressive interpersonal engagements that feature in our early childhood and the interrelations of non-human animals. Attending to these in their own right, if we are freed from the straight-jacket of ToM thinking, allows us to understand them in a non-derivative way. We need not regard them, as is the cognitivist wont, as merely early, weak, pseudo or precursor forms of ToM-based attributions.[10] Our *basic* ways of engaging with others are not based on making cold inferences (of any sort). Nor do they require or rely on the use of high-level mental concepts. Thus they are not detached and removed in the way theorists who adopt the ToM framework would have it.

Nevertheless, it is deeply implausible to suppose that these proposed alternatives can shoulder the burden of explaining the full spectrum of kinds of interpersonal understanding. In particular, they are not able to account for complex ways we make sense of others when we do so in terms of FP *senso strictu*. Take an everyday case. I ask a student casually why she has decided to join the MA programme and I get the following short answer: 'My job isn't very intellectually stimulating.' I immediately understand her reason. But this is because, in some sense, I am familiar with how reason explanations work and because I take a great deal about my student's psychological set for granted. This is brought out by the fact that were she to go on to announce that she does not find the offerings on the MA programme intellectually stimulating either, then her initial explanation would be undercut; her stated reason for attending would be inexplicable (it would be no reason at all). But if she were to go on to say that when she first signed up for the programme she thought or believed that it would have the relevant property, then we would be back in business. Or, she might say something more elaborate about her desires that would make sense of her first remark. And so on. The example is simple but the situation is familiar enough. It should remind us that making sense of actions in terms of reasons is a complicated business. It is something that children are not readily prepared for, but they apparently master it somehow.

What should we make of this? More and less aggressive responses have been canvassed. On the extreme end of the spectrum, it has been suggested that there really is no such thing as the practice of making sense of actions in FP terms at all. According to one utterly deflationary appraisal, *'FP is not strictly speaking false*. It is, rather, an abstraction from social life that is misleading in various respects and *has no psychological reality*. At best, it is a convenient way of talking in certain areas of philosophy' (Ratcliffe, 2007b, p. 23; emphases added). An advantage of this, if true, is that there is no discernable practice involving the systematic use of mentalistic terms that needs to be explained and hence no domain of interpersonal understanding that situated approaches cannot handle.

> I hope to have shown that FP is not a part of everyday interpersonal understanding *at all* but rather a theoretically motivated and misleading abstraction that has been imposed upon it.
>
> (Ratcliffe, 2007b, p. 57; emphasis added)

The idea of our language as embodying a folk psychology is a *wholly unnecessary* shuffle super-imposed on the (problematic) notion that we can demarcate a portion of our vocabulary as 'mentalistic'.

(Sharrock and Coulter, 2004, p. 591;
emphasis added; see also pp. 581, 595)

These claims represent the most interesting and powerful challenge to FP to date. For if we take these claims at face value not only is the ToM interpretation of FP misguided, folk psychological practice does not exist at all (other than – at best – in the fevered imagination of some philosophers): there is no such thing. If so, one must deal with FP in the way one deals with any other kind of myth – by exposing and exploding it; since it has no content, it cannot be demonstrated to be false by appeal to evidence. By comparison those, such as the Churchlands, who hold that folk psychology is a radically false theory and exists in at least this sense, are 'weak' eliminativists; even they allow that FP really plays a role in everyday social life. They merely hold that it ought not, since they regard it as being out of tune with our best scientific world-view. But interesting or not, extreme eliminativism about FP appears to be a mistaken over-reaction.[11]

It is not credible to hold that understanding reasons in complex ways involving the distinctive and systematic use of well-defined mentalistic predicates – the sort of thing that belief-desire psychology is meant to characterize – never takes place. We should instead ask: What truth exactly is there to the idea that we make sense of each other in FP terms, once that activity is freed from the philosophical tyranny of the ToM framework?

A better resolution

A more positive approach is to regard 'folk psychology as a form of life' (Costall and Leudar, 2004, p. 625). Of late, constructivist accounts of developmental psychology that emphasize the role social scaffolding plays have grown in popularity. Their guiding insight is that 'it is only in the context of the social matrix [...] that we can make sense of cognitive development' (Garfield, Peterson and Perry, 2001, p. 532; Carpendale and Lewis, 2004, p. 80). Accordingly, for the proponents of such views it is important to realize that:

> Language changes everything [...] Language does not just make a linear difference, as it were, forward or upwards. Rather its effects wash back over activities and capacities that are not themselves in origin or nature intrinsically linguistic [...] language transforms.

(Bavidge and Ground, this volume, p. 187)

I have recently advanced a very specific proposal along these lines, arguing that engaging in one particular kind of socio-cultural practice – narrative practices of a distinctive sort – is the apparent source of our mature FP abilities. Narratives of a specific kind are the crucial medium for engendering FP understanding. I call this the Narrative Practice Hypothesis (or NPH) and advance it in detail elsewhere (Hutto, 2007, 2008). A great virtue of the NPH is that it acknowledges that there are structural and mentalistic aspects at the core of our folk psychological practice, but without conceding that this – in any way – implies that the practice is theoretical or theory-like. Equally, it highlights the fact that although we make use of mentalistic vocabulary in understanding intentional actions, the origin of this practice did not involve postulating 'inner mental entities' in the context of explicit theorizing.

It is part of the folklore of analytic philosophy of mind that FP is a 'term-introducing theory [...] invented long before there was an institution of professional science' (Lewis, 1972). According to Sellar's creation myth, a lone genius – Jones – develops folk psychology in order to better deal with his compatriots (who are, as yet, diehard methodological behaviourists). The scene is as follows:

> [In] the attempt to account for the fact that his fellow men behave intelligently not only when their conduct is threaded on a string of overt verbal episodes [...] but also when no detectable verbal output is present, Jones develops a theory according to which overt utterances are but the culmination of a process which begins with certain inner episodes [... His] model for these episodes which initiate the events which culminate in overt behaviour is that of overt verbal behaviour itself.
>
> (Sellars, 1956/1997, p. 186)

How seriously should we take this? Not very seriously it seems. Even the progenitors of 'theory theory' reduced this sort of claim to the status of a myth.[12] But what then becomes of the status of TT if we don't take the myth at all seriously (as we shouldn't) – that is, if we do not accept the story that primary function of FP in our actual pre-history was that of accurate third-personal mind-reading (as opposed, say, to mind-shaping)? I contend that we lose any firm grip we may have had on what is supposed to put the first use of 'theory' in 'Theory Theory'. And even if we should take it seriously, it shows only that – at best – the intersubjectively grounded activity of modelling our understanding of one domain on that of another has certain parallels in the practices of advanced theoretical science. If we consider the logic of such an observation, it hardly shows that FP is theoretical at root (see Hutto, 2008; see also McGeer, 2007).

It is no accident that public linguistic expressions of beliefs and desires exhibit precisely the features that such psychological states are thought to characterize when they are less readily visible. It is quite plausible that our everyday understanding of beliefs as propositional attitudes is directly modelled on the expressive attitudes we take to linguistically mediated representations of states of affairs. But accepting this supplies no reason for thinking that the concept of belief is theoretical *per se* in its nature or origin. Thus, to the extent that beliefs and desires denote 'inner' states of mind at all, it is only in this innocent and derivative sense. Even Sellars, the arch theory-theorist would agree to this. Our characterization of mentalistic states is derived and borrowed – to be sure – but it is hardly a form or outcome of systematic, hypothetical theorizing.

Putting aside questions about the origins of our mentalistic concepts, isn't on-the-hoof theorizing at the heart of FP practice? To be sure, when others are not in a position to tell us their thoughts, motives or reasons (or when they are unwilling to do so) we may have to guess at them. This takes the form of supposition and speculation. Doing this clearly requires, *inter alia*, reliance on some loose knowledge about what people (and types of people) tend to do on specific occasions. Does this indicate that such speculation is a form of theoretical activity? Clearly not – that is, unless we are prepared to bleed the notion of 'theory' of all interesting content.

Still it might be argued that in attributing reasons, we are necessarily assuming that the mental states in question are the causes of the person's action. After all, isn't it right to assume that everyday FP explanations, which cite reasons, are in fact a species of causal explanation (typically construed as singular causal statements about event interactions). The idea is that they function by identifying causes, albeit rational causes.[13] Many leap on this train of thought without querying its ultimate destination. Yet it is also a train of thought that is easy enough to de-rail by questioning the contentious, though popular, idea that to ascribe a reason is tantamount to ascribing an inner mental state that can act as a kind of *efficient* or *Humean* cause (Sehon, 2005). Without that assumption in play there is no direct route from accepting that reasons are causal *in some sense* to endorsing the sort of intentional realism that treats mental causes as inner happenings; intermediate states standing in characteristic input and output relations. It is possible to deny that functionalist story while accepting, nevertheless, that reasons are causes and reason explanations are causal; for they may be so in only a weak Aristotelian sense that lacks the usual implications (see Hutto, 1999).

Even so, don't mentalistic ascriptions come with ontological commitments – commitments that surely could turn out to be wrong-headed?

> if the meaning of our common observation terms is determined not by sensations, but by the network of common beliefs, assumptions, and principles in which they figure, then, *barring some (surely insupportable) story about the incorrigibility of such beliefs, assumptions, and principles*, our common observation terms are semantically embedded within a framework of sentences that has all the essential properties of a theory.
>
> (Churchland 1979, p. 37; emphasis added)

Churchland begins the above passage by emphasizing the meaning that the holistic character of folk psychological predicates (a view no longer widely endorsed today). The implication is that it is the having of meaning-constituting network properties that distinguishes something as being essentially theoretical. But to suppose this is to commit a simple logical fallacy; for even if all theories have such properties, it would not follow that everything with such properties was a theory.

Really, it is the idea that the FP principles might be false that captured the imagination of philosophers who insist on its having a theoretical status. For, if this should be so, the mental states mentioned in FP laws (here thought of as posits of FP) – belief and desires playing distinctive causal roles – might turn out not to exist. In this light, it has to be remembered that insisting on FP's theoretical status suited the eliminativist agenda. Churchland and his followers wanted to establish FP's theoretical status precisely because they wanted to show that it was ripe for replacement. Yet beyond serving this purpose there seems to be no independent motivation to suppose FP is any kind of theory. Note that FP might not be theoretical even if it is logically possible that we might turn out to be radically mistaken about the nature of beliefs and desires or even their existence (should the latter prove possible).

Without doubt, FP is a stable practice which is predicated on our taking the existence of the entities it describes for granted, but it is not thereby a theory. In this respect beliefs and desires enjoy a status more akin to chairs and tables than photons and quarks. We have many practices that operate with distinctive classificatory schemes and, as such, have 'ontological commitments'. This is true of many mundane activities such as sporting, gaming and gardening and it runs straight through to the sciences themselves – but this does not mean that there is a 'theory' embedded in *every* such practice (unless, yet again, the term applies so generally as to be virtually meaningless).[14]

The point is that to deny that FP is a theory *in this respect*, does not necessarily afford it or its charges any protected status. If FP is a distinct kind of socio-cultural practice, it is still subject to elimination. Practices come and they go; they fall into and out of use. But whether they do or not is neither driven by discoveries about the non-existence of their 'central posits', nor is their continued use normally decided by their specifically intellectual virtues (such as, their fit or lack thereof with the world-view of growing modern science) at all.

And so, we come to the crux. Costall and Leudar (2004) ask the crucial question: 'Where is the "Theory" in Theory of Mind?' Or, in just what sense is our adult capacity to give and receive reason explanations best understood as a kind of theory? As we have just seen, all the possible candidate answers are weak, at best. Moreover, consideration of the existing experimental evidence gives us no reason to accept such a characterization. In sum, the idea that FP is a kind of theory can be justifiably eliminated – being nothing other than a philosophical picture that clouds our understanding of one of our most familiar everyday practices.

Notes

1   It is an unfortunate title because of certain illicit comparisons that it tends (and was intended) to invoke with more mature, scientifically well-established ways of explaining behaviour.
2   These labels can be found, for example, in Churchland (1979), Baker (1999), Sehon (2005) and Goldman (2006).
3   To take but one example, it is an open question as to exactly how and when our distinctive FP ability is acquired. These issues are hotly debated even *within* the various TT/ST camps. Thus with respect to the former, it is divided between those who favour nativist proposals (typically involving some kind of ToM module or ToMM) and those who advocate a certain brand of constructivist story, according to which our ToMs are forged by active, evidence-sensitive theorizing during childhood; theorizing which is both rational and – at times – revolutionary.
4   Fodor, like Chomsky, helped resurrect mentalism and representationalism in what the latter has identified as the 'second' cognitive revolution (Chomsky, 2007).
5   This verdict respects the existing evidence even if it goes against the impression fostered by some philosophers who, ironically enough, regard themselves as the true champions of scientific naturalism.
6   The distinction is meant to capture the difference between capacities to represent merely representational states of mind (such as desires, which have a mind-to-world direction of fit) and those for representing metarepresentational states of mind such as beliefs (which are more complex because they have a world-to-mind direction of fit).
7   They are equally right to observe that 'This is true even for enlanguaged creatures like ourselves. In expressive language, we speak out our experience before we speak about it' (Bavidge and Ground, this volume, Chapter 9, p. 181).
8   The trouble is that such Cartesianism is deep rooted and has found its way into other foundational domains of thought too, including that of our understanding of linguistic behaviour itself. For example, Leudar and Costall (2004b) identify Grice and Chomsky as promoting a 'mentalized understanding of communication'; both in different ways. At root they promote the 'inner process' model of communication which promotes a Cryptographer model of the mind (see Putnam, 1988, ch. 2; Rowlands, 2003). According to this communicative view of language, linguistic comprehension proceeds by decoding useful, but ultimately meaningless, public signs by translating them into meaningful mental symbols. Thus 'For Jones to have (know) a particular language is simply for the language faculty of Jones' mind to be in a particular state. If the state of your language faculty is similar enough to the state of mine, you may understand what I say. Spelling it out a bit further, when my mind produces something that induces my articulatory apparatus to produce noises, and those signals hit your ear, they stimulate your mind to construct some sort of an "image" (a symbolic structure of some sort), your counterpart to what I am trying to express. If our systems are similar enough you may understand me, more or less, comprehension being a "more or less" affair' (Chomsky, 2007, p. 50). It is easy to see from this passage how certain standard

assumptions about the form and nature of linguistic communication have 'established a niche for the Theory of Mind' (Leudar and Costall, 2004b, p. 605).

9 Accordingly, 'sensory overload and under-reactivity inhibit their ability to engage in [relevant] co-regulated interactive experiences' (Shanker, 2004b, p. 685).

10 My own contribution to this movement has been to stress that expressive and unprincipled engagements best characterize our basic social dealings. This claim has been defended by advancing a view of intentionality and phenomenal consciousness under the banner of radical enactivism (Hutto, 2005, 2006, 2008). At its heart is an explication of basic intentionality in terms of biosemiotics; which proceeds to explain end-directed, purposeful organismic activity without appeal to mental representations. Shunning psychosemantics, this form of enactivism provides a basis for rethinking the nature and ground of intersubjective engagements without supposing that participants are making use of propositional attitudes or the concepts of such.

11 For the purposes of questioning this strong claim, I am adopting a particular reading of Ratcliffe (2007b). In his book he makes a variety of remarks, ranging from the reasonable to the seemingly quite radical, with respect to the place of FP in our practices. And, in private correspondence, it appears that his take on this issue might be closer to mine, once certain terminological difficulties are cleared up.

12 Zimmerman, for example, writes 'History shows no record of "belief" being introduced into the lexicon by a band of proto-psychologists in the process of elaborating a highly predictive and subsequently well-confirmed theory' (Zimmerman, 2007, p. 62). Yet he goes on to list three other possible explanations of the origins of the concept that are consistent with the idea that it is theoretical in nature: (1) That the theory in question is a biological inheritance. (2) That it is forged by children during ontogeny. (3) That ancient humans developed folk psychology when the notion of belief was first introduced into the language, and that the theory has since been handed down over the ages through a process of deference.

13 One can see the central importance of considerations about the nature of mental causation by attending to the debates about the ontology of FP. Strong realists hold that the predictive success of folk psychology gives us good reason to take its mentalistic posits metaphysically seriously by our mature sciences. They hold that beliefs and desires cause action and that they deserve to be treated as real, internal events in the minds (or brains) of subjects – even though making sense of this fact presents us with a range of philosophical challenges. Everyday folk make good use of FP and our best psychological sciences should follow their lead, at least for the most part, when theorizing about the mind in a rigorous way. Instrumentalists disagree. They think that the belief/desire calculus is indeed predictively useful but hold that acknowledging this fact, in and of itself, fails to supply sufficient reason to think that the entities postulated by such a theory are ontologically real (or, at least, no more than mildly so). Eliminativists are more aggressive still. As they see it, the propositional calculus of folk psychology has no non-redundant place in the rich framework of growing modern science. To such philosophers there simply are no such things as beliefs and desires.

14 Indeed, we should remember that even with respect to belief-based or belief-incurring practices: 'Human beings, after all, have many beliefs and not many of them hang together so systematically as to merit the term "theory"' (Bavidge and Ground, this volume, Chapter 9).

References

Adrien, J. L., Faure, M., Perrot, A., Hameury, L., Garreau, B., Barthelemy, C. and Sauvage, D. (1991). Autism and family home movies: Preliminary findings. *Journal of Autism and Developmental Disorders*, 21: 43–9.

Adrien, J. L., Perrot, A., Sauvage, D., Leddet, I., Larmande, C., Hameury, L. and Barthelemy, C. (1992). Early symptoms in Autism from family home movies: Evaluation and comparison between 1st and 2nd year of life using I.B.S.E. scale. *Acta Paedopsychiatrica*, 55: 71–5.

Allen, C. (1998). Painting the passions: The *Passions de l'âme* as a basis for pictorial expression. In S. Gaukroger (ed.), *The Soft Underbelly of Reason* (pp. 79–111). London: Routledge.

Allport, G. W. (1954). *The Nature of Prejudice*. Reading, MA: Addison-Wesley.

American Psychiatric Association (1994). *Diagnostic and Statistical Manual of Mental Disorders*, 4th edn. Washington DC: American Psychiatric Association.

Antaki, C. (2004). Reading minds or dealing with interactional implications? *Theory and Psychology*, 14: 667–83.

Argyll, Duke of. (1884). *The Unity of Nature*. London: Alexander Strahan.

Asch, S. (1952). *Social Psychology*. Englewood Cliffs, NJ: Prentice-Hall.

Asperger, H. (1944). Die, 'Autistischen psychopathen' im kindesalter. *Archiv für Psychiatrie und Nervenkrankheiten*, 117: 76–136.

Asperger, H. (1991). Autistic psychopathology in childhood. In U. Frith (ed.), *Autism and Asperger syndrome* (pp. 37–92). Cambridge: Cambridge University Press.

Astington, J. W. (1994). *The Child's Discovery of the Mind*. London: Fontana Press.

Astington, J. (1995). *The Child's Discovery of the Mind*. Cambridge, MA: Harvard University Press.

Astington, J. W. (1996). What is theoretical about the child's development of mind? In P. Carruthers and P. Smith (eds), *Theories of Theories of Mind* (pp. 184–99). Cambridge: Cambridge University Press.

Astington, J. W. (2001). The future of theory-of-mind research: Understanding motivational states, the role of language and real-world consequences. *Child Development*, 72: 685–7.

Astington, J. W. (2003). Sometimes necessary, never sufficient: False-belief understanding and social competence. In B. Repacholi and V. Slaughter (eds), *Individual Differences in Theory of Mind: Implications for Typical and Atypical Development* (pp. 13–38). New York: Psychology Press.

Astington, J. W. and Gopnik, A. (1991). Theoretical explanations of children's understanding of the mind. *The British Journal of Developmental Psychology*, 9: 7–31.

Atkinson, R. L., Atkinson, R. C., Smith, E. E., Bem, D. J. and Nolen-Hoeksema, S. (2000). *Hilgard's Introduction to Psychology*, 13th edn. Fort Worth, TX: Harcourt College Publishers.

Austin, J. L. (1979). *Philosophical Papers*, 3rd edn. Oxford: Oxford University Press.

Bachevalier, J. and Loveland, K. A. (2006). The orbitofrontal-amygdala circuit and self-regulation of social-emotional behavior in autism. *Neuroscience and Biobehavioral Reviews*, 30: 97–117.

Baird, G., Simonoff, E., Pickles, A., Chandler, S., Loucas, T., Meldrum, D. and Charman, T. (2006). Prevalence of disorders of the autism spectrum in a population cohort of children in South Thames: The Special Needs and Autism Project (SNAP). *Lancet*, 368: 210–15.

Bakan, D. (1966). Behaviorism and American urbanization. *Journal of the History of the Behavioral Sciences*, 2: 5–28.

Bakan, D. (1969). *On Method: Toward a Reconstruction of Psychological Investigation*. San Francisco: Jossey-Bass.

Baker L. R. (1999). What is this thing called 'commonsense psychology'? *Philosophical Explorations*, 1: 3–19.

Bakhtin, M. M. (1979/1986). *Estetika slovesnovotvorchestva*. Moskva: Bocharov. (Trans. V. W. McGee as *Speech Genres and Other Late Essays*, in C. Emerson and M. Holquist (eds). Austin: University of Texas Press).

Bakhtin, M. M. (1981). *The Dialogic Imagination: Four essays by M. M. Bakhtin*. Austin: University of Texas Press.

Bakhtin, M. M. (1984). *Problems of Dostoyevsky's Poetics*. Manchester: Manchester University Press.

Barkow, J. H., Cosmides, L. and Tooby, J. (1992). *The Adapted Mind: Evolutionary Psychology and the Generation of Culture*. New York: Oxford University Press.

Baron-Cohen, S. (1988). Social and pragmatic deficits in autism: Cognitive or affective? *Journal of Autism and Affective Disorders*, 18: 379–402.

Baron-Cohen, S. (1989). The autistic child's theory of mind: A case of specific developmental delay. *Journal of Child Psychology and Psychiatry and Allied Disciplines*, 30: 285–97.

Baron-Cohen, S. (1992). The theory of mind hypothesis of autism: History and prospects of the idea. *The Psychologist: Bulletin of the British Psychological Society*, 5: 9–12.

Baron-Cohen, S. (1995). *Mindblindness: An Essay on Autism and Theory of Mind*. Cambridge, MA: MIT Press.

Baron-Cohen, S. (2000a). The cognitive neuroscience of autism: Evolutionary approaches. In M. S. Gazzinaga (ed.), *The New Cognitive Neurosciences* (pp. 1249–55). Cambridge, MA: MIT Press.

Baron-Cohen, S. (2000b). Theory of mind and autism: A fifteen year review. In S. Baron-Cohen, H. Tager-Flusberg and D. J. Cohen (eds), *Understanding Other Minds: Perspectives from Developmental Cognitive Neuroscience* (pp. 3–20). Cambridge, MA: MIT Press.

Baron-Cohen, S. (2002). Is Asperger syndrome necessarily viewed as a disability? *Focus on Autism and other Developmental Disorders*, 17: 186–91.

Baron-Cohen, S. (2004). *The Essential Difference*. London: Penguin.

Baron-Cohen, S., Leslie, A. and Frith, U. (1985). Does the autistic child have a 'theory of mind'? *Cognition*, 21: 37–46.

Barr, R. (2008). Developing social understanding in a social context. In K. McCartney and D. Phillips (eds), *Blackwell Handbook of Early Childhood Development* (pp. 188–207). Oxford: Blackwell.

Barresi, J. and Moore, C. (1996). Intentional relations and social understanding. *Behavioral and Brain Sciences*, 19: 107–54.

Bates, E. (1979). *The Emergence of Symbols: Cognition and Communication in Infancy*. New York: Academic Press.

Bavidge, M. and Ground, I. (1994). *Can We Understand Animal Minds?* London: Bristol Classical.

Bell, S. (1970). The development of the concept of object as related to infant-mother attachment. *Child Development*, 41: 219–311.

Bell, V., Halligan, P. and Ellis, H. (2003). Beliefs about delusions. *The Psychologist*, 16: 418–22.

Belmonte, M. (2008). Human, but more so: What the autistic brain tells us about the process of narrative. In M. Osteen (ed.), *Autism and Representation* (pp. 166–79). London: Routledge.

Bennett, J. (1976). *Linguistic Behaviour*. Cambridge: Cambridge University Press.

Bennett, M. R. and Hacker, P. M. S. (2003). *Philosophical Foundations of Neuroscience*. Oxford: Blackwell.

Bentall, R. P. (1992). *Reconstructing Schizophrenia*. London: Routledge.

Bentall, R. P. (2001). Social cognition and delusional beliefs. In P. W. Corrigan and D. L. Penn (eds), *Social Cognition and Schizophrenia* (pp. 123–48). Washington DC: American Psychiatric Association.

Bentall, R. P. (2003). *Madness Explained: Psychosis and Human Nature*. London: Penguin Books.

Bentall, R. P. and Swarbrick, R. (2003). The best laid schemas of paranoid patients: Autonomy, sociotropy and need for closure. *Psychology and Psychotherapy*, 76: 163–71.

Bernabei, P., Camaioni, L. and Levi, G. (1998). An evaluation of early development in children with autism and pervasive developmental disorders from home movies: preliminary findings. *Autism*, 2: 243–58.

Bernstein, I. S. (1998). Metaphor, cognitive belief and science. *Behavioral and Brain Sciences*, 11: 247–8.

Bialystok, E., Sherry, S. Shanker, S. and Codd, J. (2003). Executive function deficits in children with autism. *The Journal of Developmental and Learning Disorders*, 7: 37–55.

Bieberich, A. and Morgan, S. (1998). Brief report: Affective expressions in children with autism. *Journal of Autism and Developmental Delays*, 28: 333–8.

Bilmes, J. (1986). *Discourse and Behavior*. New York: Plenum Press.

Bilmes, J. (1992). Referring to internal occurrences. *Journal for the Theory of Social Behaviour*, 22: 253–62.

Blackmore, J. (1979). On the inverted uses of the terms 'realism' and 'idealism' among scientists and historians of science. *British Journal of the Philosophy of Science*, 30: 125–34.

Bleuler, E. (1911/1950). *Dementia Praecox or the Group of Schizophrenias*. New York: International Universities Press.

Bloom, P. and German, T. P. (2000). Two reasons to abandon the false belief task as a test of the theory of mind. *Cognition*, 77: 25–31.

Bolton, N. (1987). The programme of phenomenology. In A. Costall and A. Still (eds), *Cognitive Psychology in Question* (pp. 234–54). Brighton: Harvester Press.

Boucher, J. (1996). What could possibly explain autism? In P. Carruthers and P. K. Smith (eds), *Theories of Mind* (pp. 223–41). Cambridge: Cambridge University Press.

Brandt, A. M. (1985). *No Magic Bullet*. New York: Oxford University Press.

Brankovic, S. B. and Paunovic, V. R. (1999). Reasoning under uncertainty in deluded schizophrenic patients: A longitudinal study. *European Psychiatry*, 14: 76–83.

Bretherton, I., McNew, S. and Beeghly-Smith, M. (1981). Early person knowledge as expressed in gestural and verbal communication: When do infants acquire a 'theory of mind'? In M. E. Lamb and L. R. Sherrod (eds), *Infant Social Cognition* (pp. 333–73). Hillsdale, NJ: Lawrence Erlbaum Associates.

Broadbent, D. E. (1957). *Perception and Communication*. Oxford: Pergamon Press.

Broadbent, D. E. (1973). *In Defense of Empirical Psychology*. London: Methuen.

Broadbent, D. E. (1980). Autobiography. In G. Lindzey (ed.), *A History of Psychology in Autobiography* (vol. 7, pp. 39–73). San Francisco: W. H. Freeman.

Brown, R. (1958). *Words and Things*. Glencoe, IL: Free Press of Glencoe.

Brown, R. (1970). *Psycholinguistics*. New York: Free Press.

Brüne, M. (2003). Theory of mind and the role of IQ in chronic disorganized schizophrenia. *Schizophrenia Research*, 60: 57–64.

Bruner, J. (1978). Learning how to do things with words. In J. Bruner and A. Garton (eds), *Human Growth and Development: The Wolfson College Lectures 1976* (pp. 62–84). Oxford: Clarendon Press.

Bruner, J. (1988). Founding the center for cognitive studies. In W. Hirst (ed.), *The Making of Cognitive Science: Essays in Honor of George A. Miller* (pp. 90–9). Cambridge: Cambridge University Press.

Bruner, J. (1990). *Acts of Meaning*. Cambridge, MA: Harvard University Press.

Bruner, J. and Feldman, C. (1993). Theories of mind and the problem of autism. In S. Baron-Cohen, H. Tager-Flusberg and D. J. Cohen (eds), *Understanding Other Minds: Perspectives from Autism* (pp. 267–91). Oxford: Oxford University Press.

Buber, M. (1958). *I and Thou*. Trans R. G. Smith, 2nd edn. Edinburgh: T. Clark & T. Clark.

Byrne, R. W. and Whiten, A. (1990). Tactical deception in primates: The 1990 database. *Primate Report*, whole volume, 27: 1–101.

Cadinu, M. R. and Kiesner, J. (2000). Children's development of a theory of mind. *European Journal of Psychology of Education*, 15: 93–111.

Camaioni, L. (1992). Mind knowledge in infancy: The emergence of intentional communication. *Early Development and Parenting*, 1: 15–22.

Camaioni, L. (1993). The development of intentional communication: A re-analysis. In J. Nadel and L. Camaioni (eds), *New Perspectives in Early Communicative Development* (pp. 82–96). London: Routledge.

Carpendale, J. L. M. and Lewis, C. (2004). Constructing an understanding of the mind: The development of children's social understanding within social interaction. *Behavioural and Brain Sciences*, 27: 79–96.

Carpendale, J. L. M. and Lewis, C. (2006). *How Children Develop Social Understanding*. Oxford: Blackwell.

Carruthers, P. (1996). Autism as mindblindness: An elaboration and partial defence. In P. Carruthers and P. Smith (eds), *Theories of Mind* (pp. 257–73). Cambridge: Cambridge University Press.

Carruthers, P. and P. Smith (eds) (1996). *Theories of Mind*. Cambridge: Cambridge University Press.

Celani, G., Battistelli, P., Marco, E. and Battacchi, W. (1998). Inganno e comprensione delle false credenze: Conoscenza delle conseguenze ingannevoli delle proprie azioni nei bambini sotto 14 anni di et`a. *Giornale Italiano di Psicologia*, 25: 583–605.

Chandler, M. J., Fritz, A. S. and Hala, S. (1989). Small-scale deceit: Deception as a marker of 2-, 3- and 4-year olds' early theories of mind. *Child Development*, 60: 1263–77.

Charlton, B. G. (2000). The new management of scientific knowledge: A change in direction with profound implications. In A. Miles, J. R. Hampton and B. Hurwitz (eds), *NICE, CHI and the New NHS Reforms: Enabling Excellence or Imposing Control?* (pp. 13–32). London: Aesculapius Medical Press.

Cheney, D. L. and Seyfarth, R. M. (1990). Attending to behaviour versus attending to knowledge: Examining monkeys' attribution of mental states. *Animal Behaviour*, 40: 742–53.

Cherry, C. (1957). *On Human Communication: A Review, a Survey and a Criticism*. New York: The Technology Press of Massachusetts Institute of Technology.

Chomsky, N. (1959). Review of B. F. Skinner, 'Verbal Behavior'. *Language*, 35: 26–58.
Chomsky, N. (1964). Formal Discussion. In U. Bellugi and R. Brown (eds), *The Acquisition of Language*. Monograph of the Society for Research in Child Development (pp. 35–42). Lafayette, IN: Purdue University Press.
Chomsky, N. (1966). *Cartesian Linguistics: A Chapter in the History of Rationalist Thought*. Lanham, MD: University Press of America.
Chomsky, N. (1969). Quine's empirical assumptions. In D. Davidson and J. Hintikka (eds), *Words and Objections: Essays on the work of W. V. Quine* (pp. 303–11). Dordrecht: Reidel.
Chomsky, N. (1976). *Reflections on Language*. London: Maurice Temple Smith.
Chomsky, N. (1980a). *Rules and Representations*. Oxford: Basil Blackwell.
Chomsky, N. (1980b). Rules and representations. *The Behavioural and Brain Sciences*, 3: 1–61.
Chomsky, N. (1984). *Modular Approaches to the Study of the Mind*. San Diego, CA: San Diego State University Press.
Chomsky, N. (1986). Interview with Noam Chomsky. In B. J. Baars (ed.), *The Cognitive Revolution in Psychology* (pp. 341–51). New York: Guilford Press.
Chomsky, N. (2007). Language and thought: Descartes and some reflections on venerable themes. In A. Brook (ed.), *The Prehistory of Cognitive Science* (pp. 38–66). Basingstoke: Palgrave Macmillan.
Churchland, P. M. (1979). *Scientific Realism and the Plasticity of Mind*. Cambridge: Cambridge University Press.
Clements, W. A. and Perner, J. (1994). Implicit understanding of belief. *Cognitive Development*, 9: 377–95.
Colbert, S. M. and Peters, E. R. (2002). Need for closure and jumping-to-conclusions in delusion-prone individuals. *Journal of Nervous and Mental Disease*, 190: 27–31.
Collingwood, R. G. (1940). *An Essay on Metaphysics*. Oxford: Oxford University Press.
Collingwood, R. G. (1946). *The Idea of History*. Oxford: Oxford University Press.
Collingwood, R. G. (1994). *The Idea of History*, revised edn. Oxford: Oxford University Press.
Collins, S. and Marková, I. (1999). Interaction between impaired and unimpaired speakers: Intersubjectivity and the interplay of culturally shared and situation specific knowledge. *British Journal of Social Psychology*, 38: 339–68.
Cook, J. (1969). Human beings. In P. Winch (ed.), *Studies in the Philosophy of Wittgenstein* (pp. 117–51). London: Routledge.
Corcoran, R. (2000). Theory of mind in other clinical populations. In S. Baron-Cohen, H. Tager-Flusberg and D. Cohen (eds), *Understanding Other Minds: Perspectives from Autism and Developmental Cognitive Neuroscience* (pp. 391–421), 2nd edn. Oxford: Oxford University Press.
Corcoran, R. (2001). Theory of mind in schizophrenia. In: D. Penn and P. Corrigan (eds), *Social Cognition in Schizophrenia* (pp. 149–74). Washington DC: American Psychiatric Association.
Corcoran, R., Mercer, G. and Frith, C. D. (1995). Schizophrenia, symptomatology and social inference: Investigating 'theory of mind' in people with schizophrenia. *Schizophrenia Research*, 17: 5–13.
Corkum, V. and Moore, C. (1995). Development of joint visual attention in infants. In C. Moore and P. J. Dunham (eds), *Joint Attention: Its Origins and Role in Development* (pp. 61–83). Hillsdale, NJ: Erlbaum.
Corkum, V. and Moore, C. (1998). Origins of joint visual attention in infants. *Developmental Psychology*, 34: 28–38.
Costall, A. (1991). Graceful degradation: Cognitivism and the metaphors of the computer. In A. Still. and A. Costall (eds), *Against Cognitivism: Alternative*

Foundations for Cognitive Psychology (pp. 151–70). Hemel Hempstead: Harvester-Wheatsheaf.

Costall, A. (1995). Socializing affordances. *Theory and Psychology*, 5: 467–81.

Costall, A. (2006). Introspectionism and the mythical origins of modern scientific psychology. *Consciousness and Cognition*, 15: 634–54.

Costall, A. (2007). Bringing the body back to life: James Gibson's ecology of agency. In J. Zlatev, T. Ziemke, R. Frank and R. Dirven (eds), *Body, Language and Mind: Vol. 1: Embodiment* (pp. 241–70). The Hague: de Gruyter.

Costall, A. and Dreier, O. (eds) (2006). *Doing Things with Things: The Design and Use of Objects*. London: Ashgate.

Costall, A. and Leudar, I. (eds) (1996). Situating action. Special issue, *Ecological Psychology*, 8, 2: 101–87.

Costall, A. and Leudar, I. (2004). Where is the 'theory' in theory of mind? *Theory and Psychology*, 14: 625–48.

Costall, A. and Leudar, I. (2007). Getting over 'the problem of other minds': Communication in context. *Infant Behavior and Development*, 30: 289–95.

Costall, A., Leudar, I. and Reddy, V. (2006). Failing to see the irony in 'mind-reading'. *Theory and Psychology*, 16: 163–7.

Cottingham, J. (1995). *The Cambridge Companion to Descartes*. Cambridge: Cambridge University Press.

Coulter, J. (1979). *The Social Construction of Mind*. Basingstoke: Macmillan.

Coulter, J. (1983). *Rethinking Cognitive Theory*. Basingstoke: Macmillan.

Coulter, J. (1989). *Mind in Action*. Oxford: Polity Press.

Coulter, J. (1992). Bilmes on 'internal states': A critical commentary. *Journal for the Theory of Social Behaviour*, 22: 239–52.

Coulter, J. (1999). Discourse and mind. *Human Studies*, 22: 163–81.

Coulter, J. (2004). What is 'Discursive Psychology'? *Human Studies*, 27: 335–40.

Cromer, R. F. (1980). Empirical evidence in support of non-empiricist theories of mind. *The Behavioural and Brain Sciences*, 3: 16–18.

Danziger, K. (1989). *Constructing the Subject: Historical Origins of Psychological Research*. Cambridge: Cambridge University Press.

Danziger, K. (1997). *Naming the Mind*. London: Sage.

Darwin, F. (ed.) (1887). *The Life and Letters of Charles Darwin* (vol. 1). London: John Murray.

Daston, L. (1992). Objectivity and the escape from perspective. *Social Studies of Science*, 22: 597–618.

David, A. S. (1999). On the impossibility of defining delusions. *Philosophy, Psychiatry and Psychology*, 6: 17–20.

Davies, M. J. and Stone, T. (1995). *Folk Psychology: The Theory of Mind Debate*. Oxford: Blackwell.

Dawson, G., Hill, I., Spencer, A. and Galpert, L. (1990). Affective exchanges between young autistic children and their mothers. *Journal of Abnormal Child Psychology*, 18: 335–45.

Dawson, G., Meltzoff, A. N., Osterling, J., Rinaldi, J. and Brown, E. (1998). Children with autism fail to orient to naturally occurring social stimuli. *Journal of Autism and Developmental Disorders*, 28, 479–85.

Dennett, D. (1971). Intentional systems. *Journal of Philosophy*, 8: 87–106.

Dennett, D. (1987). *The Intentional Stance*. Cambridge, MA: MIT Press.

Descartes, R. (1954). Correspondence with Princess Elizabeth (1643). In E. Anscombe and P. T. Geach (eds), *Descartes: Philosophical Writings* (pp. 274–282). London: Nelson.

Descartes, R. (1649/1970). Letter to H. More. In A. Kenny (trans.), *Descartes: Philosophical Letters*. Oxford: Blackwell.

Descartes, R. and Kenny, A. J. P. (1970/1981). *Philosophical Letters*. Oxford: Blackwell.

Di Lavore, P. C., Lord, C. and Rutter, M. (1995). Pre-linguistic Autism Diagnostic Schedule, *Journal of Autism and Developmental Disorders*, 25: 355–79.

Doody, G. A., Gàtz, M., Johnstone, E. C., Frith, C. D. and Cunningham Owens, D. G. (1998). Theory of mind and psychoses. *Psychological Medicine*, 28: 397–405.

Douglas, M. (1966). *Purity and Danger*. London and Henley: Routledge & Kegan Paul.

Drew, P. (1995). Interaction sequences and anticipatory interactive planning. In E. Goody (ed.), *Social Intelligence and Interaction* (pp. 111–38). Cambridge: Cambridge University Press.

Dreyfus, H. L. and Dreyfus, S. E. (1991). The mistaken psychological assumptions underlying belief in expert systems. In A. Still and A Costall (eds), *Against Cognitivism: Alternative Foundations for Cognitive Psychology* (pp. 17–31). New York: Harvester Wheatsheaf.

Drury, V. M., Robinson, E. J. and Birchwood, M. (1998). 'Theory of mind' skills during an acute episode of psychosis and following recovery. *Psychological Medicine*, 28: 1101–12.

Dudley, R. E. J., John, C. H., Young, A. W. and Over, D. E. (1997). The effect of self-referent material on the reasoning of people with delusions. *British Journal of Clinical Psychology*, 36: 575–84.

Dunn, J. (1988). *The Beginning of Social Understanding*. Oxford: Blackwell.

Dunn, J. (1991). Young children's understanding of other people: Evidence from observations within the family. In D. Frye and C. Moore (eds), *Children's Theories of Mind* (pp. 97–114). Hillsdale, NJ: Erlbaum.

Edwards, D. (2006). Discourse, cognition and social practices: The rich surface of language and social interaction. *Discourse Studies*, 8: 41–9.

Edwards, D. and Potter, J. (2005). Discursive psychology, mental states and descriptions. In H. te Molder and J. Potter (eds), *Conversation and Cognition* (pp. 241–59). Cambridge: Cambridge University Press.

Eisenmajer, R. and Prior, M. (1991). Cognitive linguistic correlates of 'theory of mind' ability in autistic children. *British Journal of Developmental Psychology*, 9: 351–64.

Ekman, P. (1972). *Emotion in the Human Face: Guidelines for Research and an Integration of Findings*. Oxford: Pergamon.

Emde, R. N., Biringen, Z., Clyman, R. B. and Oppenheim, D. (1991). The moral self of infancy: Affective core and procedural knowledge. *Developmental Review*, 11: 251–70.

Erikson, E. (1968). *Identity: Youth and Crisis*. London: Faber & Faber.

Feyerabend, P. (1999). *Conquest of Abundance*. Chicago: The University of Chicago Press.

Fiske, S. and Taylor, S. (1991). *Social Cognition*. New York: McGraw-Hill.

Fodor, J. (1983). *Modularity of Mind*. Cambridge, MA: MIT Press.

Fodor, J. A. (1987). *Psychosemantics*. Cambridge, MA: MIT Press.

Forbes, C. D., Marková, I., Stuart, J. and Jones, P. (1982). To tell or not to tell: Haemophiliacs' views on their employment prospects. *International Journal of Rehabilitation Research*, 5: 13–18.

Foucault, M. (1989). *The Order of Things: An Archaeology of the Human Sciences*. New York: Routledge.

Freeman, D. and Garety, P. A. (2000). Comments on the content of persecutory delusions: Does the definition need clarification? *British Journal of Clinical Psychology*, 39: 407–14.

Freeman, D. and Garety, P. A. (2003). Connecting neurosis and psychosis: The direct influence of emotion on delusions and hallucinations. *Behaviour Research and Therapy*, 41: 923–47.

Freeman, D., Garety, P. A. and Kuipers, E. (2001). Persecutory delusions: Developing the understanding of belief maintenance and emotional distress. *Psychological Medicine*, 31: 1293–306.

Freud, S. (2005). *The Unconscious*. London: Penguin. (Originally published in 1915.)

Frith, C. D. (1987). The positive and negative symptoms of schizophrenia reflect impairments in perception and initiation of action. *Psychological Medicine*, 17: 631–48.

Frith, C. D. (1992). *The Cognitive Neuropsychology of Schizophrenia*. London: Lawrence Erlbaum Associates.

Frith, C. D. (1995). Functional imaging and cognitive abnormalities. *The Lancet*, 346: 615–20.

Frith, C. D. and Corcoran, R. (1996). Exploring 'theory of mind' in people with schizophrenia. *Psychological Medicine*, 26: 521–30.

Frith, U. (1989). *Autism: Explaining the Enigma*. Oxford: Blackwell.

Frith, U. and Happé, F. (1999). Theory of mind and self-consciousness: What is it like to be autistic? *Mind and Language*, 14: 1–22.

Funder, D. C. (1995). On the accuracy of personality judgment: A realistic approach. *Psychological Review*, 102: 652–70.

Galam, S. and Moscovici, S. (1991). Towards a theory of collective phenomena: Consensus and attitude changes in groups. *European Journal of Social Psychology*, 21: 49–74.

Galam, S. and Moscovici, S. (1994). Towards a theory of collective phenomena: II: Conformity and power. *European Journal of Social Psychology*, 24: 481–95.

Galam, S. and Moscovici, S. (1995). Towards a theory of collective phenomena: III: Conflicts and forms of power. *European Journal of Social Psychology*, 25: 217–29.

Gallagher, S. (2001). The practice of mind: Theory, simulation or primary interaction? *Journal of Consciousness Studies*, 8: 83–108.

Gallagher, S. (2004). Understanding interpersonal problems in autism: Interaction theory as an alternative to theory of mind. *Philosophy, Psychiatry, Psychology*, 11: 199–217.

Gallagher, S. (2007). Logical and phenomenological arguments against simulation theory. In D. Hutto and M. Radcliffe (eds), *Folk Psychology Reassessed* (pp. 63–78). Dordrecht: Springer.

Gallese, V. (2000). The acting subject: Towards the neural basis of social cognition. In T. Metzinger (ed.), *Neural Correlates of Consciousness: Empirical and Conceptual Questions* (pp. 325–33). Cambridge, MA: MIT Press.

Gallese, V. (2001). The 'Shared Manifold' hypothesis: From mirror neurons to empathy. In E. Thompson (ed.), *Between Ourselves: Second-Person Issues in the Study of Consciousness* (pp. 35–50). Charlottesville, VA: Imprint Academic.

Gallese, V. (2006). Intentional attunement: A neuropsyhiological perspective on social cognition and its disruption in autism. *Cognitive Brain Research*, 1079: 15–24.

Gallup, G. G. (1970). Chimpanzees: Self-recognition. *Science*, 167: 86–7.

Garety, P. A. (1998). Insight and delusions. In X. F. Amador and A. S. David (eds), *Insight and Psychosis* (pp. 66–77). Oxford: Oxford University Press.

Garety, P. A. and Freeman, D. (1999). Cognitive approaches to delusions: A critical review of theories and evidence. *British Journal of Clinical Psychology*, 38: 113–54.

Garfield, J. L., Peterson, C. C. and Perry, T. (2001). Social cognition, language acquisition and the development of the theory of mind. *Mind and Language*, 16: 494–541.

Garner, W. R. (1999). Reductionism reduced: Review of 'Toward a new behavior-ism: The case against perceptual reductionism' by William R. Uttal. *Contemporary Psychology*, 44: 20–1.

Garton, A. F. (2004). *Exploring Cognitive Development: The Child as Problem Solver*. Oxford: Blackwell.

Gergely, G. (2003). The development of understanding of self and agency. In U. Goswami (ed.), *Blackwell Handbook of Child Cognitive Development* (pp. 26–46). Malden, MA: Blackwell.

Gernsbacher, M. A., Davidson, R. J., Dalton, K. and Alexander, A. (2003). *Why Do Persons with Autism Avoid Eye Contact?* Paper presented at the annual meeting of the Psychonomic Society, Vancouver, BC.

Goffman, E. (1979). *Gender Advertisements*. Basingstoke: Macmillan.

Goldman, A. I. (2006). *Simulating Minds: The Philosophy, Psychology and Neuroscience of Mindreading*. New York: Oxford University Press.

Goleman, D. (1996/2006). *Emotional Intelligence: Why It Can Matter More Than IQ*. London: Bloomsbury Paperbacks.

Golinkoff, R. M. (1986). 'I beg your pardon?': The preverbal negotiation of failed mes-sages. *Journal of Child Language*, 13: 455–76.

Golinkoff, R. M. (1993). When is communication a 'meeting of minds'? *Journal of Child Language*, 20: 119–207.

Goodglass, H. (1993). *Understanding Aphasia*. New York: Academic Press.

Gopnik, A. (1993). How we know our minds: The illusion of first-person knowledge of intentionality. *Behavioral and Brain Sciences*, 16: 1–14.

Gopnik, A. (1996). Theories and modules. In P. Carruthers and P. Smith (eds), *Theories of Theories of Mind* (pp. 169–83). Cambridge: Cambridge University Press.

Gopnik, A. (1999). Theory of mind. In R. A. Wilson and F. Keil (eds), *The MIT Encyclopedia of Cognitive Sciences* (pp. 830–41). Cambridge, MA: MIT Press.

Gopnik, A. (2003). The theory theory as an alternative to the innateness hypoth-esis. In L. M. Antony and N. Hornstein (eds), *Chomsky and His Critics* (pp. 238–54). Oxford: Blackwell.

Gopnik, A. and Wellman, H. M. (1992). Why the child's theory of mind really is a theory. *Mind and Language*, 7: 145–71.

Gopnik, A. and Wellman, H. M. (1994). The theory theory. In L. A. Hirschfield and S. A. Gellman (eds), *Mapping the Mind: Domain Specificity in Culture and Cognition* (pp. 257–93). New York: Cambridge University Press.

Gopnik, A., Capps, L. and Meltzoff, A. N. (2000). Early theories of mind: What the theory theory can tell us about autism. In S. Baron-Cohen, H. Tager-Flusberg and D. J. Cohen (eds), *Understanding Other Minds: Perspectives from Developmental Cognitive Neuroscience* (pp. 21–35), 2nd edn. Cambridge, MA: MIT Press.

Gopnik, A., Meltzoff, A. and Kuhl, P. (1999). *The Scientist in the Crib: Minds, Brains and How Children Learn*. New York: William Morrow.

Gordon, R. (1992). The simulation theory: Objections and misconceptions, *Mind and Language*, 7: 11–34.

Gordon, R. (1996). 'Radical' simulationism. In P. Carruthers and P. Smith (eds), *Theories of Mind* (pp. 11–21). Cambridge: Cambridge University Press.

Grandin, T. (1995). *Thinking in Pictures*. New York: Doubleday.

Grandin, T. (1996). *Thinking in Pictures: And Other Reports from My Life With Autism*. New York: Vintage Books.

Grant, C. M., Grayson, A. and Boucher, J. (2001). Using tests of false belief with chil-dren with autism: How reliable and valid are they? *Autism*, 5: 135–45.

Greene, J. M. (1972). *Psycholinguistics*. London: Penguin.

Greenspan, S. (1979). Intelligence and adaptation: An integration of psychoanalytic and Piagetian developmental psychology. *Psychological Issues*, Monograph 47/68. New York: International Universities Press.

Greenspan, S. (1992). *Infancy and Early Childhood: The Practice of Clinical Assessment and Intervention with Emotional and Developmental Challenges.* Madison, CT: International Universities Press.

Greenspan, S. (1997). *The Growth of the Mind.* New York: Addison-Wesley.

Greenspan, S. and Shanker, S. (2004). *The First Idea.* Reading, MA: Da Capo Press/ Perseus Books.

Greenspan, S. and Wieder, S. (1998a). Developmental patterns and outcomes in infants and children with disorders in relating and communicating: A chart review of 200 cases of children with autistic spectrum diagnoses. *The Journal of Developmental and Learning Disorders*, 1: 87–141.

Greenspan, S. and Wieder, S. (1998b). *The Child with Special Needs: Intellectual and Emotional Growth.* Reading, MA: Perseus Books.

Greenspan, S., Degangi, G. and Wieder, S. (2001). *The Functional Emotional Assessment Scale (FEAS).* Bethesda, Interdisciplinary Council on Developmental and Learning Disorders.

Grice, H. P. (1957). Meaning. *The Philosophical Review*, 64: 377–88.

Grice, H. P. (1968). Utterer's meaning, sentence-meaning and word-meaning. *Foundations of Language*, 4: 225–42.

Grice, H. P. (1969). Utterer's meaning and intentions. *Philosophical Review*, 78: 147–77.

Grice, H. P. (1975). Logic and conversation. In P. Cole and J. Morgan (eds), *Syntax and Semantics, Volume 3: Speech Acts* (pp. 41–58). New York: Academic Press.

Grice, H. P. (1982). Meaning revisited. In N. V. Smith, (ed.), *Mutual Knowledge* (pp. 223–43). London: Academic Press.

Grice, H. P. (1989). *Studies in the Way of Words.* Harvard, MA: Harvard University Press.

Griffin, D. R. (1981). *The Question of Animal Awareness: Evolutionary Continuity of Mental Experience.* Los Altos, CA: Kaufmann.

Gurwitsch, A. (1978). Galilean physics in the light of Husserl's phenomenology. In T. Luckman (ed.), *Phenomenology and Sociology* (pp. 71–89). London: Penguin.

Hacker, P. M. S. (1988). Language, rules and pseudo-rules. *Language and Communication*, 8: 159–72.

Hala, S. and Russell, J. (2001). Executive control within strategic deception: A window on early cognitive development? *Journal of Experimental Child Psychology*, 80: 112–41.

Hala, S., Chandler, M. and Fritz, A. (1991). Fledgling theories of mind: Deception as a marker of three-year-olds' understanding of false-belief. *Child Development*, 61: 83–97.

Hammond, H. and Keat, R. (1991). *Understanding Phenomenology.* Oxford: Blackwell.

Happé, F. G. E. (1995). The role of age and verbal ability in the theory of mind task performance of subjects with autism. *Child Development*, 66: 843–55.

Happé, F. (1999). Understanding assets and deficits in autism: Why success is more interesting than failure. *Psychologist*, 12: 540–6.

Harré, R. and Secord, P. (1972). *The Explanation of Social Behaviour.* Oxford: Blackwell.

Harris, P. (1992). From simulation to folk psychology: The case for development. *Mind and Language*, 7: 120–44.

Harrison, P. (1998). Reading the passions: The fall, the passions and the dominion over nature. In S. Gaukroger (ed.), *The Soft Underbelly of Reason: The Passions in the Seventeenth Century* (pp. 49–79). London: Routledge.

Heal, J. (2003). *Mind, Reason and Imagination*. New York: Cambridge University Press.

Hebb, D. O. (1958). *A Textbook of Psychology*. Philadelphia and London: W. B. Saunders.

Hebb, D. O. (1966). *Textbook of Psychology*, 2nd edn. New York: Saunders.

Heritage, J. (1984). *Garfinkel and Ethnomethodology*. Cambridge: Polity Press.

Herold, R., Tenyi, T., Lenard, K. and Trixler, M. (2002). Theory of mind deficit in people with schizophrenia during remission. *Psychological Medicine*, 32: 1125–9.

Heyes, C. M. (1996). Self-recognition in primates: Irreverence, irrelevance and irony. *Animal Behaviour*, 51: 470–3.

Heyes, C. M. (1998). Theory of mind in nonhuman primates. *Behavioral and Brain Sciences*, 21: 101–14.

Hewstone, M., Cairns, E., Voci, A., Hamberger J. and Niens, U. (2006). Intergroup contact, forgiveness and experience of 'the troubles' in Northern Ireland. *Journal of Social Issues*, 62: 99–120.

Hobson, R. P. (1986). The autistic child's appraisal of expressions of emotion. *Journal of Child Psychology and Psychiatry*, 27: 321–42.

Hobson, R. P. (1989). Beyond cognition: A theory of autism. In G. Dawson (ed.), *Autism: Nature, Diagnosis and Treatment* (pp. 254–81). New York: The Guildford Press.

Hobson, R. P. (1991). Against the theory of theory of mind. *British Journal of Developmental Psychology*, 9: 33–51.

Hobson, R. P. (1993). *Autism and the Development of Mind*. Hillsdale, NJ: Lawrence Erlbaum.

Hobson, R. P. (2002). *The Cradle of Thought*. Basingstoke: Palgrave Macmillan.

Hobson, R. P. (2007a). Communicative depth: Soundings from developmental psychopathology. *Infant Behaviour and Development*, 30: 267–77.

Hobson, R. P. (2007b). We share, therefore we think. In D. D. Hutto and M. Ratcliffe (eds), *Folk Psychology Reassessed* (pp. 41–61). Dordrecht: Springer.

Holliday Willey, L. (1999). *Pretending To Be Normal: Living with Asperger's Syndrome*. London: Jessica Kingsley.

Houston, R. and Frith, U. (2000). *Autism in History: The Case of Hugh Blair of Borgue*. Oxford: Blackwell.

Howe, M. (1989). *Fragments of Genius: The Strange Feats of Idiot Savants*. London: Routledge.

Hughes, C. and Russell, J. (1993). Autistic children's difficulty with mental disengagement from an object: Its implications for theories of autism. *Developmental Psychology*, 29: 498–510.

Hull, C. L. (1943). *Principles of Behavior*. New York: D. Appleton-Century.

Hume, D. (2004). *A Treatise of Human Nature*. Mineola, NY: Dover.

Huq, S. F., Garety, P. A. and Hemsley, D. R. (1988). Probabilistic judgements in deluded and non-deluded subjects. *Quaterly Journal of Experimental Psychology: Human Learning and Memory*, 40A: 801–12.

Hutto, D. D. (1999). A cause for concern: Reasons, causes and explanations. *Philosophy and Phenomenological Research*, 59: 381–401.

Hutto, D. D. (2005). Knowing what?: Radical versus conservative enactivism. *Phenomenology and the Cognitive Sciences*, 4: 389–405.

Hutto, D. D. (2006). Unprincipled engagements: Emotional experience, expression and response. In R. Menary (ed.), *Radical Enactivism: Focus on the Philosophy of Daniel D. Hutto* (pp. 13–38). Amerstam/Philadelphia: John Benjamins.

Hutto, D. D. (2007). The narrative practice hypothesis: Origins and applications of folk psychology. In D. D. Hutto (ed.), *Narrative and Understanding Persons*, Royal Institute of Philosophy Supplement, 82: 43–68.

Hutto, D. D. (2008). *Folk Psychological Narratives: The Sociocultural Basis of Understanding Reasons*. Cambridge, MA: MIT Press.

Jaynes, J. (1978). In a manner of speaking. *Behavioral and Brain Sciences*, 1: 578–9.

Jenkins, J. J. (1986). Interview with James J. Jenkins. In B. J. Baars (eds), *The Cognitive Revolution in Psychology* (pp. 239–52). New York: Guilford Press.

Johnson, S., Booth, A. and O'Hearn, K. (2001). Inferring the goals of a nonhuman agent. *Cognitive Development*, 16: 637–56.

Johnson, M. H., Griffin, R., Csibra, G., Halit, H., Farroni, T., De Haan, M., Tucker, L. A., Baron-Cohen, S. and Richards, J. (2005). The emergence of the social brain network: Evidence from typical and atypical development. *Development and Psychopathology*, 17: 599–619.

Johnson-Laird, P. and Wason, P. C. (eds) (1977). *Thinking: Readings in Cognitive Science*. Cambridge: Cambridge University Press.

Jones, E. (1999). The phenomenology of abnormal belief. *Philosophy, Psychiatry and Psychology*, 6: 1–16.

Kanner, L. (1943). Autistic disturbances of affective contact. *Nervous Child*, 2: 217–50.

Kant, I. (2004). *Critique of Pure Reason*. Mineola, NY: Dover.

Karmiloff-Smith, A. (1998). Development itself is the key to understanding developmental disorders. *Trends in Cognitive Sciences*, 2: 389–98.

Karmiloff-Smith, A. and Inhelder, B. (1974). If you want to get ahead, get a theory. *Cognition*, 3: 195–212.

Kasari, C., Sigman, M., Mundy, P. and Yirmiya, N. (1990). Affective sharing in the context of joint attention interactions of normal, autistic and mentally retarded children. *Journal of Autism and Developmental Disorders*, 20: 87–100.

Kaye, K. (1982). *The Mental and Social Life of Babies*. London: Methuen.

Kennedy, J. S. (1992). *The New Anthropomorphism*. Cambridge: Cambridge University Press.

Kirschner, S. R. (2003). On the varieties of intersubjective experience. *Culture and Psychology*, 9: 277–86.

Kitchener, R. F. (1977). Behavior and behaviorism. *Behaviorism*, 5: 11–71.

Kojève, A. (1969). *Introduction to the Reading of Hegel*. New York and London: Basic Books.

Krzeminska, P. (2001). *Facial Emotion in Autism: Evidence for Atypical Expressions Reduced Muscle Movements*. York University (unpublished MA thesis).

Langdon, M., Davies, M. and Coulthart, M. (2002). Understanding minds and understanding communicated meanings in schizophrenia. *Mind and Language*, 17: 68–104.

Lawson, W. (2001). *Life Behind Glass: A Personal Account of Autism Spectrum Disorder*. London: Jessica Kingsley.

Leahey, T. H. (1992). The mythical revolutions of American psychology. *American Psychologist*, 47: 308–18.

LeDoux, J. (1996). *The Emotional Brain: The Mysterious Underpinnings of Emotional Life*. New York: Simon & Schuster.

Leekam, S. and Perner, J. (1991). Does the autistic child have a metarepresentational deficit? *Cognition*, 40: 203–18.

Legerstee, M. and Barillas, Y. (2003). Sharing attention and pointing to objects at 12 months: Is the intentional stance implied? *Cognitive Development*, 18: 91–110.

Leonard, L. (1998). *Children with Specific Language Impairment*. Cambridge, MA: MIT Press.

Leslie, A. (1987). Pretense and representation: The origins of 'theory of mind'. *Psychological Review*, 94: 412–26.

Leslie, A. (1994). Pretending and believing: Issues in the theory of ToMM. *Cognition*, 50: 211–38.

Leslie, A. (1995). Pretending and believing. Issues in the theory of ToMM. In J. Mehler and S. Franck (eds), *Cognition on Cognition* (pp. 193–220). Cambridge, MA: MIT Press.

Leslie, A. (2000). Theory of mind. In A. E. Kazdin (eds), *Encyclopedia of Psychology* (vol. 8, pp. 60–1). Washington, DC: American Psychological Association; New York: Oxford University Press.

Leslie, A. and Thaiss, L. (1992). Domain specificity in conceptual development: Evidence from autism, *Cognition*, 43: 225–51.

Leslie, A., Friedman, O. and German, T. P. (2004). Core mechanismsms in 'theory of mind'. *Trends in Cognitive Science*, 8: 528–33.

Leudar, I. (1991). Sociogenesis, coordination and mutualism. *Journal for the Theory of Social Behaviour*, 21: 201–20.

Leudar, I. and Antaki, C. (1996). Discourse participation, reported speech and research practices in social psychology. *Theory and Psychology*, 6: 5–29.

Leudar, I. and Browning, P. K. (1988). Meaning, maxims of communication and language games. *Language and Communication*, 8, no. 1: 1–16.

Leudar, I. and Costall, A. (eds), (2004a). Special issue: Theory of mind. *Theory and Psychology*, 14: 571–752.

Leudar, I. and Costall, A. (2004b). On the persistence of the problem of other minds in psychology: Chomsky, Grice and 'theory of mind'. *Theory and Psychology*, 14: 603–62.

Leudar, I. and Thomas, P. (2000). *Voices of Reason, Voices of Insanity: Studies of Verbal Hallucinations*. London: Routledge.

Leudar, I., Costall A. and Francis, D. (2004). Theory of mind: A critical assessment. *Theory and Psychology*, 14: 571–8.

Leudar, I., Sharrock, W., Hayes, J. and Truckle, S. (2008b). Therapy as a 'structured immediacy'. *Journal of Pragmatics*, 40: 863–85.

Leudar, I., Sharrock, W., Truckle, S., Colombino, T., Hayes, J. and Booth, K. (2008a). Conversation of emotions: On transforming play into psychoanalytic psychotherapy. In A. Perakyla, C. Antaki, S. Vehvilanen and I. Leudar (eds), *Conversation Analysis and Psychotherapy* (pp. 152–72). Cambridge: Cambridge University Press.

Lévinas, E. (1985). *Ethics and Infinity: Conversations with Philippe Nemo*. Pittsburgh: Duquesne University Press.

Lewis, D. (1972). How to define theoretical terms. *Journal of Philosophy*, 67: 427–46.

Lewis, M. D. (2005). Self-organizing individual differences in brain development. *Developmental Review*, 25: 252–77.

Lewy, A. L. and Dawson, G. (1992). Social stimulation and joint attention in young autistic children. *Journal of Abnormal Child Psychology*, 20: 555–66.

Liszkowski, U., Carpenter, M. and Tomasello, M. (2007). Reference and attitude in infant pointing. *Journal of Child Language*, 34: 1–20.

Liszkowski, U., Carpenter, M., Striano, T. and Tomasello, M. (2006). 12 and 18 month olds point to provide information for others. *Journal of Cognition and Development*, 7: 173–87.

Lorenz, K. (2002). *On Aggression*. London: Routledge.

Louch, A. R. (1966). *Explanation and Human Action*. Berkeley: University of California Press.

Loveland, K. A., Tunali-Kotoski, B., Pearson, D. A., Brelsford, K. A., Ortegon, J. and Chen, R. (1994). Imitation and expression of facial affect in autism. *Development and Psychopathology*, 6: 433–44.

Macmurray, J. (1991). *Persons in Relation*. London: Faber & Faber. (Originally published in 1961.)

Mahler, M., Pine, F. and Bergman, A. (1975). *The Psychological Birth of the Human Infant*. New York: Basic Books.

Malatesta, C. A. and Izard, C. E. (1984). The facial expression of emotion: Young, middle-aged and older adult expressions. In C. Z. Malatesta and C. E. Izard (eds), *Emotion in Adult Development* (pp. 253–73). Beverly Hills, CA: Sage.

Malcolm, N. (1977). *Memory and Mind*. Ithaca, NY: Cornell University Press.

Malle, B. F. and Hodges, S. D. (2007). *Other Minds: How Humans Bridge the Divide Between Self and Others*. New York: Guildford Press.

Mandelbaum, J. and Pomerantz, A. (1991). What drives social action? In K. Tracy and N. Coupland (eds), *Multiple Goals in Discourse* (pp. 151–66). Clevedon: Multilingual Matters.

Marková, I. (1997). The family and haemophilia. In F. Forbes, L. Aledort and R. Madhok (eds), *Textbook of Haemophilia* (pp. 335–46). London: Chapman & Hall Medical.

Marková, I. (2003). *Dialogicality and Social Representations*. Cambridge: Cambridge University Press.

Marková, I., Wilkie, P. A., Naji, S. A. and Forbes, C. D. (1990). Knowledge of HIV/ AIDS and behavioural change of people with haemophilia. *Psychology and Health*, 4: 125–33.

Mars, A. E., Mauk, J. E. and Dowrick, P. (1998). Symptoms of pervasive developmental disorders as observed in pre-diagnostic home videos of infants and toddlers. *Journal of Paediatrics*, 132: 500–4.

Martin, J., Sugarman, J. and Thompson, J. (2003). *Psychology and the Question of Agency*. Albany, NJ: State University Press of New York.

Massie, R. K. (1985). The constant shadow: Reflections on the life of a chronically ill child. In N. Hobbs and J. M. Perrin (eds), *Issues in the Care of Children with Chronic Illness* (pp. 13–22). San Francisco: Jossey-Bass.

Mazza, M., de Risio, A., Surian, L., Roncone, R. and Casacchia, M. (2001). Selective impairment of theory of mind in people with schizophrenia. *Schizophrenia Research*, 47: 299–308.

McCabe, R., Leudar, I. and Antaki, C. (2004). Do people with schizophrenia display theory of mind deficits in clinical interactions? *Psychological Medicine*, 34: 401–10.

McCabe, R., Leudar, I. and Healey, P. G. T. (2006). *What do you think I think? Theory of mind and schizophrenia*. Proceedings of the XXVIIth Annual Conference of the Cognitive Science Society (Stresa, Italy, 21–23 July 2005), pp. 1443–8.

McDonough, R. (1991). A culturalist account of folk psychology. In J. D. Greenwood (ed.), *The Future of Folk Psychology*. Cambridge: Cambridge University Press.

McDowell, J. (1994). *Mind and World*. Cambridge, MA: Harvard University Press.

McGeer, V. (2002). Psycho-practice, psycho-theory and the contrastive case of autism: How practices of mind become second-nature, In E. Thompson (ed.), *Between Ourselves: Second-Person Issues in the Study of Consciousness* (pp. 109–32). Charlottesville, VA: Imprint Academic.

McGeer, V. (2007). The regulative dimension of folk psychology. In D. D. Hutto and M. Ratcliffe (eds), *Folk Psychology Reassessed* (pp. 137–56). Doredrecht: Springer.

McGinn, M. (1997). *Wittgenstein*. London: Routledge.

McHoul, A. and Rapley, M. (2003). What can psychological terms actually do? (Or: if Sigmund calls, tell him it didn't work). *Journal of Pragmatics*, 35: 507–22.

McKlean, T. (1994). *Soon Will Come the Light: A View from Inside the Autism Puzzle*, 2nd edn. Arlington, TX: Future Horizons.

McShane, J. (1980). *Learning to Talk*. Cambridge: Cambridge University Press.

Meltzoff, A. N., Gopnik, A. and Repacholi, B. M. (1999). Toddlers' understanding of intentions, desires and emotions: Explorations of the dark ages. In P. D. Zelazo, J. W. Astington and D. R. Olson (eds), *Developing Theories of Intention* (pp. 17–41). Mahwah, NJ: Erlbaum.

Merleau-Ponty, M. (1965). *Structure of Behaviour*. London: Methuen.

Merleau-Ponty, M. (1973). *Consciousness and the Acquisition of Language*. Evanston, IL: Northwestern University Press.

Miller, G. A. (2003). The cognitive revolution: a historical perspective. *Trends in Cognitive Sciences*, 7: 141–4.

Miller, G. A., Galanter, E. and Pribram, K. H. (1960). *Plans and the Structure of Behavior*. New York: Holt, Rinehart & Winston.

Miller, P. H. (2002). *Theories of Developmental Psychology*, 4th edn. New York: Worth Publishers.

Mitchley, N. J., Barber, J., Gray, J. M., Brooks, D. N. and Livingston, M. G. (1998). Comprehension of irony in schizophrenia. *Cognitive Neuropsychiatry*, 3: 127–38.

Montagu, J. (1994). *The Expression of the Passions*. New Haven, CT: Yale University Press.

Morgan, C. L. (1892). The speech of monkeys. Review of 'The Speech of Monkeys' by R. L. Garner. *Nature*, 1892: 509–10.

Moscovici, S. (1972a). Society and theory in social psychology. In J. Israel and H. Tajfel (eds), *The Context of Social Psychology* (pp. 17–68). London: Academic Press.

Moscovici, S. (1972b). *La société contre nature*. Paris: Plon.

Moscovici, S. (1979). *Psychologie des minorités actives*. Paris: Presses Universitaires de France.

Moscovici, S. (1984). Introduction: le domaine de la psychologie sociale. In S. Moscovici (ed.), *Psychologie sociale* (pp. 5–22). Paris: Presses Universitaires de France.

Moscovici, S. (1993). The return of the unconscious. *Social Research*, 60: 39–93.

Moscovici, S. and Marková, I. (2000). Ideas and their development: A dialogue between Serge Moscovici and Ivana Marková. In G. Duveen (ed.), *Social Representations: Explorations in Social Psychology* (pp. 224–86). Cambridge: Polity Press.

Mundy, P. and Sigman, M. (1989). The theoretical implications of joint-attention deficits in autism. *Development and Psychopathology*, 1: 173–83.

Myers, J. G. (1929). Lubbock as an entomologist and comparative psychologist. In Sir John Lubbock (Lord Avebury), *Ants, Bees and Wasps: A Record of Observations on the Habits of the Social Hymenoptera* (pp. ix–xiv). London: Kegan Paul, Trench, Trubner.

Nehamas, A. (1998). *The Art of Living: Socratic Reflections from Plato to Foucault*. Berkeley: University of California Press.

Neisser, U. (1980). On 'social knowing'. *Personality and Social Psychology Bulletin*, 6: 601–5.

Neisser, U. (1997). The future of cognitive science: An ecological analysis. In D. M. Johnson and C. E. Erneling (eds), *The Future of the Cognitive Revolution* (pp. 247–60). New York: Oxford University Press.

Nelson, K. (2003). Narrative and the emergence of a consciousness of self. In G. D. Fireman, T. E. J. McVay and O. Flanagan (eds), *Narrative and Consciousness* (pp. 17–36). Oxford: Oxford University Press.

Nelson, K. (2007). *Young Minds in Social Worlds*. Cambridge, MA: Harvard University Press.

Newell, A. (1995). The serial imperative. In P. Baumgartner and S. Payr (eds), *Speaking Minds: Interviews with Twenty Eminent Cognitive Scientists* (pp. 145–156). Princeton, NJ: Princeton University Press.

Newton, P. (1992). *Theory of Mind in Practice*. Poster presented at the European Conference on Developmental Psychology, Seville, Spain.

Newton, P., Reddy, V. and Bull, R. (2000). Children's everyday deception and performance on false-belief tasks. *British Journal of Developmental Psychology*, 18: 297–317.

Oberman, L. M. and Ramachandran, V. S. (2007). The simulating social mind: The Role of the mirror neuron system and simulation in the social and communicative deficits of autism spectrum disorders. *Psychological Bulletin*, 133: 310–27.

Ochs, E. and Schieflin, B. B. (1979). *Developmental Pragmatics*. New York: Academic Press.

Ochs, E. and Solomon, O. (2007). Practical logic and autism. In C. Casey and R. B. Edgerton (eds), *A Companion to Psychological Anthropology* (pp. 140–67). Oxford: Blackwell.

Olson, D. R. (1988). On the origins of beliefs and other intentional states in children. In J. W. Astington, P. L. Harris and D. R. Olson (eds), *Developing Theories of Mind* (pp. 414–26). Cambridge: Cambridge University Press.

O'Neill, D. K. (1996). Two-year-old children's sensitivity to a parent's knowledge state when making requests. *Child Development*, 67: 659–77.

Onishi, K. H. and Baillargeon, R. (2005). Do 15-month-old infants understand false beliefs? *Science*, 308: 255–8.

Onishi, K. H., Baillargeon, R. and Leslie, A. M. (2007). 15-month-old infants detect violations in pretend scenarios. *Acta Psychologica*, 124: 106–28.

Or, M. and Yirmiya, N. (1993). Autism and theory of mind. *Psychologia: Israel Journal of Psychology*, 3: 126–39.

Osterling, J. and Dawson, G. (1994). Early recognition of children with autism: A study of first birthday home videotapes, *Journal of Autism and Developmental Disorders*, 24: 247–57.

Overgaard, S. (2006). The problem of other minds: Wittgenstein's phenomenological perspective. *Phenomenology and the Cognitive Sciences*, 5: 53–73.

Pandora, K. (1997). *Rebels Within the Ranks: Psychologists' Critique of Scientific Authority and Democratic Realities in New Deal America*. Cambridge: Cambridge University Press.

Panksepp, J. (1998). *Affective Neuroscience*. New York: Oxford University Press.

Peirce, K., Muller, R., Ambrose, J., Allen, G. and Courschene, E. (2001). Face processing occurs outside the fusiform 'face area' in autism: Evidence from functional MRI. *Brain*, 124: 2059–73.

Penn, D. C. and Povinelli, D. J. (2008). On the lack of evidence that non-human animals possess anything remotely resembling a 'theory of mind'. In N. Emery, N. Clayton and C. Frith (eds), *Social Intelligence: From Brain to Culture* (pp. 415–30). Oxford: Oxford University Press.

Pennington, B. and Ozonoff, S. (1996). Executive functions and developmental psychopathology. *Journal of Child Psychology and Psychiatry and Allied Disciplines*, 37: 51–87.

Pennington, B. F., Rogers, S. J., Bennetto, L., Griffith, E. M., Reed, D. T. and Shyu, V. (1997). Validity tests of the executive dysfunction hypothesis of autism. In J. Russell (ed.), *Autism as an Executive Disorder* (pp. 143–73). New York: Oxford University Press.

Perner, J. (1991). *Understanding the Representational Mind*. Cambridge, MA: MIT Press.

Perner, J. and Wimmer, H. (1983). Beliefs about beliefs: Representation and constraining function of wrong beliefs in young children's understanding of deception. *Cognition*, 7: 333–62.

Perner, J. and Wimmer, H. (1985). John thinks that Mary thinks that…: Attribution of second order beliefs by five to ten year old children. *Journal of Experimental Child Psychology*, 39: 437–71.

Perner, J., Frith, U., Leslie, A. M. and Leekam, S. (1989). Exploration of the autistic child's theory of mind: Knowledge, belief and communication. *Child Development*, 60: 686–700.

Peters, S. (1972). The projection problem. How is a grammar to be selected. In S. Peters, (ed.), *Goals of Linguistic Theory* (pp. 171–88). Englewood Cliffs, NJ: Prentice Hall.

Piaget, J. (1953). *The Origins of Intelligence in the Child*. London: Routledge & Kegan Paul. (Originally published in 1936.)

Piaget, J. (1972). *Play, Dreams and Imitation in Childhood*. London: Routledge & Kegan Paul. (Originally published in 1951.)

Pickup, G. J. and Frith, C. D. (2001). Theory of mind impairments in schizophrenia: Symptomatology, severity and specificity. *Psychological Medicine*, 31: 207–20.

Pillow, B. H. (1989). Early understanding of perception as a source of knowledge. *Journal of Experimental Child Psychology*, 47: 116–29.

Pinker, S. (1994). *The Language Instinct*. New York: William Morrow.

Pinker, S. (1997). *How the Mind Works*. New York: Norton.

Pomerantz, A. (1990). Mental concepts in the analysis of social action. *Research on Language and Social Interaction*, 24: 299–310.

Potter, J. and Edwards, D. (2003). Rethinking cognition: On Coulter on discourse and mind. *Human Studies*, 26: 165–81.

Poulin-Dubois, D., Sodian, B., Metz, U., Tilden, J. and Schoeppner, B. (2007). Out of sight is not out of mind: Developmental changes in infants' understanding of visual perception during the second year. *Journal of Cognition and Development*, 8: 401–25.

Pratt, C. and Bryant, P. (1990). Young children understand that looking leads to knowing (so long as they are looking into a single barrel). *Child Development*, 61: 973–82.

Premack, D. (1976). *Intelligence in Ape and Man*. Hillsdale, NJ: Lawrence Erlbaum Associates.

Premack, D. and Woodruff, G. (1978). Does the chimpanzee have a theory of mind? *The Behavioural and Brain Sciences*, 4: 515–26.

Prince-Hughes, D. (2002). *Aquamarine Blue 5: Personal Stories of College Students with Autism*. Athens, OH: Swallow/Ohio University Press.

Pring, L. (2005). Autism and blindness: Building on the sum of their parts. In L. Pring (ed.), *Autism and Blindness: Research and Reflections* (pp. 1–9). London: Whurr Publishers.

Pullum, G. K. and Scholz, B. C. (1992). Empirical assessment of stimulus poverty arguments. *Linguistic Review*, 19: 9–50.

Putnam H. (1988). *Representation and Reality*. Cambridge, MA: MIT Press.

Putnam, H. (1995). *Pragmatism*. Oxford: Blackwell.

Quine, W. V. O. (1969). Replies To Chomsky. In D. Davidson and J. Hintikka, (eds), *Words and Objections: Essays on the Work of W. V. O. Quine* (pp. 303–11). Dordrecht: Reidel.

Ratcliffe, M. (2007a). From folk psychology to commonsense. In D. D. Hutto and M. Ratcliffe. (eds), *Folk Psychology Reassessed* (pp. 223–43). Doredrecht: Springer.

Ratcliffe, M. (2007b). *Rethinking Commonsense Psychology: A Critique of Folk Psychology, Theory of Mind and Simulation*. Basingstoke: Palgrave Macmillan.

Reddy, M. (1979). The conduit metaphor – a case of frame conflict in our language about language. In A. Ortony (ed.), *Metaphor and Thought* (pp. 164–201). Cambridge: Cambridge University Press.

Reddy, V. (1991). Playing with others' expectations: Teasing and mucking about in the first year. In A. Whiten (ed.), *Natural Theories of Mind* (pp. 143–58). Oxford: Blackwell.

Reddy, V. (1992). *Proto-Declarative Pointing: Gaze Control or Shared Perceptions?* Paper presented at the Annual Conference of the Developmental Section of the British Psychological Society, September, Edinburgh.

Reddy, V. (1995). Psychologists' problems with infant communication, *First Language*, 16: 115–28.

Reddy, V. (1996). Omitting the second person in social understanding, *Behavioral and Brain Sciences*, 19: 140–1.

Reddy, V. (2003). On being the object of attention: Implications for self–other consciousness. *Trends in Cognitive Science*, 7: 397–402.

Reddy, V. (2007). Getting back to the rough ground: Deception and social living. *Philosophical Transactions of the Royal Society of London B*, 362 (1480): 621–37.

Reddy, V. and Morris, P. (2004). Participants don't need theories: Knowing mind in engagement. *Theory and Psychology*, 14: 647–65.

Reddy, V. and Simone, L. (1995). *Acting on Attention: Towards an Understanding of Knowing in Infancy*. Paper presented at the Annual Conference of the Developmental Section of the British Psychological Society, Strathclyde, UK.

Reed, T. and Peterson, C. (1990). A comparative study of autistic subjects' performance at two levels of visual and cognitive perspective taking. *Journal of Autism and Developmental Disorders*, 20: 555–67.

Rieber, R. (ed.) (1980). *Wilhelm Wundt and the Making of a Scientific Psychology*. New York: Plenum Press.

Robinson, E. J., Thomas, G. V., Parton, A. and Nye, R. (1997). Children's overestimation of the knowledge to be gained from seeing. *British Journal of Developmental Psychology*, 15: 257–73.

Rochester, S. (1979). *Crazy Talk: A Study of the Discourse of Schizophrenic Speakers*. New York: Plenum Press.

Rowlands, M. (2003). *Externalism: Putting the Mind and World Back Together*. Chesham: Acumen.

Rudin, S. A. (1959). Book reviews: Two typical books from American psychologists. *Psychological Reports*, 5: 113–14.

Ryle, G. (1949). *The Concept of Mind*. London: Hutchinson.

Ryle, G. (1960). *Dilemmas*. Cambridge: Cambridge University Press.

Ryle, G. (1971). 'Use, usage and meaning'. In *Collected Papers*, vol. 2 (pp. 407–14). London: Hutchinson.

Ryle, G. (1974). Mowgli in Babel, *Philosophy*, 49: 5–11.

Ryle, G. (1999). Reason. *The Linacre Journal*, 3: 71–84.

Sacks, O. (1995). *An Anthropologist on Mars*. London: Picador.

Samelson, F. (1994). John B. Watson in 1913: Rhetoric and practice. In J. T. Todd and E. K. Morris (eds), *Modern Perspectives on John B. Watson and Classical Behaviourism* (pp. 3–18). Wesport, CT: Greenwood Press.

Sampson, G. (2002). Exploring the richness of stimulus. *Linguistic Review*, 19: 73–104.

Sarfati, Y., Hardy-Bayle, M. C., Nadel, J., Chevalier, J. F. and Widlocher, D. (1997). Attribution of mental states to others by schizophrenic patients. *Cognitive Neuropsychiatry*, 2: 1–17.

Savage-Rumbaugh, S., Shanker, S. and Taylor, T. (1998). *Apes, Language and the Human Mind*. New York: Oxford University Press.

Schneider, E. (1999). *Discovering My Autism: Apologia pro vita sua (With Apologies to Cardinal Newman)*. London: Jessica Kingsley.

Schopler, E. and Mesibov, G. B. (eds), *High-Functioning Individuals with Autism*. New York: Plenum Press.

Schore, A. (1994). *Affect Regulation and the Origin of the Self*. Mahwah, NJ: Lawrence Erlbaum Associates.

Searle, J. (1969). *Speech Acts*. Cambridge: Cambridge University Press.

Searle, J. (1972). A Special Supplement: Chomsky's Revolution in Linguistics. *New York Review of Books*, 18, no. 12 (29 June).

Searle, J. (1980). Rules and causation. *Behaviour and Brain Sciences*, 3: 37–8.

Searle, J. and Kiefer, F. (eds) (1980). *Speech Act Theory and Pragmatics*. Dordrecht: Reidel.

Sedler, M. J. (1995). Understanding delusions. *The Psychiatric Clinics of North America*, 18: 251–62.

Segerdahl, P. (1996). *Language Use*. Basingstoke: Macmillan.

Sehon, S. (2005). *Teleological Realism: Mind, Agency and Explanation*. Cambridge, MA: MIT Press.

Sellars, W. (1956/1997). *Empiricism and the Philosophy of Mind*. Cambridge, MA: Harvard University Press.

Sennett, R. (1969). *Classic Essays on the Culture of Cities*. New York: Appleton-Century-Crofts.

Shanker, S. (2001). What a child knows when she knows what a name is: The non-Cartesian view of language acquisition. Target article. *Current Anthropology*, 42: 481–513.

Shanker, S. (2002). The generativist/interactionist debate over specific language impairment: psycholinguistics at a crossroads. *American Journal of Psychology*, 115: 415–50.

Shanker, S. (2004a). A dynamic developmental model of emotions. *Philosophy, Psychiatry and Psychology*, 11: 219–33.

Shanker, S. (2004b). The roots of mindblindness. *Theory and Psychology*, 14: 685–703.

Shanker, S. and Reygadas, P. (2002). La red de racionalidad: Emocion y lenguaje. *Cuicuilco: Revista de la Escuela Nacional de Antropologia e Historia*, 9: 37–60.

Shannon, C. E. (1949). The mathematical theory of communication. In C. E. Shannon and W. Weaver, *The Mathematical Theory of Communication* (pp. 29–125). Urbana, IL: University of Ilinois Press.

Sharrock, W. and Coulter, J. (2004). Theory of mind: A critical commentary. *Theory and Psychology*, 14: 579–600.

Shatz, M. and O'Reilly, A. (1990). Conversational or communicative skill? A reassessment of two-year-olds' behaviour in miscommunication episodes. *Journal of Child Language*, 17: 131–46.

Shelley, L. F. (1985). *Touch Me Who Dares*. Llandysul: Gomer Press.

Shwe, H. and Markman, E. (2001). Young children's appreciation of the mental impact of their communicative signals. In E. Bates and M. Tomasello (eds), *Language Development: The Essential Readings* (pp. 62–75). Malden, MA: Blackwell Publishing.

Siegal, M. (2008). *Marvelous Minds: The Discovery of What Children Know*. Oxford: Oxford University Press.

Simon, H. A. (1995). Technology is not the problem. In P. Baumgartner and S. Payr (eds), *Speaking Minds: Interview with Twenty Eminent Cognitive Scientists* (pp. 231–48). Princeton, NJ: Princeton University Press.

Simone, L. and Reddy, V. (1997). *Knowing about Knowing in Infancy*. Paper presented at the international conference of the Piaget Society, 19–21 June, Santa Monica, California.

Sinclair, J. (1992). Bridging the gaps: An inside view of autism. In E. Schopler and G. B. Mesibov (eds), *High-Functioning Individuals with Autism* (pp. 294–302). New York: Plenum Press.

Smedslund, J. (1997). *The Structure of Psychological Common Sense*. London: Erlbaum.

Smith, E. R. and MacKie, D. M. (2000). *Social Psychology*, 2nd edn. London: Psychology Press.

Smith, J. A. (1996). Beyond the divide between cognition and discourse: Using interpretative phenomenological analysis in health psychology. *Psychology and Health*, 11: 261–71.

Smith, J. A., Flowers, P. and Osborn, M. (1997). Interpretative phenomenological analysis and the psychology of health and illness. In L. Yardley (ed.), *Material Discourses of Health and Illness* (pp. 68–91). London: Routledge.

Smith, J. A., Jarman, M. and Osborn, M. (1999). Doing interpretative phenomenological analysis. In M. Murray and K. Chamberlain (eds), *Qualitative Health Psychology: Theories and Methods* (pp. 218–40). London: Sage.

Smith, N. V. (1999). *Chomsky: Ideas and Ideals*. Cambridge: Cambridge University Press.

Snow, M. E., Hertzig, M. E. and Shapiro, T. (1987). Expression of emotion in young autistic children. *Journal of American Academy of Child and Adolescent Psychiatry*, 26: 836–8.

Sodian, B. (1994). Early deception and the conceptual continuity claim. In C. Lewis and P. Mitchell (eds), *Children's Early Understanding of Mind* (pp. 385–401). Hove: Erlbaum.

Sodian, B. and Frith, U. (1992). Deception and sabotage in autistic, retarded and normal children. *Journal of Child Psychology and Psychiatry*, 33: 591–605.

Sodian, B. and Frith, U. (1993). The theory of mind deficit in autism: Evidence from deception. In S. Baron-Cohen, H. Tager-Flusberg and D. J. Cohen (eds), *Understanding other Minds: Perspectives from Autism* (pp. 158–77). Oxford: Oxford University Press.

Sparling, J. W. (1991). A prospective case report of infantile autism from pregnancy to four years. *Journal of Autism and Developmental Disorders*, 21: 229–36.

Sperber, D. (2000). Metarepresentation in an evolutionary perspective. In D. Sperber (ed.), *Metarepresentations: An Interdisciplinary Perspective* (pp. 117–37). Oxford: Oxford University Press.

Sperber, D. and Wilson, D. (1986). *Relevance: Communication and Cognition*. Oxford: Blackwell.

Sperber, D. and Wilson, D. (2002). Pragmatics, modularity and mind-reading. *Mind and Language*, 17: 3–23.

Spitzer, M. (1990). On defining delusions. *Comprehensive Psychiatry*, 31: 377–97.

Stephen, L. (1882). *Swift*. London: Macmillan.

Stich, S. (1980). What every speaker cognizes. *Behavior and Brain Sciences*, 3: 39–40.

Stich, S. (1983). *From Folk Psychology to Cognitive Science: The Case Against Belief.* Cambridge, MA: MIT Press.

Stich, S. and Nichols, S. (1992). Folk psychology: Simulation or tacit theory? *Mind and Language*, 7: 35–71.

Stich, S. and Nichols, S. (1995). Second Thoughts on Simulation. In M. Davies and A. Stone (eds), *Mental Simulation: Evaluations and Applications* (pp. 87–108). Oxford: Basil Blackwell.

Still, A. and Costall, A. (eds) (1991). *Against Cognitivism*. London: Harvester Wheatsheaf.

Stouthamer-Loeber, N. (1986). *Adults' Perception of Verbal Misrepresentations of Reality in Four Year Olds*. Unpublished manuscript, University of Pittsburgh.

Suchman, L. A. (1987). *Plans and Situated Actions*. Cambridge: Cambridge University Press.

Suddendorf, T. and Whiten, A. (2001). Mental evolution and development: Evidence for secondary representation in children, great apes and other animals. *Psychological Bulletin*, 127: 629–50.

Sully, J. (1881). Babies and science. *Cornhill Magazine*, 43: 539–54.

Sully, J. (1897). Review of 'The mental development of a child', by Kathleen Carter. *Mind*, new series, 6: 408–12.

Talwar, V. and Lee, K. (2002). Development of lying to conceal a transgression: Children's control of expressive behaviour during verbal deception. *International Journal of Behavioral Development*, 26: 436–44.

Taylor, S. E., Peplau, L. A. and Sears, D. O. (1994). *Social Psychology*, 8th edn. Englewood Cliffs, NJ: Prentice-Hall.

Taylor, T. J. (1992). *Mutual Misunderstanding*. London: Routledge.

Ter Hark, M. (2001). The inner and the outer. In Hans-Johann Glock (ed.), *Wittgenstein: A Critical Reader* (pp. 199–223). Oxford: Blackwell.

Thomas, M. (2002). Development of the concept of 'poverty of stimulus'. *Linguistic Review*, 19: 51–72.

Thomas, P. and Leudar, I. (1995). Syntactic processing and communication disorder in schizophrenia. In A. Sims (ed.), *Speech and Language Disorders in Psychiatry* (pp. 96–112). London: Gaskell.

Thomas, P., Leudar, I. et al., (1996). Syntactic complexity and negative symptoms in first onset Schizophrenics. *Cognitive Neuropsychiatry*, 1: 191–200.

Thompson, E. (2002). Empathy and consciousness. In E. Thompson (ed.), *Between Ourselves: Second-Person Issues in the Study of Consciousness* (pp. 1–32). Charlottesville, VA: Imprint Academic.

Thompson, R. A. and Lagattuta, K. H. (2008). Feeling and understanding: Early emotional development. In K. McCartney and D. Phillips (eds), *Blackwell Handbook of Early Childhood Development* (pp. 317–37). Oxford: Blackwell.

Tibbetts, P. (1973). Historical note on Descartes' psychophysical dualism. *Journal of the History of the Behavioral Sciences*, 9: 162–5.

Tomasello, M. (1999). Social cognition before the revolution. In P. Rochat (ed.), *Infant Social Cognition* (pp. 301–14). Mahwah, NJ: Erlbaum.

Tomasello, M. and Haberl, K. (2003). Understanding attention: 12- and 18-month-olds know what is new for other persons. *Developmental Psychology*, 39: 906–12.

Tooby, J. and Cosmides, L. (1995). Foreword. In S. Baron-Cohen, *Mindblindness: An Essay on Autism and Theory of Mind* (pp. ix–xviii). Cambridge, MA: MIT Press.

Toulmin, S. (1958). *The Uses of Argument*. Cambridge: Cambridge University Press.

Toulmin, S. (1972). *Human Understanding. Volume I: General Introduction and Part I*. Oxford: Clarendon Press.

Toulmin, S. (2001). *Return to Reason*. Cambridge, MA: Harvard University Press.

Tracy, J. L., Robins, R. W. and Gosling, S. D. (2004). Tracking trends in psychological science: An empirical analysis of the history of psychology. In T. C. Dalton and R. B. Evans (eds), *The Life Cycle of Psychological Ideas: Understanding Prominence and the Dynamics of Intellectual Change* (pp. 105–30). New York: Kluwer Academic/ Plenum Publishers.

Trevarthen, C. and Hubley, P. (1978). Secondary intersubjectivity: Confidence, confiding and acts of meaning in the first year. In A. Lock (ed.), *Action, Gesture and Symbol* (pp. 183–229). London: Academic Press.

Vendler, Z. (1972). *Res cogitans*. Ithaca, NY: Cornell University Press.

Villiers, de, J. (1999). Language and theory of mind: What are the developmental relationships? In S. Baron-Cohen, H. Tager-Flusberg and D. J. Cohen (eds), *Understanding Other Minds: Perspectives from Autism and Cognitive Neuroscience* (pp. 83–123). Oxford: Oxford University Press.

Vroon, P. A. (1987). Man-machine analogs and theoretical mainstreams in psychology. In W. J. Baker, M. E. Hyland, H. van Rappard and A. W. Staats (eds), *Current Issues in Theoretical Psychology* (pp. 393–414). North-Holland: Elsevier.

Waal, F. B. M. de, Macedo, S. and Ober, J. (2006). *Primates and Philosophers: How Morality Evolved*. Princeton, NJ: Princeton University Press.

Warnock, G. J. (1969). *English Philosophy since 1900*, 2nd edn. London: Oxford University Press.

Watkins, K., Strafella, A. and Paus, T. (2003). Seeing and hearing speech excites the motor system involved in speech production. *Neuropsychologia*, 41: 989–94.

Watson, J. B. (1913a). Psychology as the behaviorist views it. *Psychological Review*, 20: 158–77.

Watson, J. B. (1913b). Image and affection in behavior. *Journal of Philosophy, Psychology, and Scientific Methods*, 10: 421–8.

Watson, J. B. (1914). *Behavior: An Introduction to Comparative Psychology*. New York: Holt.

Watson, J. B. (1924). *Psychology from the Standpoint of a Behaviorist*, 2nd edn. Philadelphia: J. B. Lippincott.

Watson, J. B. (1929). Behaviourism. *Encyclopedia Britannica*, 3: 327–9.

Watson, J. B. (1930). *Behaviorism*, 2nd revised edn. New York: Norton.

Weaver, T., Tyrer, P., Ritchie, J. and Renton, A. (2003). What does the UK700 case management trial tell us about the value of assertive outreach? A qualitative study of factors influencing the implementation and outcomes of assertive casework strategies. *British Journal of Psychiatry*, 183: 437–45.

Weizenbaum, J. (1995). The myth of the last metaphor. In P. Baumgartner and S. Payr (eds), *Speaking Minds: Interview with Twenty Eminent Cognitive Scientists* (pp. 249–64). Princeton, NJ: Princeton University Press.

Wellman, H. M. (1990). *The Child's Theory of Mind*, Cambridge, MA: Bradford/MIT Press.

Wellman, H. M. and Bartsch, K. (1988). Young children's reasoning about beliefs. *Cognition*, 30: 239–77.

Wellman, H. M., Cross, D. and Watson, A. (2001). Meta-analysis of theory-of-mind development: The truth about false-belief. *Child Development*, 72: 655–84.

Welsford, E. (1966). *The Fool: His Social and Literary History*. Gloucester, MA: Peter Smith.

Whiten, A. (1994). Grades of mindreading. In C. Lewis and P. Mitchell (eds), *Children's Early Understanding of Mind* (pp. 47–70). Hove: Erlbaum.

Whiten, A. and Byrne, R. (1988). Tactical deception in primates. *Behavioral and Brain Sciences*, 11: 233–73.

Whiten, A. and Perner, J. (1991). *Fundamental Issues in the Multidisciplinary Study of Mindreading*. Oxford: Blackwell.

Wieder, D. L. (1980). Behavioristic operationalism and the life-world: Chimpanzees and the chimpanzee researchers in face-to-face interaction. *Sociological Inquiry*, 50: 75–103.

Wiener, N. (1948). *Cybernetics*. New York: John Wiley.

Williams, E. (2004). Who really needs a 'theory' of mind? An interpretative phenomenological analysis of the autobiographical writings of ten high-functioning individuals with an autism spectrum disorder. *Theory and Psychology*, 14: 704–24.

Williams, E., Reddy, V. and Costall, A. (2001). Taking a closer look at functional play in children with autism. *Journal of Autism and Developmental Disorders*, 31: 67–77.

Wilson, D. (2000). Metarepresentation in linguistic communication. In D. Sperber (ed.), *Metarepresentations: An Interdisciplinary Perspective* (pp. 411–48). Oxford: Oxford University Press.

Wilson, A. E., Smith, M. D. and Ross, H. S. (2003). The nature and effects of young children's lies. *Social Development*, 12: 21–45.

Wimmer, H. and Perner, J. (1983). Beliefs about beliefs: Representation and constraining function of wrong beliefs in young children's understanding of deception. *Cognition*, 13: 103–28.

Wimmer, H., Hogrefe, J. G. and Perner, P. (1988). Children's understanding of informational access as source of knowledge. *Child Development*, 59: 386–96.

Wimmer, H., Hogrefe, J. and Sodian, B. (1988). A second stage in children's conception of mental life: Understanding informational access as origins of knowledge and belief. In J. Astington, P. Harris and D. Olson (eds), *Developing Theories of Mind* (pp. 173–92). Cambridge: Cambridge University Press.

Wimpory, D. C., Hobson, R. P., Williams, J. M. G. and Nash, S. (2000). Are infants with autism socially engaged? A controlled study of recent retrospective parental reports. *Journal of Autism and Developmental Disorders*, 30: 525–36.

Wing, L. (1981). Language, social and cognitive impairments in autism and severe mental retardation. *Journal of Autism and Developmental Disorders*, 11: 31–3.

Winner, E., Brownwell, H., Happé, F., Blum, A. and Pincus, D. (1998). Distinguishing lies from jokes: Theory of mind deficits and discourse interpretation in right hemisphere brain-damaged patients. *Brain and Language*, 62: 89–106.

Wittgenstein, L. (1953/1958). *Philosophical Investigations*. Oxford: Blackwell.

Wittgenstein, L. (1972). *Philosophical Investigations*. Oxford: Blackwell.

Wittgenstein, L. (1997). *Philosophical Investigations*. Oxford: Blackwell.

Woodworth, R. S. (1924). Four varieties of behaviorism. *Psychological Review*, 31: 257–64.

Wootton, A. J. (1997). *Interaction and the Development of Mind*. Cambridge: Cambridge University Press.

World Health Organization. (1993). *International Classification of Diseases*, 10th edn. *Diagnostic Criteria for Research*. Geneva: WHO.

Wright, T. (1604/1971). *The passions of the minde in generall*. Facsimile reprint introduced by Thomas O. Sloan. Urbana: University of Illinois Press.

Yirmiya, N., Erel, O., Shaked, M. and Solomonica-Levi, D. (1998). Meta-analyses comparing theory of mind abilities of individuals with autism, individuals with mental retardation and normally developing individuals. *Psychological Bulletin*, 124: 283–307.

Zahavi, D. (2002). Beyond empathy. In E. Thompson (ed.), *Between Ourselves: Second-Person Issues in the Study of Consciousness* (pp. 151–68). Charlottesville, VA: Imprint Academic.

Zahavi, D. (2003). Conceptual problems in infantile autism research, *Journal of Consciousness Studies*, 10: 53–71.

Zahavi, D. (2006). *Subjectivity and Selfhood*. Cambridge, MA: MIT Press.

Zahavi, D. and Parnas, J. (2005). Conceptual problems in infantile autism research. *Journal of Consciousness Studies*, 10: 53–71.

Zeedyk, M. S. (1997). Maternal interpretations of infant intentionality: Changes over the course of infant development. *British Journal of Developmental Psychology*, 15: 477–93.

Zimmerman, A. (2007). The nature of belief. *Journal of Consciousness Studies*, 14: 61–82.

Author Index

Adrien, J. L.   165
Allen, C.   132
Allen, G.   135
Allport, G. W.   216
Ambrose, J.   135
Antaki, C.   1, 35, 112, 119, 120, 122, 123, 125, 230
Asch, S.   4, 5
Asperger, H.   145
Astington, J. W.   25, 30, 32, 33, 38, 59, 60, 75, 91, 92, 100, 106, 131, 146, 227
Atkinson, R. C.   51
Atkinson, R. L.   51
Austin, J. L.   19, 21, 22, 33, 38

Bachevalier, J.   137
Baillargeon, R.   94, 230
Baird, G.   145
Bakan, D.   46
Baker, L. R.   237
Bakhtin, M. M.   211, 215
Barber, J.   111
Barillas, Y.   98
Barkow, J. H.   142
Baron-Cohen, S.   2, 7, 33, 34, 36, 37, 38, 91, 101, 127, 128, 143, 145, 148, 160
Barr, R.   3
Barresi, J.   105
Bartsch, K.   75, 77
Bates, E.   97, 103
Battistelli, P.   93
Battacchi, W.   93
Bavidge, M.   12, 13, 167, 188, 226, 228, 229, 230, 233, 237, 238
Beeghly-Smith, M.   2, 91
Bell, S.   143
Bell, V.   119
Belmonte, M.   231
Bem, D. J.   51
Bennett, M. R.   87
Bentall, R. P.   111, 120, 121

Bergman, A.   105
Bernstein, I. S.   182
Bialystok, E.   140
Bieberich, A.   133
Bilmes, J.   21, 33, 65
Birchwood, M.   111
Biringen, Z.   143
Blackmore, J.   9
Bleuler, E.   112
Bloom, P.   7, 118
Blum, A.   111
Bolton, N.   49
Booth, A.   98
Boucher, J.   7, 8, 130
Brandt, A. M.   217
Brankovic, S. B.   121
Bretherton, I.   2, 91
Broadbent, D. E.   24, 37, 49
Brooks, D. N.   111
Brown, E.   147
Brown, R.   27, 37, 147
Brownwell, H.   111
Browning, P. K.   38
Brüne, M.   117, 118, 119
Bruner, J.   6, 20, 28, 29, 49
Bryant, P.   95
Buber, M.   103
Bull, R.   94
Byrne, R. W.   94

Cadinu, M. R.   91
Cairns, E.   216
Camaioni, L.   93, 98, 101, 164, 165
Capps, L.   145, 146, 147
Carpendale, J. L. M.   1, 106, 233
Carpenter, M.   97, 98
Carruthers, P.   129
Casacchia, M.   111
Celani, G.   93
Chandler, S.   145
Chandler, M. J.   91, 93, 106
Charlton, B. G.   55
Cheney, D. L.   101

Cherry, C.   24
Chomsky, N.   24, 25, 26, 27, 28, 29, 30, 32, 34, 37, 38, 52, 63, 73, 76, 86, 237
Churchland, P. M.   22, 235, 236, 237
Clements, W. A.   91
Clyman, R. B.   143
Codd, J.   140
Colbert, S. M.   119
Collingwood, R. G.   12, 15, 16, 21
Collins, S.   214
Cook, J.   65
Corcoran, R.   2, 109, 110, 111, 112
Corkum, V.   98
Cosmides, L.   3, 15, 41, 129, 142
Costall, A.   1, 2, 9, 10, 12, 13, 19, 20, 29, 37, 39, 41, 42, 45, 51, 52, 53, 55, 65, 92, 101, 125, 163, 209, 225, 227, 228, 229, 230, 231, 233, 236, 237, 238
Coulter, J.   12, 15, 21, 36, 56, 87, 101, 107, 118, 120, 128, 191, 193, 194, 208, 228, 233
Coulthart, M.   111
Courschene, E.   135
Cromer, R. F.   137
Cross, D.   223, 225, 229
Csibra, G.   135

Danziger, K.   9, 21
Darwin, F.   44, 45
Daston, L.   47
David, A. S.   122
Davies, M. J.   111, 167
Dawson, G.   133, 147, 165
Degangi, G.   137, 138
Dennett, D.   2, 69
Descartes, R.   2, 9, 19, 20, 22, 23, 30, 38, 51, 65, 129, 131, 132, 171
Di Lavore, P. C.   164
Doody, G. A.   111, 112, 119
Douglas, M.   217
Dreier, O.   53
Drew, P.   35
Dreyfus, H. L.   162, 165
Drury, V. M.   111, 118, 119, 120
Dudley, R. E. J.   119, 120
Dunn, J.   1, 91

Edwards, D.   21, 87, 191, 193, 194, 195, 202, 203
Eisenmajer, R.   128
Ekman, P.   131
Ellis, H.   119
Emde, R. N.   143
Erel, O.   130, 133
Erikson, E.   212

Faure, M.   165
Feldman, C.   7
Feyerabend, P.   12
Fiske, S.   35
Flowers, P.   148
Fodor, J. A.   2, 22, 38, 73, 87, 224, 237
Forbes, C. D.   217
Foucault, M.   143
Francis, D.   225, 227, 228, 229, 231
Freeman, D.   118, 119, 122
Freud, S.   37
Friedman, O.   51
Frith, C. D.   2, 108, 109, 110, 111
Frith, U.   2, 7, 36, 37, 101, 112, 117, 128, 130, 143, 145, 160, 167
Fritz, A. S.   91, 93, 106

Galam, S.   214, 215
Galanter, E.   49
Gallagher, S.   3, 84, 227, 231
Gallese, V.   141, 231
Gallup, G. G.   178
Galpert, L.   133
Garety, P. A.   118, 119, 120, 121, 122
Garfield, J. L.   233
Garner, W. R.   50
Garton, A. F.   39
Gergely, G.   101, 107
German, T. P.   7, 51, 118
Gernsbacher, M. A.   135
Goldman, A. I.   2, 3, 6, 229, 237
Goffman, E.   21
Goleman, D.   136
Golinkoff, R. M.   96
Goodglass, H.   127
Gopnik, A.   4, 73, 74, 91, 92, 101, 106, 128, 145, 146, 147, 170, 173, 180, 187

Gordon, R.   3, 36, 37, 88, 128
Gosling, S. D.   49
Grandin, T.   133, 149, 150, 153, 155, 156, 157
Grant, C. M.   130
Gray, J. M.   111
Grayson, A.   130
Greene, J. M.   27
Greenspan, S.   130, 133, 134, 137, 138, 140, 141, 143
Grice, H. P.   24, 25, 30, 31, 32, 33, 34, 37, 38, 237
Griffin, D. R.   135, 175
Ground, I.   12, 13, 167, 188, 226, 228, 229, 230, 233, 237, 238
Gurwitsch, A.   9

Haberl, K.   96
Hacker, P. M. S.   29, 87
Hala, S.   91, 93, 106
Halit, H.   135
Halligan, P.   119
Hamberger, J.   216
Hameury, L.   165
Hammond, H.   41
Happé, F. G. E.   111, 130, 145, 148, 160
Hark, Ter, M.   22
Harré, R.   193, 208
Harris, P.   3, 88
Harrison, P.   131, 132
Heal, J.   167, 170
Healey, P. G. T.   1, 125
Hebb, D. O.   15, 50, 54
Hemsley, D. R.   120
Heritage, J.   112
Herold, R.   111
Hewstone, M.   216
Heyes, C. M.   177, 178, 179, 180, 182
Hill, I.   133
Hobson, R. P.   1, 8, 103, 127, 133, 143, 163, 164, 165, 231
Hogrefe, J.   95, 169
Holliday Willey, L.   150, 151, 152, 153, 154, 157, 158, 159, 161
Howe, M.   127
Hubley, P.   97
Hughes, C.   140

Hull, C. L.   48, 49
Hume, D.   177
Huq, S. F.   120
Hutto, D. D.   1, 13, 221, 230, 234, 235, 238

Inhelder, B.   99
Izard, S.   133

Jaynes, J.   177, 178
Jarman, M.   148
Jenkins, J. J.   50
John, C. H.   119
Johnson, M. H.   135
Johnson, S.   98
Johnson-Laird, P.   27
Jones, E.   121, 122
Jones, P.   217

Kanner, L.   130, 145
Kant, I.   183, 188
Karmiloff-Smith, A.   99, 142
Kasari, C.   133
Kaye, K.   101
Keat, R.   41
Kennedy, J. S.   172, 177
Kiefer, F.   32
Kiesner, J.   91
Kirschner, S. R.   40
Kitchener, R. F.   55
Kojève, A.   213
Krzeminska, P.   133
Kuhl, P.   128
Kuipers, E.   119

Lagattuta, K. H.   3
Langdon, M.   111, 112, 118, 119
Lawson, W.   151, 152, 154, 158, 159
Leahey, T. H.   37
Leddet, I.   165
LeDoux, J.   136
Lee, K.   94
Leekam, S.   128, 143
Legerstee, M.   98
Lenard, K.   111
Leonard, L.   127
Leslie, A. M.   2, 7, 36, 37, 41, 44, 51, 91, 101, 127, 128, 143, 145, 147, 162, 230

266   *Author Index*

Leudar, I.   1, 2, 9, 10, 12, 13, 14, 19,
    20, 29, 35, 37, 38, 39, 41, 52, 65,
    92, 101, 105, 112, 119, 120, 121,
    122, 123, 125, 163, 194, 209, 225,
    227, 228, 229, 230, 231, 233, 236,
    237, 238
Levi, G.   164, 165
Lévinas, E.   188
Lewis, C.   1, 106, 233
Lewis, D.   234
Lewis, M. D.   142
Lewy, A. L.   133
Liszkowski, U.   97, 98
Livingston, M. G.   111
Lord, C.   164
Lorenz, K.   171
Louch, A. R.   161
Loveland, K. A.   133, 137

Macedo, de, S.   173
MacKie, D. M.   5
Macmurray, J.   91, 99, 103
Mahler, M.   105
Malatesta, C. A.   133
Malcolm, N.   66
Mandelbaum, J.   35
Marco, E.   93
Markman, E.   97
Marková, I.   13, 209, 210, 211, 214,
    217, 219, 227
Mars, A. E.   150, 165
Martin, J.   54, 103
Massie, R. K.   217
Mazza, M.   111, 112, 118
McCabe, R.   1, 12, 108, 112, 121,
    122, 123, 125, 226, 230
McNew, S.   2, 91
McDonough, R.   87
McDowell, J.   183, 184
McGeer, V.   128, 143, 234
McGinn, M.   198
McHoul, A.   65, 193, 194
McKlean, T.   151, 152, 155
McShane, J.   32
Meltzoff, A. N.   4, 128, 145, 146, 147
Mercer, G.   111
Merleau-Ponty, M.   22, 35, 37, 77
Mesibov, G. B.   150, 154, 156, 159
Metz, U.   96

Miller, G. A.   49, 51
Miller, P. H.   53
Mitchley, N. J.   111
Montagu, J.   132
Morgan, C. L.   43, 44
Morgan, S.   133
Morris, P.   12, 13, 53, 91, 117, 163,
    221, 224, 228
Moscovici, S.   211, 214, 215, 216, 217,
    219
Moore, C.   98, 105
Morgan, S.   133
Muller, R.   135
Mundy, P.   133
Myers, J. G.   44, 55

Naji, S. A.   217
Nash, S.   165
Nehamas, A.   22
Neisser, U.   5, 42, 49, 54
Nelson, K.   227
Newell, A.   49
Newton, P.   47, 93
Nichols, S.   81, 88, 169
Niens, U.   216
Nolen-Hoeksema, S.   51
Nye, R.   95

Ober, J.   173
Oberman, L. M.   141
Ochs, E.   1, 32
O'Hearn, K.   98
Olson, D. R.   92, 93, 101, 107
O'Neill, D. K.   95
Onishi, K. H.   94, 230
Or, M.   130
O'Reilly, A.   96, 101
Osborn, M.   148
Osterling, J.   147, 165
Over, D. E.   119
Overgaard, S.   88
Ozonoff, S.   128

Pandora, K.   55
Panksepp, J.   134
Parton, A.   95
Paunovic, V. R.   121
Paus, T.   141
Peirce, K.   135

Pennington, B. F.   128
Peplau, L. A.   5
Perner, J.   1, 91, 92, 93, 95, 97, 98,
    100, 101, 106, 127, 128, 143, 145,
    146, 224
Perrot, A.   165
Perry, T.   233
Peters, E. R.   38
Peters, S.
Peterson, C. C.   128, 233
Penn, D. C.   4
Piaget, J.   52, 97, 100, 101, 104, 105
Pickles, A.   145
Pickup, G. J.   111
Pillow, B. H.   95
Pincus, D.   111
Pine, F.   105
Pinker, S.   127, 129, 142
Pomerantz, A.   35
Povinelli, D. J.   4
Potter, J.   87, 191, 193, 194, 195, 202, 203
Poulin-Dubois, D.   95, 96
Pratt, C.   95
Premack, D.   1, 27, 28, 36, 59, 60, 69,
    145, 167, 178
Pribram, K. H.   49
Prince-Hughes, D.   150, 151, 152, 153,
    155, 156, 157, 158, 159, 160, 166
Pring, L.   3, 39
Prior, M.   128
Pullum, G. K.   26
Putnam, H.   36, 237

Quine, W. V. O.   26, 29

Ramachandran, V. S.   141
Rapley, M.   65, 193, 194
Ratcliffe, M.   227, 228, 231, 232, 238
Reddy, M.   25
Reddy, V.   1, 12, 13, 41, 53, 91, 94,
    95, 97, 98, 101, 105, 117, 163, 164,
    221, 224, 228
Reed, D. T.   128
Renton, A.   118
Repacholi, B. M.   4
Reygadas, P.   131
Rinaldi, J.   147
Risio de, A.   111
Ritchie, J.   118

Robins, R. W.   49
Robinson, E. J.   95, 111
Rochester, S.   112
Roncone, R.   111
Ross, H. S.   93, 94, 100
Rowlands, M.   237
Rudin, S. A.   8
Russell, J.   91, 140
Rutter, M.   164
Ryle, G.   20, 22, 56, 63, 64, 65,
    66, 78, 86, 120, 193, 195, 199,
    207, 208

Sacks, O.   145, 150, 193
Samelson, F.   47
Sampson, G.   26
Sarfati, Y.   120
Sauvage, D.   165
Savage-Rumbaugh, S.   128
Schieflin, B. B.   32
Schneider, E.   150, 152, 155, 156
Schopler, E.   150, 154, 156, 159
Schore, A.   135
Searle, J.   29, 32, 33
Sears, D. O.   5
Secord, P.   208
Sedler, M. J.   122
Segerdahl, P.   73
Sehon, S.   235, 237
Sellars, W.   234, 235
Sennett, R.   46
Seyfarth, R. M.   101
Shanker, S.   10, 12, 13, 30, 37, 127,
    128, 129, 130, 131, 134, 140, 141,
    153, 163, 164, 230, 231, 238
Shannon, C. E.   24
Sharrock, W.   12, 13, 14, 15, 21, 36,
    56, 101, 107, 118, 120, 128, 191,
    228, 233, 242
Shatz, M.   96, 101
Sherry, S.   140
Shwe, H.   97
Siegal, M.   40
Sigman, M.   133
Simon, H. A.   49, 160
Simone, L.   95
Simonoff, E.   145
Sinclair, J.   150, 153, 156, 159
Smedslund, J.   60

Smith, E. E.   51
Smith, E. R.   5
Smith, J. A.   148
Smith, M. D.   93, 94, 100
Smith, N. V.   25, 30
Smith, P.   129
Snow, M. E.   133
Sodian, B.   7, 93, 96, 167, 169
Solomon, O.   1
Sparling, J. W.   165
Spencer, A.   133
Sperber, D.   32, 33, 38
Spitzer, M.   121, 122
Stephen, L.   14, 36, 44, 72
Stich, S.   2, 29, 81, 88, 116, 169
Still, A.   37
Stone, T.   167
Stouthamer-Loeber, N.   93
Strafella, A.   141
Striano, T.   98
Stuart, J.   12, 126, 217
Suchman, L. A.   21
Sugarman, J.   54
Sully, J.   43, 55
Surian, L.   111
Swarbrick, R.   120

Talwar, V.   94
Taylor, S.   35
Taylor, S. E.   5
Taylor, T. J.   34, 128
Tenyi, T.   111
Thaiss, L.   127
Thomas, G. V.   95
Thomas, M.   28
Thomas, P.   37, 112, 119, 194
Thomson, E.   128
Thompson, J.   54
Thompson, R. A.   3
Tibbetts, P.   23
Tilden, J.   96
Tooby, J.   3, 15, 41, 129, 142
Tomasello, M.   96, 97, 98
Toulmin, S.   14, 22, 36
Tracy, J. L.   49
Trevarthen, C.   97

Trixler, M.   111
Tyrer, P.   118

Vendler, Z.   86
Villiers, De, J.   128
Voci, A.   216
Vroon, P. A.   24

Waal, de F. B.   173
Warnock, G. J.   11
Wason, P. C.   27
Watkins, K.   141
Watson, A.   223, 225, 229
Watson, J. B.   45, 46, 47, 48, 52, 77
Weaver, T.   118
Weizenbaum, J.   49
Wellman, H. M.   2, 75, 77, 92, 101,
     106, 143, 145, 146, 147, 223,
     225, 229
Whiten, A.   2, 94, 96, 101
Wieder, S.   10, 133, 137, 138, 143
Wieder, D. L.   10, 133, 137, 138, 143
Wiener, N.   24
Wilkie, P. A.   217
Williams, E.   12, 13, 101, 105, 144, 163
Williams, J. M. G.   165
Wilson, A. E.   43, 94, 100
Wilson, D.   32, 33, 38
Wimpory, D. C.   165
Wing, L.   148
Winner, E.   111
Wittgenstein, L.   14, 21, 26, 56, 63,
     64, 65, 66, 74, 78, 186, 188, 193,
     195, 197, 198, 199, 205, 207, 208
Woodruff, G.   2, 27, 28, 37, 59, 60,
     69, 145, 167
Woodworth, R. S.   45
Wootton, A. J.   120
Wright, T.   131

Yirmiya, N.   130, 133
Young, A. W.   119

Zahavi, D.   1, 128, 163
Zeedyk, M. S.   106
Zimmerman, A.   238

Subject Index

affect signals   136
affective neuroscience   136
agency   15, 37, 42, 180
AIDS   212, 218, 252
Alter   210–20
amygdala   136, 137, 167–88, 239
animal communication   132, 143
animal mind   167, 170–1, 175, 180,
    182, 184, 187
animal psychology   43–5, 170
animals and ToM   40, 131, 167–88,
    226, 229, 231
anthropomorphism   171–2, 176
aphasia   126
appearance and reality   9, 11, 40, 53,
    178, 196
Asperger's syndrome   144, 145, 148,
    165, 166
autism
    autobiographical accounts   144
        et seq.
    avoidance of relating   137, 138
    false-belief task and autism   7, 93,
        127
    high-functioning autism
        (HFA)   148, 149, 160–3
    Hugh Blair, an early case study   130
    metarepresentation   8
    'natural fool'   130, 131
    perseveration   137, 138
    pretend play and autism   101
    rule-following   148, 154
    self-absorption   137, 138
    self-stimulation   137, 138
    sensory impairments   134, 137
    social withdrawal   110, 133, 135, 138
    stereotyped behaviour   138
    Theory of Mind in autism   40, 117,
        126, 128, 129, 141, 144, 145, 167

behaviour
    as evidence or cue   20, 22, 25, 26, 27,
        30, 34, 35 36, 40, 41, 70, 77, 163
    as criterion   26
    as meaningful and expressive   21,
        25, 36, 48, 52, 180–5
    as 'mere' bodily movement:
        behaviourist 'behaviour'   11,
        20, 21, 30, 39, 42, 50, 51,
        53, 55, 65, 67, 91, 179,
        181, 230
behaviourism   10, 12, 14, 19, 27, 42,
    45, 48, 58, 172, 175
    as the flip-side of mentalism   63,
        67, 77, 78, 170, 176, 188, 192,
        195, 197, 207
    as methodology   175, 176, 234
    as theory   175
    children as behaviourists   101–2,
        106, 229
    neo-behaviourism   10, 49
belief-desire
    psychology   3, 21, 33, 39, 58, 67,
        68, 74, 76, 128
body-mind problem, see mind-body
    problem

Cartesian dualism   9, 14, 37, 63–8,
    71, 78, 101, 102, 107, 120,
    128–30, 138, 174–8, 192–4,
    196, 230, 237
    ontological   10, 30
    epistemic   10, 20, 23, 36, 176
    methodological   10, 50, 52, 176
circumstantial particulars   14
claim
    justification   116, 122
    warrants   21, 36, 116, 122, 123
cognitive 'revolution'   37, 42, 50,
    51, 52
cognitivism   2, 9, 20, 42, 49, 51, 58,
    78, 85, 128, 230–2
collective representations   210
collective knower   210
common sense   29, 83
communication

270 *Subject Index*

conduit metaphor of   25
'pseudo-communication' as
   'mere' behaviour/behavioural
   routines   91, 93, 97, 102, 112
concepts   59, 60, 128, 178, 183–6,
   220, 225, 232, 238
confirmation bias   121
consciousness   5, 29, 47, 136,
   175, 211
context   14, 40, 47, 66, 119, 134, 161,
   163, 186, 193, 210, 226–7
conversation
   logic of   31
   maxims of   31, 32
   organization of   21, 23, 35, 116,
     123, 137, 153, 158, 210, 214
conversation analysis   112, 123, 191

deception   93–5, 100, 120, 164, 177,
   242, 248
development
   emotional   130–47
   intrapersonal   33
   social   40, 92, 106, 126
Developmental Individual
   Relationship programme   137
dialogical approach
   to self/Ego   210–20
   to theory   210–12
discourse analysis/discursive
   psychology   191, 193, 208
dispositions   26, 70, 199

ecological validity   5, 6, 11, 100, 119, 120
Ego   210–14, 220
egocentrism   98, 99, 158
eliminativism   233, 236, 238
emotions
   emotional engagement   13, 103–5,
     126, 139, 141, 162
   emotional intelligence   131, 156
   emotional problems   109, 133, 137,
     149, 159, 231
empathy   79, 126, 130, 140, 141, 154,
   165, 167, 171, 173
epistemic detachment   11, 34, 44,
   48, 92, 162, 163
ethnomethodology   21, 191, 207, 208
ethology   167, 175, 180, 182

evolution   2, 32, 51, 53, 88, 101, 129,
   142, 145, 170, 173, 187
executive functioning   118, 119,
   128, 230
experiment, the fetish of   6–12, 15,
   33, 35, 43–5, 52, 75–7, 100, 117,
   186, 225–8
experts vs. 'ordinary people'   29, 43,
   53, 162–5, 214
explanation   85, 96, 102, 168, 183,
   221–3
expression/expressive
   behaviour   180–8, *see also*
   facial expression
eye-to-eye gaze patterns   97, 98, 133,
   135, 165

facial expression   127, 128, 130–4,
   142, 147, 152
false-belief test   6, 35, 54, 75, 93–5,
   100, 111, 117, 118, 127, 128,
   138, 224, 225, 227
false-photograph task   127
folk biology   147
folk psychology (FP)   2, 64, 69, 71,
   72, 78, 146, 169, 192, 196, 206,
   221, 222, 233
forms of life   74, 186, 195, 233
fusiform gyrus   127, 135, 142
functional/emotional model   130, 134

Gaze   97, 98, 133, 135, 165
genetic blueprints   142, 145

heteroglossia   220
hypothetical entities   66, 67, 146
hypothesis-testing/hypothetico-
   deductive method   22, 28, 54,
   70, 99, 128

illocution   31
imitation   103, 133, 146, 165, 177
implicature   31, 34
indirectness of our experience of
   others   3–7, 10, 14, 30, 35, 206
inference   10, 13, 14, 20, 22, 28, 39,
   40, 66, 77, 103, 112, 120, 129,
   161, 174, 181, 232
in-groups and out-groups   216

information theory   24, 25
interpretative phenomenological
        analysis (IPA)   148
innate endowment   26, 32, 36, 41,
        53, 61, 70, 76, 106, 131, 143,
        146, 147, 164, 213
inner, *see* internal
intellectualisation   6, 11, 19, 22, 23,
        28, 35, 98, 165
intersubjectivity   102, 107, 133,
        212, 215
intentionality   2, 11–13, 21, 35, 36,
        112, 120, 164, 230, 231, 238
internal   36, 46
    constraints   129
    events   120
    'in the head' attributions   71,
        194, 202
    representations   224
    states   3, 5, 131
    theatre   196
introspection   45, 47, 50, 51, 176,
        177, 206
I–thou and *I–you* relation   103, 104, 210

knowledge
    vs. action   21
    vs. belief   88

language   22, 28, 30, 56, 60–6, 71–8,
        112, 120, 128, 153, 181, 184,
        185–8, 227, 233
    language acquisition   27, 29, 86,
        138, 148, 191–8, 207, 209, 215
    language corpus   26, 37, 38
    language games (Wittgenstein)   31,
        123
lying, *see* deceit
linguistics   26–8, 30, 37
linguistic
    competence   29–32, 74
    performance   30

maxims of conversation, *see*
        conversation
mediation   38, 92
mental states
    attribution of   33, 35, 36, 38, 59,
        61, 71, 72, 73, 75, 76, 79, 116,

        179, 184, 205, 200, 206, 223,
        225, 226, 232
mentalism   58, 61, 63, 72, 74, 85, 88,
        101, 192, 194, 195, 197, 207,
        237
mentalist
    doctrines   63, 64, 77, 78, 191–7,
        199, 201, 207, 222, 231
    presuppositions   58, 102
    vocabulary   59, 61, 62, 71, 73, 76,
        78, 192, 196, 199, 207, 208,
        221, 233
mentalising, *see* mind-reading
meta-representation   6, 101, 106,
        109, 111, 114, 237
meta-language   25
methodological pluralism   12
mind/brain concept   14, 30, 57, 59
mindreading   1, 8, 32, 41, 119, 131,
        135, 137, 138, 141, 143, 224,
        229, 234
    deficits   110–12, 117–19,123, 128,
        130, 135, 138, 141, 147
    state-related deficits   111, 117
mind
    privileged access   30, 102, 107, 121,
        129, 203, 204, 206
minority-majority interaction   213,
        214
mirror neurons   140, 141
mindblindness   98, 126, 129, 136
modularity and modules   2, 29, 30,
        32, 34, 36, 38, 73, 74, 106,
        126–9, 136, 140–2, 145, 164
mutual understanding   10, 86, 105,
        132, 165

naturalistic studies   52, 93, 95, 112,
        117, 122
neo-behaviourism   11
neuro-Cartesianism   23
neuroconstructivism   142
non-human primates   1, 27, 59, 69,
        70, 94, 167, 177, 179
non-natural meaning   31, 32, 38

observation   10, 14, 15, 43, 55, 58,
        63–7, 103, 141, 160, 171, 173,
        176, 235

objectivism   9, 11, 33, 42, 44, 47–9,
        103, 171, 181
ontological commitments   224, 235,
        236
ontology   10, 26, 30, 73, 172, 174,
        192, 196, 210, 212, 220, 238
otherness   187, 212
outward criteria   78, 116, 120, 122,
        197, 198, 199, 213

pain   5, 21, 37, 78, 79, 177, 196–9,
    'pain behaviour'   187, 197–9
passive onlooker   5, 150, 151
personal narratives/accounts   144,
        149, 151, 151, 159, 160
perlocution   31, 38
play   101, 118, 138, 139, 216
Pleistocene   128, 142
pointing   95, 98, 102, 107
    proto-declarative   97, 102
    pseudo-   97, 98, 101
poverty of the stimulus
        argument   26, 27
pragmatics   24, 25, 30–4, 38, 116
pretence   100, 101
privacy   14, 20, 175, 176, 197, 200,
        201, 206
private
    language argument   197–200
    mental states   14, 20, 21, 26,
        41, 51, 66, 68, 71, 79, 121,
        129, 174, 193, 195, 203–6
        223
    thoughts   195, 196, 198, 19,
        200–3
privileged access   30, 107, 121, 129,
        203, 204, 206
problem of other minds   6, 11,
        19–23, 30, 34, 36, 37, 40, 41,
        51–5, 101, 105
propositional attitudes   222, 234, 238
proto-declaratives   97
psychiatric consultation   113–14
psychological vocabulary   73, 196, 207
psychosemantics   238, 245
psychotic beliefs   116
public vs. private   20, 51, 78, 119,
        195, 198, 203, 207, 237
public criteria   120, 122

radical enactivism   238
rationality   156, 209, 216, 220
reasoning   2, 11, 24, 31, 33, 34, 35,
        51, 75, 79, 112, 113, 114, 119,
        121, 122, 123, 147, 226, 241
reductionism   45, 50, 207, 247
reference to inner states   65, 72, 78,
        195, 196
reflective thinking   140
rules   13, 27, 28, 29, 32, 33, 61, 68,
        72, 73, 82, 83, 87, 112, 135,
        148, 154–62, 168, 198, 217, 219,
        224, 227
    rule-generalising   159
    if-then rules   148, 160

Sally-Anne task   118, 127, 140
scepticism   22, 40, 62, 103, 167, 171,
        196
schizophrenia   2, 9, 12, 40, 108–25,
        230
    alogia   109
    anhedonia   109
    avolition   109
    delusions   108, 109, 110, 114,
        116–23
    formal thought disorder   109
    hallucinations   109, 110, 117, 119,
        122
    negative symptoms   109, 110, 111,
        113
scientific inference   20, 22
scientism   11
second-person perspective   13, 92,
        163
Self and Other   15, 79, 82, 92, 103,
        104, 145, 146, 149, 150, 164,
        213, 216
Sense of self   135, 177, 178, 184, 186,
        188, 211, 226
sensorimotor schemes   97
sign-reading   130, 131, 132, 143
simulation theory   36, 39, 58, 60, 63,
        79, 88, 191, 223
social
    action   1, 92, 231
    brain network   134, 136
    breakdown   144, 161
    change   213

cognition   2, 6, 129, 144, 163, 224, 229
development   92, 134, 145, 164, 212
identity theory   216
interaction   4, 9, 10, 11, 13, 15, 19, 22, 23, 25, 30, 33, 34, 35, 37, 39, 99, 108, 112, 116, 133, 135, 136, 138, 144, 151, 152, 153, 156, 159, 160, 165, 209, 229
psychology   2, 5, 10, 212, 213, 216, 218, 220
representations   212, 214, 217–19
socio-cultural psychology   1, 142, 145
solipsism   99
spectators vs. participants   15, 91, 224–6
speech acts   32, 33, 38
speech act theory   32
strangeness   215
syntax   73, 181, 227

theoretical constructs   146, 161, 162
theory-testing   146
telementation   25, 30
tertiary circular reactions   97
theory of mind mechanism   126, 128, 145, 223, 229–31

theory-theory of mind   38, 79, 91–107, 144
third personal   44, 107
contexts   223, 227
attribution   23, 226
mentalizing   129, 197, 226, 228
perspective   13, 105, 109
ToM mechanism, *see* theory of mind mechanism
trial-and-error thinking   128
trust   55, 212, 213, 215, 218, 219

unobservable entities   3, 4, 14, 15, 20, 22, 34, 35, 41, 51, 59, 63, 64, 66, 67, 69, 77, 82, 87, 120, 170, 174, 175, 181
understanding
animal behaviour   181, 182, 186, 187
emotional   134, 140
social   15, 20, 22, 28, 35, 38, 40, 51, 53, 62, 76, 79–86, 91, 102, 105, 126, 127, 130, 139, 144, 164, 165, 221, 225, 227, 230–2
other cultures   85
rule-based strategies   144, 156

voices in the head   109, 194